Comparative Politics

05/06

Twenty-Third Edition

W9-CYA-118

EDITOR

Christian Søe

California State University, Long Beach

Christian Søe was born in Denmark, studied at the University of British Columbia and the University of Michigan, and received his doctoral degree in political science at the Free University in Berlin. He is professor in political science at California State University in Long Beach, where he teaches courses in comparative politics. His research deals primarily with political developments in contemporary Germany. He visits that country annually to conduct research on parties and elections, as part of an effort to follow continuities and shifts in its politics. His publications include a book he co-edited with Mary N. Hampton, *Between Bonn and Berlin: German Politics Adrift?*, that examines the last years of Helmut Kohl's center-right government and its replacement by a center-left coalition headed by Gerhard Schröder and Joschka Fischer. The milestone election of 1998 is the subject of another book that he co-edited with David Conradt and Gerald R. Kleinfeld, *Power Shift in Germany*. The same team co-edited a recent volume on the 2002 German Bundestag election and its aftermath, *Precarious Victory*. Three other publications include a biographical essay on Hans-Dietrich Genscher, Germany's foreign minister from 1974 to 1992, in *Political Leaders of Contemporary Western Europe*, a chapter on the Free Democratic Party in Germany's New Politics, and another chapter on the Danish-German relationship in *The Germans and Their Neighbors*. Dr. Søe is also co-editor of the latter two books. He has been editor of the twenty-three volumes of *Annual Editions: Comparative Politics* since the beginning of this series in 1983.

McGraw-Hill/Dushkin

2460 Kerper Boulevard, Dubuque, Iowa 52001

Visit us on the Internet
http://www.dushkin.com

Credits

1. **Pluralist Democracies: Country Studies**
   Unit photo— © Corbis/Royalty-Free
2. **Pluralist Democracies: Factors in the Political Process**
   Unit photo—Emma Lee/Life File/Getty Images
3. **Europe in Transition: West, Center, and East**
   Unit photo—Photograph by Cpl Matthew Roberson, USMC courtesy of USAID
4. **Political Diversity in the Developing World**
   Unit photo—Corbis Images/Royalty Free
5. **Comparative Politics: Some Major Trends, Issues, and Prospects**
   Unit photo—Photograph courtesy of the Audiovisual Library of the European Commission

Copyright

Cataloging in Publication Data
Main entry under title: Annual Editions: Comparative Politics. 2005/2006.
1. Comparative Politics—Periodicals. I. Søe, Christian, comp. II. Title: Comparative Politics.
ISBN 0–07–312385–4   658'.05   ISSN 0741–7233

Twenty-third Edition

Cover image © Corbis/Royalty Free
Printed in the United States of America   1234567890QPDQPD98765   Printed on Recycled Paper

Editors/Advisory Board

Members of the Advisory Board are instrumental in the final selection of articles for each edition of ANNUAL EDITIONS. Their review of articles for content, level, currentness, and appropriateness provides critical direction to the editor and staff. We think that you will find their careful consideration well reflected in this volume.

EDITOR

Christian Søe
California State University, Long Beach

ADVISORY BOARD

Staff

Preface

In publishing ANNUAL EDITIONS we recognize the enormous role played by the magazines, newspapers, and journals of the public press in providing current, first-rate educational information in a broad spectrum of interest areas. Many of these articles are appropriate for students, researchers, and professionals seeking accurate, current material to help bridge the gap between principles and theories and the real world. These articles, however, become more useful for study when those of lasting value are carefully collected, organized, indexed, and reproduced in a low-cost format, which provides easy and permanent access when the material is needed. That is the role played by ANNUAL EDITIONS.

This collection of readings brings together current articles that will help you understand the politics of foreign countries from a comparative perspective. Such a study opens up a fascinating world beyond our borders. It will also lead to deeper insights into the American political process.

The articles in unit 1 cover Britain or the United Kingdom, France, Germany, Italy and Japan in a serial manner. In terms of gross domestic product, these countries all belong with the United States among the top six market economies in the world. Each of these modern societies has an individual tradition of politics and governance within a particular institutional framework. Nevertheless, as the readings of unit 2 show, it is possible to point to some comparable patterns of political challenge and response among these and some other representative democracies.

Unit 3 deals with the impact of two major changes that continue to transform the political map of Europe. One of them is the irregular, sometimes halting, but nevertheless impressive growth of the European Union (EU). It began with six member states in 1957, grew incrementally to fifteen, and then in 2004 added ten new countries for a total membership of 25. The other and closely related major change involves the political and economic reconstruction of Central and Eastern Europe, including Russia, after the collapse of the Communist regimes in that region between 1989 and 1991. These developments underscore the continuing political importance of Europe.

Unit 4 looks first at the challenge of globalization and then turns to articles dealing with some of the developing countries and regions, including Mexico and Latin America as a whole, South Africa, Nigeria, India, China, and the Muslim world. The articles will give the careful reader a better understanding of the diversity of social and political conditions in these countries.

Unit 5 considers three major trends in contemporary politics from a comparative perspective. First, the past quarter of a century has seen a remarkable spread of democratic forms of government in the world. This recent "wave of democratization," sometimes described as the "third" of its kind in modern history, seems likely to have a lasting effect on the political process in some countries that previously knew only authoritarian governments. But some recent reversals remind us there is no simple way to construct a stable democracy anywhere—least of all in countries that are divided by deep ethnic, economic, religious and other cleavages.

Second, beginning in the 1980s there has been a major shift in economic policy toward greater reliance on private enterprise and markets, and a corresponding reduction in state ownership and regulation in much of the world, including Communist-ruled China. But there has been a reaction in the advanced industrial societies and in many developing countries against the inequalities, dislocations, and uncertainties associated with the unfettered market economy.

Third, many parts of the world have seen a surge of what has been called "identity politics." This trend has brought group identities more strongly into play when differences are being defined, played out, and resolved in the political arena.

This is an unusually interesting and important time to study comparative politics. The past fifteen years have seen a major restructuring of politics in many countries along with a generational shift in leadership. Even in a time of political transformation, however, there will be significant patterns of continuity as well as change.

This is the twenty-third edition of *Annual Editions: Comparative Politics*. Over the years, the successive editions have reflected the developments that eventually brought about the post–cold war world of today. This present volume tries to present information and analysis that are useful in the quest to understand today's political world and the parameters it sets for tomorrow's developments.

A special word of thanks goes to my own past and present students at California State University, Long Beach. They are wonderfully inquisitive and help keep me posted on matters that this anthology must address. Several of my past students have helped me gather material. As always, I am particularly grateful to Susan B. Mason, who received her master's degree in political science over a decade ago. She continues to volunteer as a superb research assistant. Once again, I also wish to thank some other past and present students at Cal State, Linda Wohlman, Erika Reinhardt, Erik Ibsen, Jon Nakagawa, Perry Oliver, Mike Petri, Richard Sherman, and Ali Taghavi. Like so many others, these individuals first encountered the anthology in comparative politics courses. It is a great joy to have worked with such fine students. Their enthusiasm for the project has been contagious.

I am very grateful also to members of the advisory board and McGraw-Hill/Dushkin as well as to the many readers who have made useful comments on past selections and suggested new ones. I ask you all to help improve future editions by keeping me informed of your reactions and suggestions for change. Please complete and return the article rating form in the back of the book..

Christian Søe

Editor

Contents

UNIT 1
Pluralist Democracies: Country Studies

Part A.   The United Kingdom

Part B.   France

The concepts in bold italics are developed in the article. For further expansion, please refer to the Topic Guide and the Index.

The concepts in bold italics are developed in the article. For further expansion, please refer to the Topic Guide and the Index.

UNIT 2
Pluralist Democracies: Factors in the Political Process

The concepts in bold italics are developed in the article. For further expansion, please refer to the Topic Guide and the Index.

UNIT 3
Europe in Transition: West, Center, and East

The concepts in bold italics are developed in the article. For further expansion, please refer to the Topic Guide and the Index.

UNIT 4
Political Diversity in the Developing World

The concepts in bold italics are developed in the article. For further expansion, please refer to the Topic Guide and the Index.

The concepts in bold italics are developed in the article. For further expansion, please refer to the Topic Guide and the Index.

UNIT 5
Comparative Politics: Some Major Trends, Issues, and Prospects

The concepts in bold italics are developed in the article. For further expansion, please refer to the Topic Guide and the Index.

The concepts in bold italics are developed in the article. For further expansion, please refer to the Topic Guide and the Index.

Topic Guide

This topic guide suggests how the selections in this book relate to the subjects covered in your course. You may want to use the topics listed on these pages to search the Web more easily.

On the following pages a number of Web sites have been gathered specifically for this book. They are arranged to reflect the units of this *Annual Edition*. You can link to these sites by going to the DUSHKIN ONLINE support site at *http://www.dushkin.com/online/*.

ALL THE ARTICLES THAT RELATE TO EACH TOPIC ARE LISTED BELOW THE BOLD-FACED TERM.

World Wide Web Sites

The following World Wide Web sites have been carefully researched and selected to support the articles found in this reader. The easiest way to access these selected sites is to go to our DUSHKIN ONLINE support site at *http://www.dushkin.com/online/*.

AE: Comparative Politics 05/06

The following sites were available at the time of publication. Visit our Web site—we update DUSHKIN ONLINE regularly to reflect any changes.

General Sources

Central Intelligence Agency
http://www.odci.gov

Use this official home page to get connections to *The CIA Factbook,* which provides extensive statistical and political information about every country in the world.

National Geographic Society
http://www.nationalgeographic.com

This site provides links to National Geographic's archive of maps, articles, and documents. There is a great deal of material related to political cultures around the world.

U.S. Agency for International Development
http://www.info.usaid.gov

This Web site covers such broad and overlapping issues as democracy, population and health, economic growth, and development about different regions and countries.

U.S. Information Agency
http://usinfo.state.gov/

This USIA page provides definitions, related documentation, and discussion of topics on global issues. Many Web links are provided.

World Bank
http://www.worldbank.org

News (press releases, summaries of new projects, speeches) and coverage of numerous topics regarding development, countries, and regions are provided at this site.

World Wide Web Virtual Library: International Affairs Resources
http://www.etown.edu/vl/

Surf this site and its extensive links to learn about specific countries and regions, to research international organizations, and to study such vital topics as international law, development, the international economy, and human rights.

UNIT 1: Pluralist Democracies: Country Studies

France.com
http://www.france.com

The links at this site will lead to extensive information about the French government, politics, history, and culture.

GermNews
http://www.germnews.de/dn/about/

Search this site for German political and economic news covering the years 1995 to the present.

Japan Ministry of Foreign Affairs
http://www.mofa.go.jp

Visit this official site for Japanese foreign policy statements and discussions of regional and global relations.

UNIT 2: Pluralist Democracies: Factors in the Political Process

Carnegie Endowment for International Peace
http://www.ceip.org

This organization's goal is to stimulate discussion and learning among both experts and the public at large on a wide range of international issues. The site provides links to the well-respected journal *Foreign Policy,* to the Moscow Center, to descriptions of various programs, and much more.

Inter-American Dialogue (IAD)
http://www.iadialog.org

This is the Web site for IAD, a premier U.S. center for policy analysis, communication, and exchange in Western Hemisphere affairs. The 100-member organization has helped to shape the agenda of issues and choices in hemispheric relations.

The North American Institute (NAMI)
http://www.northamericaninstitute.org

NAMI, a trinational public-affairs organization concerned with the emerging "regional space" of Canada, the United States, and Mexico, provides links for study of trade, the environment, and institutional developments.

UNIT 3: Europe in Transition: West, Center, and East

Europa: European Union
http://europa.eu.int

This server site of the European Union will lead you to the history of the EU; descriptions of EU policies, institutions, and goals; discussion of monetary union; and documentation of treaties and other materials.

NATO Integrated Data Service (NIDS)
http://www.nato.int/structur/nids/nids.htm

NIDS was created to bring information on security-related matters to the widest possible audience. Check out this Web site to review North Atlantic Treaty Organization documentation of all kinds, to read *NATO Review,* and to explore key issues in the field of European security.

Research and Reference (Library of Congress)
http://lcweb.loc.gov/rr/

This massive research and reference site of the Library of Congress will lead you to invaluable information on the former Soviet Union and other countries attempting the transition to democracy. It provides links to numerous publications, bibliographies, and guides in area studies.

Russian and East European Network Information Center, University of Texas at Austin
http://reenic.utexas.edu/reenic/index.html

This is *the* Web site for information on Russia and the former Soviet Union.

UNIT 4: Political Diversity in the Developing World

Africa News Online
http://allafrica.com/

Open this site for extensive, up-to-date information on all of Africa, with reports from Africa's leading newspapers, magazines, and news agencies. Coverage is country-by-country and regional. Background documents and Internet links are among the resource pages.

ArabNet
http://www.arab.net

This home page of ArabNet, the online resource for the Arab world in the Middle East and North Africa, presents links to 22 Arab countries. Each country Web page classifies information using a standardized system of categories.

Inside China Today
http://www.einnews.com/china/

Part of the European Internet Network, this site leads to information on China, including recent news, government, and related sites pertaining to mainland China, Hong Kong, Macao, and Taiwan.

Organization for Economic Cooperation and Development
http://www.oecd.org/home/

Explore development, governance, and world trade and investment issues on this OECD site. It provides links to many related topics and addresses global economic issues on a country-by-country basis.

Sun SITE Singapore
http://sunsite.nus.edu.sg/noframe.html

These South East Asia Information pages provide information and point to other online resources about the region's 10 countries, including Vietnam, Indonesia, and Brunei.

UNIT 5: Comparative Politics: Some Major Trends, Issues, and Prospects

Commission on Global Governance
http://www.sovereignty.net/p/gov/gganalysis.htm

This site provides access to *The Report of the Commission on Global Governance,* produced by an international group of leaders who want to find ways in which the global community can better manage its affairs.

IISDnet
http://www.iisd.org/default.asp

This site of the International Institute for Sustainable Development, a Canadian organization, presents information through links on business and sustainable development, developing ideas, and Hot Topics. Linkages is its multimedia resource for environment and development policy makers.

ISN International Relations and Security Network
http://www.isn.ethz.ch

This site, maintained by the Center for Security Studies and Conflict Research, is a clearinghouse for extensive information on international relations and security policy. Topics are listed by category (Traditional Dimensions of Security, New Dimensions of Security) and by major world regions.

United Nations Environment Program
http://www.unep.ch/

Consult this home page of UNEP for links to critical topics about global issues, including decertification and the impact of trade on the environment. The site leads to useful databases and global resource information.

We highly recommend that you review our Web site for expanded information and our other product lines. We are continually updating and adding links to our Web site in order to offer you the most usable and useful information that will support and expand the value of your Annual Editions. You can reach us at: *http://www.dushkin.com/annualeditions/.*

World Map

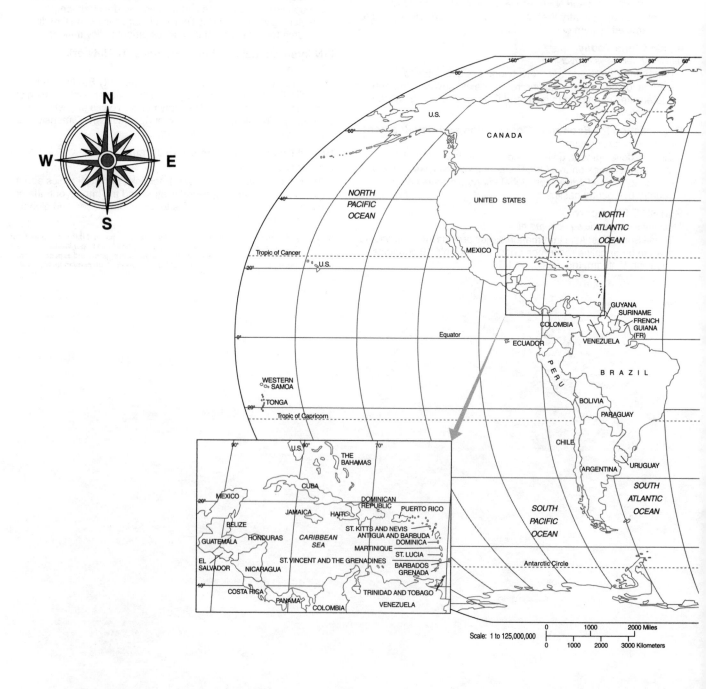

N
W   E
S

U.S.

CANADA

NORTH
PACIFIC
OCEAN

UNITED STATES

NORTH
ATLANTIC
OCEAN

Tropic of Cancer

MEXICO

U.S.

GUYANA
SURINAME
FRENCH
GUIANA
(FR)

COLOMBIA

VENEZUELA

Equator

ECUADOR

PERU

BRAZIL

WESTERN
SAMOA

BOLIVIA

TONGA

PARAGUAY

Tropic of Capricorn

CHILE

URUGUAY

ARGENTINA

SOUTH
ATLANTIC
OCEAN

SOUTH
PACIFIC
OCEAN

Antarctic Circle

U.S.

THE
BAHAMAS

CUBA

MEXICO

DOMINICAN
REPUBLIC

PUERTO RICO

JAMAICA

HAITI

BELIZE

ST. KITTS AND NEVIS
ANTIGUA AND BARBUDA
DOMINICA

GUATEMALA

HONDURAS

CARIBBEAN
SEA

MARTINIQUE

ST. LUCIA

EL
SALVADOR

NICARAGUA

ST. VINCENT AND THE GRENADINES

BARBADOS
GRENADA

COSTA RICA

TRINIDAD AND TOBAGO

PANAMA

COLOMBIA

VENEZUELA

Scale: 1 to 125,000,000

0	1000	2000 Miles
0	1000	2000	3000 Kilometers

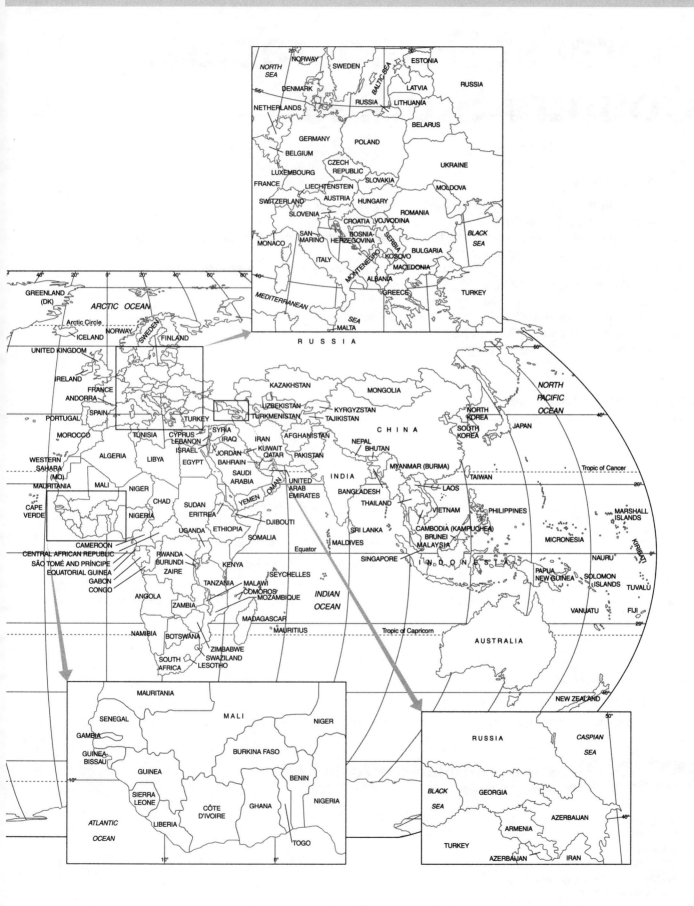

UNIT 1
Pluralist Democracies: Country Studies

Unit Selections

Key Points to Consider

- What are the main items on Prime Minister Blair's constitutional reform agenda, and how far have they become reality by now?

- What is "new" about Labour?

- How do Anthony Giddens and David Marquand differ in their perception of New Labour?

- How does Tony Blair manage to hold on to power despite his unpopular Iraq policy?

- Why did Jacques Chirac call an early parliamentary election in 1997, and how did the outcome produce a new form of "cohabitation" in the Fifth Republic?

- What are the signs that French politics have become more centrist or middle-of-the-road for the main political parties?

- How did the formula, "first time vote with the heart, next time with the head," boomerang for the Left in the French presidential elections of 2002?

- Name three unusual factors that helped the SPD and the Greens in Germany find new supporters in the parliamentary elections of 2002.

- Explain what is meant by the reform packet, *Agenda 2010*, and why it has been so controversial.

- Why has the federal council (Bundesrat) become a reform issue in Germany?

- Explain why Japan's LDP is jokingly said to be "neither liberal, nor democratic, nor a party."

- What has been the role of this party in postwar Japanese politics?

- How and why has a would-be reformer like Prime Minister Koizumi begun to resemble his predecessors?

 **Links: www.dushkin.com/online/**
These sites are annotated in the World Wide Web pages.

France.com
http://www.france.com
GermNews
http://www.germnews.de/dn/about/
Japan Ministry of Foreign Affairs
http://www.mofa.go.jp

Britain, France, Germany, and Italy are the most prominent industrial societies in Western Europe. Their modern political histories vary considerably, but all have developed from oligarchic forms of rule into pluralist democracies with representative forms of government. None of them is without democratic shortcomings, but each can point to a democratic infrastructure, with regular elections, active citizens, competing political parties, assertive interest groups and a free press. It is a key axiom that the "rule of law" must prevail, with government officials and civil servants alike bound by legal rules in their public acts. Japan appears to have developed less overt forms of pluralist expression and competition, but it too is a representative democracy and occupies a similar position of political prominence in Eastern Asia. Each of these countries has developed a distinctive set of political institutions, defined its own public agenda, and found its own dynamic balance of continuity and change. But there are intriguing similarities as well. Their individual traits, coupled with important similarities, invite cross-national comparisons. Our study of politics can usefully begin here.

The five countries all belong in the relatively small category of "older democracies." This is how political scientist Robert A. Dahl refers to the 22 countries—15 of them located in Western Europe—that have continuously maintained democratic forms of governance since at least 1950. Had Dahl set his starting point just a few years earlier, the list of "older democracies" would have been much shorter. It is sobering to remember that in our group of five, only Britain did not interrupt its democratic development at some point in the twentieth century. Three of these countries (Italy, Japan and Germany) abandoned the democratic road in the period between the two world wars, and France did the same after its defeat and partial military occupation by Germany in 1940. After World War II, these four all started out with new democratic constitutions, whereas Britain continued to function—as it had for centuries—within an evolving framework of basic laws, rules, and conventions often referred to as its "unwritten" or uncodified constitution.

The four West European countries in our group show the impact of some major developments that are changing the political, social and economic map of their continent. This was the birthplace of the modern nation-state, and it is now the location where that basic political construct is undergoing a partial and ambiguous transformation. In principle and practice, all of the member nations of the European Union (EU) have agreed to an unprecedented dilution of their traditional national sovereignty. For these countries, the fulcrum of much policy-making has been shifting away from the national arena to the EU, particularly in economic matters. As a result, some familiar aspects of their political identity, like national borders or distinctive national currencies, have been reduced in importance or entirely replaced.

None of this signals the end of the nation-state or its imminent displacement by a United States of Europe. But no student of comparative politics will want to ignore the European Union as a novel political formation—so novel, that a former Commission President once referred to the EU as an "unidentified political object" (UPO). It began with a core group of six member states in

the 1950s and grew incrementally to fifteen by 1996. In May of 2004, however, the EU in one major move almost doubled its membership to 25. Eight of its ten new members had spent the Cold War under communist governments, as integral units of the Soviet bloc in Central and Eastern Europe. With about 450 million people since this recent expansion, the EU now overshadows the United States by more than 150 million in population. One of the big questions is how this regional organization will change as a result of its enlargement and diversification. Part three returns to this topic from an EU perspective.

Europeans have begun to examine carefully another of their major contributions to contemporary politics, the modern welfare state. In practically every country there are attempts to define a new balance between economic efficiency and social justice, as governments and publics are confronted with the increasing costs of a popular and relatively generous system of welfare and service entitlements. If the funding problem were merely a cyclical one, it would lend itself more easily to solutions within the existing policy framework. But there are structural components that seem to require a thorough revamping or "reinvention" of the welfare state. The problem is exacerbated by the overall ageing of the population in these societies, where long life expectancies and low birth rates have become the rule. Almost everywhere in Europe, this is causing strains on the social budget and its "pay-as-you-go" formula that in practice involves an inter-generational transfer of wealth.

Economically, the five countries have relatively high and fairly similar rankings. They are all members of the Group of Seven (G 7), where they follow the United States in places two (Japan), three (Germany), four (Britain), five (France), and six (Italy) among the world's biggest market economies. If China's economy were included, that huge and rapidly developing country would probably rank in place three or four. On the other hand, when economies are compared in terms of gross domestic product (GDP) per capita, China falls far behind while our five countries slip somewhat lower as they are passed and become separated by a few smaller but higher performing economies. Yet even in terms of per capita product, the five countries remain at the high end of the world's economies and keep the same internal order, except that Britain moves ahead of Germany. There is little change when it comes to a standard measure of the quality of life. The Human Development Index (HDI) places Japan slightly ahead of equidistant Britain and France, closely followed by Germany, with Italy trailing slightly behind. Once again, the aggregate figures are strikingly similar for the five countries.

All five have arrived at some "mixed" form of market capitalism, but here their manner and degree of state intervention in the economy does show considerable variations. Since the "Thatcher Revolution" of the 1980s, Britain has come closer to the relatively open market conditions of the United States, while France and Germany have followed a more organized and regulated form of capitalism, often called a social market economy. The highly protected and corporatist Japanese economy is less competitive and sometimes described as neo-mercantilist.

When compared for disparity in income, as measured by the gini index, the five countries also show notable differences. Yet none of them records as high an income gap between the top 10 percent and the lowest 10 percent of the population as the one found in the United States. The income gap is lowest in Japan and highest—and thus closest to the U.S. situation—in Britain. It is noteworthy that some of Europe's smaller countries, like the five Scandinavian nations and the Netherlands, have demonstrated that it is possible to create a form of market economy that combines overall prosperity and relatively small income discrepancies. Such national differences in income distribution probably result from public policy rather than from undisturbed market outcomes or pure chance.

There are some additional developments that underscore the continuing political importance of Europe. For example, it is faced with a growing ethnic and cultural diversity brought about by the arrival of many economic migrants and political refugees during and after the cold war. This influx has had some stimulating economic and cultural effects, but it has also brought issues of multicultural co-existence and tolerance back onto the political agenda in a new and intensified form. An example is the current controversy in France over an official ban on wearing a piece of clothing that could be regarded as a religious symbol, such as a head scarf or a yarmulke, in public schools or other secular institutions.

Even as West Europeans seek to come to terms with this challenge of greater diversity, their politics has been affected by a growing ecological awareness. It shows up in widespread support for national and international initiatives to protect the environment, such as the Kyoto Treaty. They are also trying to adjust to the new information technologies and the many challenges of the global market with its opportunities for expansion and its threats of job insecurity and economic instability. It is clearly a time of dynamic change and wrenching dislocations that transcend the traditional boundaries of region and nation. In such a bewildering context, it is not surprising to encounter manifestations of discontent that also take the form of anti-establishment protest, a topic that is further explored in unit two.

The events of September 11, 2001 and its aftermath have added a new element of organized violence and unpredictability to our political world. The terrorist attacks on the World Trade Towers and the Pentagon were clearly directed at the United States, but the clandestine network of supporters and sympathizers reached deep into the immigrant communities of several European countries. Similar strikes could affect them at any time, and have already done so in the case of the train-bombing in Madrid in the spring of 2004. This awareness has affected the politics of these countries. It helped mobilize their early support for U.S.–led military counter-measures in Afghanistan. But it soon became clear that there is no trans-Atlantic consensus on the most effective strategy for dealing with the new terrorism or our own vulnerability to this type of attack. One crucial assumption of the traditional policy of containment does not apply to this kind of activity, namely that the desire for self-preservation will restrain the actions of potential opponents by making them reluctant to risk severe retaliation. The primary responsibility of the state, to provide security for its citizens in a dangerous world, has acquired a new dimension in light of the willingness of individual terrorists to risk or even seek out self-destruction (understood as noble self-sacrifice). The search for an appropriate and effective response will preoccupy our politics for a long time to come.

This became particularly evident in the controversy about the approach to be taken in dealing with Iraq and its ruler, Saddam Hussein. The U.S. government was determined to move decisively to disarm Iraq of the weapons of mass destruction, which President George W. Bush believed the Baghdad government to be developing and accumulating. In addition, the United States spoke openly of seeking a "regime change," leaving no one in doubt of its readiness to conduct what it presented as a massive preemptive strike to achieve its goals.

Chancellor Gerhard Schröder and President Jacques Chirac, the political leaders of Germany and France, both reacted critically to President Bush's position. Their preference for giving more time to UN weapon inspectors to search for hidden weapons in Iraq ran counter to the official American determination to use military pressure and intervention to force the issue. British Prime Minister Tony Blair played a markedly different role, in the tradition of his country's "special relationship" to the United States. He was largely supportive of President Bush's strategy, even as he stressed that the *casus belli* had been Iraq's failure to meet UN-backed resolutions on weapons inspection. As a result, a significant number of British troops joined the American ones in the invasion and occupation of Iraq in April 2003. Blair ended up having to pay a heavy political price for extending political and military support. In Britain, he ran into an unprecedented barrage of public criticism, much of it from within his own party.

Not surprisingly, the debate has led to reflections on more fundamental political differences between much of continental Europe and the United States. One of the most widely discussed thesis has come from the American political writer, Robert Kagan. He concludes that Europe and America are not just separated on the important issue of Iraq, but that the "older" and weaker continent no longer shares the willingness or propensity of a "younger" and more powerful United States to use military power as a means of foreign policy. In a widely quoted phrase, he sums up his perception of the difference: "Americans are from Mars and Europeans are from Venus." Europeans are more likely than Americans to stress the need for multilateral approaches, and to prefer "soft" over "hard" power in international affairs. There is little agreement between them, Kagan argues, and less and less mutual understanding. He believes that the deep lying causes are likely to endure. Kagan's thesis has set off a lively debate, much of it critical of the simple dichotomy he sometimes adopts. The issue is critically discussed from a British perspective by Timothy Garton Ash in his article in unit two.

It is important to pay attention to these major changes and new challenges. But we must not lose sight of some equally important if less dramatic elements of continuity or even inertia in our politics. In the stable democracies of Western Europe and Japan, the political process is usually defined by a relatively mild blend of change and continuity. Here political agendas are normally modified rather than discarded entirely, and shifts in the balance of power do not take the form of revolutionary displacements of a ruling group. Instead, there are occasional changes of government as a result of coalition disagreements or routine elections.

Britain has long been regarded as "the mother" of the parliamentary system of government. In contrast to a presidential system, where the chief executive and legislatures are separately elected by the voters for fixed terms of office, a parliamentary government is often described as based on the "fusion" of the executive and legislative powers. Its most distinctive trait is that the prime minister, as head of government, is in some way "chosen" by and from the popularly elected legislature and remains dependent on its sustained majority support or toleration to stay in office. Should the prime minister lose majority support in the legislature, then he or she may be replaced by someone else. The political rupture sometimes finds expression in a formal vote of "no confidence."

There are numerous variations in the institutional workings of parliamentary government over time or locale. In Britain, for example, there is no formal "election" of the prime minister in the House of Commons. Instead, the person who is the recognized leader of the majority party in the House of Commons will be asked by the monarch to form a government. In Germany, on the other hand, the federal chancellor is formally elected by the Bundestag as the result of the formation of a majority based on a coalition of two or more political parties.

In today's British version of parliamentary government, called the Westminster model, there is usually one party that wins a majority of the seats in the House of Commons. The result is single-party rule and a form of majoritarian politics in which the main opposition party of "outs" plays the adversary role of an institutionalized critic and rival of the government party of "ins." In continental Europe, where elections seldom result in a single party majority in the legislature, the prime minister is normally supported by a parliamentary coalition of parties that provide the crucial flow of majority support or toleration required for the political executive to stay in office. Under such power-sharing coalition governments, the political process tends to be less adversary and more inclusive or consensual than in the majoritarian Westminster system.

Politically, a British prime minister can stay in power between elections as long as he or she continues to receive majority support from the elected legislature. It is possible to lose the prime ministerial office through a parliamentary vote of no confidence. Such an overthrow is relatively rare in contemporary British politics, because the electoral system—based on single member districts that are won in plurality ("first past the post") elections—tends to produce a single party majority that is then kept together by political self-interest and other factors that produce a strong party discipline. A motion of no confidence can only threaten a prime minister whose own parliamentary base of supporters has for some reason—such as attrition or desertion—become too weak to ensure a dependable majority in favor of the government.

A far more likely cause for turnovers in British government is a general election that results in the governing party losing its parliamentary majority. This has happened in seven of the 16 general elections held between 1945 and 2001—compared to seven party alternations in the White House resulting from 14 U.S. presidential elections in the same period. The most recent British example took place in 1997, when Labour defeated the Conservatives and replaced them in office.

It is also fairly common for prime ministers to step down at midterm, voluntarily or as the result of political pressure from members of their own party. Since 1945, there have been four such cases of early resignation when a British prime minister has been replaced by a leading member of the same party. The most recent case is that of Margaret Thatcher, who headed a Conservative government for more than eleven years, beginning in May 1979. In November 1990, she faced a potential revolt by members of her own parliamentary party, as many Conservatives concluded that she had become a political liability. She stepped down reluctantly, making the way free for another leading Tory, John Major, to succeed her as party leader and prime minister. Such an early resignation is very rare in the U.S. system, where heads of government are elected for fixed terms of office.

Since 1945 Britain can be said to have had three major reform governments that greatly altered some key features of British society and politics. The first of these was Clement Atlee's Labour Government (1945-51) that came to power immediately after World War II and replaced the wartime coalition government led by Winston Churchill. In a nation weary of war and depression, Labour had won a sweeping victory over the Conservatives. During its first five years in office, Labour established a comprehensive welfare state in Britain, nationalized some key parts of the economy ("the commanding heights"), and took the first major steps to dismantle the large overseas empire by releasing the huge Indian subcontinent. The result was a sea change that turned Britain toward a more egalitarian form of society. Labour scraped through the general election of 1950 with a tiny parliamentary majority, too weak to continue with major new reforms. A year later, it called an early election in a bid to win a "working" parliamentary majority. The stakes were unusually high in 1951, and the result was a milestone election that recorded one of the biggest voter turnouts in British history. Labour won a narrow plurality of the popular vote, but the Conservatives won a majority of the seats in the House of Commons and formed the next government.

During the first five years in office, Atlee's Labour government had taken full advantage of the British political system's capacity for effective, comprehensive yet accountable action. This institutional trait has impressed many U.S. political scientists since Woodrow Wilson. It was much less in evidence during the next quarter of a century. Instead, the British governmental process from 1950 to the late 1970s seemed to be better captured in the phrase "muddling through." Some historians would later refer to these years as an era of "consensus politics."

Having come back to power in 1951 by a whisker, the Conservatives refrained from a "roll back" of the welfare state reforms. They returned some parts of the nationalized economy to private hands, but they engaged in no major reform program of their own. Decolonization continued and reduced Britain's international presence. When Labour finally returned to government office, between 1964 and 1970, the new government talked a lot about policy innovation but failed like its Tory predecessor to deal effectively with some mounting economic problems. In the regular confrontation between "ins" and "outs" in the House of Commons, the British tradition of adversary rhetoric continued to

3

flourish. In practice, however, the differences between the two major political parties seemed often to have been reduced to relatively minor matters.

Specific foreign policy issues continued to provide the occasion for some severe political disagreements that sometimes ran through as well as between the main political parties. In 1956, Conservative Prime Minister Eden tried in collusion with the leaders of the Fourth French Republic and Israel to wrest control of the nationalized Suez Canal from President Nasser's Egypt. The military intervention led to a deep division in British politics and caused a temporary rift in relations with the United States. Britain's embarrassed withdrawal from the Suez engagement underscored its decline as a major power. Prime Minister Eden's resignation a few months later was a key element in the resolution of this foreign policy fiasco. He was succeeded by Harold Macmillan, who turned out to be a successful practitioner of consensus politics until he too felt obliged to step down, in his case as the result of a scandal involving a member of the government.

The relationship to the European Economic Community (originally EEC, then EC, now EU) was the source of another political division. Britain had chosen not to join the original six founding members, who signed the Treaty of Rome at the beginning of 1957. The British government soon came to regret its decision and sought entry in the early 1960s. At this point, however, French President Charles de Gaulle blocked the late comer who would inevitably have challenged France's political leadership of the Community. After having been rebuffed by France a second time, Britain finally became a member in 1973, under its new Conservative Prime Minister Edward Heath. The Labour Party was deeply divided over the issue. When it returned to power in the following year, Labour therefore felt obliged to use a national referendum—the first one in British political history—to decide whether Britain should stay a member. The decision was affirmative, but there continues still today to be elements in both major parties who are, at best, reluctant "Europeans."

By the late 1960s and throughout the 1970s, Britain could no longer be said to live up to its earlier reputation for effective government. Instead, the country became notorious for its chronic governing problems. Serious observers spoke of Britain as "the sick man of Europe." They diagnosed a socio-political infirmity dubbed "Englanditis," a condition characterized by such problems as economic stagnation, social malaise, and a general incapacity of elected governments to deal effectively with such evidence of relative deterioration.

In the years before Margaret Thatcher became Prime Minister, there were several attempts to give a macro-explanation of Britain's problems. Some British political scientists, like Anthony King, defined their country's condition as one of "governmental overload." According to this diagnosis, British governments had become so entangled by socioeconomic entitlements that the country was on the edge of political paralysis or "ungovernability." In the United States, the political economist Mancur Olson developed a more general but in some ways similar explanation of political "sclerosis" in advanced pluralist democracies like Britain. He explained it in terms of the clotting effects of a highly developed interest group system that made excessive demands on government and thereby threatened its ability to perform. In a similar analysis of Western democracies that included the British case, Samuel Huntington detected what he decided to call an "excess of democracy," a jarring phrase that critics would not let him forget.

A second cluster of interpretations explained Britain's relative decline primarily in terms of structural inertia that prevented the country from keeping pace with its European neighbors. From this perspective, the problems were primarily attributed to Britain's tenacious tradition as a class-divided society and imperial power. Compared to its more modern European neighbors, supporters of this view argued, the United Kingdom was hampered at home by the remnants of an outmoded and dysfunctional social order. It needed to promote a meritocracy by way of greater equality of opportunity and a general societal "modernization." Abroad, the U.K. needed to disentangle itself from an unproductive legacy of over-commitment or "overstretch" in international affairs. The British-American historian, Paul Kennedy, later pursued the thesis about the paralyzing costs of an imperial overextension in his widely discussed book on the rise and fall of the great powers.

Yet another explanation of Britain's governing crisis focused on the unusually sharp adversarial character of the country's major party politics. It suggested that a major culprit was Britain's famed "Westminster Model" of government by a single majority party. From this perspective, the ritualized parliamentary confrontation of the two major parties served to polarize political discourse, leave the moderate center underrepresented, and disrupt the governmental process whenever the "ins" were replaced by the "outs." This interpretation, which understandably found support among centrist Liberals, sometimes idealized the broader power-sharing and consensus-seeking forms of coalition government that are found in most of the parliamentary systems in Western Europe.

By the mid-1970s, this last explanation gained some plausibility, because the mounting British problems had weakened the grip of consensus politics. The two main parties had again begun to diverge and become more polarized in their search for political answers to Britain's problems. As Labour and Conservatives moved away from their long held centrist positions, toward the political left and right respectively, some voters in the middle turned to the Liberals and thereby helped them revive as a national "third" party. In the early 1980s, British party politics became more complex, when a group of moderates defected from Labour to form a new centrist party. Led by such well known Labour politicians as Roy Jenkins, David Owen, and Shirley Williams, this Social Democratic Party (SDP) cooperated with the old Liberals in an electoral "Alliance." In this manner, the two "third" parties avoided competing against each other and managed to win about a quarter of the popular vote in 1983 and 1987. Under the plurality election rules of "first past the post," however, the two Alliance parties received only about three percent of the seats in the House of Commons.

The Conservatives, led since 1975 by Margaret Thatcher, were the immediate political beneficiaries of the fragmentation of the non-Conservative vote between Labour, the Liberals, and the Social Democrats. They swept into power in 1979 with 43 percent of the total vote but over 60 percent of the seats, and they went on to win with similar margins in the two general elections of 1983 and 1987. This could hardly have been predicted in the early 1980s, when the prime minister and her party plummeted in popularity as a result of some wrenching economic reform measures. The situation changed in 1982, when Argentina's navy invaded the British-held Falkland Islands in the South Atlantic. The move elicited a swift and determined military response from Prime Minister Thatcher. Her success in restoring British control of the distant islands had symbolic significance for many British people who had not been comfortable with a "Little England" role for their country.

This second major reform government in Britain since World War II (1979 to 1990) saw itself as an overdue corrective to the general political direction taken by Britain since Clement Atlee's earlier reform government and the consensus politics it had spawned. Prime Minister Thatcher prided herself on being a "conviction politician" with policies that were based on sound conservative principles. Thatcher was determined to replace what she saw as a sluggish socialist torpor with a dynamic entrepreneurial spirit. Her policies were designed to stimulate the private sector and the interplay of market forces, weaken the obstructing trade unions, and generally reduce the interventionist role of the government. She stayed in office for over eleven years or about twice as long as Atlee's postwar reform government. Moreover, her successor was another Conservative, John Major, whose additional six and a half years in office (1990 to 1997) served to consolidate the Thatcher legacy.

As prime minister, Thatcher dismissed the centrist path taken by Britain's "consensus politicians," as she referred to her immediate Labour and Conservative predecessors. Her radical rhetoric, non-accommodating style and somewhat less drastic policy changes spawned yet another debate about "the Thatcher Effect." The disagreement was not only about how best to achieve economic growth but also about the kind of polity and society Britain ought to be. Even among the observers who were impressed by the economic revival of Britain in the mid-1980s, there were many who became disturbed by some social and political trade-offs. In particular, the income gap between the highest and lowest 10 percent of the U.K. population grew precipitously, as compared to the West European neighbors. It began to move towards the much greater U.S. disparity between top and bottom incomes. And in the late 1980s critics could also point to the return of stagflation, or sluggish economic performance coupled with fairly high inflation.

The British debate had never been restricted to the economy only. The concerns about an alleged "ungovernability" were now joined by questions about the dislocating consequences of the Conservative government's economic and social policies. In addition, some decried what they saw as emerging authoritarian and centralizing tendencies in the governance of the country. They cited all manner of high-handed efforts by the national government—such as its imposition of central direction over education at all levels, introduction of greater cost controls in the popular National Health Service, privatization of electricity and water industries, or drastic inroads upon what had long been considered established rights in such areas as local government powers and civil liberties.

In foreign affairs, Prime Minister Thatcher had combined an assertive role for Britain in Europe and close cooperation with the United States under the leadership of Presidents Ronald Reagan and George Bush. As a patriot and staunch defender of both market economics and national sovereignty, Thatcher distrusted the drive toward monetary and greater political union in the European Community. She became known throughout the continent for her unusually sharp public attacks on what she pilloried as tendencies toward bureaucratic intervention or technocratic socialism in Brussels. There were critics in her own party who regarded her "Euro-critical" position as untenable, also because it isolated Britain and reduced its influence on questions of strategic planning for the EC's future.

For the mass electorate, however, nothing seems to have been so upsetting as Thatcher's introduction of the community charge or "poll tax." This was a tax on each adult resident that would replace the local property tax or "rates" as a means of financing local public services. Although the new tax was extremely unpopular from the start, the veteran prime minister resisted all pressure to abandon the project before its full national implementation in early 1990. Not only did such a poll tax appear inequitable or regressive, as compared to one based on property values, it also turned out to be set much higher by local governments than the national government originally had estimated.

The politically disastrous result was that, as a revenue measure, the poll tax was anything but neutral in its impact. It created an unexpectedly large proportion of immediate losers, that is, people who had to pay considerably more in local taxes than previously. The immediate winners were people who had previously paid high property taxes. Not surprisingly, the national and local governments disagreed about who was responsible for the high poll tax bills, but the voters seemed to have little difficulty in assigning blame to Margaret Thatcher and the Conservative Party as originators of the unpopular reform. Many voters were up in arms, and some observers correctly anticipated that the tax rebellion would undermine Thatcher's position in her own party and become her political Waterloo.

The feisty prime minister had weathered many previous challenges, but she was now confronted with increasing speculation that the Tories might try to replace her with a more attractive leader before the next general election. The issue that finally triggered such a development was Thatcher's stepped-up attacks on closer European integration during 1990. It led her deputy prime minister and party colleague, Sir Geoffrey Howe, to resign on November 1, 1990, with an unusually sharp public rebuke of her attitude toward the EC. There followed a leadership challenge in the Conservative Party that ended with Thatcher's resignation, in advance of an expected defeat in the internal vote taken by her own parliamentary party.

The transition in power was remarkably smooth. John Major, who was chosen by his fellow Conservatives in Parliament to be Thatcher's successor as party leader and thus prime minister, had long been regarded as one of her closest cabinet supporters. In economic policy, he basically supported her "tough love" approach, which she had often described as "dry"—in contrast to the "wet" or soft approach of accommodating "consensus" politicians like Edward Heath. Although Major seemed to prefer a somewhat more compassionate social policy than Thatcher, he followed her general rejection of the Tory tradition of welfare paternalism. Not surprisingly, he abandoned the hated poll tax. His governing style was far less dramatic or confrontational than that of his predecessor, and some nostalgic critics were quick to call him dull. During the Gulf War of 1991, he continued Thatcher's policy of giving strong British support for firm and ultimately military measures against the government of Iraq, whose troops had invaded and occupied oil-rich Kuwait.

By the time of Thatcher's resignation, Labour appeared to be in a position to capitalize on the growing disenchantment with the Conservative government. Led by Neil Kinnock, the opposition party had begun to move back toward its traditional center-left position, presenting itself as a politically moderate and socially caring agent of reform. But Labour was now troubled by a new version of the centrist alternative that had helped keep Thatcher in power by fragmenting the non-Conservative camp in the elections of 1983 and 1987. After operating as an electoral coalition or "Alliance" in those years, the Liberals and Social Democrats had finally joined together as a single party, the Liberal Democrats.

Under the leadership of Paddy Ashdown and later Charles Kennedy, the Liberal Democrats have sought to overcome the electoral system's bias against third parties by promoting themselves as an attractive alternative to the Conservatives on the right and Labour on the left. Their strategic goal has been to win the balance of power in a "hung" parliament and then, taking on the role of parliamentary majority-makers, enter a government coalition with one of the two big parties, presumably Labour. One of their main demands would then be the adoption of some form of proportional representation (PR). Such an electoral system, which is used widely in Western Europe, would almost surely guarantee the Liberal Democrats a much larger base in the House of Commons. This would in turn give them a pivotal role in the coalition politics that would henceforth replace the single party majorities in the House of Commons that Britain's plurality elections rarely fail to produce.

In the general election called by Prime Minister Major for April 9, 1992, the Conservatives delivered a surprise by winning an unprecedented fourth consecutive term of office. The Tories garnered almost the same percentage of the popular vote as in 1987 (about 42 percent), while Labour increased its total share slightly, from 31 to 34 percent. Support for the Liberal Democrats declined to 18 percent. In the House of Commons, the electoral system's bias in favor of the front-runners showed up once again. The Conservatives lost 40 seats but ended up with 336 of the 651 members, enough to form another single-party government. Labour increased its number of seats from 229 to 271, while the Liberal Democrats-with half as many voters as Labour—ended up with only 20 seats. As usual, a few remaining seats went to candidates of the small regional parties from Northern Ireland, Scotland, and Wales.

As a result, the Conservatives and Prime Minister Major stayed in office for another five years. But by now the majority party had lost its drive to continue the Thatcher Revolution. The Conservatives were divided, and their new leader was not a dynamic leader or reformer. Nevertheless, John Major's presence as prime minister for six and a half years made a big difference by essentially consolidating his predecessor's controversial reforms. Thatcher would surely have tried to push them further, while Kinnock's Labour would have wanted a partial roll back.

The extended period in opposition had a profound effect on Labour. In the years after the 1992 election, the party came under the increasingly centrist leadership first of John Smith and then, after the latter's sudden death, of Tony Blair. In the public opinion polls, Labour soon took a commanding and continuous lead over the Conservative governing party. John Major therefore had good reason to delay the next election as long as possible, until May 1997.

This time there were no surprises, except for the enormous parliamentary landslide that greeted the victor. With just over 43 percent of the British vote (or almost the same share as the Conservatives had won in their four consecutive victories), the Labour Party won a commanding majority of 418 of 659 seats in the House of Commons. The Liberal Democrats saw their share of the vote drop to 17 percent, but widespread tactical voting in swing districts more than doubled their number of parliamentary seats to 46, their best showing in about seven decades. Labour had also benefited from such tactical voting that was aimed at unseating the Conservatives. As a result, the Liberal Democrats failed once again to reach their strategic goal of becoming ma-

jority-makers in a governing coalition. Labour had a huge parliamentary majority of its own and formed a single-party government.

Labour's victory gave rise to the third reform government in Britain since World War II. Unlike Prime Ministers Atlee or Thatcher, however, Tony Blair did not focus primarily on major social and economic policy changes. Since the mid-1990s, the British economy had once again revived well ahead of those on the mainland in Western Europe. A growing number of observers seemed willing to conclude that Thatcher's "neo-liberal" policies had played a role in stimulating the U.K. economy. It had become more flexible and dynamic, leading to higher growth rates and lower unemployment. But there were serious trade-offs that Blair's government could have been expected to give more remedial attention—above all Britain's growing income disparities and the neglected and dilapidated infrastructure of the public service sector, where greater investments were badly needed for maintenance and renewal. Still, Donald Hirsch shows that there has been a reduction in poverty under Labour.

Blair's reform agenda gave prominence to the growing demand for constitutional change in Britain. In the late 1980s, an ad hoc reform coalition had launched *Charter 88*, an interest group that called for a bill of rights, electoral reform, and a modernization of the basic "rules of the game" in British politics. The chartists chose the tricentennial of Britain's Glorious Revolution of 1688 to launch their effort. It triggered a broad discussion in the country and several different proposals for constitutional reform.

The Liberal Democrats had been in the vanguard of reform efforts from the beginning. Even some Conservatives entered the fray, primarily to establish citizenship rights against state bureaucracy. Labour's position became crucial after it took office in May 1997. While he was still opposition leader, Tony Blair had identified himself and his party with the institutional modernization of the U.K. But he had expressed reservations about abandoning the plurality electoral system for the House of Commons that underpins the Westminster form of government by creating single-party majorities.

In contrast to France, Britain's evolutionary constitutional development and its piecemeal approach to institutional change have produced a remarkable pattern of asymmetry in the country's political structures. The Blair reforms fit well into that pattern. This is illustrated by the way the new government dealt with the recurrent demand for setting up special regional assemblies in Scotland and Wales. Soon after Labour took power, regional referendums resulted in majority approval of such assemblies—a regional parliament (with very limited powers of taxation) for Scotland, and a weaker assembly for Wales. In both cases, the regional assembly was to be elected by a form of proportional representation (PR), even as the United Kingdom continued to elect the House of Commons using a "first past the post" system. The Scottish case turned out to be a textbook example of the political impact of an electoral system: PR resulted in a multiparty regional parliament in Edinburgh, where majorities are only possible by way of two or more parties building a coalition. Presumably, similar conditions would prevail in Britain, if PR were adopted for the House of Commons.

The regional problem associated with the six counties that make up Northern Ireland or Ulster has long been recognized as far more intractable. It involves the coexistence of two communities of people, who espouse rival identities and in many cases would prefer not to live together. Even if only relatively few took up arms, their paramilitary organizations were responsible for many terrorist actions during the last three decades of the twentieth century. Protestants make up a majority of nearly 60 percent of the population in Ulster. They vary in the intensity of their political commitment, but they are overwhelmingly Unionist and wish to maintain Northern Ireland's ties to Britain. A very large structural minority of about 40 percent are Catholics. They are overwhelmingly in favor of seeing the six counties unite with the Republic of Ireland that makes up the main part of the island.

The Blair government worked assiduously to broker a deal for Ulster that would be acceptable to the two communities and their leaders. The negotiating process came to include outsiders, with the Irish and U.S. governments playing supportive mediating roles. Former U.S. Senator George Mitchell and a retired Canadian general invested their personal skills and reputations as honest brokers. An agreement was reached in April 1998. In the ensuing referendum, an impressive majority of 71 percent of the voters in Ulster, on an electoral turnout of 81 percent, approved this so-called Good Friday agreement. It also provides for the use of proportional representation in electing a regional assembly along with measures for power-sharing in the regional administration. The goal was to include representatives of the two communities and their several parties.

The settlement soon ran into disputes over its implementation. There followed political confrontations, a temporary suspension of the assembly and later, in 2002, of the regional government. One of the most contentious issues has revolved around the halting progress in disarming the Irish Republican Army (IRA). In view of the paramilitary activities by both sides in the recent past, it is hardly surprising that persistent mutual fear and suspicion continue to hamper relations between the two communities.

In addition to creating these new regional levels of representative institutions, the Labour government has shown interest in another devolution of power to existing or newly created local governments, such as that of London. This is a reversal of a shift in the opposite direction that took place under Prime Minister Thatcher. Yet another reform aims at a thorough revamping of the pre-democratic upper house of Parliament, the House of Lords, where the great majority of the hereditary peers have now lost their right to vote. The next step in its "modernization" will keep it as an unelected second chamber. It is still unclear how this appointed house will affect the asymmetrical balance of power with the elected House of Commons. Here and elsewhere, some critical observers invoke the "law of unanticipated consequences" when they point out that the institutional changes could bring with them some unwanted political trade-offs in terms of a reduced capacity to govern effectively or even to keep Britain together.

In his important article on Britain, Donley Studlar takes stock of these and other institutional reforms. He also reviews the reactions they have triggered until the end of the year 2004. Can one speak of a constitutional revolution in a country we usually associate with change by slow mutation? The author leaves no doubt that the series of reforms since 1997 represent important acts of constitutional engineering, even if Blair's product reflects a selective approach to change and lacks the symmetrical qualities of a complete constitutional blueprint. Clearly these matters would have been approached very differently, *if at all*, under a Conservative government.

What remains less certain is whether these institutional reforms contributed to Labour's electoral triumph in June 2001. This victory was not free of imperfections. Most serious was the very low voter turnout, which had consistently been over 70 percent since World War II but in 2001 sank by more than 10 points to only 59.4 percent. There were hardly any changes in the share of the vote received by each of the parties. The Liberal Democrats again failed to become a balancer, but they won six additional seats for a new high of 52. With close to 41 percent of the popular vote, Labour won 413 of the 659 seats in the House of Commons—another disproportional result that seemed likely to guarantee Labour its first ever full second term in office.

In the second article, Emma Duncan anticipates "judgment day," as she refers to the next general election in Britain. Like most observers, she expects a 2005 election, marked by voter apathy and a Labour victory with a reduced majority. The Labour record in office is more thoroughly reviewed and evaluated by Anthony Giddens and David Marquand, who disagree on whether the party deserves a third term.

France celebrated the bicentennial of its 1789 Revolution by preparing major public ceremonies to celebrate that formative event in modern political history. Unexpectedly, the anniversary was partly overshadowed by another great political upheaval, as several Communist regimes in Central and Eastern Europe began to totter before they eventually collapsed. This curious combination of events stimulated a discussion about the costs and benefits of the revolutionary French model for transforming society, in which one heard echoes of Edmund Burke's contemporary advocacy of an alternative British tradition of societal change by slow but steady mutation. In reality, the British experience is not without periods of accelerated and politically driven reform offset by times of consolidation or stagnation. Yet modern French political development has been far more discontinuous than its British counterpart, recording numerous attempts at a fresh start since 1789: For example, historians count between 13 and 17 French constitutions in the first two centuries that followed. French political discourse reflected the sharp ideological cleavages to which the Revolution had given birth.

By now, however, France seems to have found its own form of political stability and continuity. There are radical residues on the far Right and far Left, but moderate center-left and center-right positions have become more prevalent and respectable. The trend toward political moderation has been accompanied by a relative consolidation of the French party system. In the Third Republic (1870 to 1940) and Fourth Republic (1946 to 1958), French politics had been notorious for its multiplicity of undisciplined parties and groupings. They provided a weak and unreliable support for prime ministers and their cabinets, resulting in political paralysis and instability of the many short-lived governments. In the frequent absence of responsible political direction and oversight, a well-trained civil service maintained administrative continuity but was helpless to resolve major political issues. There developed a risky tradition, known in France as Bonapartism, of intermittently calling for strong political saviors who were to lead the country out of its recurrent crises. Ironically, it was such a Bonapartist leader who ended up delivering an institutional solution to the problem.

In 1958 a political emergency caused by the colonial war in Algeria gave Charles de Gaulle the opportunity to become architect of a new political system. He had already played a Bonapartist role in World War II and later as interim leader of postwar France before the adoption—against his strong warnings—of the constitution of the Fourth Republic. Having long viewed the unruly French parties as beyond reform, de Gaulle decided to prune their power base in the legislature and instead concentrate authority in the executive. In the constitution of the Fifth Republic, the prime minister remains responsible to the National Assembly but enjoys far more perrogatives and is far less vulnerable to legislative power plays than previously. Above all, de Gaulle strengthened the government by adding a politically powerful president in what became known as a dual executive. The president is directly elected and has powers that include the appointment and dismissal of the prime minister and the dissolution of the National Assembly. The result is a presidential-prime ministerial system in which the president played the leading role for the first quarter of a century. It has found some imitation in the post-Communist political systems set up in Central and Eastern Europe.

There is some additional historical irony in the fact that the political framework of the Fifth Republic has become the setting for a consolidation and moderation of the French party system. The Communists (PCF) were once the main party of the Left, receiving about 20 percent of the vote in parliamentary elections until the late 1970s. They were relatively late to join their colleagues elsewhere in Western Europe in the painful withdrawal from their common Leninist and Stalinist heritage. By now they are a marginal force, less than half their former strength, but they have gained a chance to play a role in coalition politics that was previously denied them. Between 1997 and 2002, they were a small partner in the coalition government dominated by the Socialists, who had overtaken them on the Left in 1978.

On the extreme Right, Le Pen's National Front (FN) seemed in recent years to be weakened by internal splits and rivalries, before it surprised many by capturing 17 percent of the vote in the first round of the presidential election in 2002. The party continues to find right-wing populist support for its authoritarian and xenophobic rhetoric directed primarily against the country's many residents of Arab origin. The apparent electoral appeal of such invective has tempted some leaders of the establishment parties of the more moderate Right to voice carefully formulated reservations about the presence of so many immigrants.

Although it has become increasingly moderate and centrist, French party politics can still be highly volatile. To gain a little perspective, it makes sense to briefly review the electoral politics of the past decade, beginning with the parliamentary contest of 1993. Here the Socialists suffered a major setback after 5 years of serving as the main government party. Together, the loosely organized center-right Giscardists of the Union for French Democracy (UDF) and the more conservative neo-Gaullists in the Rally for the Republic (RPR) won about 40 percent of the first-round vote. Beginning with that plurality, these two coalition parties ended up with an overwhelming majority of nearly 80 percent of the seats in the 577-member National Assembly.

The Socialists (PS) and their close allies were clearly the big losers in this largest electoral landslide in French democratic history. Receiving about 20 percent of the popular vote on the first round, the Socialists plummeted from their previous share of 274 seats to 61 seats or less than one-quarter of their previous parliamentary strength. The Communists, with only 9 percent of the first-round vote, were able to win 24 seats because much of their electoral support was concentrated in a few urban districts where their candidates ran ahead of all others. With a slightly higher share of the total vote, the ultra-right National Front won no seats at all, having failed to arrive "first past the post" anywhere.

Socialist president François Mitterrand's second 7-year presidential term lasted until May 1995. After the parliamentary rout of the Socialists in March 1993, he was faced with the question of whether to resign early from the presidency. Alternatively, he could appoint a conservative prime minister for a period of "cohabitation," as after a similar setback in the parliamentary elections of 1986. Mitterrand opted once again for the latter solution, making sure to appoint a moderate Gaullist, Edouard Balladur, to this position.

For a time, the new prime minister enjoyed considerable popularity, and this encouraged him to enter the presidential race in 1995. By declaring his own candidacy, Balladur in effect snubbed Jacques Chirac, the assertive Gaullist leader who had himself served as prime minister in the first period of cohabitation (1986–1988). In 1995, Chirac had expected to be the only Gaullist candidate for the presidency, as he had been 7 years earlier, in 1988, when he lost against the incumbent Mitterrand.

The presidential race in France tends to become highly individualized. Eventually the tough and outspoken Chirac pulled ahead of his more consensual and lackluster party colleague. In the first round of the 1995 presidential election, however, a surprising plurality of the vote went to the main socialist candidate, Lionel Jospin, a former education minister and party leader. In the run-off election, 2 weeks later, Chirac defeated Jospin and thereby ended 14 years of Socialist control of the presidency. He appointed another Gaullist and close political ally, Alain Juppé, to replace the faithless Balladur as prime minister.

The new conservative dominance lasted only until 1997, when France entered into a new version of "cohabitation" as the result of another electoral upset. No parliamentary elections were necessary in France until the end of the National Assembly's 5 year term in 1998, but President Chirac sensed a leftward drift in the country and decided to renew the legislature 10 months early while the conservative coalition still appeared to be ahead of the Left. As it turned out, Chirac totally underestimated how far public confidence in Juppé's government had already deteriorated. The two-stage elections for the National Assembly took place in May and early June of 1997, and the result was a major setback for the neo-Gaullists (RPR) and their increasingly divided neo-liberal allies (mainly the loosely organized UDF). Their combined share of the popular vote dropped to 31 percent, and their parliamentary strength was reduced by 200 seats, to 249. The Socialists quadrupled their strength from 61 to 245 seats, while their non-Communist allies won another 13 seats in the 577-seat National Assembly. In order to form a majority coalition government, they included the small Communist Party, with its 37 seats.

In one respect, the 1997 parliamentary election resembled all the elections to the National Assembly since 1981. Whereas the French voters had elected a conservative majority in elections before that date, they had since then thrown out the incumbent government whatever its orientation. President Chirac now appointed the Socialist leader, Lionel Jospin, as prime minister—the very politician he had narrowly defeated in the presidential race barely 2 years earlier. Thus began France's third and so far longest experiment in cohabitation. It lasted a full parliamentary term of 5 years. The novelty was that this time the president was a conservative serving with a socialist prime minister rather than vice versa.

After three separate periods of cohabitation, between 1986 and 2002, it is possible to conclude that they produce a prime ministerial form of governance that differs from the Gaullist model of a strong presidential leadership. So far, however, the end of cohabitation has always brought a return to the original dual executive of the Fifth Republic with its strong president dominating a clearly subordinate prime minister—as from 1988 to 1993, from 1995 to 1997, and again since 2002.

In some ways, the latest experiment in cohabitation can be seen as a test of how far the moderate Left and Right in France have really overcome their once very deep ideological differences. During the 1997 election campaign, the political distance between them seemed to have grown. The Socialists sharply criticized neo-Gaullist Prime Minister Juppé's austerity measures and neo-liberal measures of deregulation. Instead, they promised a more traditional program to attack unemployment by priming the economy, creating new public service jobs, and reducing the work week to 35 hours from 39 without lowering pay. Conservative political critics were quick to speak of the socialist platform as one of deceptive smoke and mirrors. Even they could not deny, however, that Jospin's government set off to an excellent start in restoring public confidence.

Meanwhile, the French parties of the Right seem to have been weakened by their internal disagreements on policy and strategy as well as personal rivalries at the leadership level. The UDF, organized by former President Giscard d'Estaing in the 1970s, has always been a loose coalition of disparate political groups and tendencies that differed from the neo-Gaullists by showing a greater support for European integration, civil rights, and economic neo-liberalism. The more conservative and nationally oriented RPR, founded by Jacques Chirac in the 1970s as well, experienced its own internecine battles. Since 2002, when he successfully ran for another term as president, Chirac and some of his followers have attempted to revitalize and modernize their party as a less traditionalist element of the French center-right. It now forms the core of a more inclusive Union for the Political Majority (UMP).

The first article in this section provides many insights on a country that one author describes as a "divided self." Few who know the nation would refer without reservation to "the new France." Instead, contemporary French politics and society combine some traits that reflect a strong sense of continuity with the past and others that suggest a spirit of innovation. One major change is the decline of the previously sharp ideological struggle between the Left and the Right. This seems to have resulted in a sense of loss among some French intellectuals who still prefer the political battle to have apocalyptic implications. They seem to find it hard to accept that the grand struggle between Left and Right has been replaced by a more moderate and seemingly more mundane party politics of competition among groups that tend to cluster fairly close to the center of the political spectrum.

In the end, French intellectuals may discover that what they have long regarded as a tedious political competition between those who promise a "little more" or a "little less" can have considerable practical consequences in terms of "who gets what, when, and how." Moreover, such incremental politics need not be without dramatic conflict, since new issues, events, or leaders often emerge to sharpen the differences and increase the stakes of politics. In the last months of 1995 and again in late 1996, for example, French politics took on a dramatic immediacy when workers and students resorted to massive strikes and street demonstrations against a new austerity program introduced by the then conservative government of Prime Minister Juppé. The proposed cutbacks in social entitlements such as pension rights were perceived by many as unnecessary, drastic, and unfair. They were difficult to explain to the public at large, and many observers saw the political confrontation in France as a major test for the welfare state or "social market economy" that is now being squeezed throughout Western Europe in the name of general affordability as well as international or global "competitiveness."

The loss of the grand ideological alternatives may help account for the mood of political malaise that many observers report about contemporary France. But the French search for political direction and identity in a changing Europe has another major origin as well. The sudden emergence of a larger and politically less inhibited Germany next door cannot but have a disquieting effect on France. French elites now face the troubling question of redefining their country's role in a post–cold war world, in which Russia has lost in power and influence while Germany has gained in both. The French resistance to a large American role in Europe adds another source of friction. Together with Germany's Chancellor Schröder, President Chirac has recently gone out of his way to emphasize Franco-German friendship and cooperation. Both have publicly disagreed with what they regard as President Bush's unilateral and militaristic approach in the Iraq Question. They seem to be searching for a distinctive European position on such international problems.

In setting, some observers have even suggested that we may expect a major new cleavage in French politics. It runs between those who favor a reassertion of the traditional French nation-state ideal—a kind of isolationist "neo-Gaullism" that can be found on both the Left and Right—and those who want the country to accept a new European order, in which the sovereignty of both the French and German nation-states would be further diluted or contained by a network of international obligations within the larger European framework.

A persistent question is whether the long-run structural problems of France—similar to those of some of her neighbors—can be handled without a resort to the very market-oriented "therapy" that seems to be alien in spirit to many French voters and political leaders. French capitalism (like its German counterpart) is significantly different from its British and American counterparts. Yet careful observers point out that in his 5 years as prime minister, Jospin engaged in a skillful political sleight of hand by introducing some economic reforms like deregulation and privatization that had the effect of reducing the traditional interventionist role of the French state. Once again, the moderate Left appears to promote a kind of "new centrism" in politics—but with due respect to what is acceptable within a particular national and cultural setting.

The French faced an electoral marathon in 2002, when there were two-stage elections for both the presidency and the National Assembly. It was expected in advance that the focus of the relatively short presidential campaign would be on the two veteran warhorses, Chirac and Jospin. The big surprise was the elimination of Jospin in the first stage: He ran a close third behind Chirac, who came first, and the far right candidate, Le Pen, who came second. As in 1995, many people on the Left had apparently voted "with their hearts" in the first round. The result was that the Left vote was split among a multiplicity of candidates, none of whom had a chance of making it into the second round. This time, however, the result was the failure of the main candidate of the Left to make it into the second round, since socialist Jospin gathered slightly fewer votes than nationalist Le Pen. In the run-off between Chirac and Le Pen, the incumbent president won an overwhelming victory by attracting moderate votes from both Right and Left. The electoral statistics can be found in the first article on France.

In the two-stage elections of the National Assembly in June of 2002, the parties of the moderate right-of-center, led by

Chirac's neo-Gaullist conservatives, won a major victory over the parties of the Left. Voter turnout was unusually low, as it had been in Britain's general election the year before. President Chirac called on the relatively obscure Pierre Raffarin (DL) to form a new, moderately conservative government in place of the defeated left-of-center government that Jospin had headed for the previous 5 years.

No matter how resilient Chirac and other established leaders of France may be, there is a generational change coming. Chirac's fellow conservative, Nicholas Sarkozy, is one of the younger politicians who are now pushing ahead. He is talented, ambitious and already accomplished as former finance minister and now leader of the president's party, the UMP.

Germany was united in 1990, when the eastern German Democratic Republic, or GDR, was merged into the western Federal Republic of Germany. The two German states had been established in 1949, 4 years after the total defeat of the German Reich in World War II. During the next 40 years, their rival elites subscribed to the conflicting ideologies and interests of East and West in the cold war. East Germany comprised the territory of the former Soviet Occupation Zone of Germany, where the Communists exercised a power monopoly and established an economy based on Soviet-style central planning. In contrast, West Germany, which had emerged from the former American, British, and French zones of postwar occupation, developed a pluralist democracy and a flourishing market economy, modified by an extensive network of social policy. West Germans generally spoke with approval of their arrangement as a "social market economy." In the 1970s, when the Social Democrats were in power at the federal level and before some structural problems had darkened the economic horizon, the political class began to refer with confidence to *Modell Deutschland*, "the German model." Communist-ruled East Germany lagged far behind, even though it had gained a reputation for being one of the most productive economies within the Soviet bloc. When the two German states were getting ready to celebrate their fortieth anniversaries in 1989, no leading politician was on record as having foreseen that the forced political division was about to come to an end. In fact, a leading American dictionary published in 1988 defined Germany as a "former country in Central Europe."

Mass demonstrations in several East German cities and the westward flight of thousands of citizens brought the GDR government to make an increasing number of concessions in the last months of 1989 and early 1990. The Berlin Wall ceased to be a hermetical seal after November 9, 1989, and East Germans began to stream over into West Berlin. Collectors and entrepreneurs soon broke pieces from the Wall to keep or sell as souvenirs, before public workers set about to remove the rest of this symbol of the cold war and Germany's division. Under new leadership, the ruling Communists of East Germany made a last-ditch stand by introducing a form of power-sharing with noncommunist groups and parties. They agreed to seek democratic legitimation by holding a free East German election in March 1990, in the hope of reducing the westward flight of thousands of people with its devastating consequences for the eastern economy.

The popular demonstrations and the willingness of East Germans to "vote with their feet" had been made possible by two major preconditions. First, the Soviet leader, Mikhail Gorbachev, had abandoned the so-called Brezhnev Doctrine, under which the Soviets claimed the right of military intervention on behalf of the established communist regimes in Central and Eastern Europe. And second, the imposed communist regimes of these countries turned out to have lost their will—and ability—to hold on to power at any cost.

At first, the East German Communists only loosened their claim to an exclusive control of power and positions in the so-called German Democratic Republic. The results of the March 1990 election, however, made it clear even to them that the pressure for national unification could no longer be stemmed. An eastern alliance of Christian Democrats, largely identified with and supported by Chancellor Helmut Kohl's party in West Germany, recorded a surprisingly decisive victory, by winning about one-half of the vote throughout East Germany. It advocated a short, quick route to unification, beginning with an early monetary union in the summer and a political union by the fall of 1990. Almost immediately a new noncommunist government was installed in East Germany. Headed by Lothar de Maizière (CDU), it followed the short-cut to a merger with the Federal Republic, under Article 23 of the West German Basic Law. The Social Democrats, or SPD, had won only 22 percent of the East German vote. That was widely interpreted as a defeat for their alternative strategy for unification that would have involved the protracted negotiation of a new German constitution, as envisaged in Article 146 of the Federal Republic's Basic Law.

During the summer and fall of 1990, the governments of the two German states and the four former occupying powers completed their so-called two-plus-four negotiations that resulted in a mutual agreement on the German unification process. The monetary union in July was quickly followed by a political merger in October 1990. In advance of unification, Bonn negotiated an agreement with Moscow in which the latter accepted the gradual withdrawal of Soviet troops from eastern Germany and the membership of the larger, united Germany in NATO, in return for considerable German economic support for the Soviet Union. The result was a major shift in both the domestic and international balance of power.

The moderately conservative Christian Democrats repeated their electoral success in the first Bundestag election in a reunited Germany, held in early December 1990. They captured almost 44 percent of the vote, against the long-time low of 33.5 percent for the rival Social Democrats. At the same time, Kohl's small coalition partner of liberal Free Democrats (FDP) did unusually well (11 percent of the vote). The environmentalist Greens, on the other hand, failed to get the required minimum of 5 percent of the vote in western Germany and dropped out of the Bundestag for the next 4 years. Under a special dispensation for the 1990 election only, the two parts of united Germany were regarded as separate electoral regions as far as the 5 percent threshold was concerned. That made it possible for two small eastern parties to get a foothold in the Bundestag. One was a coalition of political dissidents and environmentalists (Alliance 90/Greens); the other was the communist-descended Party of Democratic Socialism. The PDS was able to win about 11 percent of the vote in the East by appealing to those who felt displaced and alienated in the new order. Its voters included many former privileged party members but also some rural workers and young people. Ironically, the communist-descended party received only weak support among blue-collar workers.

The election results of December 1990 suggested that national unification could eventually modify the German party system and German politics significantly. By the time of the next national election, in October 1994, it became evident that a new east-west divide had emerged. This time, the far-left PDS was able to almost double its support and attract 20 percent of the vote in the East, where only one-fifth of Germany's total population lives. At the same time, the PDS won only about 1 percent of the vote in the far more populous West. Its total electoral support in Germany thus fell slightly below the famous "5 percent hurdle" established in Germany's electoral law as a minimum for a party to win proportional representation in the Bundestag. The PDS was nevertheless able to keep and expand its parliamentary foothold, because it met an almost forgotten alternative seating requirement of winning pluralities in at least three single-member districts under Germany's double-ballot electoral system. Thus the political descendants of the former ruling Communists were given proportional representation after all. They won seats in the Bundestag for 30 deputies, who presented themselves as a democratically sensitive, far-left party of socialists and regionalists.

Despite a widespread unification malaise in Germany, the conservative-liberal government headed by Chancellor Helmut Kohl won reelection in 1994. His Christian Democrats, who benefited from a widely perceived if only temporary improvement in the German economy, won 41.4 percent of the vote. Their Free Democratic ally barely scraped through with 6.9 percent of the vote. Together, the two governing parties had a very slim majority of 10 seats more than the combined total of the three opposition parties, the SPD (36.4 percent), the revived and united Greens (7.3 percent), and the PDS (4.4 percent).

In the federal upper house, or Bundesrat, the SPD continued to hold a majority of the seats, based on their control of many state governments. This situation gave a united SPD considerable leverage or blocking power in federal legislative politics. The Kohl government charged that the resulting parliamentary gridlock stalled its economic reform initiatives. It would be only a few years before the tables were turned.

Between 1949 and 1999, the seat of government for the Federal Republic had been the small Rhineland town of Bonn. Reunification made possible the move of the government and parliament several hundred miles eastward to the old political center of Berlin. The transfer was controversial in Germany, because of both the costs and symbolism involved. Nevertheless, it had already been approved by the Bundestag in 1991, with a narrow parliamentary majority, and was then delayed until 1999. Observers generally agree that the "Berlin Republic" will continue the democratic tradition that has been firmly established in Germany. But they also point to the need for a revamping of the economic and social arrangements that worked so well during much of the Bonn period, if the country is to meet its new obligations within Europe and in the increasingly global market arena.

Unlike their British counterparts, German governments are regularly produced by coalition politics. In the multiparty system, based on the country's modified form of proportional representation, a single party is unlikely to win a parliamentary majority at the federal level of politics. In some German states, however, single party government has become familiar or is even an embedded tradition, as in Bavaria with its powerful CSU (a Bavarian sister party of the CDU). More remarkable is the fact that between 1949 and 1998 there had never been a complete replacement of a governing coalition in Bonn. Even when there was a change of government, at least one partner of the previous coalition had always managed to hang on as majority maker in the next cabinet. This German pattern of incomplete power transfers came to an abrupt end with the clean sweep brought by the Bundestag election of September 1998.

In advance of the contest, it had been widely expected that the outcome once again would be only a partial shift in power, resulting from a "grand coalition" of Social Democrats (SPD) and Christian Democrats (CDU/CSU). In such a situation, the chancellorship would go to the leader of the front-running party—most likely the SPD. The result would have been a considerable continuity and, as interpreted by rival scenarios, either a disabling inertia or a newfound strength in the shared responsibility for dealing with Germany's backlog of social and economic reforms.

Instead, the 1998 election made possible a complete turnover in power. It brought into office what Germans like to call a "red-green" coalition by giving the Social Democrats, with 40.9 percent of the popular vote, a sufficient margin over the Christian Democrats (35.1 percent) to form a majority coalition with the small party of Greens (6.7 percent). German voters in effect decided it was "time for a change" in their country, similar to the political turnabouts that had taken place in Britain and France a year earlier. As in these neighboring countries, the main party of the Left was very careful to present itself as a moderate reform agent that would provide security along with both "continuity and change." The SPD borrowed freely from both British and American political imagery by proclaiming that it represented a decidedly non-radical "new middle" (*neue Mitte*). It was a successful, if rather vague, political formula.

The complete change in governing parties also brought a generational turnover in the top levels of German government. In the federal chancellery, Social Democrat Gerhard Schröder, born in 1944, replaced Christian Democrat Helmut Kohl, born in 1930. Most of the other leading members of the new government spent their childhood years in post–war Germany. In many cases they had their initial political experiences in youthful opposition to the societal establishment of the late 1960s. By now the "68ers" are well into middle age, but they have ascended to power as successors to Kohl's generation, whose politically formative years coincided with the founding period of the Federal Republic. The new German leaders do not have youthful memories of the Third Reich, World War II, or even, in many cases, the post–war military occupation. They are truly Germany's first post–war generation in power as well as its first left of center governing coalition.

The larger political system was affected by the shifts in the power balance of the small political parties and their leaders after the milestone election of September 1998. On the far left, the post-communist PDS managed for the first time to pass the 5 percent threshold, if only barely, by winning 21.6 percent of the vote in eastern Germany, while advancing only slightly to 1.2 percent of the vote in the far more populous West, where approximately 80 percent of the German population lives. Clearly, the PDS is still very much a party rooted in the new federal states that emerged from the communist-ruled East Germany.

The liberal Free Democrats ended up with another close scrape (6.2 percent). In contrast to the PDS, the Liberals now appeared to be a party of the West, where they received 7 percent of the vote as compared to 3.3 percent in the East. After 29 years as junior government party, their struggle for political survival now had to be conducted in the unfamiliar role as a marginal opposition party.

The third small party, the Greens, had also slid back (to 6.7 percent), but this was enough to replace the FDP as majority-maker in the federal government. Like the other small parties, the Greens bore marks of the east-west divide: They received only 4.1 percent in the East versus 7.3 percent in the West.

Germany had in effect arrived at a slightly more complex party system. It consisted of the two major parties of the moderate center-left (SPD) and the moderate center-right (CDU/CSU) along with three small parties that each had a regional concentration either in the West (Greens and FDP) or almost exclusively in the East (PDS). Some observers referred to a "two-and-three-halves" party system. Each of the three "halves" had an impact on the overall balance of power and what the Germans call the system's "coalition arithmetic," but each was also small enough to be in danger of slipping below the 5 percent mark at any time. Another important result of the 1998 Bundestag election was the continued failure of the parties of the extreme right, with their authoritarian and xenophobic rhetoric, to mobilize a significant support in the German electorate.

For the Greens, the first-time role as junior coalition partner in the national government has not been easy. In fact, some close observers have spoken of an identity crisis of the German Left that includes parts of the Social Democratic Party. It was fed by controversies linked to domestic socioeconomic and environmental issues as well as the German military participation in Kosovo in early 1999. There followed a remarkable political recovery of the SPD in the latter half of that year. The abrupt resignation of the key Social Democrat Oskar Lafontaine, as both finance minister and party leader in March 1999, gave Schröder a welcome opportunity to take over the SPD leadership. The assumption that this move would give him more authority within both the party and the cabinet did not pan out. Instead, the dual set of responsibilities turned out to be very demanding, and the battle weary chancellor soon became known for his repeated threats to resign from one or both positions.

The federal system, which now had 16 states, turned out to be a major obstacle to the new government. The staggered elections in the states had a potential for shifting the balance of power in Berlin as well. In the first year after taking power, the SPD and the Greens suffered a string of serious setbacks in state elections. They were ousted from some state governments, and this led to a loss of their majority control of the federal council or Bundesrat. Beginning in late 1999, the SPD's adverse trend came to a halt. Instead, the Christian Democrats suddenly found themselves in shambles, resulting from the sensational revelations of a major party finance scandal that had taken place under the leadership of Helmut Kohl, the veteran chancellor. Basically the problem stemmed from transfers of huge political contributions to a slush fund that was not reported as required by law.

Dubbed "Kohlgate," the finance scandal resulted in immediate setbacks for the CDU in several state elections. This had the effect of boosting the FDP, for some disaffected CDU supporters turned to the FDP as an acceptable center-right alternative. The small liberal party went through a significant leadership change, when it chose its former secretary general, the youthful Guido Westerwelle, to become its new head. With this single move, supported by a clever promotion campaign, the party seemed to experience a rejuvenation that boosted its poll standings and brought it well ahead of the Greens in advance of the September 2002 election. In a cocky mood, the FDP announced a year in advance that its election goal would be to attract 18 percent of the vote, at a time when its poll standings had improved to about 8 percent. Suddenly the small party, whose political obituary has been written repeatedly, exuded a new vigor and self-confidence. It appeared as though the FDP could regain its familiar position of balancer in German electoral and coalition politics—

a role that before 1998 had made it the most successful small party in West European politics .

As the 2002 election approached, voters shifted their attention to the lackluster economic performance of the Schröder government. The poll standings of the CDU improved and even brought the party ahead of the SPD. The conservative party introduced law and order themes and sometimes played to anti-immigrant sentiments both before and after the September 11 events. At the beginning of 2002, the Christian Democrats decided against nominating as "chancellor candidate" their own leader, Angela Merkel. She is an East German woman who as a newcomer to politics rose rapidly in the party after unification. Untainted by political scandal, she had quickly made it to the top when the CDU needed a facelift.

As chancellor candidate, the Christian Democrats decided in favor of Edmund Stoiber, the governor of Bavaria and leader of the CSU, their more conservative sister party in that large state. Stoiber's main advantage was held to be a strong economic record in his home state, but it surely helped that he was an older male politician from the West with many personal supporters in the CDU/CSU. Some observers wondered whether he was not too right-leaning to attract many voters outside Bavaria. Stoiber trailed Schröder in his individual poll ratings—as did Angela Merkl. But a parliamentary election is also about party support, and here an electoral comeback of the CDU/CSU seemed to be in the making. By the mid-summer of 2002 it was widely believed that the revived Christian Democrats were likely to return to government office in coalition with the recharged FDP. The SPD's weak economic record, most vividly dramatized by a persistent unemployment problem, seemed likely to become its Achilles' heel in the September election.

Once again, the small parties were to play a key role in the electoral and parliamentary balance of power established by the 2002 Bundestag election. Until the summer of that year, the Greens had suffered a long string of electoral setbacks at the state level of politics. They had been damaged by their internal quarrels and also lost some of their traditional backing among younger voters, as the founder generation grew older and joined the establishment. Some critical voters now seemed to be attracted by the FDP's self-promotion as the real alternative. The FDP's constant focus on "Project 18" and a "fun" campaign helped maintain the illusion that the Free Democrats were likely to pass the Greens and again become the "third force" in German party politics. The PDS had most reason to tremble at its electoral prospects. It had passed the 5 percent hurdle in only one of the three Bundestag election since unification, and only barely at that (5.1 percent in 1998). Since then, it had lost some of its previous voters and largely failed to win many new ones. The alternative route to proportional representation in the Bundestag also looked bleak for the PDS: The boundaries of the single-member districts in Berlin had recently been redrawn in a way that diluted the PDS strength and made its capture of three districts less likely.

In the end, the Bundestag election of 2002 did keep the PDS from sharing in the proportional allocation of parliamentary seats. The post-Communists won two single-member districts in eastern Berlin, enough for only two deputies. Had the PDS won a third district, the 5 percent clause would have been set aside, and its 4.0 percent share of the party vote would then have entitled it to about 24 of the 603 seats in the new Bundestag. The PDS may be headed for further marginalization at the subnational levels as well, but it is also possible that the PDS could instead begin to attract left-wing voters who have become unhappy with Chancellor Schröder and the SPD.

Ironically, it was the near shut-out of the PDS that enabled the red-green government to hold on to power in one of Germany's closest elections ever. The first article on Germany analyzes the outcome in some detail. Both SPD and CDU/CSU won 38.5 percent of the vote, but a quirk in the two-vote electoral law gave the SPD three more seats than its major rival. The SPD had overcome its poor stand in the polls to come within 2.4 percent of its result in 1998. Most observers explain the electoral recovery by referring to points earned by Chancellor Schröder through his performance in the televised debates with Edmund Stoiber, his unusually critical remarks about President Bush's "adventurous" strategy toward Iraq, and his appearance as a decisive leader in dealing with the great floods that ravaged parts of eastern Germany in the month before the Bundestag election. The FDP had lost ground with a controversial campaign since mid-summer. It fell back to 7.4 percent of the vote—an improvement over its previous share of 6.2 percent but far less than its trumpeted goal of 18 percent. The Greens probably benefited from the revival of war fears in connection with Iraq as well as the popularity of their foreign minister, Joschka Fischer. While they continued to perform poorly in the eastern states, where the SPD picked up many former CDU and PDS voters, the Greens benefited from the renewal of ecological concerns in the wake of the August floods.

In the first year after the 2002 election, Germans returned to a discussion of basic structural reform. The two main topics were the country's federal structure and its economic model. Federalism is a crucial element not only in the country's governance but also in its self-understanding, as reflected in its official name, the Federal Republic of Germany. The founders of the West German state regarded a federal arrangement as a key safeguard against a dangerous concentration and potential abuse of power in the central government. Since then, federalism has set Germany apart from France, which is still fairly centralized even after Mitterrand's regional reforms. Italy and Britain have carried out some regional devolution, but neither comes anywhere close to having a federal system like the one that was projected into the eastern part of Germany at the time of unification. Today there is a growing conviction that federal entanglements may have become an obstacle to effective governance in Germany. No matter how strong the arguments for an overhaul of the federal system may be, however, there are strong vested interests in keeping the present structures, including the federal council or *Bundesrat*, which provides a powerful check on the parliamentary government in Berlin.

It is widely agreed that there is a need for a basic socio-economic reform in Germany. In some respects, the discussion resembles that of other advanced countries, but the German version includes some special aspects linked to the challenges and accomplishments of national unification. The task of post-communist reconstruction in eastern Germany goes far beyond the transfer of institutions and capital from the West. The transition to a pluralist democracy and a market economy also requires a measure of social and cultural transformation. Not least, there is a growing awareness that Germany's generous social welfare model may have become unsustainable in its present form over the long run. Here the country faces the familiar demographic shifts at home and stiff economic competition from abroad.

On the other hand, Germans have traditionally favored a more social form of capitalism than the one that prevails in Britain or the United States. They are unlikely to accept the kind of shock therapy of massive deregulation and other market-oriented reforms that were introduced in the United States and Britain by conservative governments in the 1980s and largely accepted by their left-of-center successors in the following decade. Both the political culture and institutional framework of Germany (and much of mainland Europe) lean far more toward corporatist and communitarian solutions than their British and American counterparts.

At the beginning of 2004, Chancellor Schröder succeeded in mobilizing parliamentary support for much of a comprehensive structural reform package, *Agenda 2010*. There followed a public out as Germans began to understand and anticipate the painful reforms. At this point, Schröder decided to concentrate on governing and have a trusted supporter, Franz Müntefering, take over the leadership of the SPD. The party was certainly in need of special attention to quell its protests and stem a massive loss of members.

With his reform packet, Chancellor Schröder appears finally to have bit the bullet. His commitment to a reform of the labor market and social security provisions will be tested in the coming year, but Bertrand Benoit indicates that he cannot afford to back down now. Curiously, the widely unpopular cutbacks, envisaged by the reform legislation, coincide with an improvement in the drooping poll standings for the Chancellor and his show of leadership. Moreover, as Richard Bernstein explains, there are new problems facing the larger and more powerful Germany on the international scene. Here it must deal with an ambiguous mixture of expectations and anxieties that this European giant arouses abroad.

Italy is roughly comparable to France and Britain in population size and it is fairly close to them in gross economic output. It has a very different political tradition that includes a relatively long period of fascist rule as well as an unusually persistent and troubling element of north-south regionalism. The country became a republic after World War II. Using a system of proportional representation until the 1990s, it spawned a highly fragmented multiparty system in which two large parties together received about two-thirds or more of the total vote, while many small parties picked up the rest. The center-right Christian Democrats (DC) was the perennially dominant party in Italy's coalition governments, and usually provided the prime minister. The Italian Communists (PCI) comprised the second large party. They were persistently excluded from government at the national level, despite the fact that they received close to one-third of the popular vote during most of the Cold War era.

Yet the Italian Communists played a considerable role in local and, later, regional politics. Here they learned to engage in a more pragmatic form of politics than prescribed by their ideology. They embarked relatively early on a non-revolutionary path of seeking social reforms in a pluralist society. Under a new name adopted in 1991, the former Communists presented themselves as the Democratic Party of the Left (PDS) or, later, simply the Left Democrats (DS). They essentially came to adopt social democratic reform positions. In 1993 and 1994, they were able to leave their ghetto in national politics, as Italian voters abruptly turned away from the Christian Democrats and other corrupt establishment parties.

At the end of the cold war, Italy experienced a political earthquake that many thought would lead to a Second Republic in that country. It was triggered by a change of attitude toward a state of affairs that had long been accepted with a shrug of cynicism or helplessness. As middle class fears of a communist takeover declined, many Italians were no longer willing to tolerate the self-serving manner in which the governing parties and their leaders had prospered from all manners of side payments for political services and public contracts and services. Some vigorous prosecutors and judges played a key role in exposing the extent of what became known as tangentopoli ("kickback city") in public affairs. In local and regional elections of 1993, voter protests benefited both the PDS and some market-oriented regional leagues in the north that favored greater autonomy from Rome. A frantic political facelift by the Christian Democrats, some of whom regrouped as the Popular Party, failed to stem their huge losses. Their old center-left and center-right partners in corruption also experienced great setbacks or entered political oblivion altogether, like the Socialists.

In late 1994, Italy held what at the time was heralded as the most important parliamentary election since 1948. In effect, it ended the Christian Democratic dominance that had begun forty-six years earlier. Using a new electoral system, in which three-quarters of the members of parliament's lower house are elected on a winner-take-all basis and the rest by proportional representation, Italian voters decimated the centrist alliance, which included the former Christian Democrats. On the left, a Progressive Alliance led by the PDS won 213 of the 630 seats in the Chamber of Deputies, compared to the 46 seats for the main centrist group or Pact of Italy. But it was the Freedom Alliance of the right that triumphed by winning 366 seats. It consisted of an incongruous coalition of three main groups, of which the strongest was the *Forza Italia* (Go Italy) movement, created, funded, and led by the media magnate and multimillionaire, Silvio Berlusconi. The two other members of the Freedom Alliance were the fascist-descended National Alliance (formerly Italian Social Movement or MSI), led by Gianfranco Fini, and the strongly regionalist Northern League, headed by Umberto Bossi.

Berlusconi had catapulted himself and his new party to the front by a skillful use of his electronic media, in which he chastised the Left and propagated free market solutions to the problems of corruption and "statism." After the electoral victory, he accomplished the difficult task of stitching together a government based on a highly incongruous coalition. Very soon, the leader of the regionalist and tax-protesting Northern League showed open contempt for the nationalist and centralizing positions of its coalition partner, the post-fascist National Alliance. When Bossi pulled out of the new government, Prime Minister Berlusconi lost his parliamentary majority and soon had to resign. From January 1995 until the new elections in April 1996, Italy had a caretaker government headed by the banker Lamberto Dini.

Using the new hybrid voting system, the national election of 1996 produced an advance for the parties of the left. The PDS was by far the strongest member of the so-called Olive Tree coalition, but it entered a new coalition government headed by Romano Prodi, a banker who came from the center-left Popular Party. Prodi survived several challenges, not least from a radical left group that called itself the Refounded Communists. He finally stepped down in October 1998, after losing a parliamentary vote of confidence by a single vote. Under his skillful leadership, the government had managed to cut public spending sufficiently to have Italy meet the criteria for participation in the European Monetary Union with its euro currency. He was succeeded as prime minister by the PDS leader, Massimo D'Alema, who be-

came the first former Communist to head the government of a major West European country. His coalition government, which was Italy's fifty-sixth since 1948, closely resembled its predecessor but suffered more from infighting. Having rebuilt his cabinet after one collapse, D'Alemo finally stepped down after setbacks in the spring 2000 local elections. Another Olive Tree government muddled along until its defeat in the new parliamentary elections in the summer of 2001. At that point, it would seem that while Italy had a changed mixture of old and new players in its party system, it had not overcome the familiar pattern of governmental instability and paralysis.

In 2001, after spending more than six years in the opposition, the right-of-center Freedom Alliance won a solid parliamentary majority and returned to office with Silvio Berlusconi as prime minister. It seemed to have overcome some of the internal disarray that had cut short its earlier stay in power. Yet the conservative government has not really resolved the fundamental personal and ideological differences between Bossi's regionalist Northern League and Fini's centralist National Alliance. Berlusconi still appears to command a substantial political following, but a poll from February 2004 showed that two out of three Italians thought the conservative government's economic policies were failing. The prime minister continues to face troubles with judicial authorities that have been looking into possible corruption in his past business dealings. His response has been characteristically combative: to seek immunity while in office and to discuss the need for a reform of the justice system. In the last half of 2003, Berlusconi's six-month tenure as president of the European Union became marred from beginning to end by public gaffes, and it was climaxed by the collapse of the EU constitutional convention. The unraveling of a major accounting scandal at the food giant Parmalat threw a further shadow on his plans for economic reform through deregulation.

Italy remains an intriguing political arena. After half a century of political instability and fragmentation, it has during the past decade experienced the tentative beginnings of what could eventually become a simpler center-left and center-right dualism in its party politics. Yet infighting among a multiplicity of political parties continues to weaken the governing process, and the country seems incapable of moving on to fundamental political or socioeconomic reforms. It remains to be seen whether new national elections will produce a simpler and more consolidated party system without a prior simplification of the hybrid electoral system that replaced proportional representation in the early 1990s.

There are plenty of ideas for institutional reform afloat. On the left, some reformers favor the introduction of new electoral rules similar to the two-round system of France, in the hope of producing a simpler system of center-left and center-right blocs. Such plans run into opposition in the smaller parties that want to retain en element of proportional representation in order to guarantee their own survival. Primarily on the right, one finds a wistful interest in the adoption of a stronger executive model, again along the lines of France's Fifth Republic. So far then, the Italian political system has been deeply shaken by recent political upheavals, but it still has developed no consensus on the preferred institutional framework for what could one day become a "Second Italian Republic."

Japan has long fascinated comparative social scientists as a country that modernized rapidly without losing its non-Western, Japanese identity. The article, "Japanese Spirit, Western Things," explains how this was possible and why it is important. It begins by recounting the story of Commodore Perry's arrival in

Tokyo harbor in the 1850s and his role in forcing the country to "open up." The Japanese rulers decided in effect to learn from the West in order to strengthen Japan and maintain its independence. The special conditions that made the modernization possible have become a staple topic on the social science agenda. About one hundred years later, a few other countries in East and South Asia began taking tentative steps toward what soon became a rapid and self-sustained modernization. Soon known as the "Asian tigers" or "dragons," the New Industrial Countries include South Korea, Taiwan, and Singapore.

Japan's tentative move toward a parliamentary form of government after World War I was blocked by a militarist takeover in the early 1930s. After World War II, a parliamentary form of representative democracy was installed in Japan under American supervision. This political system soon acquired indigenous Japanese characteristics that set it off from the other major democracies examined here.

For almost four decades following its creation in 1955, the Liberal Democratic Party (LDP) played a hegemonic role in Japanese politics. The many opposition parties were divided and provided little effective competition for the LDP which, according to a popular saying, was really "neither liberal, nor democratic, nor a party." It has essentially been a conservative political machine that loosely unites several rival and delicately balanced factions. The factions in turn consist mostly of the personal followers of political bosses who stake out factional claims to benefits of office.

In 1993, the LDP temporarily lost its parliamentary majority, when a couple of its factions joined the opposition. This set the stage for a vote of no confidence, followed by new elections in which the LDP lost its parliamentary majority. Seven different parties, spanning the spectrum from conservative to socialist, thereupon formed a fragile coalition government. It was incapable of defining or promoting a coherent policy program and stood helpless as the Japanese economy continued on its course of stagnation that began at the outset of the 1990s after a long postwar economic boom.

Two prime ministers and several cabinet reshuffles later, a revived LDP managed by the summer of 1994 to return to the cabinet by way of a coalition with its former rival, the Socialists. The peculiar alliance was possible because the leadership of both these major parties had adopted a pragmatic orientation at this juncture. By December 1995, the LDP had recaptured the prime ministership. There followed a rapid succession of short-lived governments headed by LDP factional leaders. When the post once again became open in April 2001, there was a surprising number of willing candidates.

The unexpected winner of the leadership contest in the LDP and new prime minister of Japan was Junichiro Koizumi. He was no beginner in Japanese party politics, but he seemed to personify a more unconventional approach than most veteran politicians in Japan. He spoke the language of structural reform, and immediately took some symbolic steps to show that he meant business. His cabinet included five women, including the controversial Makiko Tanaka as head of the foreign ministry. Koizumi soon ran into resistance from conservative elements in the political class, including factional leaders of his own party and members of the high civil service. By January 2002, he dismissed the assertive Tanaka, who had become a favorite target of those who opposed the new political style and possible major policy changes. The move triggered widespread public dissatisfaction. Koizumi countered by appointing another prominent woman, Yoriko Kawaguchi, to head the foreign ministry. By this time, however, his own popularity rating was rapidly falling. It seemed unlikely that his remaining public support provided enough political capital to offset the entrenched foes of a reform of the Japanese economy and fiscal policy. Koizumi now seemed disinclined to try. Some observers argued that the prime minister himself had little realistic understanding of or commitment to the kind of structural change that Japan needed. Thus continuity seemed once again more likely than basic change in Japan.

There now seems to be an emerging understanding that fundamental change must be based on an "opening up" of Japanese society to more competition. From this perspective, the entrenched bureaucratic elites and their cozy relationships with business leaders need to become prime targets of reform. It is remarkable that Japan's prolonged economic stagnation has not resulted in more political protests and electoral repercussions.

It will probably take more than a flamboyant prime minister to revitalize Japanese politics and society, but reform steps are more likely under Koizumi than any of his handful of recent predecessors. A key question becomes whether the fragmented parliamentary opposition will one day take advantage of the situation and become a more coherent, alternative force for reform. There are no clear answers as yet, but the parliamentary elections of 2003 gave some positive indications.

The immediate result of the 2003 election was that Koizumi remained prime minister. His party had lost ten seats, but the LDP could record exactly one-half of the 480 se... e House of Representatives after three independent... ks. Together with its two smaller partners ... ruling coalition commanded a total of ...

The main change brough... ...tion of the hitherto fragmente... ...c Party of Japan (DPJ), formed i... of 177 in all. The young party se... jor mainstream challenger to the L... other parties. In its assessment, th... possible emergence of a two-party ... the DPJ as the clear alternative choice for ... ...ters.

The new strength of the DPJ could ... easier for Prime Minister Koizumi to neutralize resistance in his own party and the bureaucracy to the structural reforms that he intermittently advocates. In a sense, he has been given the proverbial second chance.

A Constitutional Revolution In Britain?*

Donley T. Studlar

When the New Labor government led by Tony Blair took office in May 1997, one of its most distinctive policies was its program of constitutional reform. Indeed, few British parties have ever campaigned so consistently on constitutional issues. From its first days of power, Labor promoted its constitutional reform agenda: (1) devolution to Scotland and Wales, (2) an elected mayor and council for London and possibly other urban areas, (3) removal of the voting rights of hereditary peers in the House of Lords, (4) incorporation of the European Convention on Human Rights into British law, (5) a Freedom of Information Act, and (6) electoral reform at various levels of government, including a referendum on changing the electoral system for Members of Parliament. These reforms, plus a stable agreement for governing Northern Ireland, the constitutional implications of membership of the European Union, and the question of modernization of the monarchy will be considered here. This article analyzes the nature of Labor's constitutional proposals, including their inspiration, implementation, and potential impact.

Traditional British Constitutional Principles

The United Kingdom as a state in international law is made up of four constituent parts—England, Scotland, Wales, and Northern Ireland—all under the authority of the Queen in Parliament in London. The constitution is the structure of fundamental laws and customary practices that define the authority of state institutions and regulate their interrelationships, including those to citizens of the state. Although in principle very flexible, in practice the "unwritten" British constitution (no single document) is difficult to change. The socialization of political elites in a small country leads to a political culture in which custom and convention make participants reluctant to change practices which brought them to power.

Even though Britain is under the rule of law, that law is subject to change through parliamentary sovereignty. Instead of a written constitution with a complicated amending process, a simple majority of the House of Commons can change any law, even over the objections of the House of Lords if necessary. Individual rights are protected by ordinary law and custom, not an entrenched Bill of Rights.

Officially Britain remains a unitary state, with all constitutional authority belonging to the central government, rather than a federal state with a formal, even if vague, division of powers between the center and a lower level. Some commentators argue that Britain should be considered a "union-state," since the relationship of the four parts to the central government varies rather than being on the same terms. Although limited devolution has been utilized in the past, especially in Northern Ireland, 1921–1972, central government retains the authority to intervene in lower-level affairs, including local government matters. The voters are asked once every four or five years to choose a team of politicians to rule the central authority through the parliament at Westminster. Under the single member district, simple plurality electoral system, the outcome usually has been a single-party government (prime minister and cabinet) chosen based on a cohesive majority in the House of Commons, a fusion of power between the legislature and the executive. Referendums have been few and are formally only advisory; parliament retains final authority. The judiciary seldom makes politically important decisions, and even then it can be overridden by a parliamentary majority. Thus, in the United Kingdom almost any alteration of the interrelationship of political institutions can be considered constitutional in nature.

Constitutional issues were one of the few on which there were major party differences during the 1997 General Election campaign. Labor and the third party, the Liberal Democrats, had an agreed agenda for constitutional change, developed in consultation over several years. The Conservatives upheld traditional British constitutional principles, including the unwritten constitution, no guarantees of civil liberties except through the laws of Parliament, maintenance of the unitary state, and a

House of Lords composed of hereditary peers and some life peers, the latter appointed by the prime minister.

Other features of the British constitution have also resisted change. British government has been one of the most secretive among Western democracies, with unauthorized communication of information punishable by law. Large cities did not elect their own mayors or even their own metropolitan governing councils. The House of Commons is one of the few remaining legislatures elected by the single member district, simple plurality electoral system, which rewards a disproportionate share of parliamentary seats to larger parties having geographically concentrated voting strength. Thus Britain has continued to have an overwhelmingly two-party House of Commons despite having a multiparty electorate.

Even though the elected Labor government proposed to change some of these procedures and to consider reform in others, there were good reasons to doubt its commitment. Traditionally, constitutional reform has evoked little sustained interest within the party. Like the Conservatives, it has embraced the almost untrammeled formal power that the "elective dictatorship" of British parliamentary government provides for a single-party majority in the House of Commons. Although Labor sometimes voiced decentralist and reformist concerns when in opposition, in government it usually proved to be as centralist as the Conservatives.

Labor's Constitutional Promises

There was general agreement that the most radical aspect of Labor's 1997 election manifesto was constitutional reform. This program was designed to stimulate the normally passive, relatively deferential British public into becoming more active citizens. In addition to parliamentary elections, they would vote for other levels of government with enhanced authority and have enhanced individual rights. More electoral opportunities, for different levels and within the voting process itself, would provide a wider range of choice for citizens.

Tony Blair had for some years advocated an infusion of a more participatory citizenship into British constitutional practices. In *New Britain* (Westview Press, 1997), Blair criticized British government as too centralized, secretive, and containing unrepresentative hereditary peers in the House of Lords. Blair called Labor's constitutional program "democratic renewal," argued that there had been 80 years of erosion of consent, self-government, and respect for rights under governments of both Left and Right, and contended that the mission of a Left-of-center party involves the extension of political rights as well as economic and social equality.

How and Why Labor Developed a Program for Constitutional Change

Several events and trends focused Labor's thinking on constitutional reform as never before. Labor suffered four consec-

utive general election losses (1979, 1983, 1987, 1992) even though the Conservatives never achieved above 43 percent of the popular vote. Eighteen consecutive years out of government made Labor fearful of ever returning as a single-party government, which made it more attentive to arguments for a more limited central authority.

Groups interested in constitutional reform were not difficult to find. The third party in Britain, the Liberal Democrats, have long been advocating changing the electoral system to have their voting strength better represented in parliament as well as decentralization and increased protection for civil liberties. Since 1988, a nonpartisan lobby group, Charter 88, has not only proposed most of the reforms that Labor eventually embraced but also others, such as a full-scale written constitution and a bill of rights. Other influential thinkers on the moderate left argued that a precondition for social and economic change in an increasingly middle-class Britain was to encourage citizen involvement by limiting central government authority. In Scotland, where the Conservatives had continuously declined as an electoral force, the cross-party Scottish Constitutional Convention encouraged devolution of power. Eventually Labor and the Liberal Democrats [worked together] to form a pre-election commission on constitutional matters, which continued after the election in the form of a special cabinet committee on constitutional reform.

Skeptics have argued that public support for constitutional change is a mile wide and an inch deep. Surveys indicate that the public usually supports constitutional reform proposals in principle without understanding very much about the specifics. Intense minorities, such as Charter 88 and the Electoral Reform Society, have fueled the discussion. During the 1997 election campaign constitutional issues featured prominently in elite discussions of party differences but did not emerge as a critical voting issue, except perhaps in Scotland.

New Labor had multiple incentives in developing an agenda for constitutional change. It provided a clear sense of Labor distinctiveness from the Conservatives, especially important when there were so few differences in social and economic policy between the two parties. It was designed to alleviate threats to Labor support by Scottish and Welsh nationalist parties arguing for more autonomy. There was also the longer-term prospect of possibly realigning the party system by co-opting the Liberal Democrats and their issues into a more permanent government of the center, thereby reducing both the Conservatives and die-hard socialists of the Labor party left wing to permanent minority status. Even with the large majority of parliamentary seats that Labor gained in the May, 1997 election, the government did not abandon constitutional reform.

Constitutional Change after Five Years of Labor Rule

No British government since the early twentieth century has presided over such a large agenda of constitutional reform. There are now new legislatures with devolved powers in

Northern Ireland, Scotland, and Wales. All but 92 hereditary peers have been removed from the House of Lords, and further deliberations have taken place over the second stage of Lords reform. A report from the Independent Commission on the Voting System advocated a change in the electoral system for the House of Commons, but no further government action has been taken. The European Convention on Human Rights has been incorporated into British law through the Human Rights Act. A weak Freedom of Information Act was also passed. In 1998, Londoners approved a proposal for the city to be governed by a directly-elected Mayor and the Assembly, and in 2000 the first election was held. Other cities have now adopted this measure through referendums.

New Labor immediately instituted some elements of its constitutional reform agenda. The referendums held in 1997 showed support for devolution to be stronger in Scotland than in Wales. The Scottish Parliament has more authority over policy and limited taxation powers while the Welsh Assembly has less authority and no taxation powers. Elections for both were held in 1999 under a combination of the traditional single member district, simply plurality electoral system and party list proportional representation, which yielded no clear majority in either legislature. Initially a Labor-Liberal Democrat coalition government was formed in Scotland and a minority Labor government in Wales. The latter was eventually replaced by another Labor-Liberal Democrat coalition. Labor has experienced problems in maintaining its party leaders in both governments; otherwise both have functioned largely as anticipated. No major disagreements on the constitutional allocation of powers have occurred. The second elections for the devolved legislatures will occur in May, 2003. The Welsh Assembly is expected to petition the Westminster government for greater powers, similar to those of the Scottish Parliament.

Eighty percent of the population of the United Kingdom, however, lives in England, which has been treated as a residual consideration in the plans for devolution. Tony Blair has indicated that Labor would be willing to form devolved governments in "regions with strong identities of their own," but, aside from the Northeast, there has been no substantial demand. Finally, in the Queen's Speech in fall, 2002, devolution legislation for English regions, based on a demonstrated willingness for it through a referendum vote, was promised.

The Mayor of London is the first modern directly-elected executive in the United Kingdom. The introduction of party primary elections for mayoral candidates led to less central party control over candidates and a personalization of the contest. The eventual winner was a dissident Labor MP and former London official, Ken Livingstone, who, however, has been relatively conciliatory in office.

Northern Ireland is a perennial problem, a hangover of the separation of Ireland from the United Kingdom in 1922. Six counties in the northern part of the island of Ireland, with approximately two-thirds of the population consisting of Protestants favoring continued union with Great Britain, remained in the United Kingdom. Many Catholics north and south remain convinced that there should be one, united country of Ireland on the island. This fundamental division of opinion concerning to which country the territory belongs led to organized violence by proponents of both sides, especially since the late 1960s. The Irish Republican Army (IRA) was the principal organization fighting for a united Ireland.

The current peace accord in Northern Ireland, the Good Friday Agreement of 1998, has led to new institutions there as well. In December 1999, devolution of power from the Westminster parliament to the Belfast parliament ushered in a period of what the British call "power sharing," or "consensus democracy." This entailed not only joint authority over internal matters by both Protestants (Unionists) and Catholics (Nationalists) through the requirement of super-majorities in the Northern Ireland Assembly and executive, but also some sharing of sovereignty over the territory between the United Kingdom and Ireland. Both countries have pledged, however, that Northern Ireland will remain part of the United Kingdom as long as a majority of the population in the province wishes. According to the latest census, Protestants remain in the majority, by 53 to 44 percent.

Referendums on the Good Friday Agreement passed overwhelmingly in both Northern Ireland and the Irish Republic, which repealed its constitutional claim to the province. As expected, devolved government in Northern Ireland has been rocky. Groups representing formerly armed adversaries, including Sinn Fein, closely linked to the IRA, now share executive power; some dissident factions have refused to renounce violence. The major issues have been continued; IRA terrorist activity in light of its relationship to Sinn Fein, incorporation of Catholics into the police service, and divisions among Protestants about how far to cooperate in the new government. In October, 2002, the Northern Ireland Assembly and government were suspended for the fourth time in three years, and direct rule from London was reinstituted, at least temporarily. The May, 2003 elections for a new assembly remain in place. The Northern Ireland government will continue to have a difficult path in working for peaceful solutions to long-intractable problems.

Britain signed the European Convention on Human Rights in 1951. Since 1966 it has allowed appeals to the European Court of Human Rights at Strasbourg, where it has lost more cases than any other country. Under New Labor, a law was quickly passed incorporating the European Convention on Human Rights into domestic law, but it only went into effect in October 2000. British judges rather than European judges now make the decisions about whether Britain is conforming to the Convention. This enhances the ability of British citizens to raise issues of human rights in domestic courts. Nevertheless, parliamentary sovereignty is maintained because Westminster remains the final authority on whether judicial decisions will be followed.

The tougher questions of constitutional reform—the electoral system for the House of Commons, freedom of information, and the House of Lords—were delayed. Currently the United Kingdom remains one of the most secretive democracies in the world, under the doctrine of executive prerogatives of Ministers of the Crown. The Freedom of Information Act eventually enacted is generally viewed as one which still allows the government to withhold a large amount of information.

Superficially House of Lords reform appears simple since a government majority in the House of Commons eventually can override any objections. Because of the capacity of the Lords to delay legislation, however, reform is difficult to complete in a timely fashion. In fact, discussion of reform of the Lords has been ongoing for 90 years. New Labor pledged to abolish voting by hereditary peers, initially leaving only the prime-ministerially appointed life peers, often senior political figures, as constituting a second chamber. There is fear, however, that the power of the Commons would be enhanced even further if "Tony's Cronies," as critics have dubbed prime ministerial appointees, constituted an entirely patronage-based second chamber. In order to accomplish initial reform, Prime Minister Blair accepted a temporary arrangement in 1999 allowing 92 hereditary peers to remain in the 720-member House of Lords, while eliminating 600 others. He then appointed a Royal Commission on the House of Lords (Wakeham Commission) to consider the second stage of Lords reform.

After the Wakeham Commission reported, in 2001 the government proposed a 600-member chamber, with 60 percent appointed by the prime minister on the basis of party affiliations, 20 percent nonpartisan "cross-benchers" appointed by an independent commission, and 20 percent elected on a regional basis through party list proportional representation. This would occur over a transition period of ten years. The government's plans were greeted with widespread skepticism from all parties, especially because of the low proportion of elected representatives. In an attempt to generate a cross-party consensus, a joint committee of MPs and peers was established to reexamine the question. In December, 2002, the Committee initially reported a list of seven options for further discussion, ranging from a fully elected to a fully appointed second chamber. It is now hoped that agreement on the second stage of Lords reform can be reached by the end of Labor's second term in office.

Although the Prime Minister indicated that he was not "personally convinced" that a change in the electoral system was needed, he appointed an Independent Commission on the Voting System (Jenkins Commission) to recommend an alternative to the current electoral system for the House of Commons. In 1998, the Commission recommended what is called "Alternative Vote Plus." The single-member district system would be retained, but instead of casting a vote for one person only, the electorate would rank candidates in order of preference, thus assuring a majority rather than a plurality vote for the winner. There would also be a second vote for a "preferred party." These votes would be put into a regional pool, with 15–20 percent of the total seats being awarded to parties based on their proportional share of these second votes, a favorable development for smaller parties.

Even such a relatively mild reform, however, generated substantial political controversy, as expected when the very basis on which legislators hold their seats is challenged. The proposed change has been criticized not only by the opposition Conservatives, but also by Labor members because it might make it more difficult for Labor to obtain a single-party parliamentary majority. There are no prospects for enactment of Westminster electoral system reform in the near future.

Some analysts, however, argue that the most significant constitutional change in the United Kingdom has been brought about not by Labor but by three actions of Conservative governments—joining the European Community (now European Union) in 1972, approving the *Single European Act* (1986), and signing the *Maastricht Treaty* (1992). Within the ever-expanding areas of EU competence, EU law supersedes British law, including judicial review by the European Court of Justice. Already one-third of total legislation in the United Kingdom comes from the European Union. Famously, Lord Denning observed that the European Union is an incoming tide which cannot be held back. The current process of the European Constitutional Convention may lead to further government integration among the members.

Britain remains one of only three EU members not to join the new European currency, the euro. If Britain were to join the euro, then control over monetary policy as well would effectively pass into the hands of the European Union. Tony Blair had indicated that this step would only be taken with public support in a countrywide referendum. It is widely expected that the government will call for such a referendum before the end of its second full term of office in 2006.

Although not on the Labor party agenda of constitutional change, the role of the monarchy has also come under increased scrutiny in recent years. The Queen's Golden Jubilee Year, celebrating the first 50 years of her reign (2002), was not a happy one, with two deaths and more scandals in the royal family. A resolution of the Scottish Parliament, supported by some MPs and Lords at Westminster, petitions the government to allow the monarch either to be or to marry a Catholic. Currently this is forbidden by the *Act of Settlement* (1701), passed at the end of a period of religious wars. The heir to the throne, Prince Charles, has proposed removing the monarch's particular tie to the Church of England in favor of the title of a more general "defender of faith" in what is now, despite appearances, a secularized country.

More vaguely, the government has suggested moving toward a "people's monarchy"—a simpler, slimmer, and less ritualized institution, perhaps with a gender-neutral inheritance. This would be more like the low profile "bicycle monarchs" of some other European countries. For the first time since Queen Victoria, there is substantial, if muted, public expression of anti-monarchism (republicanism). Tampering with an established and still widely revered institution such as the monarchy, however, requires extremely careful consideration, as many traditionalists are opposed to all change.

Conflicting Views on the Effects of Constitutional Change

Labor's program of constitutional renewal already has brought about some changes in Britain. Instead of near-uniform use of the single member district, simple plurality electoral system, now there are five different systems in operation: Single Transferable Vote (a form of proportional representation with candidate choice) in Northern Ireland, party list proportional representation for the June, 1999 European Parliament election, alternative member systems (a combination of single member district and party list proportional) for the devolved legislatures in Scotland and Wales and the London Assembly, and a popularly elected executive through the Supplementary Vote (voting for two candidates in order of preference) for London. Plurality elections remain the norm only for the House of Commons at Westminster and English local government elections.

Until 1997, there had been only four referendums in the history of the United Kingdom. Within nine months of taking power, Labor held four additional referendums (in Wales, Scotland, Northern Ireland, and London), with two others promised, on changing the Westminster electoral system and on joining the European single currency.

Broadly, five interpretations of these developments have been voiced by commentators, as outlined below. We might term these the (1) popular social liberalism, (2) lukewarm reform, (3) symbolic politics, (4) the doomsday scenario, and (5) constitutional incoherence. These contending explanations exist at least partially because Labor itself has never outlined a coherent theory behind its constitutional reforms beyond Blair's pre-election formulations. There has been no general constitutional convention; instead there have been a series of *ad hoc* measures.

The well-known American analyst of Britain, Samuel H. Beer, has compared Blair's reforms to the popular social liberalism of the early twentieth century Liberal governments, which included restricting the power of the House of Lords and devolving power to Ireland. After the First World War, however, electorally the Conservatives came to dominate a political Left divided between an insurgent Labor Party and the remaining Liberals. At least in the first term of office, social and constitutional reform served as a substitute for a more traditional Labor program of increased government spending. It is considered important as an element to help establish the long-term political dominance of a revitalized center-left.

Another constitutional scholar, Philip Norton, argues that New Labor's proposals are radical in concept but so far moderate in form and effects, e.g., lukewarm reform. Similarly, Anthony Barnett of Charter 88 claims that the government practices *constitutus interruptus*. Another British academic, Patrick Dunleavy, has suggested that constitutional reform for New Labor represents continuous but financially cheap activity at a time when the government is wary of alienating its middle-class supporters by appearing to be another Labor "tax and spend" administration. This amounts to little substantive change, however, until the two critical questions, electoral reform for the House of Commons and membership of the euro, are faced.

Although there has been grudging acceptance from constitutional conservatives who originally opposed change, they are still fearful of the implications of some reforms. The Conservative former editor of *The Times*, William Rees-Mogg, envisioned Labor's constitutional changes eroding democracy in the United Kingdom through a semi-permanent Labor-Liberal governing coalition in Westminster, Scotland, and Wales, a House

of Lords based on patronage, and a more centralized, bureaucratic European superstate. More sanguinely, *The Economist* foresaw a weakening of Westminster's authority through the combined forces of devolution and a more integrated European Union. But by the election of 2001, the Conservative party claimed that it could make devolved institutions work more efficiently as well as maintaining the integrity of an independent House of Lords. However, they continue to oppose a more centralized Europe and a changed electoral system.

Finally, the prominent British political scientist Anthony King has argued that Britain no longer has a coherent set of constitutional principles. Because of the piecemeal constitutional changes over the past quarter century by both Conservative and Labor governments, traditional interpretations of the British constitution no longer adequately describe contemporary practice, but there also is no set of alternative principles as a guide. Britain has moved away from majoritarian democracy without becoming a fully-fledged consensus democracy with proportional representation and coalition governments.

Despite its prominence in the election of 1997 and in New Labor's first term of government, constitutional reform was only a minor feature of the 2001 general election campaign. While the Liberal Democrats, as expected, gave it greater attention, all of the major parties deemphasized constitutional reform in their party manifestos. This was particularly surprising for Labor, which was content to claim that it had delivered on its 1997 commitments. Of Labor's "25 major goals for Britain," the only one touching on constitutional reform was a vague pledge for greater local democracy. Notably absent was any commitment to call a referendum on the Westminster electoral system. While some moves have been made to establish devolved regions in England and to complete Lords reform, as well to deal with the continuing problems in Northern Ireland, overall constitutional reform has been less prominent in Labor's second term of office.

Unintended Consequences Over the Horizon?

Institutional rearrangements often have unanticipated consequences. Although New Labor legislation on constitutional matters claims not to disturb the principle of parliamentary sovereignty, the likelihood is that this constitutional convention will be compromised even more than it already has been under Britain's membership of the European Union. Congruent with the process of decentralization in other European countries, devolution is likely to be entrenched *de facto* if no *de jure*. Some journalists have begun calling British a "federal" political system. Although specific powers are granted to each devolved government, disputes over which level has authority over certain policies are likely to arise. Even without a comprehensive Bill of Rights, incorporation of the European Convention on Human Rights may mean a stronger, more politically active judiciary, a form of creeping judicial review. House of Lords reform, if it is not to be simply an appointed chamber reflecting the wishes of the government of the day, could also lead to a more symmetrical bicameralism.

Incorporation of the European Convention on Human Rights, as well as a limited form of joint authority with Ireland over Northern Ireland and possible membership of the European common currency and central bank, suggest that Britain may be moving into new patterns of international shared authority in areas heretofore considered exclusively within the domain of the sovereign state. Regional policies of the European Union even may be helping stimulate ethnonationalist demands. If the Scottish National Party, still committed to independence for Scotland, ever wins a majority in the Scottish Parliament, the United Kingdom could be faced with a "Quebec scenario," whereby control of a level of government enhances rather than retards its secessionist claims.

The "third way" ideas of Anthony Giddens, influential in the New Labor government, advocate a restructuring of government to promote "subsidiarity" (the taking of decisions at the lowest level possible) and correcting the "democratic deficit" through constitutional reform, greater transparency, and more local democracy. In such a process, Britain would become a more complex polity institutionally. This would demand cultivating habits of conciliation, cooperation, and consent rather than the usual reliance upon parliamentary laws and executive orders. Having additional levels of elected government already has created difficulties for central party organizations attempting to exert control over who becomes the party leader in these jurisdictions.

The electoral system, however, may be the lynchpin of the British parliamentary system as it currently exists. Even the relatively modest changes proposed by the Jenkins Commission might help realign the party system. Because of the fears this arouses within the Labor party, Prime Minister Blair has dealt with electoral reform at Westminster by indefinitely postponing it.

Whatever one's view of the desirability and impact of the changes, New Labor under Tony Blair has pursued and largely fulfilled its 1997 pledges on constitutional reform. Although delays and retreats have occurred on some issues, the implications of these changes will continue to be felt in British politics for some time to come.

Donley T. Studlar is Eberly Family Distinguished Professor of Political Science at West Virginia University, Executive Secretary of the British Politics Group, and author of *Great Britain: Decline or Renewal?* (Westview Press). This article originated as the 1998 Taft Lecture, delivered to the undergraduate Honors recognition ceremony of the Political Science Department, University of Cincinnati.

---

*This is a revised version of an article which first appeared in *Harvard International Review,* Spring 1999.

Judgment day

Tony Blair will win a third term but few friends

Emma Duncan

It will be a year of reckoning for Tony Blair. The last general election took place in June 2001. The next one is therefore due by June 2006. To avoid getting trapped into holding elections at bad times (as James Callaghan was by the 1978 winter of discontent), prime ministers tend to call them after four years, and pundits who pore over the political calendar have pencilled in May 5th 2005 as the likeliest date. Mr Blair will hold off until 2006 only if things are going particularly badly for him; so not having an election in 2005 will be as much a judgment on his performance as having one.

Which groups of people will be for Mr Blair in 2005 and which groups against him? The latter are easier to identify than the former.

The left will be against Mr Blair. When he first came to power, some of them were inclined to give him the benefit of the doubt. Now it is hard to find any who are. Iraq and his close relationship with George Bush have been the biggest factors in turning them against him, but there are plenty of other reasons too. The left hates the market-oriented reforms he has introduced in the public sector; his hostility towards the unions, most sharply illustrated by his battle with the Fire Brigades Union; his failure to roll back the Tory privatisation of the railways. The left regards him as Thatcherlite.

A new licensing act, which will allow pubs to remain open around the clock, is likely to take effect in Britain towards the end of the year. And a new gambling bill may lift restrictions on gaming hours and herald the spread of big casinos.

The countryside will be against him. Rural folk have long been aware that the soul of New Labour is deeply metropolitan: its luminaries regard the countryside as an alien land populated by strange, backward, cruel people. But the countryside's hostility turned to violence over Mr Blair's determination to ban foxhunting (because it seemed a cheap bone to throw to the Labour left); and more civil disobedience is promised.

Anti-Europeans will be against him. Mr Blair once saw it as his destiny to take Britain into the euro. That hope faded, largely because Britain's economy performed so much better than those in the euro zone. But Mr Blair has promised a referendum on the European constitution and the prospect of that vote (expected in 2006) will galvanise anti-Europeans once more. Now that the United Kingdom Independence Party has successes in local and European elections behind it, there is a plausible focus for anti-European feeling.

The poor will be for Mr Blair. Thanks to the tax credits that have boosted the incomes of low earners, the poor have done well out of this government's quietly redistributionist policies. They never voted Tory much anyway; and over the past two elections the Tories' vote in the poor bits of cities has disappeared.

But nobody is fighting over these groups. Their allegiances are already largely determined. The election will be won or lost in the towns and suburbs where the great mass of middle England lives. The factors that determine which way it goes will be partly emotional and partly material.

Iraq will have most bearing on how people feel about Mr Blair. It's not so much that Britons are moved by the Iraqis' plight. Indeed, once Iraqis took over running the government, the country slipped off the front pages; it takes the deaths of foreigners, or of several dozen Iraqis, to get it back on again. What's more important for British politics is how the Iraq war eroded faith in Mr Blair. Some people no longer trust him because they think he lied, and some people because he got the assessment of the danger from Iraq disastrously wrong. Whether they think he is guilty of dishonesty or incompetence, Iraq has changed perceptions of Mr Blair.

Money will have most bearing on how people think about Mr Blair. The most remarkable feature of Labour's time in power has been the economy's performance. Growth has remained high and stable, unemployment low. That will persist going into the election. The house-price boom will be going into reverse, but not fast enough to undermine the government's reputation for sound economic management.

The crucial question in the election will be whether people feel that the improvements in the public services (health in particular) that their taxes have paid for have been sufficient

Taxes have increased, and people have noticed. The middle classes are aware that they have done worse than the poor and are grumpy about it. But the crucial question in the election will be whether people feel that the improvements in the public services (health in particular) that their taxes have paid for have been sufficient. Those improvements are beginning to come through, but it is not clear that they are coming through fast enough to impress the people paying for them.

But even if the public services don't come through for Mr Blair in 2005, one factor is fairly certain to: the Conservative Party. It will go into the next election in almost as much despair as it went into the last.

Changing leaders twice has done the Tories no good. The current one, Michael Howard, has failed to revive their fortunes, partly because Mr Blair has deftly occupied many of the policy areas—tough immigration and law-and-order policies, market-oriented public-service reforms—that are naturally the Tories', and partly because he supported the war against Iraq and has therefore been ill-placed to criticise Mr Blair's foreign policy. Charles Kennedy, the leader of the Liberal Democrats, took a strong stance against the war, and has thus benefited from the fallout. But the Lib Dems are the perennial losers in British politics, and even they do not believe that their post-war bounce will propel them into government. Apathy looks like a more serious enemy for Labour than either the Tories or the Lib Dems: many disaffected Labour voters will simply stay at home.

A credible opposition is a necessary if not a sufficient condition for defeating an incumbent government. Expect Labour to enter its third term in government with a much-reduced majority and a discredited leader. And expect the Tories, shortly thereafter, to get themselves a new leader and a new lease of life. On all sides, change will be in the air. Mr Blair has already announced that, if elected, his third term in Number Ten will be his last. In 2005 preparations for post-Blair politics in Britain will begin in earnest.

Does New Labour Deserve a Third Term?

YES: ANTHONY GIDDENS

NO: DAVID MARQUAND

Dear David
1st February 2004

The prime minister has many troubles ahead. Yet, unforeseeable crises aside, it now looks probable that Tony Blair will both lead the Labour party into the next election and that he will win it. So it is important to ask where New Labour should go from here. As I understand it, setting the Iraq war aside, you have become thoroughly disillusioned with the whole enterprise. I remain a supporter and I would like to explain why.

This government has changed Britain for the better, and will accomplish still more in a third term. What is Labour in power for? Its prime purpose is to turn a Thatcherite society into a social democratic one. By this I mean a society that is cosmopolitan rather than narrowly nationalistic; in which economic prosperity is combined with social justice; and where there are robust, effective public institutions.

Mistakes have certainly been made since 1997. In its first term the government was over-cautious. It stuck too closely to Tory policies in health and education. Devolution was not driven by a coherent vision. Little progress was made on European issues. Transport was placed too low down on the list of priorities.

However, substantial progress has been achieved towards the goals I outlined. This is the first Labour government to preside over a period of steady economic growth—the precondition for

generating revenue for social spending. Britain has low unemployment, a situation to which the New Deal has contributed. Seventy-five per cent of the working population is in employment, one of the highest levels of any industrial country. The decision to place control of interest rates in the hands of the Bank of England was a correct one.

Constitutional reform and devolution have already altered the country irrevocably. Separatism has declined since the arrival of the Scottish parliament. The advent of elected mayors is an important step. Britain has signed up to European legislation on human rights. The proposed supreme court is a worthwhile innovation.

This is a government with a better track record on the social justice front than its critics give it credit for. It is not easy to track inequalities, but the latest estimates indicate that in 2003–04 1.3m fewer children will be living in poverty than in 1996–97. Child poverty remains an endemic problem, but is at its lowest level since 1991. There were 400,000 fewer over-65s living in poverty in 2001–02 than in 1996–97, a fall of almost 20 per cent. It has been the right strategy to get as many people in work as possible, above a decent minimum wage. Those living in workless households are five times as likely to be below the poverty line than in households where at least one adult is in work. Whatever one thinks of the Iraq episode, the government has taken a lead on development is-

sues, pushing for more money to tackle global poverty.

What of public services and the public domain more generally? I know this is an area where you believe Labour has pushed on with the attack on public institutions initiated by Margaret Thatcher. The public sphere, you say in your new book, *Decline of the Public*, has been diminished rather than revived under New Labour. Citizenship has been hollowed out by an emphasis upon consumensm.

I agree that a centre-left government should stand for the renewal of public goods and institutions. But I interpret what New Labour is trying to achieve differently from you.

Although in Britain it is a risky business, the government put taxes up, channelling large amounts of money into the NHS and education. This policy in itself is a major contribution to the strengthening of the public domain, as well as lifting the morale of those who work in these sectors. However, reform of public sector institutions is crucial to making such investment pay. Many state bodies are overly bureaucratic, dominated by producer interests and unresponsive to citizens' needs. The government overdosed on targets and central regulation in its early attempts to pursue these concerns. But it has pulled back from most of these over-zealous endeavours and the general thrust of policy is right.

It is right, for example, to try to expand the range of choice that people—especially poorer people—have in health care, education and elsewhere. Such an emphasis does riot mean equating citizenship and consumerism. I argue that in the market sphere the individual is a "consumer citizen." Consumer choice is what drives a competitive market. Yet markets presume norms of trust, which markets themselves cannot generate, and require regulation to protect consumers. In the public arena, by contrast, the individual is a "citizen consumer." Choice and diversity of provision are desirable, but professional ethics and a public service ethos have a more central role.

> **Substantial progress has been made in turning Britain into a social democratic society**
> **ANTHONY GIDDENS**

The state and the public sphere are not the same. In this sense the term "public services" can be misleading. Experimenting with new ways of delivering public goods is a vital enterprise, not at all the same as "creeping privatization." The Scandinavian countries are the most advanced social democratic states in the world. Yet these are also the countries where there has been most acceptance of the need for reform and change. Foundation hospitals, for example, were pioneered in Denmark and Sweden, as was the use of vouchers in education and the provision of services for the elderly. We should be pursuing a similar nondogmatic approach here.

All best
Tony

Dear Tony
5th February 2004

I am not disillusioned with New Labour; I am un-illusioned. When Tony Blair was elected leader of the Labour party, I rejoiced. I applauded his decision to campaign for a change in clause four, and marvelled at the panache with which he did so. I marvelled so much that I rejoined the Labour party which I had left 15 years before. But well before the 1997 election I was beginning to smell a rat. The shallow rhetoric of "modernisation" and a "young country" suggested a lack of ideological conviction which seemed ominous.

All the same, you are right that this government has a far better economic record than any previous Labour government. Gordon Brown deserves the credit. He is the best Labour chancellor since Roy Jenkins, perhaps since Stafford Cripps. And whereas Jenkins and Cripps had to spend their time clearing up the mess left by their predecessors, Brown followed the best Tory chancellor for 50 years—Kenneth Clarke. I also agree with you that the Blair governments have been more redistributive than many of their critics realise. For that, too, the lion's share of the credit belongs to Brown.

> **It is preposterous to claim that Blair's governments have strengthened the public domain**
> **DAVID MARQUAND**

Where do we differ? First, over the government's attitude to the public domain. You conclude that because it has channelled large sums into the NHS and education it has strengthened the public domain. But the strength of the public domain has nothing to do with the level of public spending. Massive public spending can coexist with a crippled public domain. It did so in the old Soviet Union. In this country, the public domain was a child of the Victorian era. It grew rapidly from about 1860 until the end of the century, but public spending hardly grew at all until the 1890s. I believe the state can be an enemy of the public domain as well as a friend. On the whole, the British state was a friend in the second half of the 19th century and the first half of the 20th. By the last quarter of the 20th it had become a bitter enemy. It is still an enemy today.

> **Many on the left are too complacent about the danger posed to the west by the new terrorism**
> **ANTHONY GIDDENS**

The public domain encompasses much more than the public sector. In my book, I list many public domain activities and institutions. Here are some: the Pennine way; Amnesty International; fair trials; impartial public administration; disinterested scholarship; welcoming public spaces. Spending levels have little to do with any of these. They reflect an ethic of public service and a culture of citizenship, which the state can snuff out but cannot implant. The public domain is the domain of citizenship, equity, service and professionalism. It depends on the rule of law, and therefore on an independent judiciary, insulated from political interference and popular pressure. It also depends on disinterested professionalism, embodied in a professional ethic. These have to be protected from market pressures—not because there is anything wrong with markets in their proper place, but because the public and market domains are distinct entities. And the proxy markets which successive governments have forced on the public services in the name of reform can do even more harm to the trust relationships that lie at the heart of the public domain than real markets. The vitality of the public domain depends on strong, confident intermediate institutions, capable of resisting incursions from the central state. Democratic accountability, too, is a corollary of a culture of citizenship. In this country, its growth was connected with the emergence of a professional, non-partisan, career civil service, and the demise of the nepotism and cronyism that Radicals dubbed "old corruption."

Looked at in this light, it is preposterous to claim that the Blair governments have strengthened the public domain. One of their most obvious hallmarks is contempt for the rule of law and disdain for judicial independence. The Iraq war was fought in defiance of international law. David Blunkett can hardly open his mouth without savaging lawyers and judges. Blair has fetishised trust-corroding targets and audits as wholeheartedly as the Thatcherites did; and he has shown the same disdain for public service professionals. The Thatcherites ignited the audit explosion which has done more damage to the public domain than any other development of the last 20 years, but the Blairites have fanned its flames. And the whole culture of audit rests on the premise that professionals are inherently untrustworthy, and that the professional ethic is camouflage for monopolistic cartels.

The Blairites' approach to governance is even more disquieting. Yes, they have honoured the devolution commitments they inherited from John Smith; in truth, they had no alternative. But they disdain local government as thoroughly as the Thatcherites did. Their treatment of the House of Lords is a scandal. Britain desperately needs effective checks on the elective dictatorship in Downing Street. An entirely nominated upper house can't possibly provide that. Worst of all, they have systematically blurred the distinction between professional, career civil servants, with an ethic of public service, and the personal ministerial appointees who now pullulate allover Whitehall. That is the real moral of the Hutton inquiry. We have returned to the favouritism and cronyism that the I9th-century reforms of public administration rooted out.

Which brings me to our second difference: Iraq. The Iraq war *cannot* be set aside. It is the defining episode of Blair's premiership, as surely as Suez was for Eden's and Munich for Chamberlain's. As with Suez and Munich, it was a catastrophic blunder. However questionable John Scarlett's role in the September 2002 dossier, the intelligence services were not responsible for this. It was Blair who led Britain into war, not the joint intelligence committee. He helped to inflict dreadful damage on the UN, poisoned our relations with the two core states of the EU, and split the Labour party. His credibility is now in tatters. The Hutton inquiry has done nothing to restore his reputation because the inquiry's terms of reference were so restrictive that he could not examine the issues that really mattered. Now it looks as if the same will happen with the Butler inquiry. To appoint one inquiry with overly restrictive terms of reference might be forgiven as a lapse. To appoint two looks suspiciously like a habit. It is not a habit social democrats can condone.

All good wishes
David

Dear David
10th February 2004

I was hoping to concentrate on the domestic agenda because the Iraq war, Hutton report, proposed Butler report, 45-minute claim and so forth have been so exhaustively debated in recent weeks. My views do differ from yours. There were many reasons why Saddam's regime had to be confronted. It was Saddam, after all, who sought to hoodwink the UN over many years and who drove his country to ruin through his obsessive desire to dominate the middle east. Saddam could have stepped down—or if he didn't have any WMD, provide clear evidence—at any time in the build-up to war. If decisive action had not been taken against his regime, he would have continued to split the international community and defy the UN—and he would still be in power today. It would have been far better if the UN security council had been able to reach agreement on this. And Saddam might have acted differently if a united international community had condemned him, backed by the threat of force.

I think many on the left are too complacent about the dangers posed to western democracies by the new terrorism. It is not just an extension of the terrorism we are familiar with, such as that practised by the IRA or Eta. The new terrorism is geopolitical in its aims and ruthless in the means it will use to achieve them. Al Qaeda has cells in dozens of countries, held together by a sense of mission. September 11th now seems to be down played by many people, but other 9/11s, only worse, could happen. Blocking off possible connections between rogue states and geopolitical terrorism is crucial. Saddam's Iraq was a ticking time-bomb against this backdrop. The intervention in Iraq has certainly had some influence on Libya's decision to abandon its WMD programmes, the rethinking going on in Iran and the uncovering of the export of nuclear knowhow from Pakistan.

You say the Iraq conflict will be the defining episode of Tony Blair's premiership, implying that it will lead to his decline and fall. I presume you want Blair to stand down, as a leader whose "credibility is in tatters." There is a sort of unholy alliance of anti-war newspapers and the right-wing press apparently aiming at the same outcome. But I think it is a delusion to suppose that if Blair were somehow forced out, Labour would march on to better and greater things. Labour's prospects would be irretrievably damaged.

On the public domain, I have no quarrel with your Durkheimian point that strong intermediary groups are essential for a healthy civic life. A centre-left party should stand for the renewal of the public sphere, not for a society where everything becomes commercialised.

However you also claim that "the strength of the public domain has nothing to do with the level of public expenditure." I find this assertion extraordinary. The years of underinvestment in public services during the Thatcher period, coupled with her disdainful attitude towards them, were highly damaging. It seems to me both churlish and wrong to say that the funding Labour is putting into the health service and other areas is not a significant contribution to enhancing the public domain.

You say "trust the professionals," whether they are dons, doctors, judges or civil servants. New Labour wants to reform the state and public agencies so that they are more open, efficient and responsive to the needs of citizens. Professional power can facilitate these objectives, but clearly it can also block them. Professionals can form closed shops, resist change and innovation, act as special interest groups, be disdainful towards the public, or otherwise coast along on the privileges they enjoy. The government quite rightly has sought to change these practices, as well as introduce wider reforms in public sector provision. And with some success. There are few "Lucky Jims" in universities these days.

I agree that detailed targets and auditing are counterproductive, and tend to spawn a new layer of bureaucracy. They can corrode the very ethic of public service that promotes dedication and commitment. These points, however, have been registered and responded to. We have to find a better balance between accountability and autonomy, and serious efforts are being made to do just that.

Finally, what about the "elective dictatorship" in Downing Street? Your account ignores the changed environment in which political leaders have to function today. There are fundamental and difficult problems—which we, as a society, are far from having faced up to—in the relation between the media and democracy in an era of media saturation. The decline of parliament is directly connected to the fact that the way in which politicians respond to questions on the *Today* programme often counts for more than what they say in the chamber. The "advisers" whom you excoriate have stepped into the gap. It won't do to say that we should simply go back to how things used to work 30 years ago. Every country is struggling with these questions, but I see no easy solutions.

With all best regards
Tony

Dear Tony
11th February 2004

The differences between us are deeper than I thought. On Iraq and its sequel, I don't think Saddam's phantom WMD had much to do with Blair's decision to go to war. I think he went to war because he believed it was a vital British interest to fight alongside the world's only superpower. There is nothing dishonourable about that view, but even so it was a terrible mistake. The crux of the issue has to do with geopolitics, not Iraq or even the middle east. Blair believes in a unipolar world and is viscerally hostile to the suggestion that Europe should try to become an alternative pole of power, balancing the US (and one day China). I believe in a multipolar world: the notion of a single, permanent hegemon, to which the rest of the world must forever bend the knee, flies in the face of some of my most deeply held values—human dignity, self-determination, diversity and pluralism. Quite apart from that, I believe that a multipolar world will sooner or later come into existence whether we like it or not. The spectre that terrifies me is of a weak, divided Europe, incapable of defending its interests in a world dominated by the Americans, the Chinese and perhaps the Indians. I therefore believe that Britain's overriding interest is to stay alongside the core nations of the EU, and to work with them to consolidate and strengthen the union in the face of the centrifugal pressures let loose by an ill thought out enlarge-

ment. My reason for thinking Blair's Iraq policy catastrophic is that I believe it brought the above spectre nearer. (He is rowing back a little at the moment, but I see no evidence that he has changed his basic attitudes.)

> **The return of a third Labour government with a big majority would be a disaster for our democracy**
> **DAVID MARQUAND**

On the public domain, we are talking about different things. For you the public domain is a set of institutions. For me, it is a set of practices, embodying values. Hence our differences about the relationship between the public domain and public spending. Like you, I'm glad to see this government spending more on health and education. But however desirable it may be for other reasons, the extra spending won't, by itself, do anything for the public domain. Your suggestion that Thatcherite "underinvestment" weakened the public domain is a piece of Labour mythology. Public spending as a proportion of GDP fell very little in the Thatcher years. What damaged the public domain was the remorseless attack on professional autonomy and the equally remorseless marketisation that accompanied it. Both continue under Labour.

Of course, professionals have to be accountable. Lack of accountability was the worm in the bud of the public domain in the old days. But it's never a good idea to call in Beelzebub to drive out Satan. Accountability through markets, proxy markets and corporate sector managerialism have done infinitely more harm than good. We have to devise new forms of accountability—qualitative rather than quantitative, localist rather than centralist, bottom-up rather than top-down and involving stakeholders along with professionals in a process of social learning. This is an extraordinarily difficult task, but we haven't a hope unless we abandon the bossy, centralist mind set that New Labour shares with old Thatcherism.

However, even this is a minor matter compared with what I now realise are the

really crucial differences between us. I'll try to describe them as fairly as I can. You evidently think that anything that weakens Labour's chances of winning the next election is, by definition, a bad thing. I am afraid I don't. On the contrary, I think the return of a third Labour government with a massive parliamentary majority, on the back of little more than 40 per cent of the popular vote, would be a disaster for British democracy, and therefore for social democracy as well. The best possible result would be a hung parliament, followed by a Lib-Lab coalition, the abandonment of our antediluvian first past the post electoral system and the slow conversion of our equally antediluvian political class to a politics of pluralism, negotiation, power-sharing and mutual education. The second best would be a small Labour majority, which would force the party leadership to abandon the macho posturing and we know best triumphalism of the recent past and might—who knows?—persuade it to adopt proportional representation (PR) of its own accord. But a third Labour term with a big majority would mean more posturing, more triumphalism, more hubris—and, almost certainly, eventual nemesis.

Behind this looms an even deeper difference. Pondering your letters, I have come to see that you are committing the besetting sin of old Labour—the sin of concentrating on outcome and forgetting process. In a giveaway phrase in your first letter, you said you wanted a "social democratic society." For me, the very notion of a social democratic society is an absurdity. Social democracy is not an end state. It is a process: the process of applying the fundamental values I mentioned a moment ago to ever-changing social realities. The true lesson of old Labour's failures was that British-style majoritarian democracy, and the elective dictatorship it inevitably produces, are incompatible with such a process. New Labour has taught us the same lesson, in spades.

All the best
David

Dear David
12th February 2004

I'm a Labour supporter. I hope Labour *will* win a clear majority again. A hung parliament and a Lib-Lab coalition would not be good for the country. Look at the poor performance of the Lib-Lab coalition in Scotland, which has produced policies that skirt the core problems of the uncompetitive Scottish economy. On the whole I'm a supporter of PR, but I don't feel as passionately about it as you. The advantages are obvious, but there is a well known downside, including the space opened up for extremist parties.

There's something mildly comforting about being called old Labour again—that hasn't happened to me for some time. More seriously, I find the concluding paragraph of your letter quite mysterious. I am a social democrat, and I regard Labour as a social democratic party, which shares a great deal in common with social democratic parties elsewhere. A social democrat wants to further a society that embodies the core values of the left-solidarity, equality and protection of the vulnerable. These values, as we have discussed, can't be achieved in a society where markets are allowed free rein; they presume active government and a flourishing public sphere. But constant policy reform is needed to help realise them.

No one can possibly think that social democracy can reach a final state. Revisionism is an essential part of the history of social democracy and has to remain so. That for me is precisely what New Labour and the third way debate is about—responding positively to social change. Scandinavian social democrats have been even more innovative than New Labour. You claim that one can't talk about a "social democratic society," but it seems to me perfect sense to say that the Scandinavian countries are the most developed social democracies in the world. It also makes sense to say that we can give Britain a hefty nudge in the same direction.

I am a committed European and I want Britain to playa positive role in the ED. A multipolar world, however, could be very dangerous. The EU certainly has to reform itself. At the moment it is free-riding on US military power. The Europeans couldn't even resolve the conflicts in their own backyard, in Bosnia and Kosovo, without the US military. It isn't surprising that many in Europe simply repress the threat posed by the new terrorism. We need a stronger and more coordinated Europe, although not one that would be a military rival to the US. But we also need a US that constructively engages with the EU and the wider world community, and I hope a Democratic president will be elected who pursues such an aim.

All best
Tony

Dear Tony
13th February 2004

I can't sum up my position. I'm not sure I have a "position." What I have are instincts and values, and these point me in a very different direction from yours. I'm also a Labour supporter of sorts, but support for the Labour party comes a lot lower down my list of priorities than the health of British democracy, the need to replace the backward-looking and corrupting political system of this country with a new framework in which we can practise a different politics, and the need for an independent and powerful European presence in the dangerously unbalanced global political economy of our time. I would like to see a hung parliament after the next election because two terms of overweening and unrepresentative Labour majorities have taught me that the party will not move in the direction I want it to take unless it is forced to.

So why do I believe all these things? Essentially because my core values are not solidarity, equality and protection of the vulnerable—important as the first and last are. (Equality is a very dodgy notion; in the last 100 years more crimes have been committed in its name than in that of any other political ideal, with the exception of racial purity.) My core values are human dignity, self-expression, self-respect, self-realisation, diversity, pluralism and, above all, tolerance. I rejoice in difference. I rejoice in the marvellous diversities of human cultures and traditions, and I want to protect them from the monstrous regiment of universalists. The political theorist from whom I have learned most is Isaiah Berlin—though I don't like to see him treated as an icon, as too many people in Oxford seem to do—and like him, I bristle at the very notion of a single, all-embracing, universally applicable ideology. No creed will ever do justice to human diversity; no creed will ever arm us against the inherently unpredictable contingencies of political life. GK Chesterton was right when he said mankind's favourite game was "cheat the prophet."

That's why I took you to task for talking about a "social democratic society." The very notion seems to me to belong to the destructive and dysfunctional family of notions that includes a "socialist society," a "classless society," a "market economy," a "Christian country" and a "Jewish state." It implies that we know how to remake society, when we don't and can't; and that we know where history is heading, which we also don't and can't. For the same reason I bristle at the prospect of perpetual US hegemony, and the assumption of successive British prime ministers that we have no option but to hunt with the Americans. By the same token, I want to junk majoritarian democracy *a l'Anglaise*, together with the elective dictatorship associated with it, and come into line with the overwhelming majority of our European neighbours. I'm astonished by the insular parochialism that leads you to support a patently bankrupt system found nowhere else in the democratic world. I do, however, agree with you about the desirability of a Democratic victory in the US election. If the Democrats do win, Tony Blair will be the only significant head of government in the world who still supports the Iraq war. A nice irony.

All the best
David

ANTHONY GIDDENS is a former director if the LSE. He is a fellow of King's College, Cambridge. DAVID MARQUAND is the author of "Decline of the Public" (Polity) and a visiting fellow at Oxford University.

A divided self:
A Survey of France

France has an identity problem. It needs to find the courage to redefine itself, says John Andrews

"I HAVE heard and understood your call: that the republic should live, that the nation should reunite, that politics should change." On a cold evening in early May, Jacques Chirac found the right words for the moment. He had just been re-elected president of the French republic, with 82% of the vote, in a run-off with Jean-Marie Le Pen, the leader of the extreme-right National Front. Two weeks earlier, in the first round of the election, Mr Le Pen had eliminated the Socialist candidate (and incumbent prime minister), Lionel Jospin, from the contest. For left-leaning voters, Mr Chirac was clearly the lesser evil, so in the run-off they joined forces with Mr Chirac's centre-right to humble Mr Le Pen. Hence Mr Chirac's carefully chosen words: his victory may have been sweet, but it was hardly unqualified.

Doubtless that is why as prime minister of his "government of mission", Mr Chirac appointed Jean-Pierre Raffarin, a pudgy and amiable former senator from the Poitou-Charentes region. Mr Raffarin's motto is *la France d'en bas*, grassroots France, which is supposed to mean not only a government closer to the people but a government that comes from the people.

So six months later, is the nation "reunited"; has politics changed; is the republic "alive"? The answers are horribly muddled, mainly because the French themselves are muddled: over France's place in Europe, over the impact of globalisation and, at root, over what it means to be French. In their hearts they want precious little to change; in their heads they suspect change is inevitable.

If it is, their worry is not just what the change will be, but how and when it will come. On June 17th, the day after a parliamentary election in which Mr Chirac's supporters (most of them members of the newly assembled and aptly named Union for the Presidential Majority) won 399 of the National Assembly's 577 seats, the headline of the conservative *Le Figaro* proclaimed: "Five years to change France". Given that there will be no significant elections before the next presidential and parliamentary polls, due in 2007, the opportunity is there. But if change does come, many will not like it: the leftist *Libération*'s headline sarcastically predicted "A five-year sentence".

Whatever the headlines say, for most of France's 59m people not much has changed since the bout of elections in the spring. Around 9% of the workforce is still without a job; the rest troop off to their offices and factories just as before, cosseted by laws that protect them from quick lay-offs, provide them with one of the world's shortest working weeks—just 35 hours—and give them holiday entitlements Americans can only dream of. Meanwhile, their country remains as beautiful and seductive as ever, and the two-hour lunch is alive and well. Add trains that run fast and on time, modern motorways in good repair, and a med-

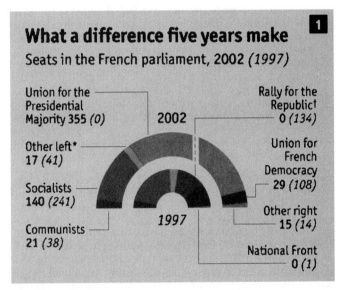

What a difference five years make

Seats in the French parliament, 2002 *(1997)*

Union for the Presidential Majority 355 *(0)*

2002

Rally for the Republic[†] 0 *(134)*

Other left* 17 *(41)*

Union for French Democracy 29 *(108)*

Socialists 140 *(241)*

Other right 15 *(14)*

1997

Communists 21 *(38)*

National Front 0 *(1)*

*Includes Radical Party of the Left, 7 *(12)*; Greens, 3 *(7)*
[†]In 2002 it was absorbed into the Union for the Presidential Majority
Sources: French interior ministry; *The Economist*

ical system at the top of the World Health Organisation's international rankings. Surely the French have a right to feel pleased with themselves?

Not altogether superior

So why do they feel so insecure? Why do politicians, pundits and philosophers (a breed revered on French television) feel a need to bolster the country's collective morale by pointing out the deficiencies of the "Anglo-Saxon" way, be they fraudulent accountancy practices in America or decrepit private railways in Britain?

One reason is doubtless a dash of *Schadenfreude*. Within the lifetime of its senior citizens, France has been occupied by Germany, rescued by America and Britain, and then divested—bloodily in the case of Algeria and Indochina—of almost all its colonies. Since then English has become the world's common language (so much so that France's own politicians will now

Same bed, different dreams

Better to cohabit than be out in the cold

IS IT sensible for France to have a president from one side of the political divide and a government from the other? Olivier Schrameck, chief of staff to Mr Jospin from 1997 until May this year, devoted much of a recent book, "Matignon Rive Gauche, 1997–2001", to denouncing such "cohabitation" as a waste of energy and a recipe for immobility. Under cohabitation, the government would run the country, but the president, who retains traditional authority over defence and foreign policy (the constitutional authority is rather vague), would be tempted to snipe from the sidelines.

Yet French voters have forced such liaisons on their country three times since the birth of the Fifth Republic in 1958. The first time was when the left was defeated in the parliamentary elections of 1986. The Socialist François Mitterrand, who had been elected president in 1981, had to put up with a centre-right government led by Jacques Chirac as prime minister. In 1988 Mitterrand was re-elected president and dissolved parliament. In the ensuing elections the Socialists returned to power. In 1993, however, the left-wing government was voted out and Mitterrand had to cohabit with the centre-right once again, this time with Edouard Balladur as prime minister. Two years later this cohabitation ended with the election of Mr Chirac as president. But in 1997 Mr

Chirac provoked the third cohabitation—much tenser than the first two—by calling early parliamentary elections that the left, led by Mr Jospin, won handsomely.

Such cohabitations could happen because the presidential term was for seven years and that of the lower house of parliament, the National Assembly, for five. But in future there will be less opportunity for these oddball relationships. In September 2000, after an arcane debate between constitutional experts and self-interested politicians, a bemused electorate decided in a referendum (in which only 30% cast a vote) that, beginning with the elections of 2002, the president would have the same five-year term as the parliament.

Since a president might die in office, or might dissolve parliament early, there could still be cohabitations in the future. But as long as President Chirac remains in the post, he is unlikely to call early elections again. For the record, he used to be a fierce opponent of reducing the seven-year presidential term, but changed his mind. His critics say he feared that voters in 2002 might think him too old for another seven-year term but young enough for five years (he will be 70 later this month). He himself claims he supported the change in order to modernise France.

speak it in public), America has turned into the world's only superpower and Hollywood has come to dominate the world's entertainment industry. For France, a country which believes that its revolution, just as much as America's, bears a universal message, these changes have not been easy to accept. Seeing someone else having a hard time provides some light relief.

But there are also more troubling reasons for this lack of confidence. One is the feeling, especially among industrialists and businessmen, that France's economic formula, involving higher taxes and social charges than in most of the countries its firms compete with, will not work forever. Indeed, it is already fraying at the edges. At the start of the 1990s, France ranked eighth in the world in terms of economic output per person, but by the end of the decade it had slipped to 18th.

The most important reason, however, is a lurking suspicion that French society itself is not working. Go back to the first round of the presidential election on April 21st, with its 16 candidates, and ask a few simple questions. Why did Mr Jospin, arguably France's most effective prime minister in the 44 years of the Fifth Republic, get only 16.2% of the vote? Why, in that round, did Mr Chirac get only 19.9%, the lowest ever for an incumbent president? Why did 13 no-hoper candidates gather up 47% of the vote between them? And why did a record 28.4% of the electorate abstain? Most bothersome of all, why did Mr Le Pen, ostracised throughout his 40-odd years in politics, win 16.9% of the vote and so pass through to the second round?

There are plenty of superficial answers: Mr Jospin lacked charm; Mr Chirac was stained by alleged corruption; the electorate felt free to indulge its whims because it assumed that a run-off between Messrs Jospin and Chirac was pre-ordained; and Mr Le Pen is a brilliant orator. But there is a more fundamental explanation. As one French journalist, Philippe Manière, puts it in a recent book, the first-round result was "the vengeance of the people".

A question of colour, a matter of faith

France must face up to its immigrant problems

JEAN-MARIE LE PEN, at ease in his drawing room, waves an arm as if to state the obvious: "The greatest challenge is demographic. The countries of the north—the world of the white man, or let's say the non-black world—have an ageing population. They are rich, and they are facing a third world of 5 billion people, maybe more tomorrow, who are very young and dynamic. This dynamism will be translated into immigration."

Outside the room, the guard-dogs are asleep. In the urban plain below the Le Pen mansion (inherited from a political admirer) in Saint-Cloud, the Paris evening rush-hour is under way. The National Front leader goes on: "The rise of Islam is more the result of its youth and dynamism than its religious values. It's a demographic problem which will lead to immigration, whose consequences could lead, if nothing is done, to the submersion of our country, our people, our civilisation… No government, whether by ideology or by blindness, has realised the danger."

France's far-right bogeyman gained second place in the presidential election by saying what few other politicians would either want to or dare to: that the French republic has too many immigrants, who in turn have too many children. But that is putting it politely. What the National Front and the National Republican Movement, its rival on the extreme right, really mean is that France has too many inhabitants who are black, brown and Muslim. And lots of them are not immigrants at all, but were born in France and are French citizens.

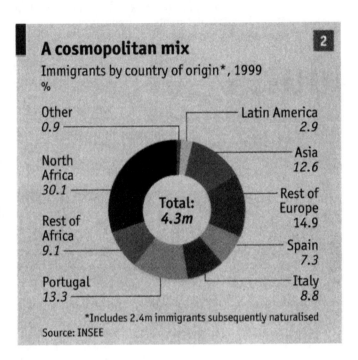

A cosmopolitan mix

Immigrants by country of origin*, 1999
%

Other 0.9

Latin America 2.9

Asia 12.6

North Africa 30.1

Rest of Europe 14.9

Rest of Africa 9.1

Total: 4.3m

Spain 7.3

Portugal 13.3

Italy 8.8

*Includes 2.4m immigrants subsequently naturalised

Source: INSEE

There are plenty of other politicians who have dabbled in the politics of race. Governments of the right have over the years enacted increasingly strong laws to restrict immigration, and governments of the left have for the most part accepted them. Mr Chirac, definitely not a racist himself, found it useful in the 1988 presidential election campaign to refer to the "odours" of immigrant cooking.

What makes Mr Le Pen different is that he has consistently preached the same xenophobic message ever since he entered politics. He became France's youngest member of parliament in 1956, at the age of 27, and first stood for the presidency in 1974. France's ills, he has said all along, are the fault of foreigners, including fellow members of the European Union. The remedy is to keep out foreigners, produce more French children, build more prisons, cut taxes and leave the EU.

The question is why that message suddenly found more resonance with the voters in last spring's presidential election than ever before in Mr Le Pen's political career. Mr Le Pen's previous best score was 14.4% in the first round in 1988, and the only time his party has ever gained more than one seat in the National Assembly was in 1986, when the elections, exceptionally, were held by proportional representation.

The answer is surely not that nearly a fifth of the voters suddenly decided that Mr Le Pen's programme made practical sense, nor that all those who cast their ballot for him are anti-Semitic fascists (Mr Le Pen has described the gas chambers as a "detail" of the second world war, and thinks that Maurice Pa-

pon, the Vichy official who in the late 1990s was eventually convicted for crimes against humanity, was innocent). More likely, the voters wanted to jog the governing elite into action. As a former Socialist prime minister, Laurent Fabius, once said, "Le Pen poses good questions and offers bad solutions."

So what might a good solution look like? A useful start would be, literally, to enumerate France's problems. Malek Boutih, the French-born son of Algerian immigrants and now the president of SOS-Racisme, an anti-racism organisation, argued in a recent book that "France is wrong not to publish, as other countries like America do, statistics of criminality by social category, age, place, type of city development and so on. It is even more wrong not to establish a public debate on the question, as though the French are so irrational that they cannot calmly consider the reality of their problems."

Crime matters

But should that mean a debate on crime as well? Polls before the election showed that the subject topped the list of their concerns, ahead of the state of the economy or pensions or even unemployment. Whether crime in France is worse than in other countries is a moot point: criminal statistics are hard to compare, and although one study showed that France in 2000 had proportionately more crimes than America, other studies suggest that it did a little better than, say, Germany or Belgium. However, what matters to French people is what happens in France.

Or more precisely, what they think is happening. Nicolas Sarkozy, the interior minister, has won plaudits for not only identifying crime as a serious problem but being seen to be doing something about it. Barely a week goes by without him being photographed with a smiling collection of police or gendarmes. Mr Sarkozy has secured the money to add another 6,500 police to the 146,000 he took over from his predecessor. And Mr Raffarin has appointed a junior minister in the justice ministry specifically to supervise a building programme that will add 11,000 prison places to the 47,000 already occupied.

In terms of public perception, such measures will help. One poll in September found that the proportion of those questioned who felt they were "often" at risk of crime was 49%—shockingly high in absolute terms but actually slightly less than in the autumn of last year. Mr Sarkozy has been able to trumpet a reduction in reported crime, by 4.5% in August compared with a year earlier, the first such fall for five years. In Paris, where the tourist industry has long complained about the plague of pickpockets, the fall was 11%.

Whether the momentum can be sustained is another matter. In the country that produced the Declaration of Human Rights (in 1789, a satisfying two years before America's Bill of Rights), the new enthusiasm for "zero tolerance" becomes hard to swallow when it means giving the authorities greater powers of arrest and punishment.

According to critics, many of them well placed in the judiciary and the media, the government is eroding the presumption of innocence (never particularly robust in France, which has no Anglo-Saxon protection of *habeas corpus*); it casually treats many young offenders as though they were adults; and it is callously cracking down on France's most marginal residents, from Romanian beggars to African prostitutes. In other words, the critics allege that the Raffarin government—and Mr Sarkozy in particular—is doing the work of Mr Le Pen for him.

Press Mr Boutih on whether criminal statistics should include a breakdown by race or religion, and he immediately says no: "I remain convinced that ethnic origin is less relevant than the level of education and social status." He has a point: a well-educated Arab or black Frenchman with a decent job is unlikely to turn to petty drug-dealing or car-stealing. The trouble, according to Tahar Ben Jelloun, a Moroccan who is one of France's finest writers, is that only 4% of the children of immigrants get to university, compared with 25% of their native contemporaries.

Our ancestors the Gauls

But the main reason for Mr Boutih's resistance is that to collect information by race or religion would offend the very French concept of "republican values", because it would discriminate between citizens rather than treat them as equal. France makes no allowance for cultural differences: "our ancestors the Gauls" applies to schoolchildren of every hue. In this secular republic, the idea of collecting racial and religious statistics is a virtual taboo across the whole of the political spectrum. Such statistics, it is feared, will lead France along the Anglo-Saxon road of "communautarisme" (in which the idea of separate communities within the country as a whole is acceptable). In the words of the constitution, the French republic is indivisible, and having separate communities is seen as automatically leading to divisions.

Yet the sad reality is that France's race relations are no better than anyone else's. Arab and black minorities are as much as ever excluded from the mainstream. In opinion polls in the late 1990s, two-fifths of the respondents admitted to being at least "a little bit" racist (more than in any other European Union country except Belgium), and just over half thought there were "too many Arabs" in France.

The lack of solid figures leads to the sort of guesswork that plays into the far-right's hands. The state statistics office, INSEE, reckons that in 1999 (the year of the most recent census) the total number of foreign-born residents in metropolitan France, including 2.4m who have acquired French nationality, was 4.3m, or 7.4% of the metropolitan population of 58.5m. Of these, 1.3m had come from Algeria, Morocco and Tunisia. But the official figures end with that breakdown by country of origin.

The best estimate for the religious breakdown that INSEE is not allowed to publish comes from a scholarly report presented to the prime minister two years ago by the High Council for Integration, a committee of academics and experts. The report reckoned that France is home to 4m–5m Muslims—defined by culture rather than religious observance—of whom up to half have French nationality. Of the Muslim total, almost 3m are of North African origin or ancestry, with 1.5m from Algeria, 1m from Morocco and the rest from Tunisia. Of the other Muslims, Turks probably number 350,000, sub-Saharan Africans about 250,000, and assorted Middle Easterners (Iranians and Kurds, as well as Arabs) the remainder. So France's Muslims make up at most one in 12 of the population—and its Arabs one in 20.

Yet the media keep repeating that there are at least 6m Arabs in France, and quite possibly as many as 8m, who are regularly accused of crime, vandalism, the abuse of social services and other wrongdoings. It is easy for the elite and the comfortable middle classes to dismiss Mr Le Pen's view of the world, but less so for those—especially *les petits blancs* (poor whites)—who live in crime-ridden working-class neighbourhoods. According to the analysts, in the first round of the presidential election Mr Le Pen won the support of only 8% of those with a college education, but 30% of blue-collar voters and 38% of the unemployed.

Chronic or curable?

Pessimists argue that the situation will get worse before it gets better. France's high rate of unemployment is not about to tumble overnight. Nor are the high-rise public housing blocks built from the 1950s to the 1970s in the *banlieue*, or suburbs, of most French towns. At the time, they were intended to provide affordable housing to the influx of workers from the countryside

and from the colonies or ex-colonies. Now they have all too often become virtual ghettoes, each storey dotted with satellite dishes pointed towards the television stations of the Maghreb. But the problem extends far beyond the *banlieue*. The same combination of poverty, race and social exclusion can be found in the medieval villages of Provence, or in some down-at-heel parts of Paris such as the 10th or 19th *arrondissements*.

The passage of time, say the pessimists, is not healing cultural rifts but making them worse. The generation of immigrants from the Maghreb were often illiterate peasants, keen to work hard in a country whose language they could barely understand. By contrast, their children, and now their children's children, are French-born and French-educated, and have lost respect for their immigrant parents or grandparents. That has caused a loss of parental authority, and often a multitude of behavioural problems in the disciplined world of French schools.

How French can you get?

Moreover, being French-born and French-educated does not mean that an Abdel-Karim or a Samira will be treated the same as a Jean-Pierre or a Marianne. To be white and born in France of French parents and grandparents means you are a *Français de souche*—of "French stock". But to be born in France of Arab ancestry makes you a *beur*, a word which for most Arab Frenchmen has no pejorative undertone (there is, for example, the Beur-FM radio station). The word is a kind of inversion of the word *Arabe*, part of an argot of inversion called *verlan* (*l'envers*, or back-to-front), which turns *français* into *cefran* and *café* into *féca*. This is undoubtedly of linguistic interest, but the language is also a sign of exclusion, sometimes self-imposed. *Beur* is now so universal that the new word among the *beurs* is *rebeu*, a *verlan* of a *verlan*.

How to end that exclusion? In America the answer might be affirmative action or positive discrimination, but in France such notions are seen as a threat to a republic which presumes its citizens to be free, equal and brotherly to begin with. When Sciences-Po, an elite university, last year began a special entry programme for a handful of bright students from the "zones of priority education" in the *banlieue* around the cities of Paris and Nancy, current and former students reacted with horror: their beloved meritocratic institution was slipping down the Anglo-Saxon slope.

Mr Boutih understands the gap between republican theory and everyday practice all too well: "The republican model is not a natural one. It exists through political will. Communautarisme is the natural model." So why not adopt the natural one instead? "Because society will explode from within. Each community will define itself against another, as in the United States."

Arguably, that process is already under way. In October last year, at a soccer match in Paris between France and Algeria, young *beurs* greeted the French national anthem with a storm of whistles and later invaded the pitch, brandishing Algerian flags. Young *beurs* are increasingly turning to Islam, not so much as a faith but as a symbol of identity: they fast during the month of Ramadan, insist on religiously correct food in their school canteens and stay at home to mark religious holidays.

A small minority go a lot further, falling under the influence of extremist imams from the Gulf or North Africa. In their fight to dismantle al-Qaeda, Europe's and America's intelligence services have uncovered a disturbing number of French suspects, not least Zacarias Moussaoui, currently on trial in America for his alleged role in the September 11th attacks on America last year. And a number of young *beur* layabouts have used the excuse of the Arab-Israeli conflict to indulge in anti-Jewish violence and vandalism (at over 600,000, France's Jewish minority is Europe's largest).

The *Français de souche* are accomplices in this process, not just in the April 21st vote for Mr Le Pen or in their reluctance to offer Arabs (and blacks) the same job prospects as whites, but also in the open antagonism some of them display towards the Arabs in their midst. To justify their stance, they quote the inferior status of Muslim women, or the dreadful gang-rapes of "easy" Muslim girls that some Muslim boys regard as a rite of passage. It is no accident that Oriana Fallaci's book "The Rage and the Pride", an extremist tirade against Muslims in general and Arabs in particular, spent so many weeks on this year's French bestseller list.

Could the pessimists be wrong? Back in 1998, France rejoiced in the World Cup victory of a French soccer team starring plenty of blacks and *beurs* (including the incomparable Zinedine Zidane, born of Algerian parents in the Marseilles *banlieue*). Sami Naïr, an Algerian-born member of the European Parliament and formerly an adviser on immigration to the Jospin government, points out that in an earlier wave of immigration into France, in the early part of the 20th century, Roman Catholics from Italy and Poland were accused of "trying to impose religion on our secular state". Yet in the end, he says, the discrimination fades and the newcomers' descendants end up as *Français de souche*: "I think it will be solved in a generation."

Yet there is an obvious difference between the present wave of migrants and previous waves: the *beurs* and their parents are the first minority that can be physically distinguished from the *Français de souche*. Their assimilation cannot be achieved by fading into the background. Instead, Mr Naïr proposes a pact: the government must live up to the values of the republic when dealing with its Arabs—and the *beurs* must accept the duties that go with them, including equality of the sexes. That might be easier if the economy could deliver more jobs.

A new kind of solidarity

France needs more jobs and less state. The two are not unconnected

Now is not a good time to be prime minister of France, and Jean-Pierre Raffarin knows it only too well. The world economy is in the doldrums, and the French economy is becalmed with it; investor confidence is low; and the trade unions are restive. Last month, for example, thousands of public-sector workers (80,000 according to the unions; 40,000 according to the police) marched through the centre of Paris to defend their privileges as public servants or agents of the state, and to denounce modest plans for privatisation. On the same day, INSEE, the government statistical office, announced that economic growth for this year was now likely to be only 1%, compared with its forecast in June of 1.4% (and the previous government's self-serving prediction of 2.5% before the elections).

If INSEE is right, then the budget for next year presented in October by the finance minister, Francis Mer, becomes an exercise in fiction. It assumes growth of 1.2% this year and 2.5% next, and a budget deficit of 2.6% of GDP. Instead, the deficit could well break through the 3% limit set by the European Union in its collective quest for economic stability. In other words, crisis looms: the EU will want French belts to be tightened, whereas the voters, worried about their jobs and mortgages, want them loosened.

Engraved in the country's political consciousness is the memory of 1995, the last time a centre-right president was elected with a centre-right majority in parliament. The prime minister of the day was the intellectually brilliant but aloof Alain Juppé; he was determined that France should qualify for membership of the euro zone, which meant keeping the franc closely in line with the D-mark while simultaneously cutting the budget deficit (then running at 5% of GDP). This he hoped to do by reforming the public sector, which would restrain public spending. Instead, he saw hundreds of thousands of public-sector workers taking to the streets in a wave of protests and strikes, with the sympathy of most of the population. Two years later, when President Chirac rashly called an early general election to obtain a popular mandate for the EU's single currency, the right was swept from power.

Not surprisingly, Mr Raffarin and his colleagues are keen to prevent history repeating itself. Their strategy is to tread softly, even to speak softly. In opposition, the right accused Lionel Jospin of "immobility". Now the bosses' association, Medef (Mouvement des Entreprises de France), lays the same charge

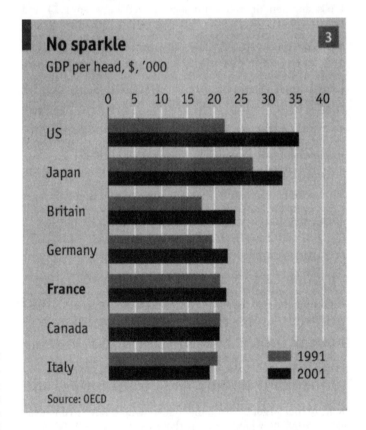

No sparkle

GDP per head, $, '000

	1991	2001
US		
Japan		
Britain		
Germany		
France		
Canada		
Italy		

Source: OECD

against Mr Raffarin: it accuses him of being too timid in dealing with the consequences of the 35-hour working week, introduced by Mr Jospin (who cut it from 39 hours with no loss of pay), or with the previous government's "Law on Social Modernisation" (which makes it harder than ever for employers to fire people, thus discouraging them from hiring in the first place). The bosses fear that if Mr Raffarin shows the same timidity in other areas, notably slimming down the civil service and reforming

33

pensions, the country will continue its slide down the international scale of GDP per person.

Just as this is a bad time for Mr Raffarin to be prime minister, the previous period was a good time for Mr Jospin. The world economy, powered by America and its dotcom infatuation, was growing strongly, and France, the world's fifth-biggest exporter, reaped the benefits. A series of partial privatisations (or "openings of capital", in the words of Mr Jospin, an ex-Trotskyist well aware of the need to placate the Communists in his coalition) helped to keep the country's finances in excellent shape. Inflation, the public debt and the budget deficit were all low, and economic growth in 1998–2000 averaged 3.3% a year. Successive finance ministers basked in the plaudits of the International Monetary Fund and the OECD.

Growing jobs

All this may have encouraged Mr Jospin to believe that full employment had become a realistic target for France. Certainly a report in December 2000 by Jean Pisani-Ferry, of the Council of Economic Analysis, a body of experts set up by Mr Jospin to give him independent advice, seemed to be suggesting as much. The report noted that in the four years from the start of 1997 France had created 1.6m jobs, "twice as many as during the 1960s and ten times the number created between 1974 and 1996". The drop in the jobless, it said, was "unprecedented".

The government was keen to take the credit. In the run-up to this year's elections, it claimed that the 35-hour week, which came into effect in February 2000 for firms with more than 20 employees (it has yet to be fully applied to small firms), had already created 400,000 jobs. The idea was that to compensate for the shorter week, bosses would have to take on more employees, and could be encouraged to do so through temporary relief on their payroll taxes. The government noted, too, that 320,000 young people had found work since 1997 through the youth employment scheme, under which young people were given five-year contracts in the public sector, for example as school playground assistants or as guards at railway stations and other public buildings. At the beginning of 2001 the government had also taken steps to lessen the poverty trap, in which recipients of state benefits lose out if they take a low-paid job.

A success of sorts

But how much of the credit for all these extra jobs did the Jospin government really deserve? On closer scrutiny, the Pisani-Ferry report reads less like a congratulatory pat on the government's back and more like a warning that things must change. For a start, much of the job creation was simply the result of economic growth. Further, full employment was defined as a jobless rate of 5% or less of the workforce, a rate that in happier days for the world economy would have been considered fairly disastrous in, say, Japan or Singapore. The report also argued that to achieve this target by 2010, the country would have to create at least 300,000 new jobs a year, perhaps as many as 400,000.

That, however, would require large-scale liberalisation, of the sort introduced by Margaret Thatcher, Britain's radical prime minister of the 1980s—and French vested interests are most unlikely to allow that to happen. Besides, there is little sign of a French Lady Thatcher emerging. Only Alain Madelin, of the Liberal Democrats, currently speaks a Thatcherite language of free markets and a minimalist state, and he won a mere 3.9% of the vote on April 21st.

All this puts a different perspective on the labour-market "success" of the Jospin term. True, unemployment fell from the 12.2% of the workforce inherited from the right in 1997, but only

to 9%, getting on for twice as much as in Britain or America—at a time when the economy was booming and employers had jobs they could not fill. The economists concluded that 9%, or a smidgen less, was—and is—France's "structural" rate of unemployment, which can be reduced only by changing the make-up of the economy.

Go to the lovely Place du Capitole in Toulouse, or ride the subway system in Lyons, or watch a game of street-soccer in a Marseilles housing estate, and the economic jargon translates into bored young men whiling away their days doing nothing in particular: no wonder many of them trade drugs to supplement their meagre state benefits. People over 25 receive the RMI (*revenu minimum d'insertion*), created in 1988 to provide a "minimum income for inclusion in society". For a single man with no dependants, this amounts to €406 ($405) a month. In a land of plenty, some 1m of France's 24m households rely on the income of the country's 2.2m *eremistes*.

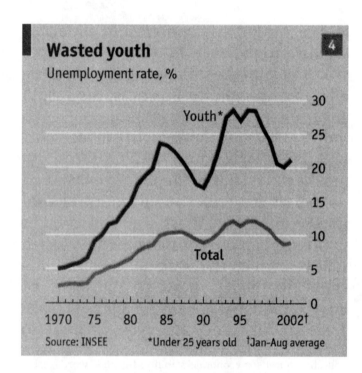

Wasted youth 4
Unemployment rate, %

Youth*
Total

1970 75 80 85 90 95 2002†

Source: INSEE   *Under 25 years old   †Jan-Aug average

That is a waste of young energy and talent; but a similar waste goes on at the other end of the age range too. In Antibes, a town on the Côte d'Azur sandwiched between Cannes and Nice, men in their 50s and 60s go down to the seafront each afternoon to play *boules*, as do thousands of other perfectly healthy contemporaries throughout the country (albeit perhaps in less pleasant surroundings). In most other industrialised countries, they would still be toiling at the office desk or on the factory floor; in France, they are enjoying a comfortable retirement.

In other words, France's unemployment rate, already bad enough by international standards, is even worse than it looks. In Switzerland, more than 70% of the 55–64 age group are in the labour market; in Japan two-thirds; and in Britain just over half. The average for the OECD group of rich countries is 51%. But in France the share is a mere 37%.

So what, you might say with a Gallic shrug. One of France's many attractive features is that its people work to live, not the other way round (which is what critics say is wrong with the Anglo-Saxon model). Patrick Artus, the chief economist of the Caisse de Dépôts et Consignations, a venerable state-owned bank, makes a joke of it: "No one wants to increase the [labour-market] participation rate except economists over the age of 55.

As the Pisani-Ferry report notes: "Inactivity was viewed in France for many years as an alternative to unemployment." In other words, the government encouraged mothers to stay at home and workers over 50 to retire. This was particularly true for the Mitterrand era of the 1980s and early 90s: legislation to protect workers' rights and the proliferation of payroll charges created an exceptionally illiquid labour market. As a result, *les trentes glorieuses* (the 30 years from 1945 to 1975 when the economy boomed and jobs were there for the taking) were followed by a quarter-century in which high unemployment, especially among the young, became part of the economic landscape.

Embracing business

Could the Raffarin government begin to turn things round? Not in the short term, but at least Mr Raffarin and his team have understood a vital precondition: it is business that must create the jobs of the future, not government. The daily *Le Figaro* went to the trouble of analysing the words used by Mr Raffarin in a recent television programme about his future plans, and found that the second most frequent subject on his lips was *"entreprise"* (business)—surpassed only by the word "France". Compared with Mr Jospin, who spent little time with business bosses during his five-year tenure, Mr Raffarin's interest in *entreprise* seems promising. On the other hand, words are not the same as deeds. For all its alleged antipathy to business, the Jospin government privatised far more of French industry than its centre-right predecessors had done. Mr Raffarin will have to show that he can do better than Mr Jospin.

In part, this will involve more privatisation. Amazingly, there are still around 1,500 companies—compared with 3,500 in 1986—in which the state has a controlling share. In theory, most of the icons of French industry are up for grabs—France Telecom, Air France and even the hitherto sacrosanct Electricité de France (EDF) and Gaz de France (GDF). But at least three things could get in the way.

One is a disinclination on the part of the government to let key industries such as electricity escape from its control, which means that in practice only minority stakes will be sold; a second is union opposition to any loss of pension and other privileges if control goes to the private sector; and the third is the abysmal state of the stockmarket. Air France, 54% owned by the state, may—when market conditions eventually suit the government—be a safe enough bet to fly further into private ownership; France Telecom, 55.5% owned by the state, risks a flop thanks to its debt of around €70 billion.

But the main challenge for Mr Raffarin goes far beyond selling the family silver: it involves lightening the government's hold on the economy in general and the private sector in particular. Government spending accounts for over 53% of GDP, way above the OECD average of 38%. A steeply progressive system of income tax, for example, can claim as much as 60% of an individual's pay-packet, and even the moderately rich have to pay a wealth tax. Virtually every French citizen gripes about taxes or social charges. Admittedly, because of various exemptions, only half of all wage-earners have to pay income tax; the trouble is that the non-paying half are still subject to a variety of payroll charges that make no allowances for income differentials. Value-added tax, levied at 19.6%, also has to be paid by rich and poor alike.

Taxes on business were reduced by the Jospin government, but employers complain that heavy payroll charges still make it hard for them to compete internationally. Medef has calculated that the Jospin government's measures, if they had been fully implemented by their 2003 deadline (in fact some changes will be made), would still have left France bottom out of 14 EU countries. For example, for every €100 an employee takes home, a French employer would still have had to shell out €288, compared with €227 for a German boss and €166 for a British one. Only a Belgian employer would pay more.

Individual taxpayers who are rich and mobile enough vote with their feet. For instance, Laetitia Casta, a model whose face now graces the country's stamps as the national figurehead, Marianne, lives for the most part outside the country; so do virtually all of the French soccer team who won the World Cup for France in 1998 (and lost it so ingloriously in 2002). It is said that up to 300,000 French people now live in south-east England, where the taxes are lower. There is clear evidence that fewer foreigners want to set up business in France, and more French people want to shift their investment abroad.

The government seems to have accepted the need to act. During his election campaign, President Chirac promised to cut income tax by 5% this year and by 30% over his five-year term; to reduce bureaucracy; and to create a million new businesses. Last month Mr Raffarin and his minister for small and medium-sized businesses, Renaud Dutreil, announced that from next autumn the charge for setting up a limited-liability company will be cut from €7,500 to just €1; the company will be able to operate from the entrepreneur's home for up to five years, instead of two (which still raises the question why this kind of restriction should be imposed at all); the tax-exemption limit for capital gains will rise by a third or more; and payment of the first year's social charges can be spread over five years.

French entrepreneurs will be grateful for any lightening of their load. Two years ago the OECD found that France had more business red tape than any other member, and more barriers to entrepreneurs than all but Italy. For example, simply to register a company could take four months.

Let 1m flowers bloom

Will Mr Dutreil's measures meet Mr Chirac's target for 1m new businesses by the next election? At present more than 170,000 companies are created each year, so another 30,000 a year does not look out of the question. It is not as though the country lacked talent and initiative: the Côte d'Azur science park of Sophia-Antipolis is full of high-technology start-ups and foreign investment.

The question is whether France wants that business badly enough. Back in 1925, an American president, Calvin Coolidge, famously declared: "The chief business of the American people is business." It is hard to imagine a French politician ever embracing that sentiment on behalf of his countrymen. In an opinion poll last year, 56% of the respondents said their idea of France was "a country of solidarity and social justice".

They are deluding themselves. According to Timothy Smith, a Canadian historian who specialises in French social policy, "a truly solidaristic society is one which pays the price for its solidarity in the here and now, instead of leaving the bill for future generations, instead of taking raises and an extra month of paid vacation (which is the consequence of the shift from the 39-hour to the 35-hour week) or an expensive pension at 55 years of age, on the backs of 2m-3m unemployed people—most of them under the age of 40." But in France that sort of solidarity still seems a long way off.

The French exception

From agriculture to Europe, France gets away with doing its own thing

THE vineyards bake in the sun of Provence; vast cornfields stretch golden across the plains of Picardy; in Brittany the cattle slowly munch their way from one deep green field to another; in the Dordogne the geese are having their livers fattened for the world's best foie gras. All this is *la France profonde*, that entrancing country of picturesque villages and revered cuisine. No wonder France is by far the world's most popular tourist destination for foreigners. And no wonder the French themselves, not least President Chirac, are determined to preserve it.

Yet the pastoral idyll is in part a myth. The country towns are surrounded by hypermarkets and car-lots; the villages have garish kiosks dispensing videos; and, all too often, the fields and rivers are polluted with pesticides. Meanwhile, the true *paysans* (the word translates better as "country folk" rather than "peasants") are dwindling in number: down to 627,000 in the 1999 census, a drop of 38% on ten years earlier. Their place has been taken by the modern barons of industrialised agriculture (the average farm now is half as large again as in 1988); or the workers who commute to the nearest town; or the Parisians and foreigners who have bought second homes in the country.

Rus in urbe

So why is the myth so important? The answer is a mix of nostalgia, culture and economic self-interest. Only two generations ago, agriculture accounted for one-third of the nation's workforce, which explains why even the most confirmed city types usually still have some rural connection. Mr Chirac once said: "The farmers are the gardeners of our country and the guardians of our memory." But there is rather more to it than gardening: helped by an EU Common Agricultural Policy designed with French farmers in mind, France has become the world's fourth-biggest producer of cereals and meat and pockets a quarter of the CAP's funds.

That does not please José Bové, the pipe-smoking, moustachioed leader of the Confédération Paysanne. Mr Bové, a former student activist turned occasional goat-cheese maker, is demanding a more literal interpretation of the myth. He has become a popular hero by attacking globalisation and the CAP for industrialising agriculture at the expense of the small farmer. Two years ago, when he appeared in court for trashing the site for a new McDonalds restaurant, 30,000 demonstrators gathered in his support. He was briefly imprisoned earlier this year.

By contrast, the politicians think the myth is best served by holding on to the status quo. When the European Commission earlier this year proposed replacing production subsidies for farmers with direct payments geared to their care for the environment, Hervé Gaymard, France's agriculture minister, led the counter-attack. Gathering the signatures of six other EU agriculture ministers, Mr Gaymard sent a letter to several European newspapers, noting: "For us, agricultural products are more than marketable goods; they are the fruit of a love of an occupation and of the land, which has been developed over many generations... For us, farmers must not become the 'variable adjustment' of a dehumanised and standardised world."

Cri de coeur or hypocritical power politics? Perhaps a bit of both. Mr Gaymard's argument is that the CAP has served Europe well, and that its reform should not be rushed, but should involve a debate going back to first principles. Then again, the letter was published on September 24th, to coincide with a meeting of agriculture ministers in Brussels. Moreover, it guaranteed a French victory: the signatories represented a minority big enough to defeat not just the commission's plans but also the wish of several northern countries, particularly Britain, to renegotiate the CAP before the present agreement on the EU's finances expires at the end of 2006.

What kind of Europe?

All this, say the critics, is proof that France, a founder member of the EU, sees it only as a vehicle for its own national interests. But that hardly seems a damning verdict. After all, why join a club if it does not serve your interests? For France, the European club has always served two purposes: to ensure peace with Germany after three wars within a century; and to provide a counterweight to America's power.

Still, the French seem to have a way of bending the club rules to their advantage. For example, back in 1965, when the France of President De Gaulle boycotted Europe's institutions for six months, its "empty chair" policy successfully checked Europe's supranational course, guaranteeing each nation the right to a veto if its vital interests were at stake. And in the early 1990s France held the Uruguay Round of trade negotiations hostage until it won the right to a "cultural exception", allowing it, in effect, to subsidise French films and discriminate against American ones.

In the same vein, Mr Raffarin's finance minister, Francis Mer, blithely told his EU colleagues last June that their "Stability and Growth Pact", a 1997 accord under which all countries had pledged to balance their public-sector budgets by 2004, was "not set in stone." The commission and the other EU members agreed, giving France until 2006 to meet the deadline. But the medium-term budget plans which Mr Mer announced in September show that France will still have a 1% deficit in 2006, prompting open criticism by the commission. Mr Mer seemed unfazed. After a meeting with his EU counterparts last month, he declared: "We decided there were other priorities for France—for instance, increased military spending. Other countries have not taken this kind of decision, but we are still in a Europe where budgetary policy and political decisions are under national control."

It sounds rather like a Europe in which France remains an independent nation-state, choosing for itself when and how to cooperate with the rest of the club. That is one reason why the tie with Gerhard Schröder's federalist-minded Germany has come under strain. However, the tie still holds: last month in Brussels, Mr Chirac, outmanoeuvring—and enraging—Britain's prime minister, Tony Blair, persuaded Mr Schröder that the CAP should remain unchanged until 2006.

Back home, François Bayrou, leader of the Union for French Democracy and a member of the European Parliament, is one of very few French politicians to share the Belgian, Italian or German vision of a powerfully supranational EU. Other visions for the future of the EU, from a confederation of nation-states to a "hard core" of "the willing and the able", all have one thing in common: in essence, France will retain its freedom of action and Europe will serve France's purpose. How else could De Gaulle and his political descendants, including Mr Chirac, have accepted the notion of a communal Europe? Nor are such attitudes confined to Gaullists: the Socialists' François Mitterrand may

High and mighty

France's elite is too clever by half

ALL nations—even those who once believed in Marx—have their elites, so why should France be any different? Philippe Méchet, a well-known opinion pollster, jokes: "We're a very royalist country, and we killed the king. So now we've monarchised the republic."

You can see his point. The American president lives in the White House, but the French president lives in the Elysée Palace, a choice of noun that conjures up a whole retinue of courtiers and uniformed flunkies. Indeed, when the Socialist François Mitterrand inhabited the Elysée, he lavished so much public money on grand schemes for the capital and its monuments that he was often compared to Louis XIV, the "Sun King".

Take the analogy a touch further and you have a modern nobility, products of the *grandes écoles*, a handful of universities—such as Sciences-Po in Paris or the Polytechnique just south of the capital—that are acknowledged to be centres of excellence. In particular, you have the *énarques*, graduates of the Ecole Nationale d'administration (ENA), a postgraduate school established by De Gaulle in 1945 to train a civil service untarnished by the Vichy regime's collaboration with the Nazis.

It has long been fashionable, even among *énarques*, to criticise ENA as being too elitist for the national good. Recruiting through fiercely competitive written and oral exams, the school has an intake of just 120 students a year for its 27-month-long curriculum. Multiply that by the number of years since ENA was established, allow for some natural wastage, and you get a total figure for living *énarques* of perhaps 5,000.

Monarchs of all they survey

That elite, minuscule compared with the massed alumni of Britain's Oxbridge or America's Ivy League, commands most of what matters in France. Mr Chirac is an *énarque*, as is Mr Jospin (but not Mr Raffarin); so too the head of the employers' association, Ernest-Antoine Seillière, and many of the bosses of leading banks and businesses, from Jean Peyrelevade of Crédit Lyonnais to Jean-Cyril Spinetta of Air France.

Is this a good or a bad thing? It depends how you look at it. As one *énarque* at the finance ministry says scathingly, "*Énarques* are pretty smart individually, and pretty dumb collectively." ENA's graduates can hardly help being clever: the meritocratic recruitment process is designed to draw bright children from humble backgrounds into the elite (one example is Hervé Gaymard, the agricultural minister). They are also competent: having been groomed for the task of administering the state, by and large they make a good job of it.

The reason that they can be "collectively dumb" is that they all come from the same educational mould, which makes their responses somewhat predictable. Their civil-service instinct is to mistrust the private sector and private initiative. Given their predominance in so many key posts, they have been criticised for holding back France's energy and creativity. But perhaps the dumbest thing they do is to ignore the views of lesser mortals, and assume that they always know best.

---

have talked of "the European project" and "the European construction", but in his alliance with Germany's Chancellor Kohl he preserved France's role as the architect.

Quite contrary

The same streak of Gaullist independence is evident in the way France so often disagrees in public with the United States, in particular over the Middle East. The most obvious example is the squabbling over what kind of UN resolution to use against Iraq, but there are plenty of others. When President Bush linked Iraq, Iran and North Korea in an "axis of evil", the Socialist foreign minister of the day described the American approach as "simplistic"—the same adjective Mr Raffarin now uses for America's policy.

All this is fine for France's *classe politique*, trained to deal with the intellectual contortions of being an insider in the rich world's councils yet an outside critic at the same time. Earlier this year, for example, both the Jospin government and the opposition sent representatives to the World Economic Forum in New York—but also sent twice as many to the rival, anti-globalisation summit in Porto Alegre, Brazil.

But what of those lesser mortals who make up the electorate? For them it smacks of double-talk. No wonder so many, either by abstaining or by casting a protest vote, took their revenge in the presidential election last spring. They felt lost, and the elite had not bothered to show them the way.

A magic moment

President Chirac has five years in which to reform France

THE French body politic has had quite a momentous year, but the sense of shock is now fading. The new obsession of the chattering classes is Iraq and American foreign policy (which has catapulted two thoughtful books on French anti-Americanism into the bestseller list). For the political right, the obsession is unity: let the rival parties that coalesced into the Union for the Presidential Majority become a single vehicle to elect the next president in 2007 (Mr Juppé, or Mr Sarkozy, or—some now whisper—Mr Chirac again?). For the opposition, so much in retreat that the Communist Party, once the largest party of the left, is now struggling to survive with just 21 supporters in the National Assembly, the task is not so much to bind its wounds, but to fight it out until the would-be modernisers of the Socialist Party, such as Dominique Strauss-Kahn and Laurent Fabius, either win or lose.

The government, for its part, talks of "decentralisation". Patrick Devedjian, the "minister of local freedoms", argues that it is time to give power to local officials and to get away from the Napoleonic military logic of a "chain of command" that always leads to Paris. In that way, perhaps a solution could at last be found for Corsica, whose bomb-planting extremists are bent on secession.

But does any of this indicate that the country is facing up to its problems? Sadly, not enough. The *fracture sociale*—a campaign slogan of Jacques Chirac's in his first bid for the presidency, in 1995—still divides the nation; the elites still pontificate at an arrogant distance from *la France d'en bas*; necessary economic reforms still remain a matter of talk rather than achievement; and policy is all to often a consequence of confrontation rather than negotiation. Worst of all, perhaps, is the temptation to seek refuge in a false comfort zone: France as an independent nuclear power, as a permanent member of the UN Security Council, as a member of the G8 club of economic powers—and, of course, as a country that takes culture seriously. France may not match the Anglo-Saxons for Nobel laureates in economics, but in literature it comes top.

Yet there is no need for such a comfort zone. France's engineers are among the best in the world—witness not just high-technology triumphs such as the Ariane rocket programme or the TGV railway system, but also lower-technology successes such as Michelin tyres or the cars of Citroën and Renault (a good enough company to take over Japan's Nissan and return it to profit). The same is true of some of its bankers, insurers and retailers, who successfully compete on the world stage. AXA, for example, will insure your life in America; Carrefour will sell you groceries whether you live in China or Chile.

The disappointment is that such assets are undervalued in the public mind, especially since the fall from grace of Jean-Marie Messier (a graduate both of ENA and the Polytechnique), with his improbable dream of turning a sewage and water company into the Vivendi Universal media giant. Denis Ranque, the boss of Thalès, a French defence and electronics group operating in more than 30 countries, has an explanation: "Popular knowledge of the economy is weak in France. We have important industries, but the French don't like them. They associate them with pollution, not jobs."

Elie Cohen, the economist at Sciences-Po, argues that France has been an ordinary market economy since the mid-1980s, when the folly of Mitterrand's nationalisation programme of 1981–82 became obvious even to the president, but: "The spirit of Gallo-capitalism remains. Each time there's a problem, you appeal to the state." Yet surely an "ordinary" market economy would not go to the lengths France does to resist the liberalising demands of the EU, in particular in the energy market, where EDF is protected at home even as it creates an empire abroad.

Face up to reality

No matter, you might say: France has prospered regardless. Indeed, there is a certain pragmatism behind the rhetoric: criticise globalisation but profit from it too; criticise America but support it at the same time. The problem is that sooner or later this form of self-deception could turn into self-destruction. In 1995, it prevented France's government from getting the popular backing to carry out reforms that have now become all the more necessary.

During his first presidential term, Jacques Chirac's critics had a common taunt: he was a man who knew how to win power, but now how to wield it. But there was a reason: from 1995 he was locked by the voters into cohabitation with his political opponents. For the next five years, he has no such excuse: having promised to reform France, he now has the power to do so. May he use it wisely.

French Secularism Unwraps Far More than Headscarves in the Classroom

ROBERT GRAHAM

New laws have a nasty habit of creating more problems than they pretend to resolve. Could this be the case with President Jacques Chirac's decision this week to use legislation to ban the wearing of "conspicuous" religious symbols in French schools?

By invoking the principles of France as a secular republic, the new law is supposed to be impartial towards Christians Jews and Muslims. Mr. Chirac was careful to say a large cross, a headscarf and skullcap all fall within the category of "conspicuous".

But this cannot hide the context. This is the first time a European head of state has intervened so directly on an issue involving church and state.

Mr. Chirac is anxious to defuse a battle over the Islamic headscarf in the classroom which has highlighted France's failure to integrate its large immigrant community — much of which is made up of Muslims of mainly north African origin.

The move therefore risks being seen as discriminatory: not just against Islamic custom but against Islam itself, now France's second biggest religion.

Using the law to resolve a sensitive religious issue reflects both the current confusion about the wearing of the headscarf and the way the French establishment prefers to hide behind the courts to enforce rules.

Chirac is anxious to defuse a battle that has highlighted France's failure to integrate its large immigrant community. Using the law risks being seen as discriminatory against Islam

Mr. Chirac this week even urged a law to prohibit patients in state hospitals from refusing treatment from doctors of the opposite sex.

The roots of the headscarf controversy are common to many European nations trying to assimilate immigrant cultures. But this affair has acquired an intensely French flavour. The drama and debate triggered by the refusal of a relatively small group of girls to remove their headscarves at school is now seen as a threat to two fundamental tenets of the republic.

The first is that of *laicité* or secularism: a rigid separation of the state from organized religion. This harks back to 1905 when the proponents of a secular republic severed all church-state links through a law that prevented the Catholic hierarchy from meddling in politics.

The anti-clerical spirit of 1905 has infused subsequent political thinking. It explains Mr. Chirac's refusal to entertain any reference to Europe's Christian heritage in the text of the proposed European Union constitution.

At another level, secularism has led the national statistics office to exclude any question on religious denomination in its population census. Hence, the generally accepted number of 6m Muslims in France is just a rough estimate.

The second principle under challenge is the indivisible nature of French citizenship shaped around the revolutionary ideal "Liberty, Equality, Fraternity". For immigrants, this means adapting to France rather than France adapting to them.

The authorities discourage any move to retain ethnic identity in the belief it fosters *communitarisme* — literally, trying to establish a "community". The term is political shorthand for refusing to integrate into French society by adhering to traditional customs.

Such is the fear of encouraging *communitarisme* that a recent proposal for affirmative action employment policies put forward by Nicholas Sarkozy, the outspoken interior minister, was immediately shouted down. Affirmative action risked laying bare the fiction of France as a homogenous nation with equal opportunities for all.

These reflexes have become more defensive as the ultra-right National Front successfully exploits fears about France losing its "Frenchness". But at a deeper level, they result from the conservatism of a French political establishment that has been slow to accept an increasingly multi-cultural society where immigrants have difficulty adapting.

The initial 19th-century immigration flows assimilated well - Italians, Armenians, east European Jews, Spaniards and Portuguese. Not so the recent waves from north and sub-Saharan Africa, people who mostly live in outer-city ghettoes and account for the bulk of unemployed youth.

It is therefore unsurprising that politicians and opinion polls generally favour a law banning "conspicuous" religious symbols. This clearly upholds *laicité* and curbs *communitarisem*. Besides, the French president would never have taken the initiative without being assured that public opinion was against allowing the classroom to become a platform for asserting religious identity.

Teachers in particular have been in the firing line, having to mediate between parents, pupils and the state in applying ambiguous legislation on classroom dress codes. Indeed, the Islamic headscarf first surfaced as an issue in the late 1980s, largely due to a constitutional judgment that the wearing of symbols of religious identity was not *per se* "incompatible" with the republic's secular principles.

This allowed a more liberal interpretation of school dress rules, permitting, for example, the wearing of headscarves in school grounds but not in the classroom itself. The appointment in the early 1990s of Hanifa Cherifi, the daughter of Algerian immigrants, as the education ministry mediator in difficult cases has also been a successful palliative. She now deals with about 150 cases a year where girls refuse to remove their headscarves.

"With young girls it is usually under parental pressure that they wear the headscarf; but with teenagers they are often doing it as a gesture against their parents more than the school," she says. What worries Ms Cherifi is the rise of active proselytising by well-organized groups close to Islamic fundamentalist movements.

Other groups, too, including the Christian Churches and the National Muslim Council, argue that a strict headscarf ban will stigmatise Muslims. If girls are ejected from state schools for refusing to remove headscarves, they risk being disadvantaged while the rise of private religious schools is encouraged. And why should obvious religious symbols be banned while prominent clothing brand names such as Nike are tolerated?

Fewer than 10 girls have been expelled from state schools this year for refusing to remove headscarves. Legislation might seem an overreaction if it were not for the many related issues beneath the surface that could now become more visible: religious tolerance, race relations, women's rights and the place of Islam in a modern European society.

In the suburbs of French cities today, a young Muslim girls can be taunted by youth gangs for wearing a headscarf or, if she removes it, threatened by fundamentalists for not being a devout Muslim. No law, however wise, can neatly resolve that dilemma.

The writer is the FT's Paris bureau chief

The Nicolas v Jacques show

Paris

The consequences of Nicolas Sarkozy taking over the president's party

THE centre-right politician was restless, hungry for the top job, keen to build himself a platform for a presidential bid while still in his 40s. His relations with the sitting president were dreadful. The centre-right had done disastrously in recent regional polls. So he quit the government, and built up a party machine to promote his own electoral ends.

The year was 1976, and the politician was Jacques Chirac. It took him another 19 years to get to the presidency. Today, his most bitter rival and the man who so eerily resembles him in his early days, Nicolas Sarkozy, is hoping that he can achieve the same goal in a fraction of the time.

The deal between the veteran Gaullist president and his brazen young finance minister was finally tied up quietly last week, as the country was distracted by the kidnapping of two French journalists in Iraq. Under the pact, Mr Chirac agreed not to block Mr Sarkozy's candidature to be head of the ruling party, the Union for a Popular Movement (UMP). In return, Mr Sarkozy agreed to leave the government.

For Mr Chirac, this was a much-needed reassertion of his authority. In July he declared firmly that he would fire any minister who became the party head, since this would undermine the prime minister's authority. Although Mr Sarkozy at first hoped that he could flout such a rule, in the end he agreed to go.

Yet the greater victory, symbolically and substantively, has gone to Mr Sarkozy. Symbolically, the upstart outsider has grabbed hold of the president's personal war machine (other minor candidates may stay in the race, but the result of the party members' vote in November is now a foregone conclusion). This party, after all, is the direct descendant of the one that Mr Chirac founded in 1976. In its most recent incarnation, as the UMP, it was designed solely to elect a centre-right government and then become a platform for Mr Chirac's chosen successor, Alain Juppé.

When, instead, Mr Juppé had to quit politics after being convicted of political corruption in January, la chiraquie, the president's circle, stepped up efforts to keep the party out of Mr Sarkozy's hands. *"Tout sauf Sarkozy"* (Anyone but Sarkozy) was its mantra, as it sought to marginalise the man whom the president has distrusted ever since he backed a rival presidential candidate, Edouard Balladur, in 1995. Yet a few months on, Mr Chirac has proved powerless to stop the party falling into Mr Sarkozy's hands.

Substantively, the UMP will supply Mr Sarkozy with a useful electoral war-chest—parties now get a state subsidy and cannot accept private donations—plus a power base from which to prepare his 2007 presidential bid. Between now and November, when Mr Sarkozy leaves the finance ministry, he will build up his own team to replace the *juppéistes* now installed at party headquarters. Handily, he will also be able to design the procedure for selecting a presidential candidate for 2007. He intends to reinvigorate the party, clean up its image, and turn it into a sort of think-tank that can refresh the political right. In short, Mr Sarkozy's UMP will be his personal campaign-team-in-waiting.

There are risks in all this for the ambitious Mr Sarkozy, however. One is that he will struggle, as UMP head, to sustain his gravity-defying popularity. At 54%, he comfortably beats other government figures, such as Dominique de Villepin (36%) and Jean-Pierre Raffarin (25%), the prime minister, according to TNS Sofres, a pollster. While in government, both at finance and, previously, at the interior ministry, Mr Sarkozy impressed voters with his hyperactive work rate and ability to make things happen, whatever the issue. The crime rate fell; prostitutes were driven from the streets; supermarkets agreed to drop prices; Alstom, an industrial firm, was saved from bankruptcy. At the UMP, he will have no such results to show off.

Second, Mr Sarkozy will have to tread a fine line between the obligations of loyalty and the temptations of independence. Mr Raffarin loaded a speech this weekend welcoming his finance minister's candidacy with nervous appeals for "loyalty". *"Tout sauf la division"* (Anything but division) is the new rallying cry. Mr Sarkozy's response? He agreed in principle to support the government, but not through "constraint, habit, or discipline".

This could spell trouble not only for the president but also for Mr Raffarin, whose credibility and, indeed, job have been at stake throughout the Chirac-Sarkozy struggle. Even under Mr Juppé, the UMP occasionally defied Mr Chirac: for instance, it is against Turkey's entry into the European Union, which the president supports. Under Mr Juppé's far less biddable successor, such clashes are likely to multiply. Although mindful of the risk that a split right might help the left, Mr Sarkozy's popular appeal depends heavily on his differences with the president.

All of which makes for uncertain policymaking ahead. Mr Sarkozy's own credibility as finance minister is waning. He made much of an agreement this week that he had secured from French insurance firms to invest a further €6 billion ($7 billion) in French private equity, to help stimulate small businesses and high-tech start-ups. Yet this measure, based on the curious assumption that such funds cannot spot good financial returns by themselves, is largely empty. It carries no means of enforcement and refers simply to a target of boosting such investment by 2007, by which time Mr Sarkozy will be gone.

As for his successor, not yet chosen, he is unlikely to have the same clout. Possibilities include Philippe Douste-Blazy, the health minister, and François Fillon, at education. But more likely may be Hervé Gaymard, the 44-year-old farm minister and former junior finance minister, whose loyalty to Mr Chirac is absolute.

Furthermore, the presidential candidate-in-waiting may be even more tempted by shameless populism when outside government than he has been within it. As it is, Mr Sarkozy's economically liberal convictions have been tempered by the realities of French politics, where protectionism and interventionism are easy vote-winners. To popular acclaim, he bailed out Alstom, and pulled off a French private-sector drugs merger to fend off a foreign bid.

To the indignation of new EU members and the bafflement of others, Mr Sarkozy floated a proposal this week to deny EU regional aid to countries with low corporate-tax rates. Given fears of competition, this was an attempt to portray himself as protector of French jobs. Sadly, despite his demonstrated talent for confounding such misguided thinking by explaining, in lay terms, the harsh realities of a global economy, there may be more such appeals to populism in store.

Germany's general election:

Gerhard Schröder clings on

The incumbent German chancellor has won a cliff-hanging election but with no real mandate for reform

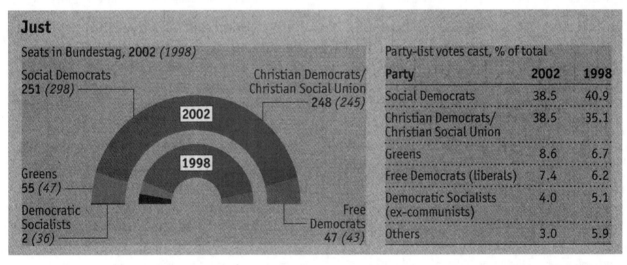

Party-list votes cast, % of total		
Party	**2002**	**1998**
Social Democrats	38.5	40.9
Christian Democrats/ Christian Social Union	38.5	35.1
Greens	8.6	6.7
Free Democrats (liberals)	7.4	6.2
Democratic Socialists (ex-communists)	4.0	5.1
Others	3.0	5.9

Source: Bundeswahlleiter

BERLIN

IN ONE of the tightest German elections for half a century, Chancellor Gerhard Schröder's coalition of Social Democrats and Greens managed to cling on to power by its fingertips. Together the pair have 306 seats, a majority of nine in the Bundestag, the lower house of parliament. In the outgoing one, they had a majority of 21, and could usually count on at least the abstention of the 36 ex-communist Democratic Socialists who this time failed to clear the hurdle to obtain any seats by proportional representation and got only two directly elected seats.

Mr Schröder's slim majority will not only make it harder for his government to push through painful reforms but also puts a question-mark over its longevity. Previous governments, notably Helmut Kohl's after 1994, have had equally thin majorities yet have survived; a sitting chancellor can be displaced in mid-term only by a "constructive vote of no confidence", meaning that parliament has to vote for an alternative administration and not just ditch a beleaguered one.

Still, Mr Schröder will find the going tough. Discipline within the left-wing parties is often loose, particularly among the idiosyncratic Greens. The conservative opposition has gained ground. It already controls the Bundesrat, Germany's upper house, where about half of federal legislation has to be passed. And the economy is continuing to stagnate. Edmund Stoiber, the defeated conservative challenger, says he expects the new government's life to be "very, very short".

Charlemagne: Europe marching left, right, left

Why political taboos are being broken in Europe

The Germans invented the word *Zeitgeist,* but anyone hoping that their latest election would confirm a new "spirit of the age" in Europe will have been disappointed. In the past year or so, a clear trend seemed visible. Left-wing governments were ousted by the right in Italy, France, the Netherlands, Denmark, Portugal and Norway. Germany looked like the next and biggest domino to fall. But though Gerhard Schröder's "red-Green" coalition wobbled, it refused to topple. Just the week before Mr Schröder's victory, Sweden's Social Democrats also bucked the trend, easily winning another stint in office. Now Austria's Social Democrats have a chance of regaining power later this year. So much for Europe's inexorable move to the right.

The broader truth, however, is that on the big economic and social issues facing Europe the differences between centre-right and centre-left—between Christian democracy and social democracy—are pretty paltry. Certainly the right is still closer to business, the left to the trade unions. But the resulting differences in policy have more to do with nuance than deep philosophy. In Germany, for example, Edmund Stoiber on the right proposed a top rate of income tax of 40%, while Mr Schröder wants to bring it down to 42%. Mr Stoiber said the state should consume no more than 40% of GDP, Mr Schröder stuck to his own favourite number, 42%. Economists and businessmen may clamour for a drastic revamp of Germany's generous welfare state and for decisive moves to tackle public pensions, but neither candidate was prepared to risk suggesting anything daring. As Mr Stoiber drily remarked, he had not noticed anyone demonstrating for a radical overhaul of social security.

What is true of Germany is true of the rest of Europe. Italy's Silvio Berlusconi admires Margaret Thatcher but has done nothing to tackle Italy's pensions problem and little to free up the labour market. France's new centre-right government has moved cautiously to mitigate the worst effects of its Socialist predecessor's introduction of a 35-hour week but is committed to an extensive welfare state and shows no desire to take on the unions.

Faced with such tiny differences between left and right on the big issues of social and economic management, voters tend to plump for the most appealing personalities. One big reason why Mr Schröder and Sweden's Goran Persson won while Lionel Jospin, a French socialist, lost is that the winning pair are highly effective politicians while Mr Jospin came across as dull and stiff. Tony Blair's mastery of British politics relies at least as much on his personality—and his Schröder-like sense of what people want to hear—as on any particular policies.

It was Mr Blair who made the last real attempt to define a new pan-European (and indeed transatlantic) political *Zeitgeist.* When the centre-left held sway on both sides of the ocean, he earnestly pushed forward his big idea—"the third way". Mr Schröder tried briefly to echo him with cosy talk of a "new middle". But the whole Blairite philosophy was too vague to catch on and much of the European left disliked what little it understood of it, assuming it was code for a kind of soft-edged Thatcherism. Mr Blair has now almost given up talking about the third way. In a recent interview in *Prospect,* a British magazine, he was reduced to claiming that "in parts of Latin America [the third way] is seen as a ground-breaking moment." (They speak of little else in the queues outside Argnetina's banks.)

But while a welfarist consensus may still hold sway across the European Union, consensus politics are fraying around the edges in other ways. The most striking recent trend has been the rise of populist parties openly hostile to immigration. When Austria's People's Party became the first such party to join a governing coalition, there was outrage across the EU. But the rise of politicians making similar appeals elsewhere in other EU countries has muted the outcry. The Pim Fortuyn list in the Netherlands and Umberto Bossi's Northern League in Italy have both joined governing coalitions after campaigns that highlighted the supposedly bad effects of immigration. The new centre-right Danish government relies on the votes of an anti-immigration party. As Bertel Haarder, Denmark's immigration minister, points out, there may be a connection between addiction to welfarism and hostility to immigrants. Partly because of high minimum wages and welfare benefits, there are very few jobs for unskilled immigrants: around 60% of them in Denmark have no job. So they are easily stigmatised as free-loading parasites.

Mainstream politicians have reacted in different ways to the rise of anti-immigration parties. In France the National Front's Jean-Marie Le Pen won close to 20% of the votes in the presidential election but remains firmly beyond the pale. The new French government has nonetheless begun to toughen both rhetoric and actions against illegal immigrants. All across the EU, asylum-seekers are getting a frostier welcome.

Vox populi, a pox on civility?

The rise of anti-immigration populists has demonstrated the political potential of voicing sentiments often heard in the street but rarely in parliamentary chambers. Mr Schröder's campaign was a variation on this theme. Struggling in the polls, he decided to express the anti-Americanism that is a strong current of public opinion in Germany and the rest of the EU. Warning against "adventures" in Iraq and carping at the American economic model was just a mild version of commonplace feelings. Mr Schröder's supporters took the hint—and helped him cling on to power. However, as with the immigration debate elsewhere in Europe, once a political taboo is broken it is hard to control the consequences. German relations with America have nosedived. And new and queasy-making sentiments are popping out of the closet at home, such as the ill-fated comparison between George Bush and Hitler allegedly made by Mr Schröder's justice minister. Sometimes taboos are there for a reason.

On a night of nerves, with both leaders at different moments claiming victory, the two main formations—the Social Democrats and the combined Christian Democrats and their Bavarian sister party, the Christian Social Union—each got 38.5% of the vote. In the end, the Social Democrats pipped the conservatives, by almost 9,000 votes and three seats. The new Bundestag is expected to have its first sitting in the week that starts on October 14th, with the formal re-election of Mr Schröder as chancellor on the same day or soon after.

With the Social Democrats losing ground since the previous election, in 1998, it was the Greens who kept the ruling coalition afloat. They emerged as the election's only real winners, with 8.6% of the vote, their highest score since they first won seats in parliament in 1983. They are now clearly the country's third force.

Barely a year ago, after a string of electoral setbacks, they seemed tired, bland and on the way out. Mr Schröder had even begun eyeing the Free Democrats, Germany's liberals, as alternative coalition partners. But the combined effect of recent floods in the east (which revived many voters' environmental concerns), of the chancellor's stand against a war in Iraq, and of a strong campaign by Joschka Fischer, the Greens' foreign minister and Germany's most popular politician, helped them bounce back. Mr Schröder can thank the Greens for letting him keep his crown. In turn, they will now expect more influence, and say they will press the chancellor to raise the tempo of reform.

The liberals, despite doing a little better than last time, were the election's losers. Their expectations had been high. Pollsters throughout the campaign had put them ahead of the Greens. Only last month, one poll gave them 13%, double the Greens' projected score. They had begun to assume that no government could be formed without them. But they ended up with a modest 7.4%, a point behind the Greens and a far cry from the 18% they had set themselves. A renewed rumpus over anti-Israeli comments by Jürgen Möllemann was partly to blame. He has now resigned as the liberals' deputy leader. But the "fun party" image projected by their leader, Guido Westerwelle, though attracting young voters, may well have put off many of the party's older, more earnest supporters. Many Germans think Mr Westerwelle lacks gravitas.

Despite failing to hit all three of his proclaimed targets—to have the biggest group in parliament, to win more than 40% of the vote, and to topple the government—Mr Stoiber has emerged beaten but unbowed. His conservatives upped their 1998 vote by more than three percentage points, while the Social Democrats dipped by a couple. In Mr Stoiber's Bavarian homeland, his party's share shot up by 10.9 points to 58.6%, its best score in nearly two decades. Indeed, with 9% of the total national vote, Mr Stoiber's Christian Social Union can claim to be Germany's third biggest party, ahead of the Greens. He says he has no intention of retiring quietly back to his home state but stands ready to take the chancellor's job should the government collapse.

Were it not for last month's floods in the east and the threat of an American-led war in Iraq, Mr Schröder would probably have failed to win a second term. Neither event was of his making, of course. But he exploited them both to his benefit. As a result, says Donald Rumsfeld, the American defence secretary, relations between Germany and the United States have been "poisoned". He refused even to talk to his German counterpart at this week's meeting of NATO defence ministers in Warsaw, and President George Bush failed to send Mr Schröder the customary congratulations. The chancellor is eager for reconciliation and has even asked Britain's Tony Blair to help. But he insists that there will be "no change" in his opposition to Germany's participation in an attack on Iraq, even under a United Nations mandate.

This, says Mr Schröder, is "a difference of opinion" that should be accepted among friends; the relationship, he insists, is "intact". That is not the view in Washington. Matters were not helped last week by the German justice minister, who was accused of lumping Mr Bush with Hitler by saying that the American president has sought to distract voters from problems at home by talk of war—tactics, she is said to have added, that were once used by "Adolf Nazi". She has denied making the remarks, but says she will resign anyway. Relations between the countries, and between Mr Schröder and Mr Bush, who have not talked since June, remain strained.

It is on the home front, however, that Mr Schröder faces his hardest task. Speeding up Germany's dismal growth rate, creating jobs and loosening the country's labour rigidities should be his top priorities. But the election does not suggest that the German people have an appetite for radical reform. Mr Schröder has no mandate for it. Nor would Mr Stoiber, if he had won. That is the election's gloomiest lesson.

From *The Economist*, September 28, 2002, pp. 45, 46, 53. © 2002 by The Economist, Ltd. Distributed by the New York Times Special Features. Reprinted by permission.

SCHRÖDER LOOKS AT THE STARS AGAIN

By Bertrand Benoit

Germany in 2004 may not be 14th century Italy, but having gone to hell and back twice since becoming chancellor in 1998, Gerhard Schröder is turning into the Dante Aligbieri of modern German politics.

Four months ago, he and his Social Democratic Party seemed stuck at the bottom of the abyss. Having pushed through Agenda 2010, a visionary but unpopular package of structural reforms, Mr Schröder was being repaid with popularity ratings at post-war lows and a string of debacles at regional elections.

Having entered the second half of his four-year term, however, the chancellor, like the medieval poet at the end of his Divine Comedy, is emerging from the depths of hell and can look at the stars again. It is not the first time he has performed such an act. In the summer of 2002, he turned what looked like certain defeat at the general election into a narrow victory by ruling out Germany's participation in the coming Iraq war while his opponent prevaricated, a cynical but effective ploy. The lesson for students of Germany, it seems, is that one should think twice before writing off Mr Schröder.

With approval ratings for the SPD oscillating around the 33 per cent mark, Mr Schröder and his Green coalition partners would probably lose a national poll today. But the figure is a considerable improvement on the 25 per cent low the party touched before the summer and the opposition Christian Democrats, while still ahead, have dropped by 10 percentage points from their peak ratings.

In September the SPD put an end to the trend that had seen it lose almost all significant regional elections since 2002. Its scores at regional polls in two eastern states were weak in historic terms but because the centre-right opposition performed badly the SPD managed to return Matthias Platzeck as premier of Brandenburg and force the Christian Democratic Union into a grand coalition in Saxony, ending the conservatives' 14-year rule in the state.

"A lot could happen before the next general election in 2006," says Manfred Güllner, head of the Forsa polling group. "But Schröder's chances have improved significantly. People trust him more than they do the opposition leaders." Mr Güllner credits the chancellor's stubborn refusal to scrap or water down the far-reaching labour

market and social security reforms he unveiled in March 2003, his decision in February to relinquish the chairmanship of the SPD and his high-profile appearances abroad, such as his participation in the ceremonies in Normandy commemorating the 60th anniversary of the D-Day landings last June. "Schröder is now perceived as a statesman; something of a presidential chancellor."

But there is more to the story. Angela Merkel, while still the unchallenged leader of the Christian Democratic Union, the biggest opposition party, has found it hard to impose her radical reformist ideas on her party and do away with its tradition of social paternalism. Endless bickering with the socially-conscious Christian Social Union, the CDU's sister party ill Bavatia over healthcare and labour market reforms, have made even the fractious SPD look as disciplined as a military band.

Like the opposition, the economy has been playing on Mr Schröder's side.

After three years of stagnation that sent unemployment rocketing and brought public finances to their knees, growth has been picking up, lifted by robust exports. Quarter-on-quarter gross domestic product growth since the second half of 2003 has been between 0.3 and 0.4 per cent.

Five of the country's six leading economic institutes forecast growth of 1.8 per cent in 2004 and 1.5 percent in 2005. Stripped of the distorting effect of additional holidays next year, growth should remain constant this year and next.

Mr Schröder's return from the politically dead, however, could also be down to clever tactics. These suggest the chancellor's most urgent priority is no longer to reform a bankrupt welfare state and bring down labour costs that are the highest in the world after Norway's, but to win a third term in 2006.

Since the summer the chancellor has been broadcasting the same finely-calibrated message: opponents of reform should know there is no going back but they should also be reassured no more painful measure will come in the life of this parliament.

"The reform process we are talking and fighting about will never end," Mr Schröder told the cream of German business at the annual congress of the BDA employers' federation last month, "because in a society whose economic foundations change so fast and radically, political systems cannot be static." Yet, he hastened to add, welfare systems "cannot be rebuilt overnight but only step by step. And that means those who overestimate the readiness of people to embrace change can also make mistakes."

This caveat, economists fear, could spell trouble for Germany. "There is a huge risk that the reform process could come to a standstill when it should be accelerating," says Jurgen Michels, Germany economist at Citigroup.

"Social security contributions are still too much of a burden on labour costs, the labour market needs additional flexibility, business is smothered by red tape, and the state is wasting money on consumption instead of investing." In recent months, business has grabbed the reformist's baton from Mr Schröder, turning the overhaul of the "social-market economy," a word coined by Ludwig Ehrard, the rotund Bavarian who shaped the country's economic post-war reconstruction, from a top-down into a grassroots exercise.

Employers' federations and trade unions have struck historically flexible wage agreements recently, which companies, ranging from DaimlerChrysler to Siemens and Volkswagen, have used to reach pay and working time deals with their workforce that should result in considerable savings.

Long-time underperformers, such as Opel, the carmaker owned by General Motors of the US, and KatStadtQuelle, the ailing retail group, have unveiled audacious restructuring plans. More successful businesses, such as BASF, and countless smaller ones whose efforts rarely register in the national media, have done the same.

This "silent corporate revolution" Goldman Sachs, the investment bank, wrote in a recent note, could raise working time in western. Germany to the level of the more industrious east within four years, and lift the country's potential growth rate from 1.4 to 1.7 per cent in a decade.

Meanwhile the tightening of bank lending that saw funding to small companies dry up in the 1990s, is being circumvented as businesses resort to sophisticated fund-raising techniques such as mezzanine financing or appeal to foreign private equity groups for backing. Recent statistics suggest companies, encouraged by rising profits, have begun to invest again after a three-year lull.

"Reforms are being adopted and labour contracts are being rewritten," a US banker and former official of the International Monetary Fund recently commented while on a business trip to Berlin. "There are more signs of change in Germany than we are inclined to give credit for in the US."

Yet there are some worrying clouds too: consumer spending, the German economy's Achilles' heel, remains anaemic as disposable income continues to stagnate and unemployment refuses to shrink; durably high oil prices are weighing on the global economy and, together with the strength of the euro against the dollar, harming German exports. Growth was worryingly weak in the third quarter.

Starting next month, the implementation of Hartz IV, a law that significantly cuts benefits for the long-term unemployed, could prove politically sensitive and a source of negative headlines for the chancellor. As Mr Güllner puts it, "the Federal Labour Agency [which hands out unemployment benefits and finds placements for the jobless] is the most inefficient administration in Germany".

For Mr Schröder, the biggest cloud of all, however, could be the chancellor himself. His wavering commitment to radical reforms has revived memories of the second half of his first term, when his government slid into inaction, a lack of initiative that nearly cost it the 2002 general election. In private, and despite the recent rise in opinion polls, pro-reform SPD parliamentarians are beginning to question the chancellor's commitment to a far-reaching overhaul of the German welfare state.

Not a bad time, it would seem, for the chancellor to reflect on this other line from Dante Alighieri: "The secret of getting things done is to act."

The German Question

It may be good news that
Germany is reasserting itself
in world affairs. But is it
bad news for American diplomacy?

By RICHARD BERNSTEIN

It's not often that world leaders are bluntly contradicted in public by other world leaders, but that is what happened at the Bayerischer Hof, Munich's grand 19th-century hotel, where a bit over a year ago, in what came to be an almost epochal event in Germany, Secretary of Defense Donald H. Rumsfeld and Germany's foreign minister, Joschka Fischer, had a sort of clash of civilizations over the war in Iraq. The setting was the 2003 Munich Conference on Security Policy, an annual event attended by a who's who of European and American diplomacy, business and politics. At the time, Rumsfeld was at the height of his European unpopularity, thanks to his statements likening Germany to Libya and Cuba in their nonsupport of what was then the imminent Iraq war and his declaration that "Old Europe" was irrelevant. As Rumsfeld spoke, demonstrators led by Munich's mayor gathered on the snowy streets of the city.

Munich, of course, is a historically and metaphorically freighted place, the city where Neville Chamberlain made his notorious gesture of appeasement to Hitler, and that was Rumsfeld's theme as he made the case for the war. To fail to overthrow the regime of Saddam Hussein, he argued, would be to fail to learn the lesson of Munich. Rumsfeld then sat in the front row of the audience, his face set in an almost theatrical glower, as Fischer took the podium to argue the contrary point of view. An intensely intellectual man who happens to be both a former street-fighting left-wing radical and Germany's most popular politician, Fischer argued what had by then become the standard Old European point of view: that starting a war against Iraq before the peaceful alternatives had been exhausted was both unnecessary and rank with possibilities for unintended consequences.

In midspeech, Fischer broke into extemporaneous English. "Excuse me," he said, while Rumsfeld sat and glared, "but I'm not convinced." The phrase, reproduced in English in the headlines of many German newspapers

the next morning, quickly acquired an almost Delphic significance in Germany, as a declaration of independence from the United States, the end point of a half-century of nearly automatic compliance with the American wish. Effusions of joy greeted the comment all over anti-George Bush and anti-Rumsfeld Germany.

But by the time of the next Munich security conference, in February, the atmosphere was much changed. There were no mass demonstrations outside the hall and no abrupt confrontations within. Of course, there were reminders of the disagreements of the past—"We were not, and are still not, convinced of the validity of the reasons for war," Fischer said. Yet he avoided repeating the old arguments. He has said frequently that the debate over Iraq was always a matter of tactics, not goals, and that even though the United States went ahead with a war that Germany opposed, it is now in the German interest for the Americans to succeed. It is certainly not in Germany's interest for its major ally, the United States, to become bogged down in a quagmire. Fischer used his Munich appearance to put forward a strategic vision that is actually very close to the American one. We face a common threat, Fischer said, and he attached a clear name to it: "destructive jihadist terrorism with its totalitarian ideology." Facing that threat, Fischer declared, it is imperative that "the coalition's efforts must be successful; the forces of violence and terror in Iraq must not win the upper hand."

Fischer's Munich 2004 speech was clearly an attempt to realign Germany with the United States after the worst period in their relations since the end of World War II, a few months during which President Bush didn't talk to Chancellor Gerhard Schröder. A few weeks after this year's Munich conference, in fact, Schröder went to Washington and, in a public display of camaraderie with President Bush, seemed to put the freeze of 2003 into the past. The chancellor proposed a sort of Marshall Plan for the Muslim world, a multifaceted effort—that was first outlined by Fischer in Munich—to address the poverty and desperation that are, in the German view, at the heart of the problem. But Fischer understands, and has said, that winning the war on terrorism will require something more than a program for what he calls the modernization of the Islamic world. "You fight terrorism with police, with armies, with intelligence, but also with transformation and by addressing the root causes," he has said. His belief, and Germany's belief, is that the old trans-Atlantic alliance is indispensable, probably for both sides, certainly for Germany.

So the question is, Is everything back to normal between the United States and Germany? Given Germany's centrality to the Western alliance's entire network of agreements and institutions, it is an important question at any time, but it seems especially important in the wake of the devastating terror attacks in Madrid on March 11. Germany is the geographical, economic and strategic heart of Europe, and it will be even more so as the European Union, newly enlarged from 15 to 25 members, strives to forge common positions in foreign affairs and defense. For 40 years, what was then West Germany was, outside of England, America's closest European ally, our chief cold-war partner, the country that owed its flourishing and vigorous democracy to what might perhaps be the most benign and successful postwar occupation in history. Germany is the country that has always prevented France from transforming the European Union into an instrument of French policy, which was, and still seems to be, to create a counterweight to the American superpower. Germany has always been, so to speak, the counterweight to the counterweight, the rudder that has kept the alliance on course.

It is this background that makes the question of German-American relations so important once again as the West confronts Islamic terrorism. The people on both sides of the Atlantic now understand that they are vulnerable to what Fischer has aptly called a transmogrified sort of totalitarianism, which strikes in a new, terrifyingly random and unpredictable way.

So, yes, normal relations between Germany and the United States have been restored, but with some new uncertainties and questions. There is no important disagreement between the United States and Germany, or the rest of Europe, over the existence and nature of the terrorist threat. But the freeze of 2003 resulted from some deep disagreements over the tactics to adopt against the threat, and these disagreements are rooted not just in different conceptions of the role of force but also in the widespread conviction that Europe and the United States belong to two very different universes of culture and values. European governments, in the wake of the Madrid bombings, have mostly reaffirmed their solidarity in the antiterror fight. Even the newly elected Spanish prime minister, José Luis Rodriguez Zapatero, pledged his support, despite his plans to withdraw his country's military contingent from Iraq. But as Zapatero's victory itself suggests,

some Europeans seem to believe that the more they distance themselves from American policies, the safer they will be. In this context, the German-American relationship will determine much about the endurance and effectiveness of the trans-Atlantic alliance that won the cold war, kept the peace, spread democracy throughout Europe and is now being called on to protect the West and the penumbra of states dependent on it from the new menace of terrorism.

THERE WAS A telling moment at Munich 2004 that indicates some of the ways in which German-American ties are still weaker than they were before the divisions over the war in Iraq. It came when William Cohen, former secretary of defense, did a bit of politely phrased public grilling of Fischer. If Germany agrees that it is essential to win the peace in Iraq, and if winning the peace is so essential to the security of Europe and America, Cohen asked, why would Germany rule out sending troops to Iraq to help the coalition in its struggle? Germany, as Cohen surely knew, has stated clearly that it will not send a single soldier to Iraq. With troops already stationed in places like Bosnia and Kosovo, in addition to Afghanistan (where more than 2,000 German soldiers serve in the NATO-commanded international force), German officials persuasively make the point that their contribution to European peacekeeping and the war on terrorism is being made elsewhere. Germany has agreed to run a training program for Iraqi police officers (though not in Iraq itself), and figures like Fischer have certainly made clear that they want the United States to prevail in making Iraq a self-sustaining democracy.

To the critics of the Schröder government, however, Germany's vigorous campaign in the United Nations and NATO against the war in Iraq was behavior unbefitting an ally. There has of course been opposition, even very passionate opposition, to the United States in the not-too-distant German past. Just look at the protests during the Vietnam War, when the posters showed the letters USA written so that the S looked like a swastika, or the mass marches against the installation of Pershing II medium-range nuclear missiles on German soil in the early 80's. What was different in the Iraq debate was that opposition to a policy that the United States deemed critical to its national interest was headquartered in the German government itself, in the office of the chancellor. (By contrast, Chancellor Helmut Schmidt, who as a Social Democrat was himself on the left, supported the installation of the missiles in the 80's.)

Schröder not only spoke out strongly against the war but also was the first major European leader to do so, inveighing against it at a time when President Jacques Chirac of France seemed uncertain what to do. Then he went further than Chirac ever did, saying that Germany would oppose a war even if the United Nations sanctioned military action. It was Schröder, not Chirac or President Vladimir Putin of Russia, who crystallized what came to be called the Moscow-Berlin-Paris antiwar axis, and it was this tripartite opposition that made Security Council approval of the American plan well-nigh impossible. Worst of all, perhaps, Schröder did this not by leading German public opinion but by following it at a time when anti-American sentiment had reached a postwar peak. As Michael Mertes, a former foreign-policy adviser to Chancellor Helmut Kohl, put it in an article in the journal Internationale Politik, "If anti-Americanism pays domestically, how reliable is Germany as an ally when the moment of truth finally comes?"

It is one of the paradoxes of the Iraq debate that despite Germany's more categorical opposition to war, Americans were, and still are, far angrier at France. One explanation for this is that as the debate heated up in the early months of 2003, Germany happily allowed France—mostly in the person of its flamboyant foreign minister, Dominique de Villepin—to lead the coalition of the unwilling. When de Villepin was applauded after a rousing antiwar speech in the Security Council, Fischer knew immediately that it was going to be very expensive applause—expensive in American annoyance. Fischer has told German journalists that in his own speeches he tried to remain academic, precise, a little bit boring. He acted that way mainly because he had no interest in allowing the war in Iraq to spoil the bilateral relationship but also because of the ineradicable German instinct, since World War II, to play a subdued role on the world stage, not to be like France. The German interest since the end of the war has been to allay fears that someday it will allow history to repeat itself, to create a Fourth Reich, to use its power to dominate Europe. It wants, as conspicuously as possible, to be nonnationalistic, nonmilitaristic, anchored in Europe and in the NATO alliance.

'The whole leftist movement was a failure,' says Otto Schily, Germany's interior minister. 'But the result—the transformation of the German collective consciousness—was a success.'

This does not mean that Germany and its foreign policy have been static since 1945. The fall of the Berlin Wall in 1989 fundamentally altered the strategic equation that had governed both German-American relations and Germany's own single-issue foreign policy for more than 40 years. Almost overnight, Germany was under no military threat. After the fall of the wall, said Karsten Voigt, the German foreign ministry's coordinator for German-American cooperation, "Germany became less dependent on the United States, but we became less relevant to the United States at the same time." In fact, the disappearance of the cold-war threat and German reunification have brought changes, most notably a slow but steady German progress toward being what the Germans often call a normal country, a country like others, even though

the Germans seem to understand that the mere fact that they aspire to be normal means that in at least some ways they still can't be. The Germans move slowly and hesitantly toward accepting that their country has interests and responsibilities like other countries even as they worry that their past disentitles them to have these things.

The liberation of Germany from its American dependency also brought it into confrontation with an unknown. "Before, it was automatic that we would be part of the game," Voigt said, meaning the cold-war game. "Now, we have to decide if and where we want to be relevant. It's a psychological shift. We need to change the mentality of the German people, not just the mind-set of a few leaders."

AMONG THE MAIN THINGS that had to change was the almost theological pacifism of the German public, that recoil from the horrors that the Germans once inflicted on the Jews, on their European neighbors and on themselves. "We have an excellent democracy, but there are terrible things in our past," Fischer once said to me, and that sentence is indeed German history in a nutshell, the bad followed by a real attempt to come to grips with what went wrong and to not repeat it. But at the same time, once democracy was firmly established, and once the Western alliance needed a German military contribution, the pacifism that was once a reassurance became a kind of failing. "Germany's pacifism was a relic of a moral superiority for Germany, another kind of arrogance," said Heinrich August Winkler, one of Germany's most prominent historians. "It was the inverse of the former German arrogance, vastly better, but an arrogance nonetheless." By all accounts it has been Fischer, the foreign minister, who is chiefly responsible for ridding Germany of this postwar legacy.

Fischer's biography is one of those things that everybody in Germany knows, a sort of metaphor for Germany itself and its transformation. He is a member of the generation born just after World War II, which demanded an accounting of Germany's wartime crimes and forced the previously taboo subject of the Holocaust into the open. As a teenager, unable to tolerate the conformity demanded in the schools, he dropped out, became a political radical and then, in the early 80's, a member of the nascent Green Party, the peace and environmentalist group whose members wore jeans, listened to Dylan and, in some cases, breast-fed their babies during meetings. In other words, Fischer belonged to a movement that failed in its stated objective, notably to bring about a revolution, but nonetheless fractured Germany's formerly stiff, heel-clicking authoritarianism and led to its replacement with a more open, more democratic and, above all, more self-critical society. When Fischer became environment and energy minister of the state of Hesse in 1985, he famously wore sneakers to his inauguration, and the shoes, emblems of Germany's cultural transformation, are now on permanent exhibit in the historical museum in Bonn. "The whole leftist movement was a failure," said Otto Schily, Germany's interior minister, who was once a lawyer for members of the terrorist Red Army Faction. "But the result—the transformation of the German collective consciousness—was a success."

Fischer never seemed primarily interested in Green issues, most notably the environment, though certainly the Greens were the only party unorthodox enough to allow a high-school dropout like him to rise to power. His interest was in foreign policy, the Middle East, in German relations inside Europe and, of course, in doing well enough in elections to become part of the national government. He and the Greens did so in 1998, coming to power as the minor partner in coalition with Schröder's Social Democrats—what's known locally as the Red-Green Coalition.

Once Fischer was in power, his former radicalism continued to fade, and he became a liberal interventionist, in favor of the use of force when all other options have been exhausted. Specific events pushed him along, especially the Serbian massacre of some 8,000 Bosnian Muslims in the supposed United Nations safe area of Srebrenica in 1995 and later the Serbian threat of ethnic cleansing against Albanian Kosovars in 1998. Both incidents left a deep mark on Fischer, who led the Greens, kicking, screaming and protesting, away from pacifism to an acceptance of the use of military force outside Germany's borders. When German pilots took part in the 1995 NATO bombardment of Serbian positions in Bosnia, it was the first time German forces had been used in a combat situation outside Germany since World War II.

Essentially, Fischer brought the left into line with a foreign policy favoring a stronger and more active German role in the trans-Atlantic alliance, and in so doing, he helped enable two German chancellors, Kohl from the right, Schröder from the left, to engage German troops abroad without instigating mass demonstrations and mass resistance at home.

SEPT. 11, 2001, moved Germany even further in the direction of greater engagement in the world and solidarity with the United States. Most important, Germany dispatched troops all the way to Afghanistan. Defense Minister Peter Struck offered a succinct definition of Germany's new strategic position. "Our security must also be defended on the Hindukush," he said in December 2002, referring to the Afghan mountain range. "We must face up to threats where they arise," he said more recently.

Struck would have committed political suicide if he'd said that a few years before, Voigt said. "We are now defining our security way outside our boundaries, and I think the German people will have to accept it," he continued. "It's no longer a debate about morality, which it used to be previously. It's now a debate about interests."

These days, Germans do indeed debate their interests, especially when those interests involve the United States.

After Sept. 11, for example, Schröder criticized the foreign policy of the preceding government of the conservative chancellor Helmut Kohl for undertaking only "secondary assistance measures." Schröder said he would have Germany behave like "a great power." But then came August 2002, when Schröder himself, campaigning hard for re-election as chancellor, announced his fundamentalist anti-Iraq-war position, and soon thereafter, Schröder, Chirac and Putin created their own alliance, whose main purpose, it was feared in Washington, would be to confront any unilateral exercise of American power.

"Both sides became very ideological, articulating positions rather than searching for the truth," said Gary Smith, the director of the American Academy in Berlin, of the fierce disagreement over Iraq. "And both sides indoctrinated themselves; they imbibed what they said at the time, and it's naive to think that suddenly either side is going to go back to the way they saw things before."

Indeed, it is not difficult to find reasons that Germany and the United States may slowly drift apart, at least enough to end up on opposite sides of more than just the Iraq-war question. Already the Germans share the wider European sense of a growing cultural gap with the United States, seen in disagreements over such matters as the death penalty, the Kyoto Protocol on global warming and the International Criminal Court. On all three, Europeans and Americans have opposing positions. There is also what has become the four-year-old stagnation of the German economy. The specter of 10 percent unemployment and the prospect of a shrunken Social Security system will probably dampen the German enthusiasm for more foreign engagements or new troop deployments. "It all comes together, and it gives you the feeling that there's less common ground than there used to be," said Wolfgang Biermann, a Social Democratic Party senior foreign-policy adviser. "The feeling in Germany is that the Americans end up doing what they want with only their national interest counting, while the Germans don't feel that only their national interest counts."

Finally, Germany has new distractions and new priorities, most important the effort to build an integrated Europe. It is a project that doesn't necessarily mean a drifting away from the Atlantic alliance, but many people suspect that the future will be determined by a contest between the German trans-Atlanticists, who see the American relationship as fundamental, and the Europeanists, who see the future with the European Union.

"I'd say that, essentially, the non-Atlanticists have won," said Jeffrey Gedmin, director of the Aspen Institute Berlin. "The deans of the Social Democratic Party are not anti-American, but none of them are full-blooded, heart-and-soul Atlanticists. They're at least as interested in the E.U. as they are in an alliance with the United States." More generally, Gedmin said, "German foreign policy in the next 10 years will look more French. The Germans will still be allies. They'll still be members of the alliance.

But Germany will be far from the old, loyal, helpful junior partner it was under Kohl."

'German foreign policy in the next 10 years will look more French,' one scholar says. 'Germany will be far from the old, loyal, helpful junior partner it was.'

Many Germans, including Fischer himself and his counterparts in the conservative opposition, repudiate the notion that foreign policy either can or should drift into a sort of Gaullism by default. "This is a complete misunderstanding," he told me. "Germany is completely different," he said, meaning different from France, and the difference lies, as so much does in Germany, in the burden of the past. "We have the responsibility of having fought for hegemony in the first half of the 20th century. We destroyed ourselves during the Nazi dictatorship. We are responsible for the Shoah. Our country was divided. And postwar Europe was not only built against the Soviet Union but also against the German threat. So, yes, we'd be more Gaullist if we hadn't had the Nazi period and the Second World War. Of course, why not? Because then we would have had a different history. But given our real history, we don't only look to the trans-Atlantic relationship because it's in our interest but also because it is in our institutions; it is part of our way of life."

There are large areas of strategic consensus—rebuilding Afghanistan, bringing Turkey into the E.U., in part to prevent it from drifting toward Islamic fundamentalism, keeping Iran from obtaining nuclear weapons. More important is the widespread assumption in Germany, despite the jaundiced view millions of Germans still take of the Bush administration, that the United States must remain Germany's most important ally. If, as many expect, the conservative parties come into power in the next national elections in 2006, Germany would probably be more trans-Atlanticist than before. "If you try to unite Europe against the United States, you will fail," said Wolfgang Schauble, vice chairman of the Christian Democratic Union, Germany's largest conservative party. "Most people in Germany understand that the better way for Germany is to cooperate very closely with the United States. Without a strong partnership, it would be much more difficult and much more insecure for us."

Perhaps the key concept for the future is very simple: a less compliant, more European-oriented Germany is the almost inevitable price that the United States will pay for one of history's greatest foreign-policy triumphs, the forging of a peaceful, democratic, united Germany. For the first time in modern history, Germany is surrounded by friendly countries; it has no territorial claims or imperial ambitions. It is, in short, a happy story, with the consequence that Germany will go its own way, even when that displeases the United States. Egon Bahr, a Social Democratic Party foreign-policy analyst who was a chief adviser to Chancellor Willy Brandt, said, "Now the Soviet Union doesn't exist anymore, so logically Europe can only get its emancipation vis-à-vis the United States."

Otto Schily put it this way: "Leaving aside the question of who was right on Iraq—there were arguments on both sides—the fact that we didn't simply follow the American position was a very big difference for German policy. We have a mature relationship now, and sometimes a relationship between a father and a son becomes a friendship." And, it might be added, sometimes it becomes a rivalry, and sometimes a little of both.

Richard Bernstein is chief of the Berlin bureau of *The New York Times*.

Japanese spirit, western things

When America's black ships forced open Japan, nobody could have predicted that the two nations would become the world's great economic powers

OPEN up. With that simple demand, Commodore Matthew Perry steamed into Japan's Edo (now Tokyo) Bay with his "black ships of evil mien" 150 years ago this week. Before the black ships arrived on July 8th 1853, the Tokugawa shoguns had run Japan for 250 years as a reclusive feudal state. Carrying a letter from America's president, Millard Fillmore, and punctuating his message with cannon fire, Commodore Perry ordered Japan's rulers to drop their barriers and open the country to trade. Over the next century and a half, Japan emerged as one of history's great economic success stories. It is now the largest creditor to the world that it previously shunned. Attempts to dissect this economic "miracle" often focus intently on the aftermath of the second world war. Japan's occupation by the Americans, who set out to rebuild the country as a pacifist liberal democracy, helped to set the stage for four decades of jaw-dropping growth. Yet the origins of the miracle—and of the continual tensions it has created inside Japan and out—stretch further back. When General Douglas MacArthur accepted Japan's surrender in 1945 aboard the battleship Missouri, the Americans made sure to hang Commodore Perry's flag from 1853 over the ship's rear turret. They had not only ended a brutal war and avenged the attack on Pearl Harbour—they had also, they thought, won an argument with Japan that was by then nearly a century old.

America's enduring frustration—in the decades after 1853, in 1945, and even today—has not been so much that Japan is closed, but that it long ago mastered the art of opening up on its own terms. Before and after those black ships steamed into Edo Bay, after all, plenty of other countries were opened to trade by western cannon. What set Japan apart—perhaps aided by America's lack of colonial ambition—was its ability to decide for itself how to make the process of opening suit its own aims.

One consequence of this is that Japan's trading partners, especially America, have never tired of complaining about its economic practices. Japan-bashing reached its most recent peak in the 1980s, when American politicians and businessmen blamed "unfair" competition for Japan's large trade surpluses. But sim-

ilar complaints could be heard within a few decades of Commodore Perry's mission. The attitude was summed up by "Mr Dooley", a character created by Peter Finley Dunne, an American satirist, at the close of the 19th century: "Th' trouble is whin the gallant Commodore kicked opn th' door, we didn't go in. They come out."

Nowadays, although poor countries still want Japan (along with America and the European Union) to free up trade in farm goods, most rich-country complaints about Japan are aimed at its approach to macroeconomics and finance, rather than its trade policies. Japan's insistence on protecting bad banks and worthless companies, say its many critics, and its reluctance to let foreign investors help fix the economy, have prevented Japanese demand from recovering for far too long. Once again, the refrain goes, Japan is unfairly taking what it can get from the world economy—exports and overseas profits have been its only source of comfort for years—without giving anything back.

While these complaints have always had some merit, they have all too often been made in a way that misses a crucial point: Japan's economic miracle, though at times paired with policies ranging from protectionist to xenophobic, has nevertheless proved a huge blessing to the rest of the world as well. The "structural impediments" that shut out imports in the 1980s did indeed keep Japanese consumers and foreign exporters from enjoying some of the fruits of that miracle; but its export prowess allowed western consumers to enjoy better and cheaper cars and electronics even as Japanese households grew richer. Similarly, Japan's resistance to inward investment is indefensible, not least because it allows salvageable Japanese companies to wither; but its outward investment has helped to transform much of East Asia into a thriving economic region, putting a huge dent in global poverty. Indeed, one of the most impressive aspects of Japan's economic miracle is that, even while reaping only half the potential gains from free trade and investment, it has still managed to do the world so much good over the past half-century.

Setting an example

Arguably, however, Japan's other big effect on the world has been even more important. It has shown clearly that you do not have to embrace "western" culture in order to modernise your economy and prosper. From the very beginning, Japan set out to have one without the other, an approach encapsulated by the saying "Japanese spirit, western things". How did Japan pull it off? In part, because the historical combination of having once been wide open, and then rapidly slamming shut, taught Japan how to control the aperture through which new ideas and practices streamed in. After eagerly absorbing Chinese culture, philosophy, writing and technology for roughly a millennium, Japan followed this with 250 years of near-total isolation. Christianity was outlawed, and overseas travel was punishable by death. Although some Japanese scholars were aware of developments in Europe—which went under the broad heading of "Dutch studies"—the shoguns strictly limited their ability to put any of that knowledge to use. They confined all economic and other exchanges with Europeans to a tiny man-made island in the south-western port of Nagasaki. When the Americans arrived in 1853, the Japanese told them to go to Nagasaki and obey the rules. Commodore Perry refused, and Japan concluded that the only way to "expel the barbarians" in future would be to embrace their technology and grow stronger.

But once the door was ajar, the Japanese appetite for "western things" grew unbounded. A modern guidebook entry on the port city of Yokohama, near Tokyo, notes that within two decades of the black ships' arrival it boasted the country's first bakery (1860), photo shop (1862), telephone (1869), beer brewery (1869), cinema (1870), daily newspaper (1870), and public lavatory (1871). Yet, at the same time, Japan's rulers also managed to frustrate many of the westerners' wishes. The constant tension between Japan's desire to measure up to the West—economically, diplomatically, socially and, until 1945, militarily—and its resistance to cultural change has played out in countless ways, good and bad, to this day. Much of it has reflected a healthy wish to hang on to local traditions. This is far more than just a matter of bowing and sleeping on futons and tatami, or of old women continuing to wear kimonos. The Japanese have also clung to distinct ways of speaking, interacting in the workplace, and showing each other respect, all of which have helped people to maintain harmony in many aspects of everyday life. Unfortunately, however, ever since they first opened to the West, anti-liberal Japanese leaders have preferred another interpretation of "Japanese spirit, western things". Instead of simply trying to preserve small cultural traditions, Japan's power-brokers tried to absorb western technology in a way that would shield them from political competition and protect their interests. Imitators still abound in Japan and elsewhere. In East Asia alone, Malaysia's Mahathir Mohamad, Thailand's Thaksin Shinawatra, and even the Chinese Communist Party all see Japan as proof that there is a way to join the rich-country club without making national leaders or their friends accountable. These disciples of Japan's brand of modernisation often use talk of local culture to resist economic and political threats to their power. But they are careful to find ways

to do this without undermining all trade and investment, since growth is the only thing propping them up.

Japan's first attempt to pursue this strategy, it must never be forgotten, grew increasingly horrific as its inconsistencies mounted. In 1868, while western writers were admiring those bakeries and cinemas, Japan's nationalist leaders were "restoring" the emperor's significance to that of an imaginary golden age. The trouble, as Ian Buruma describes in his new book, "Inventing Japan" (see article), is that the "Japanese spirit" they valued was a concoction that mixed in several bad western ideas: German theories on racial purity, European excuses for colonialism, and the observation from Christianity that a single overarching deity (in Japan's case the newly restored emperor) could motivate soldiers better than a loose contingent of Shinto gods. This combination would eventually whip countless young Japanese into a murderous xenophobic frenzy and foster rapacious colonial aggression.

It also led Japan into a head-on collision with the United States, since colonialism directly contradicted America's reasons for sending Commodore Perry. In "The Clash", a 1998 book on the history of American-Japanese relations, Walter LaFeber argues that America's main goal in opening Japan was not so much to trade bilaterally, as to enlist Japan's support in creating a global marketplace including, in particular, China. At first, the United States opened Japan because it was on the way to China and had coal for American steamships. Later, as Japan gained industrial and military might, America sought to use it as a counterweight to European colonial powers that wanted to divide China among their empires. America grew steadily more furious, therefore, as Japan turned to colonialism and tried to carve up China on its own. The irony for America was that at its very moment of triumph, after nearly a century of struggling with European powers and then Japan to keep China united and open, it ended up losing it to communism.

A half-century later, however, and with a great deal of help from Japan, America has achieved almost exactly what it set out to do as a brash young power in the 1850s, when it had barely tamed its own continent and was less than a decade away from civil war. Mainland China is whole. It has joined the World Trade Organisation and is rapidly integrating itself into the global economy. It is part of a vast East Asian trade network that nevertheless carries out more than half of its trade outside the region. And this is all backed up by an array of American security guarantees in the Pacific. The resemblance to what America set out to do in 1853 is striking.

For both Japan and America, therefore, the difficult 150-year relationship has brought impressive results. They are now the world's two biggest economies, and have driven most of the world's technological advances over the past half-century. America has helped Japan by opening it up, destroying its militarists and rebuilding the country afterwards, and, for the last 50 years, providing security and market access while Japan became an advanced export dynamo. Japan has helped America by improving on many of its technologies, teaching it new manufacturing techniques, spurring on American firms with its competition, and venturing into East Asia to trade and invest.

And now?

What, then, will the continuing tension between Japanese spirit and western things bring in the decades ahead? For America, though it will no doubt keep complaining, Japan's resistance to change is not the real worry. Instead, the same two Asian challenges that America has taken on ever since Commodore Perry sailed in will remain the most worrying risks: potential rivalries, and the desire by some leaders to form exclusive regional economic blocks. America still needs Japan, its chief Asian ally, to combat these dangers. Japan's failure to reform, however, could slowly sap its usefulness.

For Japan, the challenges are far more daunting. Many of them stem from the increasing toll that Japan's old ways are taking on the economy. Chief among these is Japan's hostility towards competition in many aspects of economic life. Although competitive private firms have driven much of its innovation and growth, especially in export-intensive industries, Japan's political system continues to hobble competition and private enterprise in many domestic sectors.

In farming, health care and education, for example, recent efforts to allow private companies a role have been swatted down by co-operatives, workers, politicians and civil servants. In other inefficient sectors, such as construction and distribution, would-be losers continue to be propped up by government policy. Now that Japan is no longer growing rapidly, it is harder for competitive forces to function without allowing some of those losers to fail.

Japan's foreign critics are correct, moreover, that its macroeconomic and financial policies are a disgrace. The central bank, the finance ministry, the bank regulators, the prime minister and the ruling-party politicians all blame each other for failing to deal with the problems. All the while, Japan continues to limp along, growing far below its potential as its liabilities mount. Its public-sector debt, for instance, is a terrifying 140% of GDP.

Lately, there has been much talk about employing more western things to help lift Japan out of its mess. The prime minister, Junichiro Koizumi, talks about deregulatory measures that have been tried in North America, Europe and elsewhere. Western auditing and corporate governance techniques—applied in a Japanese way, of course—are also lauded as potential fixes. Even inward foreign direct investment is held out by Mr Koizumi as part of the solution: he has pledged to double it over the next five years. The trouble with all of these ideas, however, is that nobody in Japan is accountable for implementing them. Moreover, most of the politicians and bureaucrats who prevent competitive pressures from driving change are themselves protected from political competition. It is undeniable that real change in Japan would bring unwelcome pain for many workers and small-business owners. Still, Japan's leaders continue to use these cultural excuses, as they have for 150 years, to mask their own efforts to cling to power and prestige. The ugly, undemocratic and illiberal aspects of Japanese traditionalism continue to lurk behind its admirable elements. One reason they can do so is because Japan's nationalists have succeeded completely in one of their original goals: financial independence. The desire to avoid relying on foreign capital has underlain Japan's economic policies from the time it opened up to trade. Those policies have worked. More than 90% of government bonds are in the hands of domestic investors, and savings accounts run by the postal service play a huge role in propping up the system.

Paradoxically, financial self-reliance has thus become Japan's curse. There are worse curses to have, of course: compare Japan with the countless countries that have wrecked their economies by overexposing themselves to volatile international capital markets. Nevertheless, Japan's financial insularity further protects its politicians, who do not have to compete with other countries to get funding.

Theories abound as to how all of this might change. Its history ought to remind anyone that, however long it takes, Japan usually moves rapidly once a consensus takes shape. Potential pressures for change could come from the reversal of its trade surpluses, an erosion of support from all those placid postal savers, or the unwinding of ties that allow bad banks and bad companies to protect each other from investors. The current political stalemate could also give way to a coherent plan, either because one political or bureaucratic faction defeats the others or because a strong leader emerges who can force them to cooperate. The past 150 years suggest, however, that one important question is impossible to answer in advance: will it be liberalism or its enemies who turn such changes to their advantage? Too often, Japan's conservative and nationalist leaders have managed to spot the forces of change more quickly than their liberal domestic counterparts, and have used those changes to seize the advantage and preserve their power. Just as in the past, East Asia's fortunes still greatly depend on the outcome of the struggle between these perennial Japanese contenders.

UNIT 2
Pluralist Democracies: Factors in the Political Process

Unit Selections

Key Points to Consider

- What is meant by the term, social capital, as used by Robert Putnam?

- How do you explain the apparent shifts toward the political center made by parties of the moderate Left and moderate Right in recent years?

- Why are women so poorly represented in Parliament and other positions of political leadership? In what way has this begun to change, where, and why?

- Would you agree with the inventory of democratic essentials as discussed by Philippe Schmitter and Terry Lynn Karl? What do you regard as most and least important in their inventory?

- What are some of the major arguments made in favor of the parliamentary system of government?

- Why do you think Christopher S. Allen includes a multiparty system in his discussion of institutional transplantation?

- Why did de Gaulle include a national referendum in the constitution of the Fifth Republic?

- How does the use of judicial review in a country like Germany compare with our own?

- Do you agree with Robert Kagan, that "Americans are from Mars, Europeans are from Venus?" Why or why not?

 **Links: www.dushkin.com/online/**
These sites are annotated in the World Wide Web pages.

Carnegie Endowment for International Peace
http://www.ceip.org
Inter-American Dialogue (IAD)
http://www.iadialog.org
The North American Institute (NAMI)
http://www.northamericaninstitute.org

Observers of contemporary Western societies frequently refer to the emergence of a new politics in these countries. They are not always very clear or in agreement about what is supposedly novel in the political process or why it is significant. Although no one would dispute that major changes have taken place in these societies during the last three decades or more, affecting both political attitudes and behavior, it is very difficult to establish clear and comparable patterns of transformation or to gauge their impact and endurance. Yet making sense of continuities and changes in political values and behavior must be one of the central tasks of a comparative study of government.

In two of the most important lines of comparative inquiry, political comparativists have examined the rise and spread of a new set of "postmaterial" values and, more recently, the growing signs of political disaffection in both "older" and "newer" democracies. The articles in this reader also explore some other trends with major impacts on contemporary politics. Very high on the list is the recent wave of democratization—that is, the uneven, incomplete, and unstable but nevertheless remarkable spread of democratic forms of governance to many countries during the last three decades. An important place must also go to the controversial "paradigm shift" toward a greater reliance on some kind of market economics in much of the world. This move, which has created its own problems and conflicts, also comes in different forms that span the gamut from partial measures of deregulation and privatization in some countries to the practical abandonment of central planning in others. Finally, political scientists recognize the important rise or revival of various forms of "identity politics." This shift has intensified the political role of ethnicity, race, gender, religion, language, and other elements of group identification that go beyond more traditional social, economic, and ideological lines of political division.

Since the early 1970s, political scientists have followed Ronald Inglehart and other careful observers who first noted a marked increase in what they called postmaterial values, especially among younger and more highly educated people in the skilled service and administrative occupations in Western Europe. Such voters showed less interest in the traditional material values of economic well-being and security, and instead stressed participatory and environmental concerns in politics as a way of improving democracy and the general "quality of life." Studies of postmaterialism form a very important addition to our ongoing attempt to interpret and explain not only the so-called youth revolt but also some more lasting shifts in lifestyles and political priorities. It makes intuitive sense that such changes appear to be especially marked among those who grew up in the relative prosperity of Western Europe, after the austere period of reconstruction that followed World War II. The shift in the post-material direction has not been complete, nor is it necessarily permanent. It is possible to find countervailing trends such as the apparent revival of material concerns among some younger people, as economic prosperity and security seem to have become less certain. There are also some indications that political

reform activities evoke considerably less interest and commitment than they did in the 1970s.

None of this should be mistaken for a return to the political patterns of the past. Instead, we may be witnessing the emergence of a still somewhat incongruent new mix of material and post-material orientations, along with "old" and "new" forms of political self-expression by the citizenry. Established political parties appear to be in somewhat of a quandary in redefining their positions, at a time when the traditional bonding of many voters to one or another party seems to have become weaker, a phenomenon also known as dealignment. Some observers perceive a condition of political malaise in advanced industrial countries, suggesting that the decline of confidence in public officials and government show up not only in opinion polls but also in voting behavior.

The readings in this unit begin with three political briefs that present a comparative perspective on public disillusionment and the decline in voter turnout, the partial weakening of the political parties, and the apparent growth of special interest lobbying. These briefs contain a rich assortment of comparative data and interpretation.

Without suggesting a simple cause-effect relationship, the British observer Martin Jacques has pointed to possible connections between electoral "dealignment" and the vague rhetoric offered by many political activists and opinion leaders. He believes that the end of the cold war and the collapse of communism in Europe have created a situation that demands a reformulation of political and ideological alternatives. In light of the sharpened differences between much of Europe and the United States over how to approach the Middle East and some other topics such as the Kyoto Accords, some observers wonder whether the end of the cold war will also mean the permanent weakening of the familiar trans-Atlantic relationship. At this point, the situation is still in flux.

Most established parties seem to have developed an ability to adjust to change, even as the balance of power within each party system shifts over time and occasional newcomers are admitted to the club—or excluded from it. Each country's party system remains uniquely shaped by its political history, but it is possible to delineate some very general patterns of development. One frequently observed trend is toward a narrowing of the ideological distance between the moderate Left and Right in many European countries. Because of this partial political convergence, it now often makes more sense to speak of the Center-Left and Center-Right respectively.

There are still some important ideological and practical differences between the two orientations. Thus the Right is usually far more ready to accept as "inevitable" the existence of social or economic inequalities along with the hierarchies they reflect and reinforce. The Right normally favors lower taxes and the promotion of market forces—with some very important exceptions intended to protect the nation as a whole (national defense and internal security) as well as certain favorite interest groups (clienteles) and values within it. In general, the Right sees the state as an instrument that should provide security, order, and protection for an established way of life. The Left, by contrast, traditionally emphasizes that government has an important task in opening greater opportunities or life chances for everyone, delivering affordable public services, and generally reducing social inequalities. On issues such as higher and more progressive taxation, or their respective concern for high rates of unemployment and inflation, there continue to be considerable differences between moderates of the Left and Right.

Even as the ideological distance between Left and Right narrows but remains important, there are also signs of some political differentiation within each camp. On the center-right side of the party spectrum in European politics, economic neoliberals (who often seem to speak for high riding and self-confident elements in the business sector) must be clearly distinguished from the social conservatives (who are more likely to advocate traditional values and authority). European liberalism has its roots in a tradition that favors civil liberties and tolerance but that also emphasizes the importance of individual achievement and laissez-faire economics. In both European and Latin American politics one encounters neoliberals. For them, the state has an important but limited role to play in providing an institutional framework within which individuals and social groups pursue their interests without much government intervention—or, as they might say, "interference."

Traditional social conservatives, by contrast, emphasize the importance of societal stability and continuity, and point to the social danger of disruptive change. They often value the strong state as an instrument of order, but many of them also show a paternalist appreciation for welfare state programs that will help keep "the social fabric" from tearing apart. For them, there is a conservative case for a limited welfare state that is not rooted in social liberal or socialist convictions. Instead, it is supported by traditional sentiments of "noblesse oblige" (roughly translated as "privilege has its obligations") and a practical concern for maintaining social harmony.

In British politics, Margaret Thatcher promoted elements from each of these traditions in what could be called her own mix of "business conservatism." The result was a peculiar tension between "drys" and "wets" within her Conservative Party, even after she ceased to be its leader. In France, on the other hand, the division between neoliberals and conservatives until recently ran more clearly between the two major center-right parties, the very loosely united Giscardist UDF (Union for French Democracy), and the more stable neo-Gaullist RPR (Rally for the Republic). They have been coalition partners in several governments and also form electoral coalitions at the second, run-off stage in French elections. In Germany, the Free Democrats (FDP) most clearly represent the traditional liberal position, with its compro-

mises on behalf of special clienteles, while traditional conservative elements can be found alongside business conservatives among the country's Christian Democrats (CDU/CSU).

On the Left, democratic socialists and ecologists stress that the sorry political, economic, and environmental record of communist-ruled states in no way diminishes the validity of their own commitment to social justice and environmental protection in modern industrial society. For them, capitalism will continue to produce its own social problems and dissatisfactions. No matter how efficient capitalism may be, they argue, it will continue to result in inequities that require politically directed redress. Today, many on the Left show a pragmatic acceptance of the modified market economy as an arena within which to promote their goals of redistribution. Social Democrats in Scandinavia and Germany have long been known for taking such positions. In recent years their colleagues in Britain and, to a lesser degree, France have followed suit by abandoning some traditional symbols and goals, such as major programs of nationalization. The moderate Socialists in Spain, who governed that new democracy after 1982, also adopted business-friendly policies before they lost office in early 1996. They were returned to government in a stunning electoral upset in March 2004 that appears to have been a protest against the support of the invasion of Iraq by the conservative incumbents. The socialists had trailed the conservatives until a few days before the election, when terrorist train bombings in Madrid killed about 200 people and injured many hundreds more. The new socialist Prime Minister, Jose Luis Rodriguez Zapatero, quickly carried out his promise to withdraw Spanish troops from Iraq.

Some other West European parties, further to the left, have also moved in the centrist direction in recent years. Two striking examples of this shift can be found among the Greens in Germany and in what used to be the Communist Party of Italy. The German Greens are by no means an establishment party, but they have served as a pragmatic coalition partner with the Social Democrats in several state governments and have gained respect for their mixture of practical competence and idealism. Members of their so-called realist faction (sometimes called the Realos) appear to have out maneuvered their more radical or "fundamentalist" rivals (the Fundis). The Greens were finally able to enter government at the national level in 1998. In Gerhard Schröder's government of Social Democrats and Greens, the leading "realo" Joschka Fischer is foreign minister and two other cabinet posts are held by fellow environmentalists. Many German Greens have had a difficult time accepting their country's military involvement in the Kosovo conflict in 1999 and, more recently, in Afghanistan. There were additional policy compromises by the new government that were difficult to square with the idealist and pacifist origins of the Greens, but Germany's public disagreement with the United States on the invasion of Iraq helped them recover after a string of electoral setbacks. They now appear to have become a firmly established small party with a distinctive program and a solid record in coalition politics.

The Italian Communists have come an even longer way in reaching their present center-left position. In 1991, they renamed themselves the Democratic Party of the Left (PDS), now Left Democrats (DS). Already years before, they had begun to abandon the Leninist revolutionary tradition and adopt reformist politics that resembled those of social democratic parties elsewhere in Western Europe. They were long kept out of national coalition politics, but they gained credibility through their pragmatic and competent performance in local and regional politics. Not every Italian Communist went along with the deradicalization, and a fundamentalist core broke away to set up a new far-left party of Refounded Communists. In 1998, however, the post-Communists fully joined the establishment they had once fought, when their leader, Massimo D'Alema became Italy's new prime minister, who for more than a year headed an unusually broad coalition of several parties.

Both center-left and center-right moderates in Europe face a challenge from the populist tendency on the Far Right that usually seeks to curtail or halt immigration. There is sometimes a separate neo-fascist or fascist-descended challenge as well. In Italy, for example, the populist Northern League and the fascist-descended National Alliance represent positions that seem to be polar opposites on such key issues as government devolution (favored by the former, opposed by the latter). Sometimes a charismatic leader can speak to both orientations, by appealing to their shared fears and resentments. That seems to be the case of Jörg Haider, whose Freedom Party managed to attract over one-quarter of the vote in Austria in the late 1990s. The electoral revival of the far-right parties can be linked in considerable part to anxieties and tensions that affect some socially and economically insecure groups in the lower middle class and some sectors of the working class.

Ultra-right nationalist politicians and their parties typically eschew a complex explanation of the structural and cyclical problems that beset the European economies. Instead, their simple answer blames external scapegoats, namely the many immigrants and refugees from Eastern Europe as well as developing countries in Africa and elsewhere. These far-right parties can be found in many countries, including some that have an earned a reputation for tolerance like the Netherlands and Denmark. Almost everywhere some of the established parties and politicians have been making concessions on the refugee issue, in order to prevent it from becoming monopolized by extremists.

Women in politics is the concern of the second section in this unit. There continues to be a strong pattern of under representation of women in positions of political and economic leadership practically everywhere. Yet there are some notable differences from country to country, as well as from party to party. Generally speaking, the parties of the Left have been readier to place women in positions of authority, although there are some remarkable exceptions, as the center-right cases of Margaret Thatcher in Britain, Angela Merkl in Germany, and Simone Weil in France illustrate. Far-right parties tend to draw markedly less support from female voters, but at least one of them is led by a woman: Pia Kjaersgaard founded and still heads the People's Party of Denmark.

On the whole, the system of proportional representation gives parties both a tool and an added incentive to place female candidates in positions where they will be elected. But here too, there can be exceptions, as in the case of France in 1986 when women did not benefit from the one-time use of proportional representation in the parliamentary elections. Clearly it is not enough to have a relatively simple means, such as proportional representation, for promoting women in politics: There must also be an organized will and a strategy among decision makers to use the available tool for the purpose of such a clearly defined reform.

This is where affirmative action can become a decisive strategic element for promoting change. The Scandinavian countries illustrate better than any other example how the breakthrough may occur. There is a markedly higher representation of women in the parliaments of Denmark, Finland, Iceland, Norway, and Sweden, where the political center of gravity is somewhat to the Left and where proportional representation makes it possible to set up party lists that are more representative of the population as a whole. It is of some interest that Iceland has a special women's party with parliamentary representation, but it is far more important that women are found in leading positions within most of the parties of this and the other Scandinavian countries. It usually does not take long for the more centrist or moderately conservative parties to adopt the new concern of gender equality, and these may even move toward the forefront. Thus women have in recent years held the leadership of three of the main parties in Norway (the Social Democrats, the Center Party, and the Conservatives), which together normally receive roughly two-thirds of the total popular vote. And the present Swedish government of Social Democrats has an equal number of women and men in the cabinet.

In another widely reported sign of change, the relatively conservative Republic of Ireland several years ago chose Mary Robinson as its first female president. It is a largely ceremonial post, but it has a symbolic potential that Mary Robinson, an outspoken advocate of liberal reform in her country, was willing to use on behalf of social change. In 1998, a second woman president was elected in Ireland. Perhaps most remarkable of all, the advancement of women into high political ranks has now also touched Switzerland, where they did not get the right to vote until 1971. It is equally noteworthy that Prime Minister Koizumi of Japan appointed five women to his cabinet when he assumed office in 2001, an absolute first in that male-dominated society.

Altogether, there is a growing awareness of the pattern of gender discrimination in most Western countries, along with a greater will to do something to rectify the situation. It seems likely that there will be a significant improvement over the course of the next decade if the pressure for reform is maintained. Several countries have now passed the 30 percent level in their national parliaments, regarded by some observers as a "critical mass." In France, it was lack of political will that derailed one of the most remarkable recent attempts at reform, at least on the first try. It took the form of a statute, promoted by the recent socialist-led government of France, which required the country's political parties to field an equal number of male and female candidates for office in most elections. The first major test of this new party measure came in the French parliamentary elections of 2002, where it was widely flouted, as Megan Rowling reports in her article.

Changes that erode gender inequality have already occurred in other areas, where there used to be significant political differences between men and women. At one time, for example, there used to be a considerably lower voter turnout among women, but this gender gap has been practically eliminated in recent decades. Similarly the tendency for women to be somewhat more conservative in their party and candidate preferences has given way to a more liberal disposition among younger women in their foreign and social policy preferences than among their male counterparts. These are aggregate differences, of course, and it is important to remember that women, like men, do not represent a monolithic bloc in political attitudes and behavior but are divided by other interests and priorities. One generalization seems to hold: namely, that there is much less inclination among women to support parties or candidates that have a decidedly "radical" image. Thus the support for extreme right-wing parties in contemporary Europe tends to be considerably higher among males.

In any case, there are some very important policy questions that affect women more directly than men. Any careful statistical study of women in the paid labor force of Europe would supply evidence to support three widely shared impressions: (1) There has been a considerable increase in the number and relative proportion of women who take up paid jobs; (2) These jobs are more often unskilled and/or part-time than in the case of men's employment; and (3) Women generally receive less pay and less social protection than men in similar positions. Such a study would also show that there are considerable differences among Western European countries in the relative position of their female workers. The findings would support the argument that political intervention in the form of appropriate legislation can improve the employment status of women.

The socioeconomic status of women in other parts of the world is often far worse. According to reports of the UN Development Program, there have been some rapid advances for women in the field of education and health opportunities, but the doors to economic opportunities are barely ajar. In the field of political leadership, the picture is more varied, as the UN reports indicate, but women generally hold few positions of importance in national politics. Rwanda is an exception. Here genocide has left women, who now make up nearly two-thirds of the country's population, in positions of leadership.

The institutional framework of representative government is the subject of the third section of this unit. Here the authors examine and compare a number of institutional arrangements: (1) essential characteristics and elements of a pluralist democracy, (2) two major forms of representative government, (3) the varying use of judicial review, and (4) the use of national and regional referendums as well as other forms of direct democracy.

The topic of pluralist democracy is a complex one, but Philippe Schmitter and Terry Lynn Karl present a very comprehensive discussion of the subject in a short space. The next two political briefs examine the remarkable growth and variety of forms taken by judicial review in recent years as well as the arguments for and against the use of the referendum as a way of increasing the electoral involvement with policy making.

American Politics in Comparative Perspective

The last three articles in this unit show some ways in which American politics can be usefully included in our comparative studies. Timothy Garton Ash critically reviews Robert Kagan's argument about the "Great Divide" between the United States and Western Europe in the prevailing approach to international relations. He does not dismiss the alleged differences, but modifies them and points to some shared values and interests that continue to link the two. In its discussion of American beliefs and values, *The Economist* also sees areas of similarity and dissimilarity. It singles out the high incidence of traditional beliefs in the U.S. that contrasts with the more secular orientation prevailing in Europe. Americans, for example, are far more likely to express patriotic sentiments and religious beliefs.

Finally, Christopher S. Allen brings U.S. political institutions into our comparative framework. His article can be seen as part of a long tradition of American interest in the parliamentary form of government and, to a lesser degree, in a multiparty system. Allen organizes his argument as a mental experiment in institutional transplantation, in order to explore how a multiparty parliamentary system would change the American political process. His intriguing rearrangement of our familiar political setting serves as a reminder that institutions are not neutral but have important consequences for the political process.

Public Opinion: Is there a crisis?

After the collapse of communism, the world saw a surge in the number of new democracies. But why are the citizens of the mature democracies meanwhile losing confidence in their political institutions? This is the first in a series of articles on democracy in transition.

Everyone remembers that Winston Churchill once called democracy the worst form of government—except for all the others. The end of the cold war seemed to prove him right. All but a handful of countries now claim to embrace democratic ide-

als. Insofar as there is a debate about democracy, much of it now centers on how to help the "emerging" democracies of Asia, Africa, Latin America and Eastern Europe catch up with the established democratic countries of the West and Japan.

The new democracies are used to having well-meaning observers from the mature democracies descend on them at election time to ensure that the voting is free and fair. But is political life in these mature democracies as healthy as it should be?

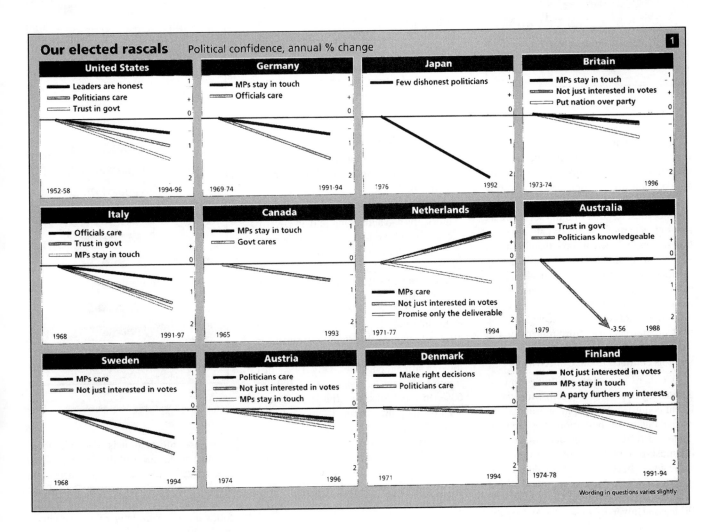

Our elected rascals — Political confidence, annual % change

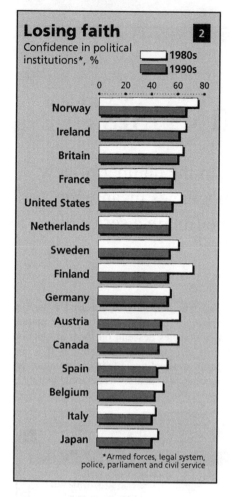

Losing faith

Confidence in political institutions*, %

☐ 1980s
■ 1990s

Norway
Ireland
Britain
France
United States
Netherlands
Sweden
Finland
Germany
Austria
Canada
Spain
Belgium
Italy
Japan

*Armed forces, legal system, police, parliament and civil service

Sources: R. Dalton; World Values Surveys

If opinion research is any guide, the mature democracies have troubles of their own. In the United States in particular, the high opinion which people had of their government has declined steadily over the past four decades. Regular opinion surveys carried out as part of a series of national election studies in America show that the slump set in during the 1960s. The civil-rights conflict and the Vietnam war made this an especially turbulent decade for the United States. But public confidence in politicians and government continued to decline over the next quarter-century. Nor (remember the student unrest in Paris and elsewhere in 1968) was this confined to the United States.

It is hard to compare attitudes toward democracy over time, and across many different countries. Most opinion surveys are carried out nation-by-nation: they are conducted at different times and researchers often ask different sorts of questions. But some generalizations can be made. In their introduction to a forthcoming book "What is Troubling the Trilateral Democracies?", Princeton University Press, 2000) three ac-

ademics—Robert Putnam, Susan Pharr, and Russell Dalton—have done their best to analyze the results of surveys conducted in most of the rich countries.

Chart 1 summarises some of these findings. The downward slopes show how public confidence in politicians seems to be falling, measured by changes in the answers voters give to questions such as "Do you think that politicians are trustworthy?"; "Do members of parliament (MPS) care about voters like you?"; and "How much do you trust governments of any party to place the needs of the nation above their own political party?" In most of the mature democracies, the results show a pattern of disillusionment with politicians. Only in the Netherlands is there clear evidence of rising confidence.

Nor is it only politicians who are losing the public's trust. Surveys suggest that confidence in political institutions is in decline as well. In 11 out of 14 countries, for example, confidence in parliament has declined, with especially sharp falls in Canada, Germany, Britain, Sweden and the United States. World-wide polls conducted in 1981 and 1990 measured confidence in five institutions: parliament, the armed services, the judiciary, the police and the civil service. Some institutions gained public trust, but on average confidence in them decreased by 6% over the decade (see chart 2). The only countries to score small increases in confidence were Iceland and Denmark.

Other findings summarised by Mr Putnam and his colleagues make uncomfortable reading:

• In the late 1950s and early 1960s **Americans** had a touching faith in government. When asked "How many times can you trust the government in Washington to do what is right?", three out of four answered "most of the time" or "just about always". By 1998, fewer than four out of ten trusted the government to do what was right. In 1964 only 29% of the American electorate agreed that "the government is pretty much run by a few big interests looking after themselves". By 1984, that figure had risen to 55%, and by 1998 to 63%. In the 1960s, two-thirds of Americans rejected the statement "most elected officials don't care what people like me think". In 1998, nearly two-thirds agreed with it. The proportion of Americans who expressed "a great deal of" confidence in the executive branch fell from 42% in 1966 to 12% in 1997; and trust in Congress fell from 42% to 11%.

• **Canadians** have also been losing faith in their politicians. The proportion of Canadians who felt that "the government doesn't care what people like me think" rose from 45% in 1968 to 67% in 1993. The proportion expressing "a great deal of" confidence in political parties fell from 30% in 1979 to 11% in 1999. Confidence in the House of Commons fell from 49% in 1974 to 21% in 1996. By 1992 only 34% of Canadians were satisfied with their system of government, down from 51% in 1986.

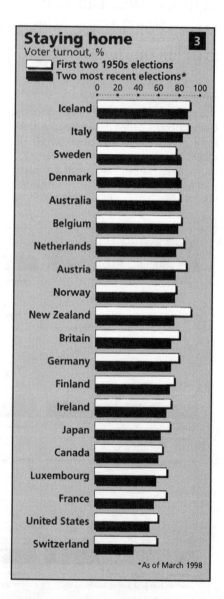

Staying home

Voter turnout, %

☐ First two 1950s elections
■ Two most recent elections*

Iceland
Italy
Sweden
Denmark
Australia
Belgium
Netherlands
Austria
Norway
New Zealand
Britain
Germany
Finland
Ireland
Japan
Canada
Luxembourg
France
United States
Switzerland

*As of March 1998

Source: Martin P. Wattenberg, University of California, Irvine

• Less information is available about attitudes in **Japan**. But the findings of the few surveys that have been carried out there match the global pattern. Confidence in political institutions rose in the decades following the smashing of the country's old politics in the second world war. Happily for democracy, the proportion of Japanese voters who agree that "in order to make Japan better, it is best to rely on talented politicians, rather than to let the citizens argue among themselves" has been falling for 40 years. However, the proportion who feel that they exert at least "some influence" on national politics through elections or demonstrations also fell steadily between 1973 and 1993.

• Although it is harder to generalize about **Western Europe**, confidence in political institutions is in decline in most countries. In 1985 48% of Britons expressed quite a lot of confidence in the House of Commons. This number had halved by 1995. The proportion of Swedes disagreeing with the statement that "parties are only interested in people's votes, not in their opinions" slumped from 51% in 1968 to 28% in 1994. In 1985 51% expressed confidence in the Rikstad (parliament); by 1996 only 19% did. In Germany, the percentage of people who said they trusted their Bundestag deputy to represent their interests rose from 25% in 1951 to 55% in 1978, but had fallen again to 34% by 1992. The percentage of Italians who say that politicians "don't care what people like me think" increased from 68% in 1968 to 84% in 1997.

Such findings are alarming if you take them at face value. But they should be interpreted with care. Democracy may just be a victim of its own success. It could just be that people nowadays expect more from governments, impose new demands on the state, and are therefore more likely to be disappointed. After all, the idea that governments ought to do such things as protect or improve the environment, maintain high employment, arbitrate between moral issues, or ensure the equal treatment of women or minorities, is a relatively modern and still controversial one. Or perhaps

the disillusionment is a healthy product of rising educational standards and the scepticism that goes with it. Or maybe it is caused by the media's search-light highlighting failures of government that were previously kept in the dark. Whatever the causes, the popularity of governments or politicians ought not to be the only test of democracy's health.

Moreover, there is encouraging evidence to put beside the discouraging findings. However much confidence in government may be declining, this does not seem to have diminished popular support for democratic principles. On average, surveys show, more than three out of four people in rich countries believe that democracy is the best form of government. Even in countries where the performance of particular governments has been so disappointing as to break up the party system itself (such as Japan and Italy in 1993–95), this has brought no serious threat to fundamental democratic principle. It may seem paradoxical for people to express strong support for democracy even while their confidence in politicians and political institutions crumbles. But it hardly amounts to the "crisis of democracy" which political scientists tend to proclaim from time to time.

Nor, though, is it a ringing endorsement, especially given that the evidence of opinion surveys is reinforced by other trends. These include a decline both in the membership of political parties and in the proportion of people who turn out to vote. Numbers compiled by Martin Wattenberg, also at the University of California, show that in 18 out of 20 of the rich established democracies the proportion of the electorate voting has been lower than it was in the early 1950s (see chart 3), with the median change being a decline of 10%. More controversially, some political scientists see the growth of protest movements since the

1960s as a sign of declining faith in the traditional institutions of representative democracy, and an attempt to bypass them. Others reckon that the most serious threat comes from the increasingly professional pressure groups and lobbying organisations that work behind the scenes to influence government policy and defend special interests, often at the expense of the electorate as a whole.

What is to be done? Those who believe that government has over-reached itself call on governments to become smaller and to promise less. Thus, it is hoped, people will come to do more for themselves. But whatever the appropriate size and reach of governments, there is also scope for making the machinery of democracy work better.

Indeed, some commentators see the public's declining confidence in political institutions as an opportunity for democratic renewal. Pippa Norris, at Harvard University's Kennedy School of Government, hails the advent of a new breed of "critical citizens" (in a book of that name, Oxford University Press, 1999) who see that existing channels of participation fall short of democratic ideals and want to reform them.

There are some signs of this. Countries as different as Italy, Japan, Britain and New Zealand have lately considered or introduced changes in their electoral systems. Countries around the world are making growing use of referendums and other forms of direct democracy. Many are reducing the power of parliaments by giving judges new powers to review the decisions that elected politicians make. And governments everywhere are introducing new rules on the financing of politicians and political parties. The rest of the articles in this series will look at some of these changes and the forces shaping them.

Political Parties: Empty vessels?

Alexis de Tocqueville called political parties an evil inherent in free governments. The second of our briefs on the mature democracies in transition asks whether parties are in decline

WHAT would democracy look like if there were no political parties? It is almost impossible to imagine. In every democracy worth the name, the contest to win the allegiance of the electorate and form a government takes place through political parties. Without them, voters would be hard put to work out what individual candidates stood for or intended to do once elected. If parties did not "aggregate" people's interests, politics might degenerate into a fight between tiny factions, each promoting its narrow self-interest. But for the past 30 years, political scientists have been asking whether parties are "in decline". Are they? And if so, does it matter?

Generalising about political parties is difficult. Their shape depends on a country's history, constitution and much else. For example, America's federal structure and separation of powers make Republicans and Democrats amorphous groupings whose main purpose is to put their man in the White House. British parties behave quite differently because members of Parliament must toe the party line to keep their man in Downing Street. An American president is safe once elected, so congressmen behave like local representatives rather than members of a national organisation bearing collective responsibility for government. Countries which, unlike Britain and America, hold elections under proportional representation are different again: they tend to produce multi-party systems and coalition governments.

Despite these differences, some trends common to almost all advanced democracies appear to be changing the nature of parties and, on one view, making them less

influential. Those who buy this thesis of decline point to the following changes:

People's behaviour is becoming more **private**. Why join a political party when you can go fly fishing or surf the web? Back in the 1950s, clubs affiliated to the Labour Party were places for Britain's working people to meet, play and study. The Conservative Party was, among other things, a marriage bureau for the better-off. Today, belonging to a British political party is more like being a supporter of some charity: you may pay a membership fee, but will not necessarily attend meetings or help to turn out the vote at election time.

Running out of ideas

Politics is becoming more **secular**. Before the 1960s, political struggles had an almost religious intensity: in much of Western Europe this took the form of communists versus Catholics, or workers versus bosses. But ideological differences were narrowing by the 1960s and became smaller still after the collapse of Soviet communism. Nowadays, politics seems to be more often about policies than values, about the competence of leaders rather than the beliefs of the led. As education grows and class distinctions blur, voters discard old loyalties. In America in 1960, two out of five voters saw themselves as "strong" Democrats or "strong" Republicans. By 1996 less than one in three saw themselves that way. The proportion of British voters expressing a "very strong" affinity with one party slumped from 44% to 16% between 1964 and 1997. This process of **"partisan de-**

alignment" has been witnessed in most mature democracies.

The erosion of loyalty is said to have pushed parties towards the **ideological centre**. The political extremes have not gone away. But mainstream parties which used to offer a straight choice between socialists and conservatives are no longer so easy to label. In the late 1950s Germany's Social Democrats (SPD) snipped off their Marxist roots in order to recast themselves is a *Volkspartei* appealing to all the people. "New" Labour no longer portrays itself as the political arm of the British working class or trade-union movement. Bill Clinton, before he became president, helped to shift the Democratic Party towards an appreciation of business and free trade. Neat ideological labels have become harder to pin on parties since they have had to contend with the emergence of what some commentators call **post-material issues** (such as the environment, personal morality and consumer rights) which do not slot elegantly into the old left-right framework

The **mass media** have taken over many of the information functions that parties once performed for themselves. "Just as radio and television have largely killed off the door-to-door salesman," says Anthony King, of Britain's Essex University, "so they have largely killed off the old-fashioned party worker." In 1878 the German SPD had nearly 50 of its own newspapers. Today the mass media enable politicians to communicate directly with voters without owning printing presses or needing party workers to knock on doors. In many other ways, the business of winning elections has become more capital-intensive and less labour-intensive, making political donors matter more and political activists less.

Another apparent threat to the parties is the growth of **interest and pressure groups**. Why should voters care about the broad sweep of policy promoted during elections by a party when other organisations will lobby all year round for their special interest, whether this is protection of the environment, opposition to abortion, or the defence of some subsidy? Some academics also claim that parties are playing a smaller role, and **think tanks** a bigger one, in making policy. Although parties continue to draw up election manifestos, they are wary of being too specific. Some hate leaving policymaking to party activists, who may be more extreme than voters at large and so put them off. Better to keep the message vague. Or why not let the tough choices be taken by **referendums**, as so often in Switzerland?

Academics have found these trends easier to describe than to evaluate. Most agree that the age of the "mass party" has passed and that its place is being taken by the "electoral-professional" or "catch-all" party. Although still staffed by politicians holding genuine beliefs and values, these modern parties are inclined to see their main objective as winning elections rather than forming large membership organisations or social movements, as was once the case.

Is this a bad thing? Perhaps, if it reduces participation in politics. One of the traditional roles of political parties has been to get out the vote, and in 18 out of 20 rich countries, recent turnout figures have been lower than they were in the 1950s. Although it is hard to pin down the reasons, Martin Wattenberg, of the University of California at Irvine, points out that turnout has fallen most sharply in countries where parties are weak: Switzerland (thanks to those referendums), America and France (where presidential elections have become increasingly candidate- rather than party-centred), and Japan (where political loyalties revolve around ties to internal factions rather than the party itself). In Scandinavia, by contrast, where class-based parties are still relatively strong, turnout has held up much better since the 1950s.

Running out of members

It is not only voters who are turned off. Party membership is falling too, and even the most strenuous attempts to reverse the decline have faltered. Germany is a case in point. The Social Democrats there increased membership rapidly in the 1960s and 1970s, and the Christian Democrats responded by doubling their own membership numbers. But since the end of the 1980s membership has been falling, especially among the young. In 1964 Britain's Labour Party had about 830,000 members and the Conservatives about 2m. By 1997 they had 420,000 and 400,000 respectively. The fall is sharper in some countries than others, but research by Susan Scarrow of the University of Houston suggests that the trend is common to most democracies (see chart). With their membership falling, ideological differences blurring, and fewer people turning out to vote, the decline thesis looks hard to refute.

Or does it? The case for party decline has some big holes in it. For a start, some academics question whether political parties ever really enjoyed the golden age which other academics hark back to. Essex University's Mr King points out that a lot of the evidence for decline is drawn from a handful of parties—Britain's two main ones, the German SPD, the French and Italian Communists—which did indeed once promote clear ideologies, enjoy mass memberships, and organise local branches and social activities. But neither of America's parties, nor Canada's, nor many of the bourgeois parties of Western Europe, were ever mass parties of that sort. Moreover, in spite of their supposed decline, parties continue to keep an iron grip on many aspects of politics.

In most places, for example, parties still control **nomination for public office**. In almost all of the mature democracies, it is rare for independent candidates to be elected to federal or state legislatures, and even in local government the proportion of independents has declined sharply since the early 1970s. When state and local parties select candidates, they usually favour people who have worked hard within the party. German parties, for example, are often conduits to jobs in the public sector, with a say over appointments to top jobs in the civil service and to the boards of publicly owned utilities or media organisations. Even in America, where independent candidates are more common in local elections, the parties still run city, county and state "machines" in which most politicians start their careers.

Naturally, there are some exceptions. In 1994 Silvio Berlusconi, a media tycoon, was able to make himself prime minister at the head of Forza Italia, a right-wing movement drawing heavily on his personal fortune and the resources of his television empire. Ross Perot, a wealthy third-party candidate, won a respectable 19% vote in his 1992 bid for the American presidency. The party declinists claim these examples as evidence for their case. But it is notable that in the end Mr Perot could not compete against the two formidable campaigning and money-raising machines ranged against him.

This suggests that a decline in the membership of parties need not make them weaker in **money and organisation**. In fact, many have enriched themselves simply by passing laws that give them public money. In Germany, campaign subsidies to the federal parties more than trebled between 1970 and 1990, and parties now receive between 20% and 40% of their income from public funds. In America, the paid professionals who have taken over from party activists tend to do their job more efficiently. Moreover, other kinds of political activity—such as donating money to a party or interest group, or attending meetings and rallies—have become more common in America. Groups campaigning for particular causes or candidates (the pro-Republican Christian Coalition, say, or the pro-Democrat National Education Association) may not be formally affiliated with the major party organisations, but are frequently allied with them.

The role of the mass media deserves a closer look as well. It is true that they have weakened the parties' traditional methods of communicating with members. But parties have invested heavily in managing relations with journalists, and making use of new media to reach both members and wider audiences. In Britain, the dwindling of local activists has gone hand-in-hand with a more professional approach to communications. Margaret Thatcher caused a stir by using an advertising firm, Saatchi & Saatchi, to push the Tory cause in the 1979 election. By the time of Britain's 1997 election, the New Labour media operation run from Millbank Tower in London was even slicker.

Another way to gauge the influence of parties is by their **reach**—that is, their power, once in office, to take control of the governmental apparatus. This is a power they have retained. Most governments tend to be unambiguously under the control of people who represent a party, and who would not be in government if they did not belong to such organisations. The French presidential system may appear ideal for independent candidates, but except—arguably—for Charles de Gaulle, who claimed to rise above party, none has ever been elected without party support.

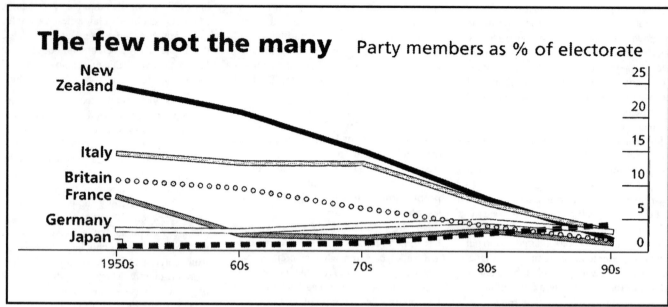

The few not the many Party members as % of electorate

Source: Susan E. Scarrow, Centre for German and European Studies Working Paper 2.59, University of California, Berkeley

The fire next time

Given the cautions that must be applied to other parts of the case for party decline, what can be said about one of the declinists' key exhibits, the erosion of ideological differences? At first sight, this is borne out by the recent movement to the centre of left-leaning parties such as America's Democrats, New Labour in Britain, and the SPD under Gerhard Schröder. In America, Newt Gingrich stoked up some fire amongst Republicans in 1994, but it has flickered out. The most popular Republican presidential hopefuls, and especially George W. Bush, the front-runner, are once again stressing the gentler side of their conservatism.

Still, the claim of ideological convergence can be exaggerated. It is not much more than a decade since Ronald Reagan and Mrs Thatcher ran successful parties with strong ideologies. And the anecdotal assumption that parties are growing less distinct is challenged by longer-term academic studies. A look at the experience of ten western democracies since 1945 ("Parties, Policies and Democracy", Westview Press, 1994) concluded that the leading left and right parties continued to keep their distance and maintain their identity, rather

than clustering around the median voter in the centre. Paul Webb of Britain's Brunel University concludes in a forthcoming book ("Political Parties in Advanced Industrial Democracies", Oxford University Press) that although partisan sentiment is weaker than it was, and voters more cynical, parties have in general adapted well to changing circumstances.

Besides, even if party differences are narrowing at present, why expect that trend to continue? In Western Europe, the ending of the cold war has snuffed out one source of ideological conflict, but new sparks might catch fire. Battered right-wing parties may try to revive their fortunes by pushing the nationalist cause against the encroachments of the European Union. In some places where ideas are dividing parties less, geography is dividing them more. Politics in Germany and Britain has acquired an increasingly regional flavour: Labour and the Social Democrats respectively dominate the north, Conservatives and Christian Democrats the south. Disaffected *Ossis* are flocking to the Party of Democratic Socialism in eastern Germany. Britain, Italy, Canada and Spain have strong separatist parties.

So there is life in the party system yet. But the declinists are on to something. The

Germans have a word for it. One reason given for the rise of Germany's Greens in the 1980s and America's Mr Perot in 1992 was *Parteienverdrossenheit*—disillusionment with mainstream parties that seemed to have abandoned their core beliefs and no longer offered meaningful choices. A "new politics" of citizens' protests appeared to be displacing conventional politics.

In the end, far from undermining the domination of the parties, the German Greens ended up by turning themselves into one and joining the government in an uneasy coalition with the SPD. The balance of evidence from around the world is that despite all the things that are changing them, parties continue to dominate democratic politics.

Indeed, there are grounds for wondering whether their continuing survival is more of a worry than their supposed decline. Is it so very comforting that parties can lose members, worry less about ideas, become detached from broader social movements, attract fewer voters and still retain an iron grip on politics? If they are so unanchored, will they not fall prey to special-interest groups? If they rely on state funding instead of member contributions, will they not turn into creatures of the state? The role of money in politics will be the subject of another brief.

Interest Groups:
Ex uno, plures

The last article in our series on the mature democracies asks whether they are in danger of being strangled by lobbyists and single-issue pressure groups

PREVIOUS briefs in this series have looked at the imperfections in democracy as it is currently practised in the rich countries, and at some of the efforts that different countries are making to overcome them. Evidence that all is not well includes declining public confidence in politicians, falling membership of political parties and smaller turnouts for elections. Ideas for improvement range from making greater use of referendums and other forms of direct democracy, to giving more power to courts to check the power of politicians. This article asks a different question: far from being too powerful, are elected politicians in modern democracies too weak?

When Alexis de Tocqueville visited the United States in the 19th century, he was impressed by the enthusiasm of Americans for joining associations. This, he felt, spread power away from the centre and fostered the emergence of democratic habits and a civil society. Until quite recently, most political scientists shared De Tocqueville's view. Lately, however, and especially in America, doubts have set in. At a certain point, say the doubters, the cumulative power of pressure groups, each promoting its own special interests, can grow so strong that it prevents elected politicians from adopting policies that are in the interest of the electorate as a whole.

A hitch-hiker's guide

A key text for such critics was a short book published in 1965 by Mancur Olson, an American economist. Called "The Logic of Collective Action", this took issue with the traditional idea that the health of democracy was served by vigorous competition between pressure groups, with governments acting as a sort of referee, able to choose the best policy once the debate between the contending groups was over. The traditional view, Olson argued, wrongly assumed that pressure groups were more or less equal. In fact, for a reason known to economists as the free-rider problem, they weren't.

Why? Take the example of five car firms, which form a lobbying group in the hope of raising the price of cars. If they succeed, each stands to reap a fifth of the gains. This makes forming the group and working for its success well worth each firm's investment of time and money. If the car makers succeed, of course, motorists will suffer. But organising millions of individual motorists to fight their corner is a great deal harder because it involves co-ordinating millions of people and because the potential gain for each motorist will be relatively small. Individual motorists will be tempted to reason that, with millions of other people involved, they do not need to do anything themselves, but can instead hitch a "free ride" on the efforts of everyone else.

This simple insight has powerful implications. Indeed, in a later book Olson went on to argue that his theory helped to explain why some nations flourish and others decline. As pressure groups multiply over time, they tend to choke a nation's vitality by impairing the government's ability to act in the wider interest. That, he argued, is why countries such as Germany and Japan—whose interest groups had been cleared away by a traumatic defeat—had fared better after the second world war than Britain, whose institutions had survived intact. With its long record of stability, said Olson, "British society has acquired so many strong organisations and collusions that it suffers from an institutional sclerosis that slows its adaptation to changing circumstances and changing technologies."

Olson's ideas have not gone unchallenged. But they have had a big impact on contemporary thinking about what ails American democracy. In "Demosclerosis" (Times Books, 1994), Jonathan Rauch, a populariser of Olson's work, says that America is afflicted by "hyperpluralism". With at least seven out of ten Americans belonging to at least one such association, the whole society, not just "special" parts of it, is now involved in influence peddling.

The result is that elected politicians find it almost impossible to act solely in the wider public interest. Bill Clinton wants to reform the health system? The health-insurance industry blocks him. China's membership in the World Trade Organisation would benefit America's consumers? America's producers of textiles and steel stand in the way. Jimmy Carter complained when he left the presidency that

Americans were increasingly drawn to single-issue groups to ensure that, whatever else happened, their own private interest would be protected. The trouble is, "the national interest is not always the sum of all our single or special interests".

Pressure groups are especially visible in the United States. As Oxford University's Jeremy Richardson puts it ("Pressure Groups", Oxford University Press, 1993), "pressure groups take account of (and exploit) the multiplicity of access points which is so characteristic of the American system of government—the presidency, the bureaucracy, both houses of Congress, the powerful congressional committees, the judiciary and state and local government."

Nevertheless pressure groups often wield just as much influence in other countries. In those where parliaments exercise tighter control of the executive—Canada, Britain or Germany, say—the government controls the parliamentary timetable and the powers of committees are much weaker. This means that pressure groups adopt different tactics. They have more chance of influencing policy behind closed doors, by bargaining with the executive branch and its civil servants before legislation comes before parliament. In this way pressure groups can sometimes exert more influence than their counterparts in America.

Political tribes

Many European countries have also buttressed the influence of pressure groups by giving them a semi-official status. In Germany, for example, the executive branch is obliged by law to consult the various big "interest organisations" before drafting legislation. In some German states, leading interest groups (along with political parties) have seats on the supervisory boards of broadcasting firms.

French pressure groups are also powerful, despite the conventional image of a strong French state dominating a relatively weak civil society. It is true that a lot of France's interest groups depend on the state for both money and membership of a network of formal consultative bodies. But a tradition of direct protest compensates for some of this institutional weakness. In France, mass demonstrations, strikes, the blocking of roads and the disruption of public services are seen as a part of normal democratic politics.

In Japan, powerful pressure groups such as the Zenchu (Central Union of Agricultural Co-operatives) have turned large

areas of public policy into virtual no-go areas. With more than 9m members (and an electoral system that gives farming communities up to three times the voting weight of urban voters), farmers can usually obstruct any policy that damages their interests. The teachers' union has similarly blocked all attempts at education reform. And almost every sector of Japanese society has its *zoku giin* (political tribes), consisting of Diet members who have made themselves knowledgeable about one industry or another, which pays for their secretaries and provides campaign funds. A Diet member belonging to the transport tribe will work hand-in-glove with senior bureaucrats in the transport ministry and the trucking industry to form what the Japanese call an "iron triangle" consisting of politicians, bureaucrats and big business.

Pressure groups are also increasingly active at a transnational level. Like any bureaucracy, the European Union has spawned a rich network of interest groups. In 1992 the European Commission reckoned that at least 3,000 special-interest groups in Brussels employing some 10,000 people acted as lobbyists. These range from big operations, such as the EU committee of the American Chamber of Commerce, to small firms and individual lobbyists-for-hire. Businesses were the first to spot the advantages of influencing the EU's law making. But trade unions swiftly followed, often achieving in Brussels breakthroughs (such as regulations on working conditions) that they could not achieve at home.

The case for the defense

So pressure groups are ubiquitous. But are they so bad? Although it has been influential, the Olson thesis has not swept all before it. Many political scientists argue that the traditional view that pressure groups create a healthy democratic pluralism is nearer the mark than Olson's thesis.

The case in favour of pressure groups begins with some of the flaws of representative democracy. Elections are infrequent and, as a previous brief in this series noted, political parties can be vague about their governing intentions. Pressure groups help people to take part in politics between elections, and to influence a government's policy in areas that they care and know about. Pressure groups also check excessive central power and give governments expert advice. Although some groups may flourish at the expense of the common weal, this danger can be guarded against if there are

many groups and if all have the same freedom to organise and to put their case to government

Critics of Olson's ideas also point out that, contrary to his prediction, many broad-based groups have in fact managed to flourish in circumstances where individual members stand to make little personal gain and should therefore fall foul of his "free-rider" problem. Clearly, some people join pressure groups for apparently altruistic reasons—perhaps simply to express their values or to be part of an organisation in which they meet like-minded people. Some consumer and environmental movements have flourished in rich countries, even though Olson's theory suggests that firms and polluters should have a strong organisational advantage over consumers and inhalers of dirty air.

Moreover, despite "demosclerosis", well-organised pressure groups can sometimes ease the task of government, not just throw sand into its wheels. The common European practice of giving pressure groups a formal status, and often a legal right to be consulted, minimises conflict by ensuring that powerful groups put their case to governments before laws are introduced. Mr Richardson argues in a forthcoming book ("Developments in the European Union", Macmillan, 1999) that even the pressure groups clustering around the institutions of the EU perform a valuable function. The European Commission, concerned with the detail of regulation, is an eager consumer of their specialist knowledge. As the powers of the European Parliament have grown, it too has attracted a growing band of lobbyists. The parliament has created scores of "intergroups" whose members gain expertise in specific sectors, such as pharmaceuticals, from industry and consumer lobbies.

Governments can learn from pressure groups, and can work through them to gain consent for their policies. At some point, however, the relationship becomes excessively cosy. If pressure groups grow too strong, they can deter governments from pursuing policies which are in the wider public interest. The temptation of governments to support protectionist trade policies at the behest of producer lobbies and at the expense of consumers is a classic example supporting Olson's theories. But problems also arise when it is governments that are relatively strong, and so able to confer special status on some pressure groups and withhold it from others. This puts less-favoured groups at a disadvantage, which they often seek to redress by finding new and sometimes less democratic ways of making their voices heard.

In Germany, for example, disenchantment with what had come to be seen as an excessively cosy system of bargaining between elite groups helped to spark an explosion of protest movements in the 1980s. In many other countries, too, there is a sense that politics has mutated since the 1960s from an activity organised largely around parties to one organised around specialised interest groups on the one hand (such as America's gun lobby) and broader protest and social movements on the other (such as the women's movement, environmentalism and consumerism). One reason for the change is clearly the growth in the size and scope of government. Now that it touches virtually every aspect of people's lives, a bewildering array of groups has sprung up around it.

Many of Olson's disciples blame pressure groups for making government grow. As each special group wins new favours from the state, it makes the state bigger and clumsier, undermining the authority of elected parties, loading excessive demands on government in general, and preventing any particular government from acting in the interest of the relatively disorganised majority of people. By encouraging governments to do too much, say critics on the

right, pressure groups prevent governments from doing anything well. Their solution is for governments to do less. Critics on the left are more inclined to complain that pressure groups exaggerate inequalities by giving those better-organised (ie, the rich and powerful) an influence out of all proportion to their actual numbers.

So what is to be done? A lot could be, but little is likely to be. There is precious little evidence from recent elections to suggest that the citizens of the rich countries want to see a radical cut in the size or scope of the state. As for political inequality, even this has its defenders. John Mueller, of America's University of Rochester, argues that democracy has had a good, if imperfect, record of dealing with minority issues, particularly when compared with other forms of government But he claims that this is less because democratic majorities are tolerant of minorities and more because democracy gives minorities the opportunity

to increase their effective political weight—to become more equal, more important, than their arithmetical size would imply—on issues that concern them. This holds even for groups held in contempt by the majority, like homosexuals. Moreover, the fact that most people most of the

time pay little attention to politics—the phenomenon of political apathy—helps interested minorities to protect their rights and to assert their interests.

Adaptability

This series of briefs has highlighted some of the defects in the practice of democracy, and some of the changes that the mature democracies are making in order to improve matters. But the defects need to be kept in perspective.

One famous critic of democracy claimed that for most people it did nothing more than allow them "once every few years, to decide which particular representatives of the oppressing class should be in parliament to represent and oppress them". When Marx wrote those words in the 19th century, they contained an element of truth. Tragically, Lenin treated this view as an eternal verity, with calamitous results for millions of people. What they both ignored was democracy's ability to evolve, which is perhaps its key virtue. Every mature democracy continues to evolve today. As a result, violent revolution in those countries where democracy has taken deepest root looks less attractive, and more remote, than ever.

Women
in National Parliaments

The data in the table below has been compiled by the Inter-Parliamentary Union on the basis of information provided by National Parliaments by 30 November 2004. **183 country** are classified by **descending order of the percentage of women in the lower or single House**. Comparative data on the world and regional averages as well as data concerning the two regional parliamentary assemblies elected by direct suffrage can be found on separate pages. You can use the PARLINE database to view detailed results of parliamentary elections by country.

New: you can now consult an archive of statistical data on women in Nationl Parliaments.

WORLD CLASSIFICATION

Rank	Country	Lower or single House				Upper House or Senate			
		Elections	Seats*	Women	% W	Elections	Seats*	Women	% W
1	Rwanda	09 2003	80	39	48.8	09 2003	20	6	30.0
2	Sweden	09 2002	349	158	45.3	---	---	---	---
3	Denmark	11 2001	179	68	38.0	---	---	---	---
4	Finland	03 2003	200	75	37.5	---	---	---	---
5	Netherlands	01 2003	150	55	36.7	06 2003	75	25	3.3
6	Norway	09 2001	165	60	36.4	---	---	---	---
7	Cuba	01 2003	609	219	36.0	---	---	---	---
"	Spain	03 2004	350	126	36.0	03 2004	259	60	23.2
8	Costa Rica	02 2002	57	20	35.1	---	---	---	---
9	Belgium	05 2003	150	52	34.7	05 2003	71	27	38.0
10	Austria	11 2002	183	62	33.9	N.A.	62	13	21.0
11	Argentina	10 2001	256	86	33.6	10 2001	72	24	33.3
12	Germany	09 2002	601	197	32.8	N.A.	69	13	18.8
"	South Africa (1)	04 2004	400	131	32.8	04 2004	54	?	?
13	Iceland	05 2003	63	19	30.2	---	---	---	---
14	Mozambique	12 1999	250	75	30.0	---	---	---	---

Rank	Country	Lower or single House				Upper House or Senate			
		Elections	Seats*	Women	% W	Elections	Seats*	Women	% W
15	Belarus	10 2004	109	32	29.4	11 2004	57	18	31.6
"	Seychelles	12 2002	34	10	29.4	---	---	---	---
16	New Zealand	07 2002	120	34	28.3	---	---	---	---
17	Viet Nam	05 2002	498	136	27.3	---	---	---	---
18	Grenada	11 2003	15	4	26.7	11 2003	13	4	30.8
19	Bulgaria	06 2001	240	63	26.2	---	---	---	---
20	Timor-Leste (2)	08 2001	88	23	26.1	---	---	---	---
21	Turkmenistan	12 1999	50	13	26.0	---	---	---	---
22	Namibia (5)	11 2004	72	18	25.0	11 1998	26	2	7.7
"	Switzerland	10 2003	200	50	25.0	10 2003	46	11	23.9
23	Australia (4)	10 2004	150	37	24.7	10 2004	76	27	35.5
"	Uganda	06 2001	304	75	24.7	---	---	---	---
24	Lao People's Democratic Rep.	02 2002	109	25	22.9	---	---	---	---
25	Tunisia	10 2004	189	43	22.8	---	---	---	---
26	Saint Vincent & the Grenadines	03 2001	22	5	22.7	---	---	---	---
27	Mexico	07 2003	500	113	22.6	07 2000	128	20	15.6
28	Eritrea	02 1994	150	33	22.0	---	---	---	---
29	Pakistan	10 2002	342	74	21.6	03 2003	100	18	18.0
30	United Rep. of Tanzania	10 2000	295	63	21.4	---	---	---	---
31	Canada	06 2004	308	65	21.1	N.A.	105	33	31.4
32	Lativa	10 2002	100	21	21.0	---	---	---	---
33	Monaco	02 2003	24	5	20.8	---	---	---	---
34	Nicaragua	11 2001	92	19	20.7	---	---	---	---
35	Lithuania	10 2004	141	29	20.6	---	---	---	---
36	China	03 2003	2985	604	20.2	---	---	---	---
"	Poland	09 2001	460	93	20.2	09 2001	100	23	23.0
37	Dem. People's Rep. of Korea	08 2003	687	138	20.1	---	---	---	---
38	Bahamas	05 2002	40	8	20.0	05 2002	16	7	43.8
"	Guyana	03 2001	65	13	20.0	---	---	---	---
"	Luxembourg	06 2004	60	12	20.0	---	---	---	---
39	Dominica	01 2000	31	6	19.4	---	---	---	---
"	Trinidad and Tobago	10 2002	36	7	19.4	10 2002	31	10	32.3
40	Guinea	06 2002	114	22	19.3	---	---	---	---
41	Senegal	04 2001	120	23	19.2	---	---	---	---
42	Portugal	03 2002	230	44	19.1	---	---	---	---
43	Estonia	03 2003	101	19	18.8	---	---	---	---
44	Bolivia	06 2002	130	24	18.5	06 2002	27	4	14.8

Rank	Country	Lower or single House				Upper House or Senate			
		Elections	Seats*	Women	% W	Elections	Seats*	Women	% W
45	Burnudi	06 1993	179	33	18.4	01 2002	53	10	18.9
46	Peru	04 2001	120	22	18.3	---	---	---	---
"	The F.Y.R. of Macedonia	09 2002	120	22	18.3	---	---	---	---
47	United Kingdom	06 2001	659	118	17.9	N.A.	707	126	17.8
48	Croatia	11 2003	152	27	17.8	---	---	---	---
49	Suriname	05 2000	51	9	17.6	---	---	---	---
50	Dominican Republic	05 2002	150	26	17.3	05 2002	32	2	6.3
51	Czech Republic	06 2002	200	34	17.0	10 2004	81	?	?
52	Bosnia and Herzegovina	10 2002	42	7	16.7	11 2002	15	0	0.0
"	Panama	05 2004	78	13	16.7	---	---	---	---
"	San Marino	06 2001	60	10	16.7	---	---	---	---
"	Slovakia	09 2002	150	25	16.7	---	---	---	---
53	Ecuador	10 2002	100	16	16.0	---	---	---	---
"	Singapore	11 2001	94	15	16.0	---	---	---	---
54	Angola	09 1992	220	34	15.5	---	---	---	---
55	Philippines	05 2004	236	36	15.3	05 2004	24	4	16.7
56	Israel	01 2003	120	18	15.0	---	---	---	---
57	United States of America	11 2004	435	65	14.9	11 2004	100	14	14.0
58	Malawi	04 2004	185	27	14.6	---	---	---	---
59	Sierra Leone	05 2002	124	18	14.5	---	---	---	---
60	Andorra	03 2001	28	4	14.3	---	---	---	---
61	Equatorial Guinea	04 2004	100	14	14.0	---	---	---	---
"	Greece	03 2004	300	42	14.0	---	---	---	---
62	Barbados	05 2003	30	4	13.3	05 2003	21	5	23.8
"	Ireland	05 2002	166	22	13.3	07 2002	60	10	16.7
63	Gambia	01 2002	53	7	13.2	---	---	---	---
64	Republic of Korea	04 2004	299	39	13.0	---	---	---	---
65	Republic of Moldova	02 2001	101	13	12.9	---	---	---	---
66	Tajikistan	02 2000	63	8	12.7	03 2000	34	4	11.8
67	Chile	12 2001	120	15	12.5	12 2001	48	2	4.2
68	France	06 2002	574	70	12.2	09 2004	331	56	16.9
"	Slovenia	10 2004	90	11	12.2	---	---	---	---
69	Uruguay	10 2004	99	?	?	10 2004	31	?	?
70	Colombia	03 2002	166	20	12.0	03 2002	102	9	8.8
"	Dem. Republic of the Congo	08 2003	500	60	12.0	08 2003	120	3	2.5
"	Liechtenstein	02 2001	25	3	12.0	---	---	---	---

Rank	Country	Lower or single House				Upper House or Senate			
		Elections	Seats*	Women	% W	Elections	Seats*	Women	% W
"	Syrian Arab Republic	03 2003	250	30	12.0	---	---	---	---
"	Zambia	12 2001	158	19	12.0	---	---	---	---
71	Indonesia	04 2004	550	65	11.8	---	---	---	---
72	Burkina Faso	05 2002	111	13	11.7	---	---	---	---
"	Jamaica	10 2002	60	7	11.7	10 2002	21	4	19.0
"	Lesotho	05 2002	120	14	11.7	N.A.	33	12	36.4
73	Italy	05 2001	618	71	11.5	05 2001	321	26	8.1
74	Botswana	10 2004	63	7	11.1	---	---	---	---
"	Cape Verde	01 2001	72	8	11.1	---	---	---	---
"	Saint Lucia	12 2001	18	2	11.1	12 2001	11	4	36.4
75	Djibouti	01 2003	65	7	10.8	---	---	---	---
"	Morocco	09 2002	325	35	10.8	10 2003	270	3	1.1
"	Swaziland	10 2003	65	7	10.8	10 2003	30	9	30.0
76	Cyprus	05 2001	56	6	10.7	---	---	---	---
"	El Salvador	03 2003	84	9	10.7	---	---	---	---
77	Antigua and Barbuda	03 2004	19	2	10.5	03 2004	17	3	17.6
"	Azerbaijan	11 2000	124	13	10.5	---	---	---	---
78	Kazakhstan	09 2004	77	8	10.4	09 2004	39	3	7.7
79	Mali	07 2002	147	15	10.2	---	---	---	---
80	Kyrgyzstan	02 2000	60	6	10.0	02 2000	45	1	2.2
"	Paraguay	04 2003	80	8	10.0	04 2003	45	4	8.9
"	Zimbabwe	06 2000	150	15	10.0	---	---	---	---
81	Cambodia	07 2003	123	12	9.8	03 1999	61	8	13.1
"	Hungary	04 2002	386	38	9.8	---	---	---	---
"	Russian Federation	12 2003	450	44	9.8	N.A.	178	6	3.4
82	Sudan	12 2000	360	35	9.7	---	---	---	---
"	Venezuela	07 2000	165	16	9.7	---	---	---	---
83	Ghana	12 2000	200	19	9.5	---	---	---	---
84	Georgia	03 2004	235	22	9.4	---	---	---	---
85	Bhutan	N.A.	152	14	9.2	---	---	---	---
"	Gabon	12 2001	119	11	9.2	02 2003	91	14	15.4
"	Malta	04 2003	65	6	9.2	---	---	---	---
"	Thailand	01 2001	500	46	9.2	03 2000	200	21	10.5
86	Malaysia	03 2004	219	20	9.1	03 2004	70	18	25.7
"	Sao Tome and Principe	03 2002	55	5	9.1	---	---	---	---
87	Cameroon	06 2002	180	16	8.9	---	---	---	---
88	Brazil	10 2002	513	44	8.6	10 2002	81	10	12.3

Rank	Country	Lower or single House				Upper House or Senate			
		Elections	Seats*	Women	% W	Elections	Seats*	Women	% W
89	Congo	05 2002	129	11	8.5	07 2002	60	9	15.0
"	Cote d'Ivoire	12 2000	223	19	8.5	---	---	---	---
90	India	04 2004	545	45	8.3	06 2004	242	28	11.6
91	Guatemala	11 2003	158	13	8.2	---	---	---	---
92	Serbia and Montenegro (3)	09 2003	126	10	7.9	---	---	---	---
93	Ethiopia	05 2000	547	42	7.7	05 2000	120	10	8.3
94	Togo	10 2002	81	6	7.4	---	---	---	---
95	Benin	03 2003	83	6	7.2	---	---	---	---
"	Uzbekistan	12 1999	250	18	7.2	---	---	---	---
96	Japan	11 2003	480	34	7.1	07 2004	242	33	13.6
"	Kenya	12 2002	224	16	7.1	---	---	---	---
97	Mongolia	06 2004	74	5	6.8	---	---	---	---
98	Algeria	05 2002	389	24	6.2	12 2003	144	28	19.4
99	Nigeria	04 2003	360	22	6.12	04 2003	109	3	2.8
"	Samoa	03 2001	49	3	6.1	---	---	---	---
100	Maldives	11 1999	50	3	6.0	---	---	---	---
101	Nepal	05 1999	205	12	5.9	06 2001	60	5	8.3
102	Chad	04 2002	155	9	5.8	---	---	---	---
103	Albania	06 2001	140	8	5.7	---	---	---	---
"	Fiji	08 2001	70	4	5.7	08 2001	32	2	6.3
"	Mauritius	09 2000	70	4	5.7	---	---	---	---
104	Honduras	11 2001	128	7	5.5	---	---	---	---
"	Jordan	06 2003	110	6	5.5	11 2003	55	7	12.7
105	Liberia	10 2003	76	4	5.3	---	---	---	---
"	Ukraine	03 2002	450	24	5.3	---	---	---	---
106	Sri Lanka	04 2004	225	11	4.9	---	---	---	---
107	Kiribati	05 2003	42	2	4.8	---	---	---	---
108	Armenia	05 2003	131	6	4.6	---	---	---	---
109	Turkey	11 2002	550	24	4.4	---	---	---	---
110	Madagascar	12 2002	160	6	3.8	03 2001	90	10	11.1
"	Vanuatu	07 2004	52	2	308	---	---	---	---
111	Mauritania	10 2001	81	3	3.7	04 2002	56	3	5.4
112	Haiti	05 2000	83	3	3.6	05 2000	27	7	25.9
113	Belize	03 2003	30	1	3.3	03 2003	13	3	23.1
114	Iran (Islamic Rep. of)	02 2004	290	9	3.1	---	---	---	---
115	Comoros	04 2004	33	1	3.0	---	---	---	---
"	Marshall Islands	11 2003	33	1	3.0	---	---	---	---

Rank	Country	Lower or single House				Upper House or Senate			
		Elections	Seats*	Women	% W	Elections	Seats*	Women	% W
116	Egypt	11 2000	454	11	2.4	05 2004	264	18	6.8
117	Lebanon	08 2000	128	3	2.3	---	---	---	---
118	Bangladesh	10 2001	300	6	2.0	---	---	---	---
119	Papua New Guinea	06 2002	109	1	0.9	---	---	---	---
120	Yemen	04 2003	301	1	0.3	---	---	---	---
121	Bahrain	10 2002	40	0	0.0	11 2002	40	6	15.0
"	Kuwait	07 2003	65	0	0.0	---	---	---	---
"	Micronesia (Fed. States of)	03 2003	14	0	0.0	---	---	---	---
"	Nauru	05 2003	18	0	0.0	---	---	---	---
"	Palau	11 2000	16	0	0.0	11 2000	9	0	0.0
"	Saint Kitts and Nevis	10 2004	15	0	0.0	---	---	---	---
"	Saudi Arabia	05 2001	120	0	0.0	---	---	---	---
"	Solomon Islands	12 2001	50	0	0.0	---	---	---	---
"	Tonga	03 2002	30	0	0.0	---	---	---	---
"	Tuvalu	07 2002	15	0	0.0	---	---	---	---
"	United Arab Emirates	02 2003	40	0	0.0	---	---	---	---
?	Guinea-Bissau	03 2004	102	?	?	---	---	---	---
?	Libyan Arab Jamahiriya	03 1997	760	?	?	---	---	---	---
?	Niger	11 2004	83	?	?	---	---	---	---
?	Romania	11 2004	345	?	?	11 2004	140	?	?

* Figures correspond to the number of seats currently filled in Parliament

(1) South Africa: the figures on the distribution of seats do not include the 36 special rotating delegates appointed on an ad hoc basis, and the percentages given are therefore calculated on the basis of the 54 permanent seats

(2) Timor-Leste: The purpose of elections held on 30 August 2001 was to elect members of the Constituent Assembly of Timor-Leste. This body became the National Parliament on 20 May 2002, the date on which the country became independent, without any new elections

(3) Serbia and Montenegro: For the first time since Yugoslavia ceased to exist and the new State, Serbia and Montenegro, was created, indirect elections were held in the two assemblies of the two member states.

(4) Australia: The figures for the Senate reflects its composition to 1 July 2005.

(5) Namibia: The 6 additional non-voting members will be appointed by the President of the Republic after he will be sworn in on 21 March 2005.

***** Elections were held in November 2003. However, on 25 November 2003, the election results were annuled by the Supreme Court of Georgia. New elections will be held in March 2004.

EUROPE CRAWLS AHEAD...

By Megan Rowling

As Speaker of the Riksdagen, the Swedish parliament, Birgitta Dahl holds Sweden's second-highest political office. But when she was first elected back in 1969, as a 30-year-old single mother, she was regarded as "very odd."

"To be accepted and respected, you had to act like a bad copy of a man," Dahl recalls of her early years in politics. "But we tried to change that, and we never gave up our identity. Now women have competence in Parliament, and they have changed its performance and priorities."

Back then, women of her generation were eager for change. From the beginning, they based their demands on the right of the individual—whether male or female—to have equal access to education, work and social security. And as politicians, they fought hard to build a legal framework for good childcare and parental leave, for fathers as well as mothers. "We got this kind of legislation through," Dahl says, "even though it took 15 years of serious conflict, debate and struggle."

And their efforts paid off. Sweden now has the highest proportion of women parliamentarians in the world, at 42.7 percent—up from just 12 percent in 1969. Two of its three deputy speakers are also women. Other Nordic countries too have high levels of female representation: In rankings compiled by the Inter-Parliamentary Union (IPU), Denmark takes second place behind Sweden, with women accounting for 38 percent of parliament members, followed by Finland and Norway with around 36.5 percent. (Finland also has one of the world's 11 women heads of state.) These nations' Social Democratic and far-left governing coalitions have made impressive progress toward equality in all areas of society in the past 40 years. But the nature of their electoral systems is also very important.

Julie Ballington, gender project officer at the Stockholm-based International Institute for Democracy and Electoral Assistance (IDEA), points out that the top 10 countries in the IPU ranking all use some form of proportional representation. This kind of voting system, in which parties are allocated seats in multi-member districts according to the percentage of votes they win, Ballington says, "offers a way to address gender imbalance in parliaments." With single-member districts, parties are often under pressure to choose a male candidate. But where they can contest and win more than one seat per constituency, they tend to be more willing to field female candidates. And by improving the gender balance on their slates, they widen their appeal among women voters.

Most European countries now use proportional representation or a combination of proportional representation and majoritarian voting, the system in use in the United States and the United Kingdom. In Europe, the widespread use of proportional representation has boosted the number of women politicians—particularly in the past three decades. And in the Nordic countries, where left-wing parties have enjoyed long periods in power and feminism has received strong support, the combination of these factors has led to significant progress toward gender parity in politics.

But even within Europe, some countries continue to lag behind. In Britain, which uses a single-member district plurality system, women members of parliament make up just 17.9 percent of the House of Commons. In the general elections of 2001, the ruling Labour Party stipulated that half those on its candidate shortlists be women. But research conducted by the Fawcett Society, a British organization that campaigns for gender equity, showed that some female hopefuls experienced overt discrimination and even sexual harassment when interviewed by local party members during the selection process.

"You are told things like 'your children are better off with you at home'... 'you are the best candidate but we are not ready for a woman.' They would select the donkey rather than the woman," said one candidate. Another complained: "They are absolutely adamant they will not consider a woman.... It was said to me... 'we do enjoy watching you speak—we always imagine what your knickers are like.' It is that basic." In light of such attitudes, it is not surprising that women candidates were selected for only four out of 38 vacant seats.

Thanks to new governmental legislation, however, the party is set to reintroduce the controversial method of all-women shortlists it used in the general election of 1997. The use of these shortlists saw the number of British women MPs double to 120 in that election, which swept

Labour to power with a landslide victory. The technique was later ruled illegal because it was judged to discriminate against men. But in early 2002, the government returned to the idea, passing a bill that will allow political parties to take measures in favor of women when choosing parliamentary candidates—what's often referred to as "positive discrimination."

"Critical mass," or the level of representation above which women make a real difference to the political agenda, is widely judged to be around 30 percent.

Judith Squires, a political researcher at Bristol University, believes that the new legislation got such an easy ride partly because it does not stipulate that parties must take action: "We had expected it to be a hard battle. But there has been a change of mood in the Conservative Party, and the fact that it is permissive, and there is a sunset clause [the legislation expires in 2015], all helped to push it through."

In France, where until the recent election women accounted for only 10.9 percent of National Assembly members, the government opted for a more extreme method: a law aimed at securing political parity between men and women. Now half of all contesting parties' candidates in National Assembly elections and most local ballots must be women. In National Assembly elections, which do not use proportional representation, parties that deviate from the 50 percent target by more than two percent are fined a proportion of their public financing.

The law's first test in the municipal elections of March 2001 saw the percentage of elected women councilors in towns of more than 3,500 almost double, to 47.5 percent. But in June's National Assembly elections, the proportion of women deputies increased by less than 1.5 points, to just 12.3 percent—way below expectations. The main factor behind this disappointing result was the success of right-wing parties that ignored the new law, says Mariette Sineau, research director at the Center for the Study of French Political Life. "The big parties decided it was better to incur the financial penalty than to sacrifice their 'favored sons.' And this was particularly so with parties on the right."

Another problem with the law, Sineau explains, is that it does not apply to regional assemblies, "which is a shame, because most National Assembly deputies are recruited there." And the recent victory of the right suggests that France's ruling—and predominantly male—elite are in no hurry to change the system that has allowed them to hold on to power up until now, law or no law. As Chantal Cauquil, a French deputy at the European Parliament and member of the Workers' Struggle Party, argues, other aspects of French society must change before real

parity can be achieved. "There's no doubt that economic and social conditions—which weigh on women earning the lowest salaries, in the most precarious situations, and with the biggest problems caused by a notable lack of childcare infrastructure—have a negative impact on women's political participation," she says. Moreover, governing parties of both the right and left are influenced by social prejudices and are not inclined to regard women as full citizens. It requires real political will to go against such prejudices and allow women to take on the same responsibilities as men."

Such deep-rooted but hidden obstacles, faced by women everywhere, are precisely why proponents of the use of gender quotas on lists for both party and national elections believe positive discrimination is essential. "Everybody hates quotas, and everyone wishes they weren't necessary,"says Drude Dahlerup, professor of politics at the University of Stockholm. "But we have to start from the point that there are structural barriers. Then quotas can be seen as compensation." Currently, political parties in some 40 countries appear to agree, with quota systems in operation from Argentina and India to Uganda.

The use of quotas in Europe varies significantly from country to country and from party to party, but where a quota system is applied, it tends to lead to a rise in women's representation. In 1988, for example, Germany's Social Democrats adopted a system of flexible quotas, under which at least one-third of all candidates for internal party election must be female—and between 1987 and 1990, the number of Social Democratic women in the German parliament, the Bundestag, doubled. In Sweden, parties didn't introduce quotas until the '90s, but the principle of "Varannan Damernas" ("Every Other Seat A Woman's Seat") has been widespread since the '80s. Dahl, the Swedish speaker, argues that "it is not only legislation that changes the world, but convincing people that change is necessary."

Yet, as Dahlerup notes, women in some Scandinavian countries have worked to improve gender equality since the end of World War I, and "other countries are not going to wait that long—they are showing impatience." "Critical mass," or the level of representation above which women make a real difference to the political agenda, is widely judged to be around 30 percent. And in countries such as France and the United Kingdom, where that is still a long way off, measures such as parity laws and all-women shortlists are a way to speed up progress.

Even in countries that are close to achieving political parity, however, women are quick to warn against complacency. Dahlerup emphasizes the case of Denmark, where quotas have been abandoned. "Young women say they don't want and don't need quotas. The discourse is that equality has already been achieved. But I think Denmark could go backward again, and that is dangerous."

Squires of Bristol University also talks about a backlash in Britain's Liberal Democratic Party against what younger women regard as "old-fashioned feminist policies." At the party conference last year, she says, many women in their twenties and early thirties lobbied against any form of positive discrimination, wearing pink T-shirts emblazoned with the words "I'm not a token woman." But Squires suggests that this attitude is somewhat misguided: "All parties [in the United Kingdom] have set criteria that discriminate against women. It is not a supply-side problem, it is a demand-side problem."

"People are waking up and saying that it's not right that there are so few women in politics."

In an attempt to address this "demand-side problem," activists are targeting not only national political institutions, but also those of the European Union. The number of women members of the European Parliament increased from 25.7 percent in 1994 to 29.9 percent in the 1999 elections—not very impressive considering that some countries introduced proportional representation voting, and some parties alternated women and men on their lists to boost women's chances. More worrying perhaps is the gender imbalance in the convention on the Future of Europe, a body charged with the important task of drafting a new treaty for the European Union. Its presidium includes only two women among its 12 members, and the convention itself only 19 out of 118 members.

"The establishment of the convention is a response to the need for transparency and democracy. How can we explain the fact that women are not included?" asks Denise Fuchs, president of the European Women's Lobby. "It is simply not coherent." The EWL has launched a campaign to rectify the problem and is lobbying to achieve parity democracy across all other European institutions as well.

Yvonne Galligan, director of the Belfast-based Center for Advancement of Women in Politics, points out that "there has been a groundswell of support for women in political life across Western Europe, but this has not yet translated into numbers in the United Kingdom, Ireland and the European Union." In May's elections in the Irish Republic, for example, women parliamentarians in Ireland's Dail gained just one seat, and are now at 12.7 percent, according to the IPU.

Galligan is now working with political parties to set targets for Ireland's local elections in a couple of years' time—a tough job, because most parties oppose any form of positive discrimination. Parity in Ireland isn't likely to happen for a long while yet, but Galligan believes the social backdrop is improving. She cites a controversial referendum in March, in which the Irish electorate narrowly voted against a proposal to tighten the country's strict abortion laws even further. "That raised the status of women," she explains. "The underlying question was, how do we perceive the role of women? Now that is carrying over into elections. People are waking up and saying that it's not right that there are so few women in politics."

But where a sea-change in attitudes has not already occurred, it is almost certainly emerging. Naturally, there are fears that the apparent resurgence of the right in Europe could reverse the trend. But most of those interviewed for this article say women have already progressed far enough to prevent a significant decline in representation.

As Linda McAvan, deputy leader of Britain's Labour MEPs, argues: "If we look at how things were 20 years ago, they have changed enormously. Young women are different now. They see what has been done by women politicians before them, and they want to do it too."

From *In These Times*, July 22, 2002. © 2002 by In These Times. Reprinted by permission.

WHAT DEMOCRACY IS... AND IS NOT

Philippe C. Schmitter & Terry Lynn Karl

For some time, the word democracy has been circulating as a debased currency in the political marketplace. Politicians with a wide range of convictions and practices strove to appropriate the label and attach it to their actions. Scholars, conversely, hesitated to use it—without adding qualifying adjectives—because of the ambiguity that surrounds it. The distinguished American political theorist Robert Dahl even tried to introduce a new term, "polyarchy," in its stead in the (vain) hope of gaining a greater measure of conceptual precision. But for better or worse, we are "stuck" with democracy as the catchword of contemporary political discourse. It is the word that resonates in people's minds and springs from their lips as they struggle for freedom and a better way of life; it is the word whose meaning we must discern if it is to be of any use in guiding political analysis and practice.

The wave of transitions away from autocratic rule that began with Portugal's "Revolution of the Carnations" in 1974 and seems to have crested with the collapse of communist regimes across Eastern Europe in 1989 has produced a welcome convergence toward [a] common definition of democracy.[1] Everywhere there has been a silent abandonment of dubious adjectives like "popular," "guided," "bourgeois," and "formal" to modify "democracy." At the same time, a remarkable consensus has emerged concerning the minimal conditions that polities must meet in order to merit the prestigious appellation of "democratic." Moreover, a number of international organizations now monitor how well these standards are met; indeed, some countries even consider them when formulating foreign policy.[2]

WHAT DEMOCRACY IS

Let us begin by broadly defining democracy and the generic *concepts* that distinguish it as a unique system for organizing relations between rulers and the ruled. We will then briefly review *procedures*, the rules and arrangements that are needed if democracy is to endure. Finally, we will discuss two operative *principles* that make democracy work. They are not expressly included among the generic concepts or formal procedures, but the prospect for democracy is grim if their underlying conditioning effects are not present.

One of the major themes of this essay is that democracy does not consist of a single unique set of institutions. There are many types of democracy, and their diverse practices produce a similarly varied set of effects. The specific form democracy takes is contingent upon a country's socioeconomic conditions as well as its entrenched state structures and policy practices.

Modern political democracy is a system of governance in which rulers are held accountable for their actions in the public realm by citizens, acting indirectly through the competition and cooperation of their elected representatives.[3]

A *regime or system of governance* is an ensemble of patterns that determines the methods of access to the principal public offices; the characteristics of the actors admitted to or excluded from such access; the strategies that actors may use to gain access; and the rules that are followed in the making of publicly binding decisions. To work properly, the ensemble must be institutionalized—that is to say, the various patterns must be habitually known, practiced, and accepted by most, if not all, actors. Increasingly, the preferred mechanism of institutionalization is a written body of laws undergirded by a written constitution, though many enduring political norms can have an informal, prudential, or traditional basis.[4]

For the sake of economy and comparison, these forms, characteristics, and rules are usually bundled together and given a generic label. Democratic is one; others are autocratic, authoritarian, despotic, dictatorial, tyrannical, totalitarian, absolutist, traditional, monarchic, obligarchic, plutocratic, aristocratic, and sultanistic.[5] Each of these regime forms may in turn be broken down into subtypes.

Like all regimes, democracies depend upon the presence of *rulers*, persons who occupy specialized authority roles and can give legitimate commands to others. What distinguishes democratic rulers from nondemocratic ones are the norms that condition how the former come to power and the practices that hold them accountable for their actions.

"However central to democracy, elections occur intermittently and only allow citizens to choose between the highly aggregated alternatives offered by political parties..."

The *public realm* encompasses the making of collective norms and choices that are binding on the society and backed by state coercion. Its content can vary a great deal across democracies, depending upon preexisting distinctions between the public and the private, state and society, legitimate coercion and voluntary exchange, and collective needs and individual preferences. The liberal conception of democracy advocates circumscribing the public realm as narrowly as possible, while the socialist or social-democratic approach would extend that realm through regulation, subsidization, and, in some cases, collective ownership of property. Neither is intrinsically more democratic than the other—just *differently* democratic. This implies that measures aimed at "developing the private sector" are no more democratic than those aimed at "developing the public sector." Both, if carried to extremes, could undermine the practice of democracy, the former by destroying the basis for satisfying collective needs and exercising legitimate authority; the latter by destroying the basis for satisfying individual preferences and controlling illegitimate government actions. Differences of opinion over the optimal mix of the two provide much of the substantive content of political conflict within established democracies.

Citizens are the most distinctive element in democracies. All regimes have rulers and a public realm, but only to the extent that they are democratic do they have citizens. Historically, severe restrictions on citizenship were imposed in most emerging or partial democracies according to criteria of age, gender, class, race, literacy, property ownership, tax-paying status, and so on. Only a small part of the total population was eligible to vote or run for office. Only restricted social categories were allowed to form, join, or support political associations. After protracted struggle—in some cases involving violent domestic upheaval or international war—most of these restrictions were lifted. Today, the criteria for inclusion are fairly standard. All native-born adults are eligible, although somewhat higher age limits may still be imposed upon candidates for certain offices. Unlike the early American and European democracies of the nineteenth century, none of the recent democracies in southern Europe, Latin America, Asia, or Eastern Europe has even attempted to impose formal restrictions on the franchise or

eligibility to office. When it comes to informal restrictions on the effective exercise of citizenship rights, however, the story can be quite different. This explains the central importance (discussed below) of procedures.

Competition has not always been considered an essential defining condition of democracy. "Classic" democracies presumed decision making based on direct participation leading to consensus. The assembled citizenry was expected to agree on a common course of action after listening to the alternatives and weighing their respective merits and demerits. A tradition of hostility to "faction," and "particular interests" persists in democratic thought, but at least since *The Federalist Papers* it has become widely accepted that competition among factions is a necessary evil in democracies that operate on a more-than-local scale. Since, as James Madison argued, "the latent causes of faction are sown into the nature of man," and the possible remedies for "the mischief of faction" are worse than the disease, the best course is to recognize them and to attempt to control their effects.[6] Yet while democrats may agree on the inevitability of factions, they tend to disagree about the best forms and rules for governing factional competition. Indeed, differences over the preferred modes and boundaries of competition contribute most to distinguishing one subtype of democracy from another.

The most popular definition of democracy equates it with regular *elections*, fairly conducted and honestly counted. Some even consider the mere fact of elections—even ones from which specific parties or candidates are excluded, or in which substantial portions of the population cannot freely participate—as a sufficient condition for the existence of democracy. This fallacy has been called "electoralism" or "the faith that merely holding elections will channel political action into peaceful contests among elites and accord public legitimacy to the winners"—no matter how they are conducted or what else constrains those who win them.[7] However central to democracy, elections occur intermittently and only allow citizens to choose between the highly aggregated alternatives offered by political parties, which can, especially in the early stages of a democratic transition, proliferate in a bewildering variety. During the intervals between elections, citizens can seek to influence public policy through a wide variety of other intermediaries: interest associations, social movements, locality groupings, clientelistic arrangements, and so forth. *Modern democracy, in other words, offers a variety of competitive processes and channels for the expression of interests and values—associational as well as partisan, functional as well as territorial, collective as well as individual. All are integral to its practice.*

Another commonly accepted image of democracy identifies it with *majority rule*. Any governing body that makes decisions by combining the votes of more than half of those eligible and present is said to be democratic, whether that majority emerges within an electorate, a parliament, a committee, a city council, or a party caucus.

For exceptional purposes (e.g., amending the constitution or expelling a member), "qualified majorities" of more than 50 percent may be required, but few would deny that democracy must involve some means of aggregating the equal preferences of individuals.

A problem arises, however, when *numbers* meet *intensities*. What happens when a properly assembled majority (especially a stable, self-perpetuating one) regularly makes decisions that harm some minority (especially a threatened cultural or ethnic group)? In these circumstances, successful democracies tend to qualify the central principle of majority rule in order to protect minority rights. Such qualifications can take the form of constitutional provisions that place certain matters beyond the reach of majorities (bills of rights); requirements for concurrent majorities in several different constituencies (confederalism); guarantees securing the autonomy of local or regional governments against the demands of the central authority (federalism); grand coalition governments that incorporate all parties (consociationalism); or the negotiation of social pacts between major social groups like business and labor (neocorporatism). The most common and effective way of protecting minorities, however, lies in the everyday operation of interest associations and social movements. These reflect (some would say, amplify) the different intensities of preference that exist in the population and bring them to bear on democratically elected decision makers. Another way of putting this intrinsic tension between numbers and intensities would be to say that "in modern democracies, votes may be counted, but influences alone are weighted."

Cooperation has always been a central feature of democracy. Actors must voluntarily make collective decisions binding on the polity as a whole. They must cooperate in order to compete. They must be capable of acting collectively through parties, associations, and movements in order to select candidates, articulate preferences, petition authorities, and influence policies.

But democracy's freedoms should also encourage citizens to deliberate among themselves, to discover their common needs, and to resolve their differences without relying on some supreme central authority. Classical democracy emphasized these qualities, and they are by no means extinct, despite repeated efforts by contemporary theorists to stress the analogy with behavior in the economic marketplace and to reduce all of democracy's operations to competitive interest maximization. Alexis de Tocqueville best described the importance of independent groups for democracy in his *Democracy in America*, a work which remains a major source of inspiration for all those who persist in viewing democracy as something more than a struggle for election and re-election among competing candidates.[8]

In contemporary political discourse, this phenomenon of cooperation and deliberation via autonomous group activity goes under the rubric of "civil society." The diverse units of social identity and interest, by remaining independent of the state (and perhaps even of parties), not only can restrain the arbitrary actions of rulers, but can also contribute to forming better citizens who are more aware of the preferences of others, more self-confident in their actions, and more civic-minded in their willingness to sacrifice for the common good. At its best, civil society provides an intermediate layer of governance between the individual and the state that is capable of resolving conflicts and controlling the behavior of members without public coercion. Rather than overloading decision makers with increased demands and making the system ungovernable,[9] a viable civil society can mitigate conflicts and improve the quality of citizenship—without relying exclusively on the privatism of the marketplace.

Representatives—whether directly or indirectly elected—do most of the real work in modern democracies. Most are professional politicians who orient their careers around the desire to fill key offices. It is doubtful that any democracy could survive without such people. The central question, therefore, is not whether or not there will be a political elite or even a professional political class, but how these representatives are chosen and then held accountable for their actions.

As noted above, there are many channels of representation in modern democracy. The electoral one, based on territorial constituencies, is the most visible and public. It culminates in a parliament or a presidency that is periodically accountable to the citizenry as a whole. Yet the sheer growth of government (in large part as a byproduct of popular demand) has increased the number, variety, and power of agencies charged with making public decisions and not subject to elections. Around these agencies there has developed a vast apparatus of specialized representation based largely on functional interests, not territorial constituencies. These interest associations, and not political parties, have become the primary expression of civil society in most stable democracies, supplemented by the more sporadic interventions of social movements.

The new and fragile democracies that have sprung up since 1974 must live in "compressed time." They will not resemble the European democracies of the nineteenth and early twentieth centuries, and they cannot expect to acquire the multiple channels of representation in gradual historical progression as did most of their predecessors. A bewildering array of parties, interests, and movements will all simultaneously seek political influence in them, creating challenges to the polity that did not exist in earlier processes of democratization.

PROCEDURES THAT MAKE DEMOCRACY POSSIBLE

The defining components of democracy are necessarily abstract, and may give rise to a considerable variety of institutions and subtypes of democracy. For democracy to thrive, however, specific procedural norms must be followed and civic rights must be respected. Any polity that fails to impose such restrictions upon itself, that fails to follow the "rule of law" with regard to its own procedures, should not be considered democratic. These procedures alone do not define democracy, but their presence is indispensable to its persistence. In essence, they are necessary but not sufficient conditions for its existence.

Robert Dahl has offered the most generally accepted listing of what he terms the "procedural minimal" conditions that must be present for modern political democracy (or as he puts it, "polyarchy") to exist:

1. Control over government decisions about policy is constitutionally vested in elected officials.
2. Elected officials are chosen in frequent and fairly conducted elections in which coercion is comparatively uncommon.
3. Practically all adults have the right to vote in the election of officials.
4. Practically all adults have the right to run for elective offices
5. Citizens have a right to express themselves without the danger of severe punishment on political matters broadly defined....
6. Citizens have a right to seek out alternative sources of information. Moreover, alternative sources of information exist and are protected by law.
7. ... Citizens also have the right to form relatively independent associations or organizations, including independent political parties and interest groups.[10]

These seven conditions seem to capture the essence of procedural democracy for many theorists, but we propose to add two others. The first might be thought of as a further refinement of item (1), while the second might be called an implicit prior condition to all seven of the above.

1. Popularly elected officials must be able to exercise their constitutional powers without being subjected to overriding (albeit informal) opposition from unelected officials. Democracy is in jeopardy if military officers, entrenched civil servants, or state managers retain the capacity to act independently of elected civilians or even veto decisions made by the people's representatives. Without this additional caveat, the militarized polities of contemporary Central America, where civilian control over the military does not exist, might be classified by many scholars as democracies, just as they have been (with the exception of Sandinista Nicaragua) by U.S. policy makers. The caveat thus guards against what we earlier called "electoralism"—the tendency to focus on the holding of elections while ignoring other political realities.
2. The polity must be self-governing; it must be able to act independently of constraints imposed by some other overarching political system. Dahl and other contemporary democratic theorists probably took

this condition for granted since they referred to formally sovereign nation-states. However, with the development of blocs, alliances, spheres of influence, and a variety of "neocolonial" arrangements, the question of autonomy has been a salient one. Is a system really democratic if its elected officials are unable to make binding decisions without the approval of actors outside their territorial domain? This is significant even if the outsiders are relatively free to alter or even end the encompassing arrangement (as in Puerto Rico), but it becomes especially critical if neither condition obtains (as in the Baltic states).

PRINCIPLES THAT MAKE DEMOCRACY FEASIBLE

Lists of component processes and procedural norms help us to specify what democracy is, but they do not tell us much about how it actually functions. The simplest answer is "by the consent of the people"; the more complex one is "by the contingent consent of politicians acting under conditions of bounded uncertainty."

In a democracy, representatives must at least informally agree that those who win greater electoral support or influence over policy will not use their temporary superiority to bar the losers from taking office or exerting influence in the future, and that in exchange for this opportunity to keep competing for power and place, momentary losers will respect the winners' right to make binding decisions. Citizens are expected to obey the decisions ensuing from such a process of competition, provided its outcome remains contingent upon their collective preferences as expressed through fair and regular elections or open and repeated negotiations.

The challenge is not so much to find a set of goals that command widespread consensus as to find a set of rules that embody contingent consent. The precise shape of this "democratic bargain," to use Dahl's expression,[11] can vary a good deal from society to society. It depends on social cleavages and such subjective factors as mutual trust, the standard of fairness, and the willingness to compromise. It may even be compatible with a great deal of dissensus on substantive policy issues.

All democracies involve a degree of uncertainty about who will be elected and what policies they will pursue. Even in those polities where one party persists in winning elections or one policy is consistently implemented, the possibility of change through independent collective action still exists, as in Italy, Japan, and the Scandinavian social democracies. If it does not, the system is not democratic, as in Mexico, Senegal, or Indonesia.

But the uncertainty embedded in the core of all democracies is bounded. Not just any actor can get into the competition and raise any issue he or she pleases—there are previously established rules that must be respected. Not just any policy can be adopted—there are conditions that must be met. Democracy institutionalizes "normal," limited political uncertainty. These boundaries vary from country to country. Constitutional guarantees of property, privacy, expression, and other rights are a part of this, but the most effective boundaries are generated by competition among interest groups and cooperation within civil society. Whatever the rhetoric (and some polities appear to offer their citizens more dramatic alternatives than others), once the rules of contingent consent have been agreed upon, the actual variation is likely to stay within a predictable and generally accepted range.

This emphasis on operative guidelines contrasts with a highly persistent, but misleading theme in recent literature on democracy—namely, the emphasis upon "civic culture." The principles we have suggested here rest on rules of prudence, not on deeply ingrained habits of tolerance, moderation, mutual respect, fair play, readiness to compromise, or trust in public authorities. Waiting for such habits to sink deep and lasting roots implies a very slow process of regime consolidation—one that takes generations—and it would probably condemn most contemporary experiences *ex hypothesi* to failure. Our assertion is that contingent consent and bounded uncertainty can emerge from the interaction between antagonistic and mutually suspicious actors and that the far more benevolent and ingrained norms of a civic culture are better thought of as a *product* and not a producer of democracy.

HOW DEMOCRACIES DIFFER

Several concepts have been deliberately excluded from our generic definition of democracy, despite the fact that they have been frequently associated with it in both everyday practice and scholarly work. They are, nevertheless, especially important when it comes to distinguishing subtypes of democracy. Since no single set of actual institutions, practices, or values embodies democracy, polities moving away from authoritarian rule can mix different components to produce different democracies. It is important to recognize that these do not define points along a single continuum of improving performance, but a matrix of potential combinations that are *differently* democratic.

1. *Consensus*: All citizens may not agree on the substantive goals of political action or on the role of the state (although if they did, it would certainly make governing democracies much easier).
2. *Participation*: All citizens may not take an active and equal part in politics, although it must be legally possible for them to do so.
3. *Access*: Rulers may not weigh equally the preferences of all who come before them, although citizenship implies that individuals and groups should have an equal opportunity to express their preferences if they choose to do so.

4. *Responsiveness*: Rulers may not always follow the course of action preferred by the citizenry. But when they deviate from such a policy, say on grounds of "reason of state" or "overriding national interest," they must ultimately be held accountable for their actions through regular and fair processes.
5. *Majority rule*: Positions may not be allocated or rules may not be decided solely on the basis of assembling the most votes, although deviations from this principle usually must be explicitly defended and previously approved.
6. *Parliamentary sovereignty*: The legislature may not be the only body that can make rules or even the one with final authority in deciding which laws are binding, although where executive, judicial, or other public bodies make that ultimate choice, they too must be accountable for their actions.
7. *Party government*: Rulers may not be nominated, promoted, and disciplined in their activities by well-organized and programmatically coherent political parties, although where they are not, it may prove more difficult to form an effective government.
8. *Pluralism*: The political process may not be based on a multiplicity of overlapping, voluntaristic, and autonomous private groups. However, where there are monopolies of representation, hierarchies of association, and obligatory memberships, it is likely that the interests involved will be more closely linked to the state and the separation between the public and private spheres of action will be much less distinct.
9. *Federalism*: The territorial division of authority may not involve multiple levels and local autonomies, least of all ones enshrined in a constitutional document, although some dispersal of power across territorial and/or functional units is characteristic of all democracies.
10. *Presidentialism*: The chief executive officer may not be a single person and he or she may not be directly elected by the citizenry as a whole, although some concentration of authority is present in all democracies, even if it is exercised collectively and only held indirectly accountable to the electorate.
11. *Checks and Balances*: It is not necessary that the different branches of government be systematically pitted against one another, although governments by assembly, by executive concentrations, by judicial command, or even by dictatorial fiat (as in time of war) must be ultimately accountable to the citizenry as a whole.

While each of the above has been named as an essential component of democracy, they should instead be seen either as indicators of this or that type of democracy, or else as useful standards for evaluating the performance of particular regimes. To include them as part of the generic definition of democracy itself would be to mistake the American polity for the universal model of democratic governance. Indeed, the parliamentary, consociational, unitary, corporatist, and concentrated arrangements of continental Europe may have some unique virtues for guiding polities through the uncertain transition from autocratic to democratic rule.[12]

WHAT DEMOCRACY IS NOT

We have attempted to convey the general meaning of modern democracy without identifying it with some particular set of rules and institutions or restricting it to some specific culture or level of development. We have also argued that it cannot be reduced to the regular holding of elections or equated with a particular notion of the role of the state, but we have not said much more about what democracy is not or about what democracy may not be capable of producing.

There is an understandable temptation to load too many expectations on this concept and to imagine that by attaining democracy, a society will have resolved all of its political, social, economic, administrative, and cultural problems. Unfortunately, "all good things do not necessarily go together."

First, democracies are not necessarily more efficient economically than other forms of government. Their rates of aggregate growth, savings, and investment may be no better than those of nondemocracies. This is especially likely during the transition, when propertied groups and administrative elites may respond to real or imagined threats to the "rights" they enjoyed under authoritarian rule by initiating capital flight, disinvestment, or sabotage. In time, depending upon the type of democracy, benevolent long-term effects upon income distribution, aggregate demand, education, productivity, and creativity may eventually combine to improve economic and social performance, but it is certainly too much to expect that these improvements will occur immediately—much less that they will be defining characteristics of democratization.

Second, democracies are not necessarily more efficient administratively. Their capacity to make decisions may even be slower than that of the regimes they replace, if only because more actors must be consulted. The costs of getting things done may be higher, if only because "payoffs" have to be made to a wider and more resourceful set of clients (although one should never underestimate the degree of corruption to be found within autocracies). Popular satisfaction with the new democratic government's performance may not even seem greater, if only because necessary compromises often please no one completely, and because the losers are free to complain.

Third, democracies are not likely to appear more orderly, consensual, stable, or governable than the autocracies they replace. This is partly a byproduct of democratic freedom of expression, but it is also a reflection of the likelihood of continuing disagreement over new rules and institutions. These products of imposition or compromise are often initially quite ambiguous in nature and uncertain in effect until actors have learned how to use them. What is more, they come in the aftermath of serious struggles motivated by high ideals. Groups and individuals with recently acquired autonomy will test certain rules, protest against the actions of certain institutions, and insist on renegotiating their part of the bargain. Thus the presence of antisystem parties should be neither surprising nor seen as a failure of democratic consolidation. What counts is whether such parties are willing, however reluctantly, to play by the general rules of bounded uncertainty and contingent consent.

Governability is a challenge for all regimes, not just democratic ones. Given the political exhaustion and loss of legitimacy that have befallen autocracies from sultanistic Paraguay to totalitarian Albania, it may seem that only democracies can now be expected to govern effectively and legitimately. Experience has shown, however, that democracies too can lose the ability to govern. Mass publics can become disenchanted with their performance. Even more threatening is the temptation for leaders to fiddle with procedures and ultimately undermine the principles of contingent consent and bounded uncertainty. Perhaps the most critical moment comes once the politicians begin to settle into the more predictable roles and relations of a consolidated democracy. Many will find their expectations frustrated; some will discover that the new rules of competition put them at a disadvantage; a few may even feel that their vital interests are threatened by popular majorities.

Finally, democracies will have more open societies and polities than the autocracies they replace, but not necessarily more open economies. Many of today's most successful and well-established democracies have historically resorted to protectionism and closed borders, and have relied extensively upon public institutions to promote economic development. While the long-term compatibility between democracy and capitalism does not seem to be in doubt, despite their continuous tension, it is not clear whether the promotion of such liberal economic goals as the right of individuals to own property and retain profits, the clearing function of markets, the private settlement of disputes, the freedom to produce without government regulation, or the privatization of state-owned enterprises necessarily furthers the consolidation of democracy. After all, democracies do need to levy taxes and regulate certain transactions, especially where private monopolies and oligopolies exist. Citizens or their representatives may decide that it is desirable to protect the rights of collectivities from encroachment by individuals, especially propertied ones, and they may choose to set aside certain forms of property for public or cooperative ownership. In short, notions of economic liberty that are currently put forward in neoliberal economic models are not synonymous with political freedom—and may even impede it.

Democratization will not necessarily bring in its wake economic growth, social peace, administrative efficiency, political harmony, free markets, or "the end of ideology." Least of all will it bring about "the end of history." No doubt some of these qualities could make the consolidation of democracy easier, but they are neither prerequisites for it nor immediate products of it. Instead, what we should be hoping for is the emergence of political institutions that can peacefully compete to form governments and influence public policy, that can channel social and economic conflicts through regular procedures, and that have sufficient linkages to civil society to represent their constituencies and commit them to collective courses of action. Some types of democracies, especially in developing countries, have been unable to fulfill this promise, perhaps due to the circumstances of their transition from authoritarian rule.[13] The democratic wager is that such a regime, once established, will not only persist by reproducing itself within its initial confining conditions, but will eventually expand beyond them.[14] Unlike authoritarian regimes, democracies have the capacity to modify their rules and institutions consensually in response to changing circumstances. They may not immediately produce all the goods mentioned above, but they stand a better chance of eventually doing so than do autocracies.

Notes

1. For a comparative analysis of the recent regime changes in southern Europe and Latin America, see Guillermo O'Donnell, Philippe C. Schmitter, and Laurence Whitehead, eds., *Transitions from Authoritarian Rule*, 4 vols. (Baltimore: Johns Hopkins University Press, 1986). For another compilation that adopts a more structural approach see Larry Diamond, Juan Linz, and Seymour Martin Lipset, eds., *Democracy in Developing Countries*, vols. 2, 3, and 4 (Boulder, Colo.: Lynne Rienner, 1989).

2. Numerous attempts have been made to codify and quantify the existence of democracy across political systems. The best known is probably Freedom House's *Freedom in the World: Political Rights and Civil Liberties*, published since 1973 by Greenwood Press and since 1988 by University Press of America. Also see Charles Humana, *World Human Rights Guide* (New York: Facts on File, 1986).

3. The definition most commonly used by American social scientists is that of Joseph Schumpeter: "that institutional arrangement for arriving at political decisions in which individuals acquire the power to decide by means of a competitive struggle for the people's vote." *Capitalism, Socialism, and Democracy* (London: George Allen and Unwin, 1943), 269. We accept certain aspects of the classical procedural approach to modern democracy, but differ prima-

rily in our emphasis on the accountability of rulers to citizens and the relevance of mechanisms of competition other than elections.

4. Not only do some countries practice a stable form of democracy without a formal constitution (e.g., Great Britain and Israel), but even more countries have constitutions and legal codes that offer no guarantee of reliable practice. On paper, Stalin's 1936 constitution for the USSR was a virtual model of democratic rights and entitlements.

5. For the most valiant attempt to make some sense out of this thicket of distinctions, see Juan Linz, "Totalitarian and Authoritarian Regimes" in *Handbook of Political Science*, eds. Fred I. Greenstein and Nelson W. Polsby (Reading Mass.: Addison Wesley, 1975), 175–411.

6. "Publius" (Alexander Hamilton, John Jay, and James Madison), *The Federalist Papers* (New York: Anchor Books, 1961). The quote is from Number 10.

7. See Terry Karl, "Imposing Consent? Electoralism versus Democratization in El Salvador," in *Elections and Democratization in Latin America, 1980–1985*, eds. Paul Drake and Eduardo Silva (San Diego: Center for Iberian and Latin American Studies, Center for US/Mexican Studies, University of California, San Diego, 1986), 9–36.

8. Alexis de Tocqueville, *Democracy in America*, 2 vols. (New York: Vintage Books, 1945).

9. This fear of overloaded government and the imminent collapse of democracy is well reflected in the work of Samuel P. Huntington during the 1970s. See especially Michel Crozier, Samuel P. Huntington, and Joji Watanuki, *The Crisis of Democracy* (New York: New York University Press, 1975). For Huntington's (revised) thoughts about the prospects for democracy, see his "Will More Countries Become Democratic?," *Political Science Quarterly* 99 (Summer 1984): 193–218.

10. Robert Dahl, *Dilemmas of Pluralist Democracy* (New Haven: Yale University Press, 1982), 11.

11. Robert Dahl, *After the Revolution: Authority in a Good Society* (New Haven: Yale University Press, 1970).

12. See Juan Linz, "The Perils of Presidentialism," *Journal of Democracy* 1 (Winter 1990): 51–69, and the ensuing discussion by Donald Horowitz, Seymour Martin Lipset, and Juan Linz in *Journal of Democracy* 1 (Fall 1990): 73–91.

13. Terry Lynn Karl, "Dilemmas of Democratization in Latin America" *Comparative Politics* 23 (October 1990): 1–23.

14. Otto Kirchheimer, "Confining Conditions and Revolutionary Breakthroughs," *American Political Science Review* 59 (1965): 964–974.

Philippe C. Schmitter *is professor of political science and director of the Center for European Studies at Stanford University.* **Terry Lynn Karl** *is associate professor of political science and director of the Center for Latin American Studies at the same institution. The original, longer version of this essay was written at the request of the United States Agency for International Development, which is not responsible for its content.*

From *Journal of Democracy*, Summer 1991, p. 19. © 1991 by the National Endowment for Democracy and the Johns Hopkins University Press. Reprinted by permission.

Judicial Review:
The gavel and the robe

Established and emerging democracies display a puzzling taste in common: both have handed increasing amounts of power to unelected judges. Th[is] article examines the remarkable growth and many different forms of judicial review.

To SOME they are unaccountable elitists, old men (and the rare women) in robes who meddle in politics where they do not belong, thwarting the will of the people. To others they are bulwarks of liberty, champions of the individual against abuses of power by scheming politicians, arrogant bureaucrats and the emotional excesses of transient majorities.

Judges who sit on supreme courts must get used to the vilification as well as the praise. They often deal with the most contentious cases, involving issues which divide the electorate or concern the very rules by which their countries are governed. With so much at stake, losers are bound to question not only judges' particular decisions, but their right to decide at all. This is especially true when judges knock down as unconstitutional a law passed by a democratically elected legislature. How dare they?

Despite continued attacks on the legitimacy of judicial review, it has flourished in the past 50 years. All established democracies now have it in some form, and the standing of constitutional courts has grown almost everywhere. In an age when all political authority is supposed to derive from voters, and every passing mood of the electorate is measured by pollsters, the growing power of judges is a startling development.

The trend in western democracies has been followed by the new democracies of Eastern Europe with enthusiasm. Hungary's constitutional court may be the most active and powerful in the world. There have been failures. After a promising start, Russia's constitutional court was crushed in the conflict between Boris Yeltsin and his parliament. But in some countries where governments have long been riven by ideological divisions or crippled by corruption, such as Israel and India, constitutional courts have filled a political vacuum, coming to embody the legitimacy of the state.

In western democracies the growing role of constitutional review, in which judges rule on the constitutionality of laws and regulations, has been accompanied by a similar growth in what is known as administrative review, in which judges rule on the legality of government actions, usually those of the executive branch. This second type of review has also dragged judges into the political arena, frequently pitting them against elected politicians in controversial cases. But it is less problematic for democratic theorists than constitutional review for a number of reasons.

Democracy's referees

The expansion of the modern state has seemed to make administrative review inevitable. The reach of government, for good or ill, now extends into every nook and cranny of life. As a result, individuals, groups and businesses all have more reason than ever before to challenge the legality of government decisions or the interpretation of laws. Such challenges naturally end up before the courts.

In France, Germany, Italy and most other European countries, special administrative tribunals, with their own hierarchies of appeal courts, have been established to handle such cases. In the United States, Britain, Canada and Australia, the ordinary courts, which handle criminal cases and private lawsuits, also deal with administrative law cases.

The growth of administrative review can be explained as a reaction to the growth of state power. But the parallel expansion of constitutional review is all the more remarkable in a democratic age because it was resisted for so long in the very name of democracy.

The idea was pioneered by the United States, the first modern democracy with a written constitution. In fact, the American constitution nowhere explicitly gives the Supreme Court the power to rule laws invalid because of their unconstitutionality. The court's right to do this was first asserted in *Marbury v Madison*, an 1803 case, and then quickly became accepted as proper. One reason for such ready acceptance may have been that a Supreme Court veto fitted so well with the whole design and spirit of the constitution itself, whose purpose was as much to control the excesses of popular majorities as to give the people a voice in government decision-making.

In Europe this was the reason why the American precedent was not followed. As the voting franchise was expanded, the will of the voting majority became ever more sacrosanct, at least in theory. Parliamentary sovereignty reigned supreme. European democrats viewed the American experiment with constitutionalism as an unwarranted restraint on the popular will.

Even in the United States, judicial review was of little importance until the late 19th century, when the Supreme Court became more active, first nullifying laws passed after the civil war to give former slaves equal rights and then overturning laws regulating economic activity in the name of contractual and property rights.

After a showdown with Franklin Roosevelt over the New Deal, which the court lost, it abandoned its defence of laissez-faire economics. In the 1950s under Chief Justice Earl Warren it embarked on the active protection and expansion of civil rights. Controversially, this plunged the court into the mainstream of American politics, a position it retains today despite a retreat from Warren-style activism over the past two decades.

Attitudes towards judicial review also changed in Europe. The rise of fascism in the 1920s and 1930s, and then the destruction wrought by the second world war, made many European democrats reconsider the usefulness of judges. Elections alone no longer seemed a reliable obstacle to the rise of dangerously authoritarian governments. Fascist dictators had seized power by manipulating representative institutions.

The violence and oppression of the pre-war and war years also convinced many that individual rights and civil liberties needed special protection. The tyranny of the executive branch of government, acting in the name of the majority, became a real concern. (Britain remained an exception to this trend, sticking exclusively to the doctrine of parliamentary sovereignty. It is only now taking its first tentative steps towards establishing a constitutional court.)

While the goals of constitutional judicial review are similar almost everywhere, its form varies from country to country, reflecting national traditions. Some of the key differences:

• **Appointments.** The most famous method of appointment is that of the United States, largely because of a handful of televised and acrimonious confir-

mation hearings. The president appoints a Supreme Court judge, subject to Senate approval, whenever one of the court's nine seats falls vacant. Political horse-trading, and conflict, are part of the system. Judges are appointed for life, though very few cling to office to the end.

Other countries may appoint their constitutional judges with more decorum, but politics always plays some part in the process. France is the most explicitly political. The directly elected president and the heads of the Senate and the National Assembly each appoint three of the judges of the Constitutional Council, who serve non-renewable nine-year terms, one-third of them retiring every three years. Former presidents are awarded life membership on the council, although none has yet chosen to take his seat.

Half of the 16 members of Germany's Federal Constitutional Tribunal are chosen by the Bundestag, the lower house of parliament, and half by the Bundesrat, the upper house. Appointments are usually brokered between the two major parties. The procedure is similar in Italy, where one-third of the 15-strong Constitutional Court is chosen by the head of state, one-third by the two houses of parliament and one-third by the professional judiciary.

Senior politicians—both before and after serving in other government posts—have sat on all three constitutional courts, sometimes with unhappy results. In March Roland Dumas, the president of France's Constitutional Council, was forced to step down temporarily because of allegations of corruption during his earlier tenure as foreign minister. The trend in all three countries is towards the appointment of professional judges and legal scholars rather than politicians.

• **Powers.** Most constitutional courts have the power to nullify laws as unconstitutional, but how they do this, and receive cases, varies. Once again, the most anomalous is France's Constitutional Council which rules on the constitutionality of laws only before they go into effect and not, like all other courts, after.

The 1958 constitution of France's Fifth Republic allowed only four authorities to refer cases to the council: the president, the prime minister, and the heads of the two houses of parliament. In 1974, a constitutional amendment authorised 60 deputies or senators to lodge appeals with the council as well. Since then, the council has become more active, and most appeals now come from

groups of legislators. Individuals have no right to appeal to the council.

French jurists argue that judicial review before a law goes into effect is simpler and faster than review after a law's promulgation. But it is also more explicitly political, and leaves no room for making a judgment in the light of a law's sometimes unanticipated effect.

No other major country has adopted prior review exclusively, but it is an option in Germany and Italy as well, usually at the request of the national or one of the regional governments. However, most of the work of the constitutional courts in both countries comes from genuine legal disputes, which are referred to them by other courts when a constitutional question is raised.

The Supreme Courts of the United States, Canada and Australia, by contrast, are the final courts of appeal for all cases, not just those dealing with constitutional issues. The United States Supreme Court does not give advisory or abstract opinions about the constitutionality of laws, but only deals with cases involving specific disputes. Moreover, lower courts in the United States can also rule on constitutional issues, although most important cases are appealed eventually to the Supreme Court.

Canada's Supreme Court can be barred from ruling a law unconstitutional if either the national or a provincial legislature has passed it with a special clause declaring that it should survive judicial review "notwithstanding" any breach of the country's Charter of Rights. If passed in this way, the law must be renewed every five years. In practice, this device has rarely been used.

• **Judgments.** The French and Italian constitutional courts deliver their judgments unanimously, without dissents. Germany abandoned this method in 1971, adopting the more transparent approach of the common-law supreme courts, which allow a tally of votes cast and dissenting opinions to be published alongside the court's judgment. Advocates of unanimity argue that it reinforces the court's authority and gives finality to the law. Opponents deride it as artificial, and claim that publishing dissents improves the technical quality of judgments, keeps the public better informed, and makes it easier for the law to evolve in the light of changing circumstances.

Also noteworthy is the growth in Europe of supra-national judicial review. The European Court of Justice in Luxembourg is the ultimate legal authority for the European Union. The court's primary task is to interpret the treaties upon which the EU is founded. Because EU law now takes precedence over national law in the 15 member states, the court's influence has grown considerably in recent years. The European Court of Human Rights in Strasbourg, the judicial arm of the 41-member Council of Europe, has, in effect, become the final court of appeal on human-rights issues for most of Europe. The judgments of both European courts carry great weight and have forced many countries to change their laws.

Despite the rapid growth of judicial review in recent decades, it still has plenty of critics. Like all institutions, supreme courts make mistakes, and their decisions are a proper topic of political debate. But some criticisms aimed at them are misconceived.

Unelected legislators?

To criticise constitutional courts as political meddlers is to misunderstand their role, which is both judicial and political. If constitutions are to play any part in limiting government, then someone must decide when they have been breached and how they should be applied, especially when the relative powers of various branches or levels of government—a frequent issue in federal systems—are in question. When a court interprets a constitution, its decisions are political by definition—though they should not be party political.

Supreme courts also are not unaccountable, as some of their critics claim. Judges can be overruled by constitutional amendment, although this is rare. They must also justify their rulings to the public in written opinions. These are pored over by the media, lawyers, legal scholars and other judges. If unpersuasive, judgments are sometimes evaded by lower courts or legislatures, and the issue eventually returns to the constitutional court to be considered again.

Moreover, the appointment of judges is a political process, and the complexions of courts change as their membership changes, although appointees are sometimes unpredictable once on the bench. Nevertheless, new appointments can result in the reversal of earlier decisions which failed to win public support.

Constitutional courts have no direct power of their own. This is why Alexander Hamilton, who helped write America's constitution, called the judiciary "the least dangerous branch of government." Courts have no vast bureaucracy, revenue-raising ability, army or police force at their command—no way, in fact, to enforce their rulings. If other branches of government ignore them, they can do nothing. Their power and legitimacy, especially when they oppose the executive or legislature, depend largely on their moral authority and credibility.

Senior judges are acutely aware of their courts' limitations. Most tread warily, preferring to mould the law through interpretation of statutes rather than employing the crude instrument of complete nullification. Even the American Supreme Court, among the world's most activist, has ruled only sections of some 135 federal laws unconstitutional in 210 years, although it has struck down many more state laws.

Finally, it is worth remembering that judges are not the only public officials who exercise large amounts of power but do not answer directly to voters. Full-time officials and appointees actually perform most government business, and many of them have enormous discretion about how they do this. Even elected legislators and prime ministers are not perfect transmitters of the popular will, but enjoy great latitude when making decisions on any particular issue. Constitutional courts exist to ensure that everyone stays within the rules. Judges have the delicate, sometimes impossible, task of checking others' power without seeming to claim too much for themselves.

Referendums:
The people's voice

Is the growing use of referendums a threat to democracy or its salvation? The fifth article in our series on changes in mature democracies examines the experience so far, and the arguments for and against letting voters decide political questions directly.

WHEN Winston Churchill proposed a referendum to Clement Attlee in 1945 on whether Britain's wartime coalition should be extended, Attlee growled that the idea was an "instrument of Nazism and fascism". The use by Hitler and Mussolini of bogus referendums to consolidate their power had confirmed the worst fears of sceptics. The most democratic of devices seemed also to be the most dangerous to democracy itself.

Dictators of all stripes have continued to use phony referendums to justify their hold on power. And yet this fact has not stopped a steady growth in the use of genuine referendums, held under free and fair conditions, by both established and aspiring democracies. Referendums have been instrumental in the dismantling of communism and the transition to democracy in countries throughout the former soviet empire. They have also successfully eased democratic transitions in Spain, Greece, South Africa, Brazil and Chile, among other countries.

In most established democracies, direct appeals to voters are now part of the machinery for constitutional change. Their use to resolve the most intractable or divisive public issues has also grown. In the 17 major democracies of Western Europe, only three—Belgium, the Netherlands and Norway—make no provision for referendums in their constitution. Only six major democracies—the Netherlands, the United States, Japan, India, Israel and the Federal Republic of Germany—have never held a nationwide referendum.

The volatile voter

Frustrated voters in Italy and New Zealand have in recent years used referendums to force radical changes to voting systems and other political institutions on a reluctant political elite. Referendums have also been used regularly in Australia, where voters go to the polls this November to decide whether to cut their country's formal link with the British crown. In Switzerland and several American states, referendums are a central feature of the political system, rivalling legislatures in significance.

Outside the United States and Switzerland, referendums are most often called by governments only when they are certain of victory, and to win endorsement of a policy they intend to implement in any case. This is how they are currently being used in Britain by Tony Blair's government.

But voters do not always behave as predicted, and they have delivered some notable rebuffs. Charles de Gaulle skil-

fully used referendums to establish the legitimacy of France's Fifth Republic and to expand his own powers as president, but then felt compelled to resign in 1969 after an unexpected referendum defeat.

Francois Mitterrand's decision to call a referendum on the Maastricht treaty in 1992 brought the European Union to the brink of breakdown when only 51% of those voting backed the treaty. Denmark's voters rejected the same treaty, despite the fact that it was supported by four out of five members of the Danish parliament. The Danish government was able to sign the treaty only after renegotiating its terms and narrowly winning a second referendum. That same year, Canada's government was not so lucky. Canadian voters unexpectedly rejected a painstakingly negotiated constitutional accord designed to placate Quebec.

Referendums come in many different forms. **Advisory referendums** test public opinion on an important issue. Governments or legislators then translate their results into new laws or policies as they see fit. Although advisory referendums can carry great weight in the right circumstances, they are sometimes ignored by politicians. In a 1955 Swedish referendum, 85% of those voting said they wanted to continue driving on the left side of the road. Only 12 years later the government went ahead and made the switch to driving on the right without a second referendum, or much protest.

By contrast, **mandatory referendums** are part of a law-making process or, more commonly, one of the procedures for constitutional amendment.

Both advisory and mandatory referendums can usually be called only by those in office—sometimes by the president, sometimes by parliamentarians, most often by the government of the day. But in a few countries, petitions by voters themselves can put a referendum on the ballot. These are known as **initiatives**. Sometimes these can only repeal an already existing law—so-called "abrogative" initiatives such as those in Italy. Elsewhere, initiatives can also be used to propose and pass new legislation, as in Switzerland and many American states. In this form they can be powerful and unpredictable political tools.

The rules for conducting and winning referendums also vary greatly from country to country. Regulations on the drafting of ballot papers and the financing of Yes and No campaigns are different everywhere, and these exert a great influence over how referendums are used, and how often.

The hurdle required for victory can be a critical feature. A simple majority of those voting is the usual rule. But a low turnout can make such victories seem illegitimate. So a percentage of eligible voters, as well as a majority of those voting, is sometimes required to approve a proposal.

Such hurdles, of course, also make failure more likely. In 1978 Britain's government was forced to abandon plans to set up a Scottish parliament when a referendum victory in Scotland failed to clear a 40% hurdle of eligible voters. Referendums have also failed in Denmark and Italy (most recently in April) because of similar voter-turnout requirements. To ensure a wide geographic consensus, Switzerland and Australia require a "double majority", of individual voters and of cantons or states, for constitutional amendments.

The use of referendums reflects the history and traditions of individual countries. Thus generalising about them is difficult. In some countries referendums have played a central, though peripatetic, role. In others they have been marginal or even irrelevant, despite provisions for their use.

Hot potatoes

Although referendums (outside Switzerland and the United States) have been most often used to legitimise constitutional change or the redrawing of boundaries, elected politicians have also found them useful for referring to voters those issues they find too hot to handle or which cut across party lines. Often these concern moral or lifestyle choices, such as alcohol prohibition, divorce or abortion. The outcome on such emotive topics can be difficult to predict. In divorce and abortion referendums, for example, Italians have shown themselves more liberal, and the Irish more conservative, than expected.

One of the best single books on referendums—"Referendums Around the World" edited by David Butler and Austin Ranney, published by Macmillan—argues that many assumptions about them are mistaken. They are not usually habit-forming, as those opposed to them claim. Many countries have used them to settle a specific issue, or even engaged in a series of them, and then turned away from referendums for long periods. But this is mostly because politicians decide whether referendums will be held. Where groups of voters can also put initiatives on the ballot, as in Switzerland and the United States, they have become addictive and their use has grown in recent years.

Messrs Butler and Ranney also point out that referendums are not usually vehicles for radical change, as is widely believed. Although they were used in this way in Italy and New Zealand, referendums have more often been used to support the status quo or to endorse changes already agreed by political parties. Most referendums, even those initiated by voters, fail. In Australia, 34 of 42 proposals to amend the constitution have been rejected by voters. According to an analysis by David Magleby, a professor at Brigham Young University in Utah, 62% of the 1,732 initiatives which reached the ballot in American states between 1898 and 1992 were rejected.

Arguments for and against referendums go to the heart of what is meant by democracy. Proponents of referendums maintain that consulting citizens directly is the only truly democratic way to determine policy. If popular sovereignty is really to mean anything, voters must have the right to set the agenda, discuss the issues and then themselves directly make the final decisions. Delegating these tasks to elected politicians, who have interests of their own, inevitably distorts the wishes of voters.

Referendums, their advocates say, can discipline representatives, and put the stamp of legitimacy on the most important political questions of the day. They also encourage participation by citizens in the governing of their own societies, and political participation is the source of most other civic virtues.

The case against

Those sceptical of referendums agree that popular sovereignty, majority rule and consulting voters are the basic building blocks of democracy, but believe that representative democracy achieves these goals much better than referendums. Genuine direct democracy, they say, is feasible only for political groups so small that all citizens can meet face-to-face—a small town perhaps. In large, modern societies, the full participation of every citizen is impossible.

Referendum opponents maintain that representatives, as full-time decision-makers, can weigh conflicting priorities, negotiate compromises among different groups and make well-informed decisions. Citizens voting in single-issue referendums have difficulty in doing any of these things. And as the bluntest of majoritarian devices, referendums encourage voters to brush aside the concerns of minority groups. Finally, the frequent use of referendums can actually undermine democracy by encouraging elected legislators to sidestep difficult issues, thus damaging the prestige and authority of representative institutions, which must continue to perform most of the business of government even if referendums are used frequently.

Testing any of these claims or counter-claims is difficult. Most countries do not, in fact, use referendums regularly enough to bear out either the hopes of proponents or the fears of opponents. The two exceptions are Switzerland and some American states, where citizen initiatives are frequent enough to draw tentative conclusions on some of these points, although both examples fall far short of full-fledged direct democracy.

Voters in both countries seem to believe that referendums do, in fact, lend legitimacy to important decisions. The Swiss are unlikely now to make a big national decision without a referendum.

Swiss voters have rejected both UN membership and links with the EU in referendums, against the advice of their political leaders. Similarly, American polls show healthy majorities favouring referendums and believing that they are more likely to produce policies that most people want. Polls also show support for the introduction of referendums on the national level.

The claim that referendums increase citizen participation is more problematic. Some referendum campaigns ignite enormous public interest and media attention. Initiatives also give political outsiders a way to influence the public agenda. But in the United States, much of the activity involved in getting initiatives on the ballot, such as collecting signatures, has been taken over by professional firms, and many referendum campaigns have become slick, expensive affairs far removed from the grassroots (so far, this is much less true in Switzerland). Even more surprising, voter participation in American referendums is well below that of candidate elections, even when these are held at the same time. The average turnout for Swiss referendums has fallen by a third in the past 50 years to about 40%. On big issues, however, turnout can still soar.

Many of the fears of those opposed to referendums have not been realised in either country. Initiatives have not usually been used to oppress minorities. A proposal to limit the number of foreigners allowed to live in Switzerland was rejected by two-thirds of voters in 1988. In 1992 Colorado's voters did approve an initiative overturning local ordinances protecting gays from discrimination, but more extreme anti-gay initiatives in Colorado and California have been defeated by large majorities. Since 1990 voters have consistently upheld certain abortion rights in initiative ballots. Minorities and immigrants have been the targets of initiatives in some states, but voters have generally rejected extreme measures and have often proven themselves no more illiberal than legislators. Most initiatives are, in fact, about tax and economic questions, not civil liberties or social issues, although the latter often gain more attention.

While the frequent use of initiatives has not destroyed representative government, as some feared, it has changed it. Party loyalty among Swiss voters is strong at general elections, but evaporates when it comes to referendum voting. Initiatives, and the threat of mounting one, have become an integral part of the legislative process in Switzerland, as they have in California, Oregon and the other American states where they are most used. Referendums now often set the political agenda in both countries. In the United States they are frequently seen, rightly or wrongly, as a barometer of the national mood. And they can occasionally spark a political revolution. California's Proposition 13, for example, a 1978 initiative lowering local property taxes, set off a tax revolt across America. Elected officials themselves are often active in launching initiatives, and relatively successful in getting their proposals approved, which hardly indicates that voters have lost all faith in their politicians. Initiatives have made legislating more complicated, but also more responsive to the public's concerns.

There is some evidence that American voters, at least, are sometimes overwhelmed by the volume of information coming their way, and cast their vote in ignorance, as critics contend. Mr Magleby cites studies showing that on several ballots, 10–20% of the electorate mistakenly cast their vote the wrong way. Ballot material dropping through the letterboxes of residents in California is now often more than 200 pages long. According to one poll, only one in five Californians believes that the average voter understands most of the propositions put before him. Quite rationally, this has also bred caution. Californians approve only one-third of initiatives.

Hybrid democracy?

The Swiss and American experience suggests that in the future there is unlikely to be a headlong rush away from representative to direct democracy anywhere, but that, even so, the use of referendums is likely to grow. The Internet and other technological advances have not yet had much impact on referendums, but they should eventually make it easier to hold them, and to inform voters of the issues they are being asked to decide upon.

Representative institutions are likely to survive because of the sheer volume of legislation in modern societies, and the need for full-time officials to run the extensive machinery of government. Nevertheless in an age of mass communication and information, confining the powers of citizens to voting in elections every few years seems a crude approach, a throwback to an earlier era. In a political system based on popular sovereignty, it will become increasingly difficult to justify a failure to consult the voters directly on a wider range of issues.

The great divide

BY TIMOTHY GARTON ASH

*Robert Kagan's celebrated analysis of the widening Atlantic—in which he claims
that Europe favours peace and negotiation simply out of weakness—is half right.
But, as the split over Iraq shows, Europe is a diverse place and wields power
in other ways. Vulgar Kaganism is exacerbating division*

ANTI-AMERICANISM HAS reached a fevered intensity," Robert Kagan reported from Europe recently in the *Washington Post.* "In London . . . one finds Britain's finest minds propounding, in sophisticated language and melodious Oxbridge accents, the conspiracy theories of Pat Buchanan concerning the 'neoconservative' (read: Jewish) hijacking of US foreign policy. Britain's most gifted scholars sift through American writings about Europe searching for signs of derogatory 'sexual imagery.'"

The last sentence must be a reference to a recent essay I wrote in the *New York Review Books.* Well, thanks for the compliment but no thanks for the implication. If I'm anti-American, then Robert Kagan is a Belgian. Since he and I have never met or conversed in accents melodious or otherwise, I take it that the earlier sentence cannot refer to me; but whoever it does refer to, its innuendo is even more disturbing. That two-word parenthesis "'neoconservative' (read: Jewish)" can only be taken to imply that this criticism of "neoconservative" views has, at the least, antisemitic overtones. That is a serious charge, which should be substantiated or withdrawn. It illustrates once again how American reports of European anti-Americanism get mixed up with claims, impossible to prove or refute, of antisemitic motivation. I am disturbed to find a writer as sophisticated and knowledgeable as Robert Kagan using such innuendo.

So far as "sexual imagery" is concerned, Kagan seems to have taken offence at a passage in which, discussing the mutual stereotypes of America vs Europe (bullying cowboys vs limp-wristed pansies) I refer to his now famous sentence "Americans are from Mars and Europeans are from Venus," as in "*men* are from Mars and *women* are from Venus." Or perhaps he was irked to find his work discussed under the headline "Anti-Europeanism in America."

So let us start with a necessary clarification: Robert Kagan is no more anti-European than I am anti-American. In his brilliant *Policy Review* article (reprinted in last August's *Prospect*), now expanded into a small book, *Paradise and Power* (Atlantic Books), he gives one of the most penetrating and influential accounts of European-American relations in recent years. It is not yet quite in the Fukuyama *End of History* and Huntington *Clash of Civilisations* class for impact—both of them journal articles later turned into books—but it is heading that way. One reason it has had such an impact is his talent for bold generalisation and provocative overstatement.

"It is time to stop pretending," both article and book begin, "that Europeans and Americans share a common view of the world, or *even that they occupy the same world*" (my italics). He goes on to draw what he admits is a "dual caricature" of Europeans—Venusian, believing in a Kantian "self-contained world of laws and rules and transnational negotiation and cooperation"—and Americans—Martian and martial, knowing that decisive national use of military power is needed in the Hobbesian world beyond Europe's cute little US-protected postmodern paradise. "The reasons for the transatlantic divide," he writes, "are deep, long in development, and likely to endure." The current transatlantic controversy over Iraq, to which more reference is now made in the book, is seen to be representative, even archetypical.

Kagan gives three reasons for this divergence. The main one, to which he returns repeatedly, is European weakness and American power. (The original article was called "Power and Weakness.") By this he means military weakness and military power. Pointing to the growing gulf between US and European military spending and capacity, he argues that when you are weak you tend to favour law, peace, negotiation, and not to see the need for the use of force: "when you don't have a hammer, you don't want anything to look like a nail." Not even Saddam's Iraq. In a vivid simile, he writes that a man walking through a forest armed just with a knife will have a different response to a prowling bear than a man armed with a rifle.

His second reason is that history has led Europeans to a different ideology. Humbled and shocked by our bloody past, we place a higher premium on peace as a value in itself. We aspire, with Immanuel Kant, to a world of perpetual peace. We would like others to imitate our European model of integration. We would rather not hear the growls from the jungle outside. There is a certain tension between these two explanations: do Europeans dislike war because they do not have enough guns, or do they not have enough guns because they dislike war? Kagan favours the former, philosophically materialist view: being determines consciousness. But he also allows for an influence the other way round. Finally, he attributes some of these differences to the fact that, since the end of the cold war, Europeans have sought to define "Europe" as something apart from America, rather than seeking a common definition of "the west."

This is a clever, knowledgeable argument, and there is quite a lot in it. Kagan is right to pour scorn on European pretensions to be a world power, without the military clout or—he might have emphasised this more—the foreign policy unity to deliver. He quotes the Belgian foreign minister saying in December 2001 that the ED military force "should declare itself operational without such a declaration being based on any true capability." I would like to know where this quotation came from—unlike most of the direct quotations in the book version, it is not sourced—but if true, it is classic. We have not advanced very far in the ten years since the Luxembourger Jacques Poos pronounced, over disintegrating Bosnia, his equally ridiculous "the hour of Europe has come."

Kagan is also right to remind us how far the "European miracle" that began with Franco-German reconciliation actually depended on the external American pacifier. Even today, he suggests, the US is "manning the walls of Europe's postmodern order." So Europeans are, in Kipling's famous phrase, making mock of uniforms that guard us while we sleep.

His remedy, so far as he has one, is twofold. First, Europe should stop being a "military pygmy"—in the phrase of George Robertson, Nato secretary-general. This means all of us, and Germany in particular, spending more on defence and getting our militaries together. Second, we should follow Robert Cooper's advice and recognise that, beyond our postmodern world of the EU, there is a modern and a pre-modern world outside. We may be Kantian in our village, but we must be Hobbesian in the jungle around. Saddam Hussein lives by the law of the jungle, so we must threaten him with spears. The two parts of the remedy are connected. Like the man in the forest, once you have a rifle you may start hunting the bear—and if you want to hunt the bear, you will go get a rifle.

There are, however, major problems with the Kagan thesis. One is this: if Europe does not exist as a single, foreign policy actor, then how can you generalise about it? Belgium and Luxembourg are certainly not Martian or martial in Kagan's terms, but Britain and France are. As he acknowledges in two slightly embarrassed asides, it was Blair's Britain that pushed, against the resistance of Clinton's America, for ground troops in Kosovo. This at a time when the martial Americans were still bombing from 15,000 feet in case one of their warrior pilots got his little finger burnt. For three decades, from the end of the Vietnam war to 11th September, Britain and France were more ready to take military casualties abroad than the US was.

Moreover, the controversy over the Iraq war has shown that there is no simple divide between "Europe" and "America." American public opinion is torn and Europeans are divided. Kagan's commentary in the *Washington Post* was occasioned by the publication of an article by a European "gang of eight" reaffirming transatlantic solidarity against Saddam, as a rebuke to the Franco-German axis. The "gang of eight" included the prime ministers of Britain, Spain, Italy and Poland—that is, Europe's four most important countries after France and Germany—as well as Václav Havel, then still president of the Czech Republic and one of Europe's greatest moral authorities, and the leaders of Portugal, Denmark and Hungary. (Slovakia subsequently joined, to make it nine.) In his commentary, Kagan welcomed the "political and moral courage" of these leaders of what Donald Rumsfeld called "new Europe" as they paid tribute to "American bravery and farsightedness," against the fevered trend of European anti-Americanism. But he might also have written: "whoops, how does this fit my thesis? If Europe's so thoroughly Venusian, as I argue, how come so much of it is cheering for Mars?"

If I wished to be polemical, I would say: where has Kagan been living all these years? The answer, as I understand it, is Brussels—or between Brussels and Washington. And that may be part of the problem. Sitting in Brussels, listening to so much lofty Eurorhetoric matched by so few effective military or diplomatic deeds, one could easily feel as he does. But in the larger EU of 25 member states from 2004—an enlargement that scarcely features in his account the balance of attitudes will be different. Yes, there is a lot of anti-Americanism about, especially in France, Germany, Luxembourg, Belgium. There is also a lot of reasonable, measured scepticism about Bush's policy on Iraq. And then there is a large constituency of the Americanised and the Atlanticist, especially in the new democracies of central and eastern Europe.

In short, Europe's true hallmark is not weakness but *diversity*. It is the sheer diversity of states, nations and views, as much as the popular reluctance to spend on defence, and more than any programmatic Kantianism, that is the main reason for Europe's feebleness in foreign and security policy. If we could just pool and redirect what we what we already spend on defence, we'd have a formidable European expeditionary force to send to Iraq, or wherever. But we won't, because the French will be French, the British will be British and Belgians will be Belgian.

Kagan stresses military power where Europe is weak and ignores economic and cultural power where it is strong

Another problem with Kagan's book is his emphasis on military power, to the neglect of the two other main dimensions of power: economic and cultural social ("soft power"). He is right to remind Europeans that old-fashioned military power still counts—the postmodern continent is not living in a postmodern world. But he discounts Europe's other forms of power. On a recent trip to the US, I found that what most people are most worried about is not the war on Iraq—it is the state of the US economy. To be sure, there is a two-way interdependence here—Europe cannot be economically strong while America is economically weak, and vice versa—while in the military dimension there is a one-way dependence of Europe on the US. And yes, welfarist complacency, national differences, over-regulation, corporatism, ageing populations and our moral incompetence over immigration are all potential sources of European economic weakness. But the advent of the "Slavonic tigers" will give Europe a shot in the arm. The European economy is already roughly the same size as that of the US. Europe is also growing in a way that America cannot. Its "soft power" is demonstrated by the fact that not only millions of individuals but also whole states want to enter it. Turkey, for example.

Mention of Turkey raises a further difficulty with the Kagan argument: where does the Kantian world end and the Hobbesian begin? Turkey shares a border with Iraq. The frontier runs through the lands of the Kurds, the would-be Kurdistan. Turkey and Iraq have both been hammering their Kurds, on and off, for some time. But the US is urging the EU to take in Turkey, to encourage its adherence to the west by the European process of "conditionality leading finally to accession," while at the same time urging us to join in a war against Saddam. We are being asked to be Kantian-European-postmodern here, but HobbesianAmerican-pre-modern just a hundred yards across the border. In truth, we need to be both—especially if the democratic reconstruction of postwar Iraq is to succeed. In a now familiar quip: America does the cooking, Europe does the washing-up.

Kagan himself concludes in conciliatory fashion. Unlike his compatriot, Charles A Kupchan, he insists that there is no "clash of civilisations" between Europe and America. Europe should beef up its military and use it a bit more roughly in the jungle, and America, he avers on his last page, should manifest a bit more of what the founding fathers called "a decent respect for the opinion decent respect for the opinion of mankind." America needs Europe, Europe needs America, we both share common western values. I agree. His book is a challenge to make it so, to Europeans especially. But this is not what he said on his first page, which is that Europeans and Americans do not *even occupy the same world*. And that, not his conciliatory conclusion, is what he is being so much quoted for. That, in wider circulation, is "the Kagan thesis."

Of course this is what tends to happen with these "big issue" think pieces turned into books. As once upon a time we had vulgar Marxism, so we now have vulgar Fukuyamaism, vulgar Huntingtonism, and will soon have vulgar Kaganism. Francis Fukuyama can go on insisting until he is purple in the face that what he meant was History not history; people will still snort "well, the end of history, my foot!" Yet usually the author is to some degree complicit, abetted by editors and publishers, in making a bold overstatement to grab attention for his thesis—and to sell. The Hobbesian law of the intellectual jungle leads you, perhaps against your better judgement, to become one of what Jacob Burckhardt called the *terribles simplificateurs*.

The real danger now is that vulgar Kaganism will become popular on both sides of the Atlantic because people either believe Kagan's "dual caricature" or—and I think this is happening—are looking for ways to *emphasis* the gulf. In short, Kagan could have the opposite effect to the one he intends. His conclusion will only be proved right if Americans and Europeans agree that his starting point is wrong.

Timothy Garton Ash is director of the European Studies Centre at St Antony's College, Oxford and a senior fellow at the Hoover Institution, Stanford

---

Living With a Superpower

Some values are held in common by America and its allies. As three studies show, many others are not

"WE SHARE common values—the common values of freedom, human rights and democracy." Thus George Bush in the Czech Republic on November 21st; but it could have been him, his national security adviser or his secretary of state at almost any time.

Now consider this: "It is time to stop pretending that Europeans and Americans share a common view of the world… Americans are from Mars and Europeans are from Venus." Thus the Carnegie Endowment's Robert Kagan; but it could have been any number of transatlantic pessimists at any point in the past two years.

The question of "values" is one of the more contentious and frustrating parts of the foreign-policy debate. Obviously, values matter in themselves and in their influence on the conduct of a nation's affairs. Equally obviously, Europeans and Americans both share and dispute "basic" values. But a concept that can support flatly contradictory views of the world and transatlantic relations evidently stands in need of refinement.

Three new reports attempt to do that job. One cannot say they resolve the question of whether shared values are more important than contested ones. But at least they provide a way of thinking about and judging the so-called "values debate".

Last month, the Pew Research Centre published the broadest single opinion poll so far taken of national attitudes in 44 countries. In general, the findings bear out the president's view, rather than Mr Kagan's: more seems to unite America and its allies than divide them.

In 2002, 61% of Germans, 63% of the French and 75% of Britons said they had a favourable view of the United States. Majorities of the populations liked America in 35 of the 42 countries where this question was asked (it was banned in China).

It is true that America's image has slipped a bit. The pro-American share of the population has fallen since 2000 by between four and 17 points in every west European country bar one (France, where opinion was least favourable to begin with). All the same, the reservoir of goodwill remains fairly deep and reports of sharply rising anti-Americanism in Europe seem to be exaggerated.

This finding is at odds with the reams of editorialising about growing hostility between America and the rest of the world. But it is consistent with another recent survey by the German Marshall Fund and the Chicago Council on Foreign Relations. Asked to rate other countries on a scale of one to 100, the six European countries rated America at 64 (more than France), while Americans gave Europeans between 55 (for France) and 75 (for Britain). Feelings towards Israel diverge sharply: it is rated at only 38 in Europe, against 55 in America. But despite that divide, and whatever the elites may say, the ordinary folk on either side of the Atlantic continue to like one another.

The two sides also share a number of more specific similarities. The Pew study found that between two-thirds and three-quarters of Europeans support "the US-led war on terror". Between two-thirds and four-fifths called Iraq a serious threat. Everyone admires American science, technology and popular culture.

In both the Marshall Fund and Pew studies, there were surprisingly few significant differences in public attitudes towards the armed forces (around three-quarters think their role in their countries is positive), nor was there much difference in public readiness to use force abroad. The Marshall study found that support for multilateral institutions like the United Nations or NATO is every bit as strong in America as Europe. In the Pew study, majorities in nearly every country said the world would be less safe if there were a rival superpower. This was true even in Russia.

Strikingly, over 80% of Americans say they want strong international leadership from the European Union, while over 60% of Europeans say they want the same thing from America. And when asked whether differences between their countries and America were the result of conflicting values or conflicting policies, most respondents in west European, Latin American and Muslim countries chose policies.

Divisions of the ways

All this sounds like music to the ears of the Bush administration. It argues that the way to win hearts and minds is to emphasise universal values: explain your policies, of course, but stress that America strives for values which everyone shares. Unfortunately, there is also much in the Pew study which casts doubt on that idea.

For one thing, the reservoir of goodwill seems to run dry in the Muslim world. The Pew study found that large majorities in four of America's main Muslim allies—Egypt, Pakistan, Jordan and Turkey—dislike America. There are obviously difficulties in measuring opinion in some of these places, but the results are still striking: in Egypt, 6% were favourable, 69% unfavourable; in Jordan, 25% and 75%.

Even where opinion overall is more flattering, as in Europe, there are signs of cultural clashes. If policies were the main problem, rather than values, you would expect people to have a higher opinion of Americans than of America. But the distinction is fading. West Europeans have a slightly more positive view of the people than the country, but they are exceptions: only 14 of 43 countries expressed more positive views about Americans than of America. And even though most Europeans say they like America, between half (in Britain) and three-quarters (in France) also say the spread of American ideas and customs is bad. As many Europeans say they dislike American ideas about democracy as like them. And this is from the part of the world that knows and claims to like America best.

In other words, people outside Muslim countries like America but not some of the most important things it stands for. What is one to make of that conflicting evidence? The short answer is that Europeans and Americans dispute some values and share others. But one can do better than that. Consider the third recent report, the world values survey run by the University of Michigan.

Unlike the other two polls, this survey goes back a long way. The university has been sending out hundreds of questions for the past 25 years (it now covers 78 countries with 85% of the world's population). Its distinctive feature is the way it organises the replies. It arranges them in two broad categories. The first it calls traditional values; the second, values of self-expression.

The survey defines "traditional values" as those of religion, family and country. Traditionalists say religion is important in their lives. They have a strong sense of national pride, think children should be taught to obey and that the first duty of a child is to make his or her parents proud. They say abortion, euthanasia, divorce and suicide are never justifiable. At the other end of this spectrum are "secular-rational" values: they emphasise the opposite qualities.

The other category looks at "quality of life" attributes. At one end of this spectrum are the values people hold when the struggle for survival is uppermost: they say that economic and physical security are more important than self-expression. People who cannot take food or safety for granted tend to dislike foreigners, homosexuals and people with AIDS. They are wary of any form of political activity, even signing a petition. And they think men make better political leaders than women. "Self-expression" values are the opposite.

Obviously, these ideas overlap. The difference between the two is actually rooted in an academic theory of development (not that it matters). The notion is that industrialisation turns traditional societies into secular-rational ones, while post-industrial development brings about a shift towards values of self-expression.

The usefulness of dividing the broad subject of "values" in this way can be seen by plotting countries on a chart whose axes are the two spectrums. The chart alongside (click to enlarge it) shows how the countries group: as you would expect, poor countries, with low self-expression and high levels of traditionalism, are at the bottom left, richer Europeans to the top right.

But America's position is odd. On the quality-of-life axis, it is like Europe: a little more "self-expressive" than Catholic countries, such as France and Italy, a little less so than Protestant ones such as Holland or Sweden. This is more than a matter of individual preference. The "quality of life" axis is the one most closely associated with political and economic freedoms. So Mr Bush is right when he claims that Americans and European share common values of democracy and freedom and that these have broad implications because, at root, alliances are built on such common interests.

But now look at America's position on the traditional-secular axis. It is far more traditional than any west European country except Ireland. It is more traditional than any place at all in central or Eastern Europe. America is near the bottom-right corner of the chart, a strange mix of tradition and self-expression.

Americans are the most patriotic people in the survey: 72% say they are very proud of their country (and this bit of the poll was taken before September 2001). That puts America in the same category as India and Turkey. The survey reckons religious attitudes are the single most important component of traditionalism. On that score, Americans are closer to Nigerians and Turks than Germans or Swedes.

Of course, America is hardly monolithic. It is strikingly traditional on average. But, to generalise wildly, that average is made up of two Americas: one that is almost as secular as Europe (and tends to vote Democratic), and one that is more traditionalist than the average (and tends to vote Republican).

But even this makes America more distinctive. Partly because America is divided in this way, its domestic political debate revolves around values to a much greater extent than in Europe. Political affiliation there is based less on income than on church-going, attitudes to abortion and attitudes to race. In America, even technical matters become moral questions. It is almost impossible to have a debate about gun registration without it becoming an argument about the right to self-defence. In Europe, even moral questions are sometimes treated as technical ones, as happened with stem-cell research.

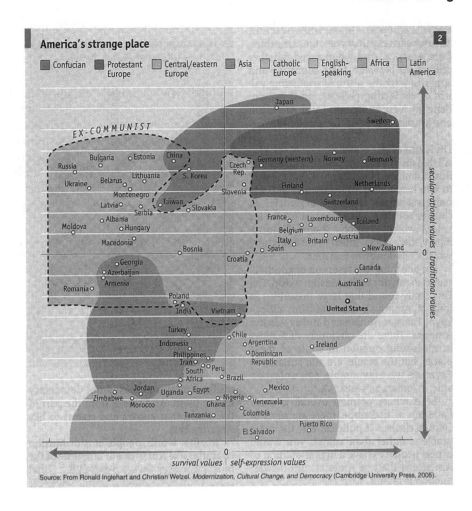

America's strange place

■ Confucian   ■ Protestant Europe   ■ Central/eastern Europe   ■ Asia   ■ Catholic Europe   ■ English-speaking   ■ Africa   ■ Latin America

Source: From Ronald Inglehart and Christian Welzel. *Modernization, Cultural Change, and Democracy* (Cambridge University Press, 2005).

The difference between the two appears to be widening. Since the first world values survey in 1981, every western country has shifted markedly along the spectrum towards greater self-expression. America is no exception. But on the other spectrum America seems to have become more traditional, rather than less. The change is only a half-step. And Italy, Spain and France have taken the same half-step. But if you look at Europe as a whole, the small movement back towards old-fashioned virtues in big Catholic countries is far outweighed by the stride the other way in post-Protestant countries such as Germany and Sweden. On average, then, the values gap between America and European countries seems to be widening.

Where evil is real

What is the significance of this? If "quality-of-life" values have political implications, helping to underpin democracy, might traditional values help explain differing attitudes to, say, the projection of power?

In principle, two things suggest they might. Patriotism is one of the core traditional values and there is an obvious link between it, military might and popular willingness to sustain large defence budgets. There may also be a link be-

tween America's religiosity and its tendency to see foreign policy in moral terms. To Americans, evil exists and can be fought in their lives and in the world. Compared with Europe, this is a different world-view in both senses: different prevailing attitudes, different ways of looking at the world.

If you go back to the Pew and Marshall Fund studies, you can see hard evidence for this difference—and it goes beyond immediate policy concerns. In the Pew study, three-quarters of west Europeans and an even higher share of east Europeans support the American-led war on terrorism—but more than half in both places say America does not take other countries into account (whereas three-quarters of Americans think their government does).

In both studies, Americans and Europeans put the same issues at the top of their concerns—religious and ethnic hatred, international terrorism and the spread of nuclear weapons. In that respect, America and Europe have more in common with each other than with African, Asian and Latin American countries, for whom the spread of AIDS and the gap between rich and poor are at least as important.

But both studies show differences in the balance of European and American anxieties. In the Pew poll, 59% of Americans think the spread of nuclear weapons is the greatest danger to the world. Between 60% and 70% of Europeans put religious and ethnic hatred first. In the Marshall

Fund study, around 90% of Americans say international terrorism and Iraq's development of weapons of mass destruction are "critical". The comparable figures for Europe are around 60%. In short, even if Americans and Europeans see one another in similar terms, they see the world differently.

One might object that such values-based judgments are still not everything. The two sides of the Atlantic have long lived with a related problem: the cultural split between "vigorous, naive" America and "refined, unprincipled" Europe. They have successfully managed that, just as they have coped with the political awkwardness that America's centre of gravity is further to the right than Europe's.

What is different now? Two things. The first is that the values gap may be widening a little, and starting to affect perceptions of foreign-policy interest on which the transatlantic alliance is based. The second is that, in the past, cultural differences have been suppressed by the shared values of American and European elites—and elite opinion is now even more sharply divided than popular opinion. It is the combination of factors that makes the current transatlantic divisions disturbing. And it is little consolation that, in the face of some mutual hostility, the Bush administration is insisting it is all just a matter of politics, and not of something deeper.

The Case for a Multi-Party U.S. Parliament? American Politics in Comparative Perspective

Abstract

This is a "mental experiment" that illuminates the role of institutions in shaping the political process. It is best viewed as part of the long history of American fascination with the parliamentary system and even multiparty politics. The larger hope is to initiate serious dialogue on the respective strengths and weaknesses of majoritarian and consensus systems with scholars of American politics and include American politics in an explicitly comparative perspective.

Christopher S. Allen

INTRODUCTION

Americans revere the constitution but at the same time also sharply and frequently criticize the government. (Dionne, 1991) Yet since the constitution is responsible for the current form of the American government, why not change the constitution to produce better government? After all, the founders of the United States did create the amendment process and we have seen 27 of them in over 200 years.

Several recent events prompt a critical look at this reverence for the constitution: unusual presidential developments, including the Clinton impeachment spectacle of 1998-1999; the historic and bizarre 2000 Presidential election; and the apparent mandate for fundamental change that President Bush inferred from this exceedingly narrow election. In the early 21st century, American politics confronted at least three other seemingly intractable problems: a significant erosion in political accountability; out of control costs of running for public office; and shamefully low voter turnout. More seriously, none of these four problems is of recent origin, as all four have eroded the functioning of the American government for a period of between 25 and 50 years! The core features of these four problems are:

- Confusion of the roles of head of state and head of government, of which the impeachment issue—from Watergate through Clinton's impeachment—is merely symptomatic of a much larger problem.
- Eroding political accountability, taking the form of either long periods of divided government, dating back to the "do nothing" 80th congress elected in 1946, to the recent "gerrymandering industry" producing a dearth of competitive elections. The result is millions of "wasted votes" and an inability for voters to assign credit or blame for legislative action.
- Costly and perennial campaigns for all offices producing "the best politicians that money can buy." This problem that had its origins with the breakdown of the party caucus system and the growth of primary elections in the 1960s; and
- The world's lowest voter turnout among all of the leading OECD countries, a phenomenon that began in the 1960s and has steadily intensified.

When various American scholars acknowledge these shortcomings, however, there is the occasional, offhand comparison to parliamentary systems which have avoided some of these pathologies. The unstated message is that we don't—or perhaps should never, ever want to—have that here.

Why not? What exactly is the problem with a parliamentary system? Durable trust in government, sense of efficacy, and approval ratings for branches in government have all declined in recent decades. Such phenomena contribute to declining voter turnout and highlight what is arguably a more significant trend toward a crisis in confidence among Americans concerning their governing institutions. So why is institutional redesign off the table?

This article examines these 4 institutional blockages of the American majoritarian/Presidential system and suggests certain features of parliamentary or consensus systems might overcome these persistent shortcomings of American politics.

Less normatively, the article is framed by three concepts central to understanding and shaping public policy in advanced industrialized states with democratic constitutional structures.

First, is the issue of comparability and 'American Exceptionalism'. (Lipset, 1996) The article's goal is to initiate a long-delayed dialogue on comparative constitutional structures with scholars of American politics. Second, the article hopes to participate in the active discussion among comparativists on the respective strengths and weaknesses of majoritarian and consensus systems. (Birchfield and Crepaz, 1998). Third, scandals surrounding money and politics in a number of democratic states (Barker, 1994) should prompt a comparison of parties and party systems and the context within which they function.

This article does not underestimate the quite significant problems associated with "institutional transplantation" (Jacoby, 2000) from one country to another. The more modest and realistic goal is to engage American and Comparative scholars in a fruitful debate about political institutions and constitutional design that (finally) includes American politics in a Comparative orbit.

This article is organized in 5 sections that address: 1) the cumbersome tool of impeachment; 2) eroding political accountability due to divided government and safe seats; 3) the costly, never-ending campaign process; 4) the continued deterioration of voter turnout, and finally, pragmatically; 5) offers a critical analysis of the quite formidable obstacles that initiating a parliamentary remedy to these problems would clearly face.

1. Impeachment: Head of State vs Head of Government

The tool of impeachment is merely a symptom of a larger problem. Its more fundamental flaw is that it highlights the constitutional confusion between the two functions of the US presidency: head of state and head of government.

Americanists have delved deeply into the minutiae of the impeachment process during the past thirty years but comparativists would ask a different question. How would other democracies handle similar crises affecting their political leaders? More than two years transpired from the Watergate break-in to Nixon's resignation (1972–74), the Iran-Contra scandal (1986–87) produced no impeachment hearings; and an entire year (1998–99) transpired from the onset of the Clinton-Lewinsky saga to the completion of the impeachment process. Comparativists and citizens of other democratic polities find this astounding, since in a parliamentary system a fundamental challenge to the executive would take the form of a vote of no confidence, (Lijphart, 1994) and the issue would be politically resolved within weeks. The executive would either survive and continue or resign.

The portrayal of the Clinton impeachment and trial is characterized as his-

toric. For only the second time in American politics, an American president has been impeached in the House and put on trial in the Senate. Yet, the *idea* of using impeachment has been much less rare, having been raised three times in the past thirty years. Yet impeachment hasn't "worked" at all. It is either not brought to fruition (Watergate), not used when it should have been (Iran-Contra), or completely trivialized (Clinton-Lewinsky) when another path was clearly needed. But impeachment itself isn't the real problem; a larger constitutional design flaw is.

The United States has a constitutional structure based on a separation of powers, while most parliamentary systems have a "fusion" of powers in that the Prime Minister is also the leader of the major party in parliament. However, within the American executive itself, there is a "fusion" of functions, which is the exact opposite of Parliamentary regimes.

The US is the only developed democracy where head of state and head of government are fused in one person. The President is the Head of State and, effectively, the Head of Government. In Parliamentary systems these two functions are performed by two different people. (Linz, 1993) Thus impeachment of one person removes two functions in one and likely explained the dichotomy of popular desire for Clinton's retention on the one hand, but also for some form of political censure on the other.

Beyond the impeachment issue, when American presidents undertake some action as head of government for which they are criticized, they then become invariably more remote and inaccessible. For example, Presidents Johnson (Vietnam), Nixon (Watergate), Reagan (Iran/Contra), Clinton (the Lewinsky Affair) and G.W. Bush (Iraq) all reduced their appearances at press conferences as criticism of their policies mounted. In short, when criticized for actions taken in their head of government capacity, they all retreated to the Rose Garden and sometimes created the impression that criticizing the President—now wearing the head of state hat (or perhaps, crown)—was somehow unpatriotic. This was especially the case with George W. Bush, who in the post 9/11 and Iraq war periods, has tried to emphasize the commander in chief aspect of the presidency rather than his role as steward of the economy and domestic politics.

Toward a Politically Accountable Prime Minister and a Ceremonial President

A parliamentary system with a separate head of state and head of government would produce two "executive" offices instead of one. It's odd that the US is so fearful of centralized power yet allows the executive to perform functions that no other leader of an OECD country (France excepted) performs alone. The US Vice President serves many of the functions of heads of state in other countries. But the United States has a comparatively odd way of dividing executive constitutional functions. One office, the Presidency, does everything while the other, the Vice Presidency, does virtually nothing and simply waits until the president can no longer serve. An American parliamentary system would redefine these 2 offices so that one person (the head of state) would serve as a national symbol and preside over ceremonial functions. The second person (the head of government) would function much like a prime minister does in a parliamentary system, namely as the head of government who could be criticized, censured and held accountable for specific political actions without creating a constitutional crisis.

Thus were it necessary to censure or otherwise take action against the head of government (i.e. prime minister), the solution would be a relatively quick vote of no confidence that would solve the problem and move on and let the country address its political business. (Huber, 1996) and unlike impeachment which is the political equivalent of the death penalty, a vote of no confidence does not preclude a politician's making a comeback and returning to lead a party or coalition. Impeachment and removal from office, on the other hand, is much more final.

Prime Ministers, unlike US presidents, are seen much more as active politicians not remote inaccessible figures. In a parliament, the prime minister as the head of government is required to engage—and be criticized—in the rough-and-tumble world of daily politics. In short, the head of government must be accountable. The British prime minister, for example, is required to participate in a weekly "question time" in which often blunt and direct inter-

TABLE 1
Trust in the Federal Government 1964–2002

	'64	'66	'68	'70	'72	'74	'76	'78	'80	'82	'84	'86	'88	'90	'92	'94	'96	'98	'00	'02
None of the Time	0	2	0	0	1	1	1	4	4	3	1	2	2	2	2	3	1	1	1	0
Some of the Time	22	28	36	44	44	61	62	64	69	62	53	57	56	69	68	74	66	58	55	44
Most of the Time	62	48	54	47	48	34	30	27	23	31	40	35	36	25	26	19	30	36	40	51
Just About Always	14	17	7	6	5	2	13	2	2	2	4	3	4	3	3	2	3	4	4	5
Don't Know, Dep.	1	4	2	2	2	2	3	3	2	3	2	2	1	1	1	1	0	1	1	0

PERCENTAGE WITHIN STUDY YEAR

Source: The National Election Studies.

QUESTION TEXT:

"How much of the time do you think you can trust the government in Washington to do what is right—just about always, most of the time or only some of the time?"

Source: The National Election Studies, University of Michigan, 2003

rogatories are pressed by the opposition. (Rundquist, 1991) There is no equivalent forum for the American president to be formally questioned as a normal part of the political process.

But could such a power might be used in a cavalier fashion, perhaps removing the head of government easily after a debilitating scandal? This is unlikely in a well-designed parliamentary system because such cynicism would likely produce a backlash that would constrain partisanship. In fact, the Germans have institutionalized such constraints in the "constructive vote of no confidence" requiring any removal of the head of government to be a simultaneous election of a new one. The context of such a parliamentary system lowers the incentives to engage in the politics of destruction. The political impact of destroying any particular individual in a collective body such as a cabinet or governing party or coalition is much less significant than removing a directly elected president.

A parliamentary head of state is above the kind of criticism generated in no confidence votes and simply serves as an apolitical symbol of national pride. In nation states that have disposed of their monarchies, ceremonial presidents perform many of the same roles as constitutional monarchs such as Queen Elizabeth do, but much more inexpensively. In fact, many of these ceremonial roles are performed by the American vice president (attending state dinners/funerals, cutting ribbons, presiding over the Sen-

ate, etc.) The problem is that the Vice President is often a political afterthought, chosen more for ticket-balancing functions and/or for inoffensive characteristics than for any expected major political contributions. On the other hand, the type of individual usually chosen as a ceremonial president in a parliamentary system is a retired politician from the moderate wing of one of the major parties who has a high degree of stature and can serve as a figure of national unity. In effect, the office of ceremonial president is often a reward or honor for decades of distinguished national service, hardly the characteristics of an American vice president.

In retrospect, one might say that President Clinton was impeached not for abusing head of government functions, but for undermining the decorum and respect associated with heads of state. The separation of head of state and head of government would have a salutary effect on this specific point. Scandals destroying heads of state would have little real political significance since the head of state would not wield real political power. Similarly, scandals destroying heads of government would have significantly less impact than the current American system. The head of government role, once separated from the head of state role, would no longer attract monolithic press and public attention or be subject to extraordinarily unrealistic behavioral expectations.

2. Political Accountability: Divided Government & "Safe Seats"

From the "do nothing" 80th Congress elected in 1946 to the 107th elected in 2002, a total of twenty nine congresses, the United States has experienced divided government for more than two-thirds of this period. In only nine of those twenty nine Congresses has the president's party enjoyed majorities in both houses of Congress. (Fiorina, 1992) Some might observe this divided government phenomenon and praise the bipartisan nature of the American system. (Mayhew, 1991) But to justify such a conclusion, defenders of the bipartisanship would have to demonstrate high public approval of governmental performance, particularly when government was divided. Based on over four decades of declining trust in government, such an argument is increasingly hard to justify

One explanation for the American preference for divided government is the fear of concentrated political power. (Jacobson, 1990) Yet in a search for passivity, the result often turns out to be simply inefficiency.

While the fear of concentrated government power is understandable for historical and ideological reasons, many of the same people who praise divided government also express concern regarding government efficiency. (Thurber, 1991) Yet divided government quite likely contributes to the very

Table 2
The Persistence of Divided Government

	President	House	Senate	Divided/Unified			President	House	Senate	Divided/Unified
1946	D Truman	Rep	Rep	d		1976	D Carter	Dem	Dem	u
1948	D Truman	Dem	Rep	d		1978	D Carter	Dem	Dem	u
1950	D Truman	Rep	Rep	d		1980	R Reagan	Dem	Rep	d
1952	R Eisenhower	Rep	Rep	u		1982	R Reagan	Dem	Rep	d
1954	R Eisenhower	Dem	Dem	d		1984	R Reagan	Dem	Rep	d
1956	R Eisenhower	Dem	Dem	d		1986	R Reagan	Dem	Dem	d
1958	R Eisenhower	Dem	Dem	d		1988	R Bush	Dem	Dem	d
1960	D Kennedy	Dem	Dem	u		1990	R Bush	Dem	Dem	d
1962	D Kennedy	Dem	Dem	u		1992	D Clinton	Dem	Dem	u
1964	D Johnson	Dem	Dem	u		1994	D Clinton	Rep	Rep	d
1966	D Johnson	Dem	Dem	u		1996	D Clinton	Rep	Rep	d
1968	R Nixon	Dem	Dem	d		1998	D Clinton	Rep	Rep	d
1970	R Nixon	Dem	Dem	d		2000	R Bush	Rep	Dem*	d
1972	R Nixon	Dem	Dem	d		2002	R Bush	Rep	Rep	u
1974	R Ford	Dem	Dem	d						

* After a 50–50 split (with Vice President Cheney as the tiebreaker), Senator Jeffords (I-VT) switched from the Republican party shortly after the 2000 election, thereby swinging the Senate to the Democrats.

inefficiencies that voters rightfully lament. Under divided government, when all is well, each of the two parties claims responsibility for the outcome; when economic or political policies turn sour, however, each party blames the other. This condition leads to a fundamental lack of political accountability and the self-fulfilling prophecy that government is inherently inefficient.

Rather than being an accidental occurrence, divided government is much more likely to result due to the American constitutional design. For it is constitutional provisions that are at the heart of divided government; 2 year terms for Congress, 4 year terms for the Presidency, and 6 year terms for the Senate invariably produce divided government.

Were it only for these "accidental" outcomes of divided government, political accountability might be less deleterious. Exacerbating the problem, however, is the decline of parties as institutions.

This has caused individuals to have weaker partisan *attachments*—despite the increased partisan *rhetoric* of many elected officials since the 1980s—and has thereby intensified the fragmentation of government. (Franklin and Hirczy de Mino, 1998) Clearly, divided government is more problematic when partisan conflict between the two parties is greater as the sharper ideological conflict and the increased party line congressional voting since the 1990s would suggest. Under these circumstances, divided government seems to be more problematic, since two highly partisan parties within the American political system seems potentially dangerous. Persistent divided government over time will likely produce a fundamental change in the relationship between Presidents and the Congress. Presidents are unable to bargain effectively with a hostile congresswitness the 1995 government shut-

down—leading the former to make appeals over the heads of Congress directly and, hence undermine the legitimacy of the legislative branch. (Kernell, 1997) This argument parallels the one made in recent comparative scholarship (Linz, 1993) regarding the serious problem of dual legitimacy in presidential systems.

A second component of the political accountability problem is the increasing uncompetitiveness of American elections. Accounts of the 2000 Presidential election stressed its historic closeness, settled by only 540,000 popular votes (notwithstanding the electoral college anomaly). And the narrow Republican majorities in the House and Senate apparently indicated that every congressional or senate seat could be up for grabs each election. The reality is something different. (Center for Voting, 2003) Out of 435 House seats, only 10% or fewer are competitive, the outcome of most Senate races is known well in advance, and the Presidential race was only competitive in 15 of 50 states. In the remaining 35, the state winners (Gore or Bush) were confident enough of the outcome to forgo television advertising in many of them. In essence, voters for candidates who did not win these hundreds of "safe seats" were effectively disenfranchised and unable to hold their representatives politically accountable.

For those who lament the irresponsibility—or perhaps irrelevance—of the two major parties, an institutional design that would force responsibility should be praised. Quite simply, those who praise divided government because it "limits the damage" or see nothing amiss when there are hundreds of safe seats are faced with a dilemma. They can not simultaneously complain about the resulting governmental inefficiency and political cynicism that ultimately follows when accountability is regularly clouded.

Political Accountability and the Fusion of Government

A number of scholars have addressed the deficiencies of divided government, but they suggest that the problem is that the electoral cycle, with its "off year" elections, intensifies the likelihood of divided government in non-presidential election years. Such advocates propose as a solution the alteration of the electoral cycle so that all congressional elections are on four year terms, concurrent with presidential terms, likely producing a clear majority. (Cutler, 1989) Yet this contains a fatal flaw. Because there is no guarantee that this proposal would alleviate the residual tension between competing branches of government, it merely sidesteps the accountability factor strongly discouraging party unity across the executive and legislative branches of government.

This suggestion could also produce the opposite effect from divided government, namely exaggerated majorities common to parliamentary regimes with majoritarian electoral systems such as the UK. The "safe seats" phenomenon would be the culprit just as in the UK. The most familiar examples of this phenomenon were the "stop-go" policies of post-World War II British governments, as each succeeding government tried to

overturn the previous election. While creating governing majorities is important for political accountability, the absence of proportional representation creates a different set of problems.

Under a fusion of power system, in which the current presidency would be redefined, the resulting parliamentary system would make the head of the legislative branch the executive, thus eliminating the current separation of powers. Yet if a government should lose its majority between scheduled elections due to defection of its party members or coalition partners, the head of state then would ask the opposition to form a new government and, failing that, call for new elections. This avoids the constitutional crises that the clamor for impeachment seem to engender in the American system.

But what if coalition members try to spread the blame for poor performance to their partners? In theory, the greater the flexibility available to in shifting from one governing coalition to another (with a different composition), the greater potential for this kind of musical cabinet chairs. The potential for such an outcome is far less than the American system, however. A century of experience in other parliamentary regimes (Laver and Shepsle, 1995) shows that members of such a party capriciously playing games with governing are usually brought to heel at the subsequent election.

In other words, the major advantage to such a parliamentary system is that it heightens the capacity for voters and citizens to evaluate government performance. Of course, many individuals might object to the resulting concentration of power. However, if voters are to judge the accomplishments of elected officials, the latter need time to succeed or fail, and then the voters can make a judgment on their tenure. The most likely outcome would be a governing party or coalition of parties that would have to stay together to accomplish anything, thereby increasing party salience. (Richter, 2002) Phrased differently, such an arrangement would likely lead to an increase in responsible government.

Many Americans might react unfavorably at the mention of the word coalition due to its supposed instability. Here we need to make the distinction between transparent and opaque coalitions. Some argue that coalition government in parliamentary systems have the reputation of increased instability. That, of course, depends on the substance of the coalition agreement and the willingness of parties

to produce a stable majority. (Strom *et al.,* 1994) But in most parliamentary systems, these party coalitions are formed transparently before an election so the voters can evaluate and then pass judgment on the possible coalition prior to election day. It's not as if there are no coalitions in the US Congress. There they take the opaque form of ad-hoc groups of individual members of Congress on an issue-by-issue basis. The high information costs to American voters in understanding the substance of such layered bargains hardly is an example of political transparency.

Table 3	
Comparative Coalitions	
American	Parliamentary
Opaque	Transparent
Issue-by-Issue	Programmatic
Back Room	Open Discussion
Unaccountable	Election Ratifies
Unstable	Generally Stable

Finally, for the concerned that the "fusion" of the executive and legislative branches—on the British majoritarian model—would upset the concept of checks and balances, a multi-party consensus parliamentary system produces them slightly differently. (Lijphart, 1984) Majoritarianism concentrates power and makes "checking difficult, while consensus democracies institutionalize the process in a different, and more accountable form. A multi-party parliamentary system would also provide greater minority representation and protection by reducing majoritarianism's excessive concentration of power. A consensus parliamentary system would also address the "tyranny of the majority" problem and allow checking and balancing by the voters in the ballot box since the multiple parties would not likely allow a single party to dominate. Consensus systems thus represent a compromise between the current US system and the sharp concentration of British Westminster systems. Americans who simultaneously favor checks and balances but decry inefficient government need to clarify what they actually want their government to do.

3. Permanent and Expensive Campaigns

The cost to run for political office in the United States dwarfs that spent in any other advanced industrialized democracy. The twin problems are time and money. More specifically a never-ending campaign "season" and the structure of political advertising that depends so heavily on TV money. (Gans, 1993) Listening to the debates about "reforming" the American campaign finance system are bizarre to students of other democratic electoral systems. More than $2 billion was raised and spent (Mann, 1997) by parties, candidates and interest groups in the 1996 campaign, and for 2000 it went up to $3 billion.

The two year congressional cycle forces members of the House of Representatives to literally campaign permanently. The amount of money required to run for a Congressional seat has quadrupled since 1990. Presidential campaigns are several orders of magnitude beyond the House of Representatives or the Senate. By themselves they are more than two years long, frequently longer. Unless a presidential candidate is independently wealthy or willing and able to raise upfront $30–$50 million it is simply impossible to run seriously for this office.

Many of the problems stem from the post-Watergate "reforms" that tried to limit the amount of spending on campaigns which then produced a backlash in the form of a 1976 Supreme Court decision (Buckley vs Valeo) that undermined this reform attempt. In essence, Buckley vs Valeo held that "paid speech" (i.e. campaign spending) has an equivalent legal status as "free speech". (Grant, 1998) Consequently, since then all "reform" efforts have been tepid measures that have not been able to get at the root of the problem. As long as "paid speech" retains its protected status, any changes are dead in the water.

At its essence this issue is a fissure between "citizens" and "consumers". What Buckley vs Valeo has done is to equate the citizenship function (campaigning, voting, civic education) with a market-based consumer function (buying and selling consumer goods as commodities). (Brubaker, 1998) Unlike the United States, most other OECD democracies

consider citizenship a public good and provide funding for parties, candidates and the electoral process as a matter of course. The Buckley vs Valeo decision conflates the concepts of citizen and consumer, the logical extension of which is there are weak limits on campaign funding and no limits on the use of a candidate's own money. We are all equal citizens, yet we are not all equal consumers. Bringing consumer metaphors into the electoral process debases the very concept of citizenship and guarantees that the American political system produces the best politicians money can buy.

Free Television Time and the Return of Political Party Dues

Any broadcaster wishing to transmit to the public is required to obtain a broadcast license because the airways have the legal status of public property. To have access to such property, the government licenses these networks, cable channels, and stations to serve the public interest. In return, broadcasters are able to sell airtimes to sponsors of various programs. Unfortunately for campaign costs, candidates for public office fall into the same category as consumer goods in the eyes of the broadcasters. (Weinberg, 1993) What has always seemed odd to observers of other democratic states is that there is no *Quid Pro Quo* requiring the provision of free public airtime for candidates when running for election.

Any serious reform of campaign finance would require a concession from all broadcasters to provide free time for all representative candidates and parties as a cost of using the public airways. Since the largest share of campaign money is TV money, this reform would solve the problem at its source. Restricting the "window" when these free debates would take place to the last two months before a general election would thus address the time dimension as well. Such practices are standard procedure in all developed parliamentary systems. Very simply, as long as "reform" efforts try to regulate the *supply* of campaign finance, it will fail. A much more achievable target would be the regulation of *demand*.

The United States could solve another money problem by borrowing a page from parliamentary systems: changing the political party contribution structure from individual voluntary contributions (almost always from the upper middle class and the wealthy) to a more broad-based dues structure common to parties in other developed democracies. This more egalitarian party dues structure would perform the additional salutary task of rebuilding parties as functioning institutions. (Allen, 1999) Rather than continuing in their current status as empty shells for independently wealthy candidates, American political parties could become the kind of dynamic membership organizations they were at the turn of the 20th century when they did have a dues structure.

4. Low Voter Turnout?

The leading OECD countries have voter turnout ranging from 70% to 90% of their adult population while the US lags woefully behind. Among the most commonly raised explanations for the US deficiency are: registration requirements, the role of television, voter discouragement, and voter contentment (although the latter two are clearly mutually exclusive). None are particularly convincing nor do they offer concrete suggestions as to how it might be overcome.

Table 4
Comparative Voting Turnout— 1945–2000 Average

Country	Turnout %
Italy	92.5
Germany	80.6
Great Britain	74.9
France	67.3
US President	55.1
US Congress "off year"	40.9
US Municipal	21.5

Source: Voter Turnout: A Global Survey (Stockholm: International IDEA, 2004)

The two party system and the electoral method that produces it: the single member district, first past the post, or winner take all system with its attendant "safe seats" often escapes criticism. The rise of such new organizations as the Reform, Libertarian, and Green parties potentially could threaten the hegemony of the Democrats and Republicans. Yet the problem of a third (or fourth) party gaining a sufficient number of votes to actually win seats and challenge the two party system is formidable. The electoral arithmetic would require any third party to win some 25% of the vote on a nationwide basis—or develop a highly-concentrated regional presence—before it would actually gain more than a token number of seats. And failing to actually win seats produces a "wasted vote" syndrome among party supporters which is devastating for such a party. (Rosenstone *et al.*, 1996) Most voters who become disillusioned with the electoral process refer to the "lesser of two evils" choices they face. In such a circumstance, declining voter turnout is not surprising.

The US is a diverse country with many regional, religious, racial, and class divisions. So why should we expect that two "catch all" parties will do a particularly good job in appealing to the interests of diverse constituencies? The solution to lower voter turnout is a greater number of choices for voters and a different electoral system.

Proportional Representation

Under electoral systems using proportional representation, the percentage of a party's vote is equivalent to the percentage of seats allocated to the party in parliament. Comparative analysis shows that those countries with proportional representation—and the multiple parties that PR systems produce—invariably have higher voter turnout. (Grofman and Lijphart, 1986) In other words, PR voting systems provide a wider variety of political choices and a wider variety of political representation.

Eliminating majoritarian single member districts (SMDs) in favor of PR voting would have several immediate effects. First, it would increase the range of choices for voters, since parties would have to develop ideological and programmatic distinctions to make themselves attractive to voters. As examples

in other countries have shown, it would lead to formation of several new parties representing long underserved interests.

Such a change would force rebuilding of parties as institutions, since candidates would have to run as members of parties and not as independent entrepreneurs. The so-called Progressive "reforms" at the turn of the 20th century and the 1960s introduction of primaries—plus TV advertising—plus the widespread use of referenda have all had powerful effects in undermining parties as coherent political organizations. (Dwyre, 1994) In trying to force market-based individual "consumer choice" in the form of high-priced candidates, the collective institutions that are political parties have been hollowed out and undermined.

Table 5
The Advantages of Proportional Representation

- Higher Voter Turnout
- No "Wasted" Votes
- Few Safe, Uncontested Seats
- More Parties
- Greater Minority Representation
- Greater Gender Diversity in Congress
- Greater Ideological Clarity
- Parties Rebuilt as Institutions
- 6% Threshold Assumed
- No More Gerrymandered Redistricting

There are, of course, a wide range of standard objections to PR voting systems by those favoring retention of majoritarian SMD systems.

The first of these, *coalitional instability*, was addressed briefly, but it needs to be restated here. The US has unstable coalitions in the Congress right now, namely issue-by-issue ones, usually formed in the House cloakroom with the "assistance" of lobbyists. Few average voters know with certainty how "their" member of Congress will vote on a given is-

sue. (Gibson, 1995) With ideologically coherent parties, they would.

An American parliament with several parties could produce self-discipline very effectively. Clearly there would have to be a coalition government since it is unlikely that any one party would capture 50% of the seats. The practice in almost all other coalition governments in parliamentary systems is that voters prefer a predictable set of political outcomes. Such an arrangement forces parties to both define their programs clearly and transparently, once entering into a coalition, and to do everything possible to keep the coalition together during the course of the legislative term.

The second standard objection to PR is the *"Too many parties"* issue. PR voting has been practiced in parliaments for almost 100 years in many different democratic regimes. There is a long history of practices that work well and practices that don't. (Norris, 1997) Two countries are invariably chosen as bad examples of PR, namely Israel and Italy. There is an easy solution to this problem of an unwieldy number of parties, namely an electoral threshold requiring any party to receive a certain minimal percentage to gain seats in the parliament. The significant question is what should this minimal threshold be? The Swedes have 4% threshold and have 6 parties in their parliament, the Germans have a 5% threshold and have 5 parties represented in the Bundestag.

The third standard objection to PR voting is *"Who's my representative?"* In a society so attuned to individualism, most Americans want a representative from their district. This argument presumes that all Americans have a member of Congress that represents their views. However, a liberal democrat who lived in House Speaker Tom Delay's district in Texas might genuinely wonder in what way he represented that liberal's interests. By the same token, conservative Republicans living in Vermont have the independent socialist, Bernard Sanders as the state's lone member of Congress representing "their" interests.

Yet if American reformers are still insistent on having individual representatives (Guinier, 1994) the phenomena of "Instant Runoff Voting" (Hill, 2003) where voters rank order their preferences could produce proportionality among parties yet retain individual single member districts.

If there were PR voting in an American parliament, what would the threshold be? The US threshold should be at least 6% and possibly as high as 7%. The goal is to devise a figure that represents all significant interests yet does not produce instability. The "shake out" of parties would likely produce some strategic "mergers" of weak parties which, as single parties, might not attain the 6%–7% threshold. For example, a separate Latino party and an African-American party might insure always attaining a 7% threshold by forming a so-called "rainbow" party. Similarly the Reform Party and the Libertarian Party might find it safer electorally to merge into one free market party.

There are four primary arguments in favor of PR.

The first is *simplicity*, the percentage of the votes equals the percentage of the seats. To accomplish this, the individualistic US could borrow the German hybrid system of "personalized" proportional representation. This system requires citizens to cast two votes on each ballot: the first for an individual candidate; and the second for a list of national/regional candidates grouped by party affiliation. (Allen, 2001) This system has the effect of personalizing list voting because voters have their own representative but also can choose among several parties. Yet allocation of seats by party in the Bundestag corresponds strongly with the party's percentage of the popular vote.

The second advantage to PR is *diversity*. The experience of PR voting in other countries is that it changes the makeup of the legislature by increasing both gender and racial diversity. Obviously, parties representing minority interests who find it difficult to win representation in 2 person races, will more easily be able to win seats under PR. (Rule and Zimmerman, 1992) Since candidates would not have to run as individuals—or raise millions of dollars—the parties would be more easily able to include individuals on the party's list of candidates who more accurately represent the demographics of average Americans. What a multi-party list system would do would provide a greater range of interests being represented and broaden the concept of "representation" to go beyond narrow geography to include representation of such things as ideas and positions on policy issues that would be understandable to voters. Moreover, as for geographic representation on a list system, it would be in the self interest of the parties to insure that there was not only gender balance—if this is what the party wanted—on their list, but also other forms of balance including geography, ideology, and ethnicity, among others.

The third advantage is *government representativeness*. Not only is a consensus-based parliamentary system based on proportional representation more representative of the voting public, it also produces more representative *governments*. (Birchfield and Crepaz, 1998) This study finds that consensus-based, PR systems also produce a high degree of "popular cabinet support," namely the percentage of voters supporting the majority party or coalition.

The fourth advantage to a PR system in the US is that it would *eliminate the redistricting circus*. Until recently, the decennial census occasioned the excruciating task of micro-managing the drawing of congressional districts. Yet, since the 2002 elections, Republicans in Texas have redistricted a second time, creating even "safer" seats by manipulating district lines to their advantage. (Veith *et al.*, 2003) Under PR however, districts would be eliminated. Candidate lists would be organized statewide, in highly populated states, or regionally in the case of smaller states like New England. To insure geographical representation, all parties would find it in their own self-interest that the candidate list included geographical diversity starting at the top of the list.

Getting from Here to There: From Academic Debates to Constitutional Reform?

Clearly, none of these four structural reforms will take place soon. But if they were, what would be the initial steps? Of the four proposals, two of them could be accomplished by simple statute: campaign reform and the voting system. The other two would require constitutional change: head of state/government and divided government. Given the above caveats, it would be easiest to effect campaign reform (the Supreme Court willing) and to alter the voting system.

The largest obstacles to such a radical change in the American constitutional system are cultural and structural. Culturally, the ethos of American individualism would have difficulty giving up features such as a single all-powerful executive and one's own individual member of congress, no matter how powerful the arguments raised in support of alternatives. Ideology and cultural practice change very slowly. A more serious obstacle would be the existing interests privileged by the current system. All would fight tenaciously to oppose this suggested change.

Finally, specialists in American politics may dismiss this argument as the far-fetched "poaching" of a comparativist on a terrain that only Americanists can write about with knowledge and expertise. However, the durability of all four of the above-mentioned problems, stretching back anywhere from 25 to 50 years, suggests that Americanists have no monopoly of wisdom on overcoming these pathologies. More seriously, what this comparativist perceives is a fundamental failure of imagination based largely on the "N of 1" problem that all comparativists struggle to avoid. If a single observed phenomenon—in this case, the American political system—is not examined comparatively, one never knows whether prevailing practice is optimal or suboptimal. In essence, those who do not look at these issues comparatively suffer a failure of imagination because they are unable to examine the full range of electoral and constitutional options.

REFERENCES

Allen, Christopher S. (2001) "Proportional Representation," in Krieger, Joel (ed): Oxford Companion to Politics of the World. *Oxford: Oxford University Press.*

Allen, Christopher S., ed. (1999) *Transformation of the German Political Party System: Institutional Crisis or Democratic Renewal?* New York: Berghahn.

Barker, A. (1994) "The Upturned Stone: Political Scandals and their Investigation Processes in 20 Democracies." *Crime Law and Social Change.* 24 1: 337–373.

Birchfield, Vicki and Crepaz, Markus M.L. (1998) "The Impact of Constitutional Structures and Collective and Competitive Veto Points on Income Inequality in Industrialized Democracies." *European Journal of Political Research.* 34 2: 175–200.

Brubaker, Stanley C. (1998) "The Limits of Campaign Spending Limits." *Public Interest*. Fall: 33–54.

Center for Voting and Democracy (2003) "Overview: Dubious Democracy 2003–2004." `http://www.fairvote.org/dubdem/overview.htm`. June.

Cutler, Lloyd (1989) "Some Reflections About Divided Government." *Presidential Studies Quarterly*. 17: 485–492.

Dionne, E.J., Jr. (1991) *Why Americans Hate Politics*. New York: Simon and Schuster.

Dwyre, Diana (1994) "Disorganized Politics and the Have-nots: Politics and Taxes in New York and California." Polity. 27 (Fall): 25–47.

Fiorina, Morris (1992) *Divided Government*. New York: Macmillan.

Franklin, Mark N. and Hirczy de Mino, Wolfgang P. (1998) "Separated Powers, Divided Government, and Turnout in U.S. Presidential Elections." *American Journal of Political Science*. 42 1 (January): 316–326.

Gans, Curtis (1993) "Television: Political Participation's Enemy #1." *Spectrum: the Journal of State Government*. 66 2: 26–31.

Gibson, Martha L. (1995) "Issues, Coalitions, and Divided Government." *Congress & the Presidency*. 22 2 (Autumn): 155–166.

Grant, Alan (1998) "The Politics of American Campaign Finance." *Parliamentary Affairs*. 51 2 (April): 223–240.

Grofman, Bernard and Lijphart, Arend (1986) *Electoral Laws and Their Consequences*. New York: Agathon Press.

Guinier, Lani (1994) *The Tyranny of the Majority: Fundamental Fairness in Representative Democracy*. New York: The Free Press.

Hill, Steven (2003) *Fixing Elections: The Failure of America's Winner Take All Politics*. New York: Routledge.

Huber, John D. (1996) *"The Vote of Confidence in Parliamentary Democracies."* American Political Science Review. 90 2 (June): 269–282.

Jacobson, Gary C. (1990) *The Electoral Origins of Divided Government: Competition in U.S. House Elections*, 1946–1988. Boulder, CO: Westview.

Jacoby, Wade (2000) *Imitation and Politics: Redesigning Germany*. Ithaca: Cornell University Press.

Kernell, Samuel (1997) *Going Public: New Strategies of Presidential Leadership*. Washington, DC: CQ Press.

Laver, Michael and Shepsle, Kenneth A. (1995) *Making and Breaking Governments: Cabinets and Legislatures in Parliamentary Democracies*. New York: Cambridge University Press.

Lijphart, Arend (1984) *Democracies: Patterns of Majoritarian and Consensus Government in Twenty-One Countries*. New Haven: Yale University Press.

Lijphart, Arend 1994) "Democracies: Forms, Performance, and Constitutional Engineering." *European Journal of Political Research*. 25: 1–17.

Linz, Juan (1993) "The Perils of Presidentialism," In Diamond, Larry and Plattner, Marc (ed): *The Global Resurgence of Democracy*. Baltimore: Johns Hopkins University Press, 109–126.

Lipset, Seymour Martin (1996) *American Exceptionalism: A Double-Edged Sword*. New York: Norton.

Mann, Thomas, ed. (1997) *Campaign Finance Reform: A Sourcebook*. Washington, DC: Brookings Institute.

Mayhew, David (1991) *Divided We Govern: Party Control, Lawmaking, and Investigations*, 1946–1990. New Haven: Yale University Press.

Norris, Pippa (1997) "Choosing Electoral Systems: Proportional, Majoritarian and Mixed Systems." *International Political Science Review*. 18 3 (July): 297–312.

Richter, Michaela (2002) "Continuity or Politikwechsel?" *Continuity or Politikwechsel? The First Federal Red-Green Coalition*. 20 1 (Spring): 1–48.

Rosenstone, Steven J., Behr, Roy L. and Lazarus, Edward H. (1996) *Third Parties in America: Citizen Response to Major Party Failure*. 2nd Princeton: Princeton University Press.

Rule, Wilma and Zimmerman, Joseph F., eds. (1992) *United States Electoral Systems: Their Impact on Women and Minorities*. New York: Praeger.

Rundquist, Paul S. (1991) *The House of Representatives and the House of Commons: A Brief Comparison of American and British Parliamentary Practice*. Washington, DC: Congressional Research Service, Library of Congress.

Strom, Kaare, Budge, Ian and Laver, Michael J. (1994) "Constraints on Cabinet formation in Parliamentary Democracies." *American Journal of Political Science*. 38 2 (May): 303–335.

Thurber, James A. (1991) "Representation, Accountability, and Efficiency in Divided Party Control of Government." PS. 24 (December): 653–657.

Veith, Richard, Veith, Norma Jean and Fuery, Susan (2003) *Oral Argument*. No. 02–1580, U.S. Supreme Court, Wednesday, December 10.

Weinberg, Jonathan (1993) "Broadcasting and Speech." *California Law Review*. 81 5: 1101–1206.

Christopher S. Allen is Associate Professor of International Affairs at the University of Georgia where he teaches courses in comparative politics and political economy. He is editor of Transformation of the German Political Party System (Berghahn, 2001) and is currently working on a project examining democratic representation in parliamentary and presidential systems.

UNIT 3
Europe in Transition: West, Center, and East

Unit Selections

Key Points to Consider

- What are the major obstacles to the emergence of a more unified Europe? Will the new constitution necessarily make matters easier?

- Why does one of the articles suggest that the enlarged EU may become a Europe 'a la carte?

- Why is the voter turnout in the elections for the European Parliament so low?

- What is the evidence that the economic problems of Western Europe could be not just cyclical but also structural in origin?

- How would you compare the plight of immigrants to Europe with immigrants to the United States?

- How do you assess Yeltsin's legacy, and how well is Putin equipped to lead his country to a better future?

- How has President Putin gone about building a strong political base for himself? What seems to be the major items on his political agenda?

 **Links: www.dushkin.com/online/**
These sites are annotated in the World Wide Web pages.

Europa: European Union
http://europa.eu.int

NATO Integrated Data Service (NIDS)
http://www.nato.int/structur/nids/nids.htm

Research and Reference (Library of Congress)
http://lcweb.loc.gov/rr/

Russian and East European Network Information Center, University of Texas at Austin
http://reenic.utexas.edu/reenic/index.html

The articles in this unit deal with two major developments that have greatly altered the political map of contemporary Europe. One is the growth and impact on the traditional nation-state and its people of the supranational project known today as the European Union (EU). The other consists of the continuing challenges and responses that have resulted from the collapse of Communist rule in Central and Eastern Europe. The year 2004 linked these two developments more closely, when the EU for the first time admitted to membership former Communist-ruled countries in the central and eastern part of the continent. While NATO had moved slightly ahead of the European Union in its own eastward expansion, the EU has very different goals and entry requirements than the defense alliance. They include a set of minimum democratic and economic criteria that new members must meet.

The present can be seen as both an important turning point and a crucial testing time for the EU. Its institutional origins go back to 1951, when France, West Germany, Italy, and the three Benelux countries integrated their coal and steel industries. In 1957 the same six nation-states founded the European Economic Community (EEC) that later became the European Union. Britain declined to join the founders, and the EU did not add new members until 1973, when Britain finally entered along with two close trading partners, Ireland and Denmark. Thereafter the European Community continued to expand incrementally in sets of three newcomers per decade. The former dictatorships, Greece, Portugal, and Spain, entered during the 1980s, after having established their credentials as new democracies and market economies. In 1995, soon after the end of the Cold War, three neutral countries—Austria, Finland, and Sweden—joined for a total membership of fifteen.

In 2004 the EU abandoned this pattern of accretion in favor of what some observers, like Kenneth Rogoff, called a great leap forward. In one swoop, the EU expanded its membership by two-thirds, from fifteen to twenty-five countries. This greatly increased the EU's economic, cultural, and political diversity, even as its population moved from 375 million to some 450 million people. Of the ten newcomers, eight lie in central or eastern Europe: Poland, Hungary, the Czech Republic, Slovakia, Slovenia, and the three Baltic states, Lithuania, Latvia, and Estonia. All have far less productive economies than any of the fifteen older EU members. The remaining two new entrants are the small Mediterranean island nations of Malta and Cyprus. Together with the smallest of the original founding states, the Grand Duchy of Luxembourg, they rank last in population in the club. But that is not all. Several additional countries are applicants who hope for future admission. They include Romania and Bulgaria as well as several smaller Balkan states and Turkey. The EU could well end up with thirty members at some point during the next decade.

The case of Turkey is special. The country has an ambiguous record on human rights and democracy, and although the state is officially secular, the Turkish population is overwhelmingly Muslim. There is strong opposition to its EU membership, not only

from Greece and the Greek-speaking population of Cyprus. Apart from culturally based reservations, the 70 million Turks are seen both as an economic dead weight and a political and demographic threat by many of their opponents. Yet, as supporters of Turkey's entry argue, the real hope for a model of democratization and modernization in the Middle East may well lie in Turkey.

The enlargement of the EU, with or without Turkey, will in any case bring changes and challenges not only to the new members of the club but to the supranational body itself as well as its older membership. It cannot be ruled out that the larger and more diverse EU could begin to depart from the founders' vision of "an ever closer union among the peoples of Europe." This evocative phrase is contained in the preamble to the Treaty of Rome, the EU's founding document. Although it echoes the goal of a "more perfect union" announced in the preamble to the U.S. Constitution, it would be a mistake to push the analogy very far. The EU has not become a political union even in the sense of a somewhat loose-knit United States of Europe. Observers like Robert Cottrell think that it is less likely to become one as it expands and diversifies. He does not rule out that the EU may become a less integrated, multi-layered framework. On the other hand, the EU until now has surprised all skeptics. It may do so again, as Kenneth Rogoff concludes.

Yet the EU is in its own right an impressive political construct that has no close parallel anywhere. It has largely dismantled national barriers to the free movement of people, goods, services, and capital among the member nations. Above all, the EU has acquired an institutional presence and authority that goes far beyond anything envisaged by NAFTA or other regional free trade arrangements. All member nations have diverted some of their traditional sovereignty to the EU. The appointed Commission uses its supranational executive authority to initiate common policy decisions and oversee their implementation. The independent European Court of Justice makes binding decisions in its adjudication of EU-related disputes. The European Parliament has seen its authority grow over the years, even though it is not a full blown legislature in the traditional sense. In the 2004 elections of a new European Parliament, the voter turnout averaged 45 percent—at least ten percent lower than the U.S. turnout in the presidential election of the same year. The powerful Council of Ministers remains an intergovernmental body, where the national government of every member nation is represented. Until now each nation has had a weighted vote related to the size of its population. Rachman and *The Economist* explain some of the intricacies of the weighted votes and the qualified and double majorities that are going to replace them under the new EU constitution. They can be compared to the far simpler contrivance of the Connecticut Compromise as a way of giving representation to all members without ignoring their considerable differences in size of population. In the case of the supranational EU, the smallest member, Malta, has a population of 400,000, while the largest member, Germany, tops 82 million.

The political process continues unabated in the individual nation states of Western Europe, as they seek to define their own public agendas. Their relative prosperity rests on a base that was built up during the prolonged postwar economic boom of the 1950s and 1960s. By political choice, a considerable portion of their wealth was channeled toward the public sector and used to develop a relatively generous system of social services and social insurance. Since the early 1970s, however, many West European countries have been beset by economic disruptions or slowdowns offset by periods of cyclical economic upturns. There are also structural reasons why they no longer can take increasing affluence for granted in a more competitive global economy.

The economic shock that first interrupted the prolonged postwar boom came in the wake of sharp rises in the cost of energy, linked to successive hikes in the price of oil imposed by the Organization of Petroleum Exporting Countries (OPEC) after 1973. In the 1980s, OPEC lost its organizational bite, as its members began to compete against each other by raising production and lowering prices rather than abiding by the opposite practices in the manner of a well-functioning cartel agreement. The exploitation of new oil and gas fields in the North Sea and elsewhere also helped alleviate the energy situation, at least for the present. The resulting improvement for the consumers of oil and gas helped the Western European economies recover, but as a whole they did not rebound to their earlier high-growth rates.

The short Gulf War in 1991 did not seriously hamper the flow of Middle East oil, but it once again underscored the vulnerability of Europe to external interruptions in its energy supply. During the year 2000, there again were signs of a petroleum shortage. It was partly a result of increased demand, and partly a result of supply limitations imposed by some of the oil producers. In the fall months of that year, irate citizens demonstrated in several countries, including France, Germany, and Britain, in protest against sharp price hikes in oil and gasoline.

Because of their heavy dependence on international trade, Western European economies are vulnerable to global cyclical tendencies. Another important challenge lies in the stiff competition they face from China and the smaller new industrial countries (NICs) of East and South Asia, where labor costs remain much lower. The emerging Asian factor probably contributed to the increased tempo of the European drive for economic integration in the late 1980s. Some observers have warned of a protectionist reaction, in which major trading blocs in Europe, North America, and Eastern Asia could replace the relatively free system of international trade established in recent decades.

Europe still feels the aftershocks from the sudden collapse of Communist rule in Central and Eastern Europe at the end of the 1980s. Here states, nations, and nationalities broke away from an imposed system of central control, by asserting their independence from the previous ruling group and its ideology. In their attempts to construct a new order for themselves, the postcommunist countries have encountered enormous difficulties. Their transition to pluralist democracy and a rudimentary market-based economy turned out to be much rockier than most had anticipated.

The prospect of membership in the EU became a major incentive to continue with the reforms. Even now that the Central and East European countries have gained entry to the club, it will be a long time before they can hope to catch up economically. Robert Cottrell reports from a study by the Economist Intelligence Unit that it will take the new entrants on average more than fifty years to draw level with the old members in average income per person. It is based on the simple assumption of relatively good growth rates of 4 percent for the new EU entrants, and lower growth rates of 2 percent for the older members from Western Europe.

In some areas of the former Soviet bloc, one encounters some nostalgia for the basic material security and "orderliness" provided by the communist welfare states of the past. This should not be understood as a wish to turn back the wheel of history. Instead, it seems to represent a desire to build buffers and safety nets into the new market-oriented systems. Communist-descended parties have responded by abandoning most or all of their Leninist baggage. They now engage in the competitive bidding for votes with promises of social fairness and security. In Poland and elsewhere, such parties have recently gained political leverage. By contrast with the recent past, they must now operate in a pluralist political setting. They have adapted by adopting new strategies and goals.

Those who attempt the big move to the "Golden West" resemble in many ways the immigrants who have been attracted to the United States in the past and present. Many Western Europeans are unwilling to accept, however, what they regard as a flood of unwanted strangers. The newcomers are widely portrayed as outsiders whose presence will further drain the generous welfare systems and threaten the economic security and established way of life. Such anxieties are the stuff of socio-cultural mistrust, tensions, and conflicts. One serious political consequence has been the emergence of an anti-immigrant populist politics on the Far Right. In response, the governments in several countries have changed their laws on citizenship, asylum, and immigration.

There can be little doubt that the issues of immigration and the accompanying cultural tensions will continue to occupy a central place on the West European political agenda in coming years. Some of the established parties have already made symbolic and substantive accommodations to appease protesting voters, for fear of otherwise losing them to extremist ultra-right movements.

It is important to remember that there are also individuals and groups who resist the xenophobic elements in their own societies. Some enlightened political leaders and commentators seek to promote the reasonable perspective that migrants could turn out to be an important asset rather than a liability. This argument may concede that the foreign influx also involves some social costs in the short run, at least during recessionary periods, but it emphasizes that the newcomers can be a very important human resource who will contribute to mid- and long-term economic prosperity. Quite apart from any such economic considerations, of course, the migrants and asylum-seekers have become an important test of liberal democratic tolerance on the continent.

The Central and East European countries continue to face the challenge of political and economic reconstruction. When they began their post-Communist journey, there were no ready-made strategies of reform. Much theoretical ink has been spilled on the problems of a transition from a market economy to state socialism, but there was little theory or practice to guide the countries that tried to make a paradigm shift in the opposite direction. Some economists familiar with Eastern Europe, like Sweden's Anders Aslund, argued that a quick transition to a market economy was a preferable course, indeed the only responsible one, even though such an approach could be very disruptive and painful in the short run. They argued that such a "shock therapy" would release human energies and bring economic growth more quickly and efficiently. At the same time, these supporters of a "tough love" strategy warned that compassionate halfway measures could end up worsening the economic plight of these countries. Yet, as David Ost has reported from Poland, tough love approaches are likely to meet with rejection, when they are seen as having failed to deliver the promised goods.

Other strategists came out in favor of a more gradual approach to economic reconstruction in these countries. They warned that the neoclassical economists, who would introduce a full-scale market economy by fiat, not only ignored the market system's cultural and historic preconditions but also underestimated the turmoil that was likely to accompany the big transition. As a more prudent course of action, these gradualists recommended the adoption of pragmatic strategies of incremental change, accompanied by rhetoric of lower expectations.

Experience and the passage of a few more years would probably have given us better insights into the relative merits of each argument. But a pluralist society rarely permits itself to become a social laboratory for controlled experiments of this kind. Moreover, decision makers must often learn on the job. They cannot afford to become inflexible and dogmatic in these matters, where the human stakes are so high. Instead, competitive politics has produced a "mix" of the two approaches as the most acceptable and practical policy outcome.

A similar debate has been carried out in the former Soviet Union. It could be argued that Mikhail Gorbachev, the last Soviet head of government (1985 to 1991), failed to opt clearly for one or the other approach to economic reform. He seems to have been ambivalent about both means and ends of his *perestroika,* or restructuring, of the centrally planned economy. In the eyes of some born-again Soviet marketers, he remained far too socialist. But Communist hard-liners never forgave him for dismantling a system in which they had enjoyed at least a modicum of security and privilege.

Gorbachev appears to have regarded his own policies of *glasnost*, or openness, and *democratization* as essential accompaniments of *perestroika* in what he perceived as his modernization program. He seems to have understood (or become convinced) that a highly developed economy needs a freer flow of information along with a more decentralized system of decision making if its component parts are to be efficient, flexible, and capable of learning and self-correction. In that sense, a market economy has some integral feedback traits that make it incompatible with the traditional Soviet model of a centrally directed "command economy."

Glasnost and democratization were clearly incompatible with a repressive political system of one-party rule as well. They served Gorbachev as instruments to weaken the grip of the Communist hard-liners and at the same time to rally behind him some reform groups, including many intellectuals and journalists. Within a remarkably short time after he came to power in 1985, a vigorous new press emerged in the Soviet Union headed by journalists who were eager to ferret out misdeeds and report on political reality as they observed it. A similar development took place in the history profession, where scholars used the new spirit of openness to report in grim detail about past Communist atrocities that had previously been covered up or dismissed as bourgeois propaganda. There was an inevitable irony to the new truthfulness. Even as it served to discredit much of the past along with any reactionary attempts to restore "the good old days," it also brought into question the foundations of the Soviet system under the leadership of the Communist Party. Yet Gorbachev had clearly set out to modernize the Soviet system, not to bring it down.

One of the greatest vulnerabilities of the Soviet Union turned out to be its multiethnic character. Gorbachev was not alone in having underestimated the potential centrifugal tendencies of a Union of Soviet Socialist Republics (USSR) erected on the territory of the old, overland Empire that the Russian tsars had conquered and governed before 1917. Many of the non-Russian minorities retained a territorial identification with their homelands, where they often lived as ethnic majorities. This made it easier for them to demand greater autonomy or national independence, when the Soviet regime became weakened. The first national assertions came from the Baltic peoples in Estonia, Latvia, and Lithuania, who had been forced under Soviet rule in 1940, after only some two decades of national independence. Very soon other nationalities, including the Georgians and Armenians, expressed similar demands through the political channels that had been opened to them. The death knell for the Soviet Union sounded in 1991, when the Ukrainians, who constituted the second largest national group in the Soviet Union after the Russians, made similar demands for independence.

Gorbachev's political reforms ended up as a mortal threat not only to the continued leadership role by the Communist Party but also to the continued existence of the Soviet Union itself. Gorbachev seems to have understood neither of these ultimately fatal consequences of his reform attempts until late in the day. This explains why he could set in motion forces that would ultimately destroy what he had hoped to make more attractive and productive. In August 1991, Communist hard-liners attempted a coup against the reformer and his reforms, but they acted far too late and were too poorly organized to succeed. The coup was defeated by a popular resistance, led by Russian President Boris Yeltsin, who had broken with Communism earlier and, as it seemed, more decisively. After his formal restoration to power following the abortive coup, Gorbachev became politically dependent on Yeltsin and was increasingly seen as a transitional figure. His days as Soviet president were numbered, when the Soviet Union ceased to exist a week before the end of 1991. The dissolution of the Soviet state took place quickly and essentially without armed conflict. It was formally replaced by the Commonwealth of Independent States (CIS), a very loose union that lacked both a sufficient institutional framework and enough political will to keep it together. Almost from the outset, the CIS seemed destined to be little more than a loosely structured transitional device.

There is an undeniable gloom or hangover atmosphere in many of the accounts of post-Communist and post-Soviet Russia. A turn to some form of authoritarian nationalist populism cannot be ruled out. Recent parliamentary and presidential elections give a picture of electoral volatility, growing voter apathy or disgruntlement, and widespread authoritarian leanings in a politically exhausted society. They also illustrate how governmental leaders can favor, manipulate, or even help create "loyal" political parties.

Duma elections 1993. The first elections of a new Russian Duma after the end of the Soviet Union did not provide a propitious start for post-Communist politics. They came in December 1993 and were preceded by a complete breakdown of relations between President Yeltsin and the parliamentary majority. The Duma had originally supported Yeltsin, but opposition had grown over some sweeping economic reforms pushed by his government. The ensuing political conflict ran the gamut from a presidential dissolution of the legislature, through an impeachment vote by the Duma, to street demonstrations. It ended with Russian soldiers entering the parliament to force out deputies who had refused to leave. Yeltsin used the opportunity to have some political parties and publications outlawed. The powers of the president in the dual executive were constitutionally strengthened.

The electoral result was something of a political boomerang for Yeltsin. It resulted in a fragmented Duma, in which nationalists and Communists occupied key positions. The forces that backed market reforms, above all Yabloko, suffered setbacks. Henceforth Yeltsin seemed to play a more subdued role, and the new government pursued far more cautious reform policies. In 1994, Russia's military intervention in Chechnya, a breakaway Caucasian republic located within the Russian Federation, failed to give Yeltsin a quick and easy victory that might have reversed his slide into political unpopularity among Russians.

Duma Elections 1995. The regular parliamentary elections in December 1995 provided a further setback for the democratic and economic reformers in Russia. However, it was far less their rivals' strength than their own disunity and rivalry both before and after the election that weakened their parliamentary position. Together, the liberal reformers received close to a quarter of the vote. That was slightly more than the Communists, led as before by Gennady Zyuganov, and it was twice as much as the far-right nationalists in Vladimir Zhirinovsky's curiously misnamed Liberal Democratic Party.

Presidential election 1996. Yeltsin still knew how to win elections as he showed in the presidential contest of 1996, albeit in a run-off against the Communist leader, Zyuganov. By this time, ill health and heavy drinking added seriously to his governing problems. His frequent and seemingly erratic replacements of prime ministers did not improve the situation.

Duma elections 1999. Always good for a political surprise, Yeltsin saved two for the end. In the latter half of 1999, he selected a stronger figure for what turned out to be his last prime minister. Vladimir V. Putin, then 47 years old, quickly turned his attention to a tough new military intervention in Chechnya. Within Russia, his strong determination to suppress the breakaway province generated widespread support, based on its presentation and perception as a counter-terrorist move. In the Duma elections of December 1999, the new prime minister's

aura of tough leadership probably helped reduce the Communist result to 113 seats, or a quarter of the Duma.

Presidential election 2000. Without warning but with impeccable timing, President Yeltsin announced his resignation on December 31, 1999, just as the century and millennium came to an end. Putin became the new acting president and easily won the presidential election a few months later. Largely due to a favorable oil market for Soviet exports, the new president inherited a much better fiscal balance than Yeltsin or, especially Gorbachev before him.

In his first term as President of Russia, Putin aroused popular support with tough measures against organized crime and political terrorism. This was also true for the judicial action taken against some of the super-rich "oligarchs," who had made huge fortunes when state owned enterprises were privatized. Their ostentatious wealth, gathered quickly in an otherwise poor country, is highly resented by many Russians. The arrest of Mikhail B. Khodorkovsky, reputedly Russia's richest man, in the fall of 2003 met with far more critical reaction abroad than in Russia. During the previous two years, the billionaire had poured money into schemes for building a civil society in Russia. His new interest in political matters had led him to support some of Putin's critics and rivals. It seemed at least politically convenient to have Khodorkovsky out of the way during the parliamentary election of December 2003.

Duma election 2003. The election was memorable in several ways. The voter turnout was low (56 percent), at least by European standards. The democratic middle class parties fared poorly, once again. The Communists received only one-half of their vote share in the previous election (dropping from 24 to 12.7 percent of the vote). And a recently created party, called United Russia, performed better than any party since the end of one-party elections in Russia. Outside observers found evidence of fraud in the election and cited media favors to United Russia. On the other hand, it seems likely that this party, which the press described as largely defined by its loyalty to President Putin, would have done well in any case.

Presidential election 2004. Putin seemed a sure bet to win the presidential election in March 2004. In advance of the contest, he asserted his authority within the dual executive by dismissing the prime minister and appointing a new one. With the dependable backing of a parliamentary majority, supplied by United Russia and a few independents, the institutional and political basis for a strong presidency until 2008 seemed to have been secured. Some Russians wonder whether Putin will at that time step aside for someone else, seek to determine his successor (as Yeltsin did), or seek a third term (a move that would require a change in the Russian Constitution).

In his survey of Russia, Gideon Lichfield explains why pluralist democracy and the open market economy have been discredited for so many Russians. Steven Lee Myers shows how Putin's reaction to the worst terrorist act in Russia since World War II—the seizure of a school that ended with more than 300 dead hostages—fits into his established pattern of authoritarian responses. Finally, Peter Lavelle examines what he calls Putin's long-term reform agenda of "managed democracy" and "managed capitalism."

A difficult birth

European leaders have, at the last gasp, drawn up a new European Union constitution—but will it ever come into force?

How, six months after the Brussels breakdown, did European leaders resolve their differences on the new EU constitution? By three means: arm-twisting, obfuscation and opt-outs.

Arm-twisting worked on the main issue that caused the failure in December: the weighting of votes. Under heavy pressure, Poland and Spain accepted a new "double majority" voting system that dilutes their power. But a degree of obfuscation smoothes the change. The original plan was that a law would pass if it had the support of half the 25 EU countries, representing 60% of the population. The new deal raises the voting thresholds to 55% of countries, representing 65% of the population, with an added provision that a blocking minority must come from four or more countries. This makes it easier for Poland and Spain to block laws they do not like, but stops the big three doing it alone.

Britain's insistence on retaining a veto in many areas was the other big obstacle. Tony Blair won a clear-cut victory on tax. Provisions to harmonise corporate taxes by majority vote were struck out, a relief to countries such as Slovakia that rely on low taxes. Obfuscation dealt with foreign policy. The draft said that, if the new EU foreign minister made a proposal, the Union could decide whether to adopt it by majority vote. Now the foreign minister can make a proposal only if EU governments unanimously ask for it. Connoisseurs of baffling diplomatic compromises are referred to Article III-201(2), sub-section (b).

Mr Blair's other red lines were dealt with by "opt-outs". Under the constitution the EU gets the right to harmonise aspects of criminal law by majority vote. But a new provision states that, if a country feels a European law threatens "fundamental aspects of its criminal justice system", it may apply an emergency brake. Initially this delays the law's passage. If a new version cannot be agreed, objectors can opt out, allowing a smaller group of countries to press ahead. This tolerance of deeper integration by a small group was a sop to federalists. An even stronger emergency brake will apply to social security.

The biggest innovation is the Charter of Fundamental Rights, which protects everything from the "right to life" to the right to strike. Two years ago, the British were reluctant to accept that the charter should be in the constitution, because it was alien to British legal traditions and might be used to overturn Thatcher-era labour-market reforms. But long before the latest summit, Britain had accepted its incorporation, with the full force of law. Instead, Mr Blair took comfort in a statement stressing that it would apply "to the member states only when they are implementing EU law", as well as a reference to the need to interpret rights in accordance with national traditions and practices.

British lawyers had also prepared an exhaustive "explanation" of the rights, to show that they all exist in some other form either in EU law or in conventions that the EU has signed. The point was to underline that the charter creates no new rights. In an effort to nail this down, the British got a new clause inserted instructing the European Court of Justice (ECJ) to pay "due regard" to these explanations. In effect, the British wanted a provision that "all of the above is meaningless and will change nothing." Have they succeeded? John Monks, general secretary of the European Trades Union Congress, complains that Britain has defanged the charter. He admits that trade unions had hoped to use the charter to attack the Thatcher labour laws, such as one barring secondary picketing, but says that is now impossible.

Even so, the charter's impact will be broad and unpredictable. Paul Craig, a law professor at Oxford, says that the key point is that there must be a European law which provides a "lock" for a legal challenge under the charter. If a plaintiff can show that a member state, or the EU itself, is violating the charter in the way it applies the law, then it is open to a challenge before the ECJ. Mr Craig thinks the ECJ will take many more cases involving "rights-based challenges" to European law. Despite the qualifications now added to the charter, these could stray into sensitive areas of domestic politics. For example, France's ban on the wearing of the Muslim veil in schools could be challenged by a Muslim child from another EU country, on the ground that the ban violates parents' rights to "teaching of their children in conformity with their religious, philosophical and pedagogical convictions".

Will all this diplomatic ingenuity ultimately prove to be pointless? Ten countries (Belgium, Britain, the Czech Republic, Denmark, Ireland, Luxembourg, the Netherlands, Poland, Portugal and Spain) now plan to hold referendums on the constitution. Others, notably France, may yet follow suit. In Britain and Poland, the voters' mood currently points to a negative vote. That may be why the British and Poles want to put off any vote for a couple of years, hoping quietly that some other country says no first. The Dutch, who plan to vote by the end of the year, may oblige. Although they were one of the original six members, the Dutch are in a tetchy mood: they are the biggest per-head contributors to the EU, their economy has been in recession, France and Germany have torn up the stability pact that set fiscal

An EU constitutional primer
What it all means

Brussels
The final legal text may not emerge before October, but here is a simplified guide

The new EU constitution:
- Consolidates all European treaties into a **single document** labelled a constitution for the European Union.
- Incorporates a **Charter of Fundamental Rights** into EU law for the first time. This includes many social as well as political rights. But its application is limited to European law.
- Contains the first formal statement of the **primacy of EU law** over national law, a principle previously established by the jurisprudence of the European Court of Justice.
- Commits the EU to the progressive framing of a **common defence policy**.
- Commits the EU to creating common rules on **asylum and immigration** by majority vote. But individual states can still control the level of immigration.
- Extends **majority voting** to many other new, if mostly trivial, areas.
- Gives the EU formal **legal personality** for the first time, enabling it to sign international agreements.
- Retains **national vetoes** over direct taxation, foreign and defence policy and financing of the EU budget.
- Adopts a new double-majority **voting system**. Laws will be passed if 55% of countries representing 65% of the EU's population approve. This will make it easier for the EU to legislate.
- Create some **important-sounding jobs.** There will be a president of the European Council and a foreign minister. The president will serve for up to five years, replacing today's six-monthly rotating presidency. The foreign minister will combine the roles of the external-affairs commissioner and the EU's high representative for foreign policy.
- Limits the size of the **European Commission,** but only from 2014. The principle that all member states must have a commissioner at all times is abandoned.
- Gives new powers to the **European Parliament** to amend laws, control the budget and approve the choice of president of the European Commission.
- Includes **subsidiary** provisions under which, if a third of national parliaments object to an EU law, the commission must reconsider it.
- Creates an explicit **right for countries to leave** the EU.

limits for the euro area, and the EU is moving into immigration law, a highly sensitive topic.

If even one country votes no, it would be legally impossible for the constitution to come into force. But any naysayers may come under enormous pressure to vote again and say yes—or leave the EU altogether. If a larger group of countries reject the constitution, the document is probably dead. But in that case the EU might split into two groups: an integrationist core that accepted the constitution, and a more loosely aligned group that opts out of many political aspects of the EU. A constitution meant to unite a Union of 25 countries could thus end up dividing it.

What the EU Constitution Says

A constitution for the European Union was agreed in Brussels on 18 June, 2004.

KEY DEVELOPMENTS

February 2002: Convention starts work
June 2003: Draft submitted to EU Thessaloniki summit
December 2003: Brussels summit fails to agree final text
May 2004: EU enlarges to 25
June 2004: Text agreed

The constitution brings together for the first time the many treaties and agreements on which the EU is based. It defines the powers of the EU, stating where it can and act and where the member states retain their right of veto.

It also defines the role of the EU institutions.

POWERS OF THE EU

What the constitution says:

The Union is said to be subsidiary to member states and can act only in those areas where "the objectives of the intended action cannot be sufficiently achieved by the member states but can rather … be better achieved at Union level." The principle is established that the Union derives its powers from the member states.

What it means:

The idea is to stop the Union from encroaching on the rights of member states other than in areas where the members have given them away. Critics say that the EU can act in so many areas that this clause does not mean much but supporters say it will act as a brake and is an important constitutional principle.

DIVISION OF RESPONSIBILITIES

What the constitution says:

The EU already has rights to legislate over external trade and customs policy, the internal market, the monetary policy of countries in the eurozone, agriculture and fisheries and many areas of domestic law including the environment and health and safety at work.

The constitution will extend its rights into some new areas, perhaps most importantly into justice policy, especially asylum and immigration. It does away with the old structure of pillars under which some policies came under the EU and some under "inter-governmental" arrangements.

What it means:

It means a greater role for the EU in more aspects of life. In some areas, the EU will have exclusive competence, in others a shared competence and in yet more, only supporting role.

DECISION MAKING
What the constitution says:

The principle of voting by qualified majority will be generally applied. It is felt that otherwise getting the agreement of all 25 members would be a recipe for inaction. There will however be a veto for members in foreign policy, defence and taxation. And there is to be what's called an "emergency brake" in which a country outvoted on an issue can take its case to the European Council, though it can still be outvoted there. The European Parliament will have an equal say on decisions requiring majority voting.

QUALIFIED MAJORITY VOTING (QMV)
What the constitution says:

"A qualified majority shall be defined as at least 55% of the members of the Council, comprising at least 15 of them and representing Member States comprising at least 65% of the population of the Union."

What it means:

This system replaces the old one under which countries got specific numbers of votes. There were objections that Spain and Poland had too many votes and this methods is felt to represent a fairer balance between large and small countries. The new one will still lead to complicated permutations of voting but the final results of the "double majority" should command more general respect.

An amendment does away with a proposed procedure under which the European Council could have changed an area of policy to QMV. Now such a proposal will have to go before national parliaments and if one objects the measure fails.

PRESIDENT

What the constitution says:

The European Council, that is the heads of state or government of the member states, "shall elect its President, by qualified majority, for a term of two and a half years, renewable once." The candidate will then have to be approved by the European Parliament. The President will "chair (the Council) and drive its work forward and ensure, at his level, the external representation of the Union."

What it means:

This is a new post. At the moment, the Council presidency rotates through the member states every six months, so continuity is lost. The new President will therefore be a permanent figure with much greater influence and symbolism. But since he or she will be subject to the Council, the powers of the post are limited.

FOREIGN MINISTER

What the constitution says:

"The European Council, deciding by qualified majority, with the agreement of the president of the Commission, shall appoint the Union Minister of Foreign Affairs . . . [who] shall conduct the Union's common foreign and security policy."

What it means:

It sounds grand, but the minister will only be able to speak on the EU's behalf when there is an agreed or common policy, for example over the Middle East roadmap which members have accepted. The post will combine the present roles of the external affairs member of the Commission with the High Representative on foreign policy so it will be more prominent, especially in negotiating trade and aid agreements. The EU is also to set up its diplomatic service which will strengthen the Minister's hand.

FOREIGN AND DEFENCE POLICY

What the constitution says:

"The Union shall have competence to define and implement a common foreign and security policy, including the progressive framing of a common defence policy."

What it means:

It does not mean that a common foreign or defence policy will be imposed on member states. Each one will retain a right of veto and can go its own way. There is nothing that could stop divisions over Iraq for example. The aim however is to agree on as much as possible. Defence is even more sensitive and has been ring-fenced by references to the primacy of Nato for relevant members.

REFORM OF THE COMMISSION

What it says:

The Commission, the body which proposes and executes EU laws, "will consist of one national from each Member State" for its first term of five years starting in November 2004. After that it will be slimmed down to "a number of members . . . corresponding to two thirds of the number of Member States, unless the European Council, acting unanimously, decides to alter this figure."

What it means:

As a transitional measure to reduce the fears of small states that they will be ignored, each member state will have a Commissioner (only one each) from November. The idea after five years is to slim down the Commission from 25 to 18 (or one or two more if there are more member states by then). It is felt that the current Commission is too big with not enough jobs to go round.

EUROPEAN PARLIAMENT

What the constitution says:

The European Parliament is to have powers of "co-decision" with the Council of Ministers for those policies requiring a decision by qualified majority.

What it means:

The European Parliament has over the years acquired real power and the constitution confirms this. If the parliament does not agree to a piece of relevant legislation, it will not pass. This idea is to strengthen democracy because the parliament is the only EU institution in which voters have a direct say.

CHARTER OF FUNDAMENTAL RIGHTS

What the constitution says:

It sets out "rights, freedoms and principles." These include a whole list from the right to life and the right to liberty down to the right to strike.

What it means:

The Charter is wide-ranging but has to be tested in the courts before its exact status is established. The British government says that rules for interpreting the Charter mean, for example, that national laws on industrial relations will not be affected.

LEGAL SUPREMACY
What the constitution says:

The EU will for the first time have a "legal personality" and its laws will trump those of national parliaments: "The Constitution and law adopted by the Union institutions in exercising competence conferred upon it by the Constitution shall have primacy over the law of the member states."

What it means:

This really just confirms the status quo, which is that if the EU is allowed to legislate in an area of policy, its law will overtake any national laws. Equally in areas where it does not legislate, national law prevails.

By having a "legal personality", the EU will be able, as an organisation, to enter into international agreements. The old European Community had this right but the EU as a whole did not so its status in world diplomacy increases.

LEAVING THE EU
What the constitution says:

A new procedure describes how a member would leave the EU: "A member state which decides to withdraw shall notify the Council of its intention . . . The Union shall negotiate and conclude an agreement with that state, setting out the arrangements for its withdrawal."

What it means:

It was always the case that a member state could leave by simply repealing its own legislation. Now there is a formal procedure designed to show that the EU is a voluntary association. However a departing member would have to agree terms so there is an implied threat that it would not be that easy.

This clause is presumably designed never to be used.

The voters take their revenge

The European elections were marked by apathy and anger. This article offers an overview; the next four look at particular regions and countries

THEY were called the European elections, but that is something of a misnomer. When voters across the European Union went to the polls between June 10th and June 13th, their task was to elect a new European Parliament, which they did. But those who actually turned out mostly took the opportunity to cast a protest vote against their governments and, to a lesser extent, against the EU in general.

In 23 of the 25 EU member countries, the largest party in the national government saw its share of the vote slump, often spectacularly. Anti-incumbency was, indeed, the main pan-European trend. Incumbents suffered whether they were on the centre-left, like Germany's Social Democrats and Britain's Labour Party, or on the right, like Italy's Forza Italia and France's UMP. The only two governing parties to escape the trend—the Spanish Socialists and Greece's centre-right New Democracy party—both won general elections this spring, and are still in their honeymoons.

Although most votes may have been cast on national lines, they have European consequences. The election confirms that the centre-right will continue to be the largest group in the European Parliament, followed by the Socialists. Because the European elections are, in effect, the composite outcome of 25 national elections, it is hard to argue that Europe's voters as a whole have a made an ideological choice for the centre-right. Nonetheless, Hans-Gert Pöttering, leader of the European People's Party—the parliament's centre-right group—is demanding that the results be taken into account in the political choices made by heads of European governments. In particular, Mr Pöttering wants European leaders to choose a centre-right politician as the new head of the European Commis-

sion at their summit, which began as we went to press.

The four biggest political groups in the parliament will be the European People's Party, the Socialists, a new Liberal and centrist group and the Greens. All four groups are likely to be led by committed federalists. And if, as many expect, the Socialists elect Martin Schulz, a German MEP, as the new leader of their parliamentary group, three of the four will have German leaders. This reflects the fact that, after a reallocation of seats to reflect population size, the Germans now make up the largest national block in the parliament, with 99 out of 732 MEPs.

Although parties traditionally committed to closer European integration will be the largest in the parliament, the other pan-European trend in the elections was a rising vote for Eurosceptic parties. The biggest breakthrough was in Britain, where the UK Independence Party took 12 seats and 16% of the vote. In Sweden a new Eurosceptic party, the Junelist, took 14.4% of the vote, and three seats. In Austria and the Netherlands new political parties campaigning against corruption in Brussels also won seats.

Yet the media picture of a Eurosceptic tide across Europe needs to be qualified. Some prominent Eurosceptics did badly. Jens-Peter Bonde, a Danish MEP who is leader of the main Eurosceptic group in parliament, saw his party reduced from three seats to just one (Mr Bonde himself). And the *souverainistes* in France, who have been bashing away at transfers of sovereignty to the EU for many years, saw their vote slump. In 1999 they got 13% of the vote; this time, they were down to about 8.5%. In Poland, the populist anti-European Selfdefence party, which some had tipped to top the polls, in fact came in

fourth—although another Eurosceptic party, the League of Polish Families, came second.

Yet though there were setbacks for some Eurosceptics, the awkward squad, broadly defined, will be much bigger in the new parliament. A narrow definition of Eurosceptic parties would give them around 10% of all MEPs. But a broader definition of Euro-awkwards, including those who oppose the new EU constitution or whose main rallying-point is a campaign against EU corruption, yields a much larger group. Professor Richard Rose, a consultant to IDEA, a Swedish think-tank, reckons that, on this definition, as many as 200 of the 732 new MEPs will be "Euro-awkwards". Inevitably, they are an ideological rag-bag, which will make it hard for them to co-operate politically. They include such groups as British Tories, who see the EU as a source of socialist regulation, and Sweden's Greens, who fear that it is a tool of ruthless global capitalism. There are far-rightists and unreconstructed Communists, as well as nationalists and populists of all political persuasions.

The presence of these Euro-awkwards, who are spread among so many countries, will make an already unwieldy European Parliament much harder to manage (see table). But it should also make it rowdier and more interesting. That is, however, if anyone is inclined to pay attention at all. For perhaps the most noticeable trend in the European elections was a widespread lack of interest in voting.

Across the EU people are far more likely to vote in national elections than in European elections. This "Euro-gap", according to Professor Rose, now stands at an average of 21.9 percentage points in the 15 old EU countries and at 29.1 in the ten new members. Average voter turnout across the

European Parliament seats, by country and political group*

	EUL/NGL (United Left, Communists)	Greens	PES (Socialists)	ELDR (Liberals)	EPP (Liberals)	UEN (Nationalists)	EDD (radicals, Eurosceptics)	Not affiliated	TOTAL SEATS
Germany	7	13	23	7	49	–	–	–	99
Britain	–	5	19	12	28	–	12	2	78
France	3	6	31	–	28	–	–	10	78
Italy	7	2	15	9	28	9	–	8	78
Poland	–	–	8	4	18	7	–	17	54
Spain	1	5	24	1	23	–	–	–	54
Netherlands	2	2	7	5	7	–	2	2	27
Belgium	–	2	7	5	7	–	–	3	24
Czech Republic	6	–	2	–	11	–	–	5	24
Greece	4	–	8	–	11	–	–	1	24
Hungary	–	–	9	2	13	–	–	–	24
Portugal	2	–	12	–	7	2	–	1	24
Sweden	2	1	5	3	5	–	–	3	19
Austria	–	2	7	–	6	–	–	3	18
Denmark	2	–	5	4	1	1	1	–	14
Finland	1	1	3	5	4	–	–	–	14
Slovakia	–	–	3	–	8	–	–	3	14
Ireland	–	1	2	–	4	4	–	2	13
Lithuania	–	–	2	3	3	–	–	5	13
Latvia	–	1	–	1	3	4	–	–	9
Slovenia	–	–	1	2	4	–	–	–	7
Cyprus	2	–	–	1	2	–	–	1	6
Estonia	–	–	3	2	1	–	–	–	6
Luxembourg	–	1	1	1	3	–	–	–	6
Malta	–	–	3	–	2	–	–	–	5
Total EU	39	42	200	67	276	27	15	66	732

Source: European Parliament/EOS Gallup Europe

*Breakdown into groups is provisional

EU fell, for the sixth election running, to just over 45%.

The ten new arrivals to the Union, who were admitted only in May and who might be expected to be flushed with enthusiasm for their common European home, were in fact the most apathetic voters. However, even in nine of the 15 older EU member countries, voter turnout was down. In France on election night just over 7.6m people turned on their televisions to watch the election-results special. By contrast 13.5m tuned in for the England-France football match in the European championships: testimony, if ever there was, to the fundamental good sense of most of the European electorate.

Europe's Quiet Leap Forward

By Kenneth Rogoff

Is the European economy sinking or swimming? The discouraging headlines are by now monotonously familiar. "Europe is lagging in global recovery," declared the New York Times recently. "U.S. Outshines Expanding EU in Economic Competitiveness Study," reported Bloomberg in April. "Most Europeans who want to watch an economic recovery," one U.S. economist quipped in September 2003, "will have to watch it on TV." (Okay, that was me during my farewell remarks as chief economist of the International Monetary Fund.) But it's not just economists and journalists who are discouraged; Europeans are as well. Beneath the veneer of exuberance surrounding the European Union's (EU) recent eastern enlargement lies deep concern over the region's economic future.

Yet, recall how just 15 years ago everyone was heralding the slowdown and ultimate collapse of the U.S. economic juggernaut. At the time, economist Paul Krugman wrote the popular Age of Diminished Expectations, which envisioned a U.S. economy in perpetually low gear. Business guru Michael Porter wrote about how U.S. companies needed to learn from the Japanese economic model. Indeed, during the 1980s, other economic models, particularly Japan's, looked pretty good. When it came to manufacturing a superior automobile, Japanese firms and workers had much to teach the rest of the world. But then the 1990s arrived with waves of technological innovation, and suddenly the free-spirited and relentlessly entrepreneurial U.S. approach proved more adept at embracing new opportunities. So Japan dropped the baton and the United States reclaimed it. Times do change, and an economic system well suited to one set of historical circumstances often proves less appropriate for another.

Fast forward to 2004. Today, if you really want to get a rise out of top European policymakers and business leaders, don't berate them about Europe's well-known economic ills. Don't mention the rigid labor markets, the aging population, or the weak state-run university systems. Instead, tell them that there is a one in three chance that the world's leading economic superpower in 2050 will not be the United States or China, but Europe. They'll stand and stare at you, waiting for the punch line.

The truth is that Europe's economy is far from hopeless. First, the notion that European firms and workers are much less productive than those in the United States is simply uninformed. The main reason why Europe's output per capita stands at only 70 percent of U.S. levels is that Europeans work less than Americans—a lot less. Europeans work fewer hours per week, take longer vacations, and retire earlier. When it comes to leisure, it is the Americans, Japanese, and even the Chinese who have plenty of catching up to do. And as they and others start "consuming" more leisure over the next 50 years, Europe's relative economic size will expand. Second, Europe still has a spectacularly well-educated and versatile work force, even if dubious labor legislation holds it back, particularly in Germany. Third, recent empirical studies have convincingly shown that strong political and legal institutions drive economic growth. Say what you want about Italian politicians and the EU's new draft constitution, but European institutions remain models of honesty and transparency compared to those in Asia, Latin America, and the Middle East.

Finally, geography is another important driver of economic destiny and, last I checked, Europe was still situated in a relatively disease-free and temperate locale that offers far better working conditions than large parts of Africa, India, or Latin America. (Even compared to the United States, Europeans save at least a couple percent of annual income on heating and cooling costs.)

What would it take to catalyze Europe's economic advantages over the next 10 to 15 years? Actually, not that much. Catching up and leapfrogging are common throughout the history of international economics, at least for those regions that display strong institutions and remain open to international trade. As the United States develops new technologies, Europe can copy them. Where the United States has to make commitments to certain technologies—such as cellular-phone technology—Europe can leapfrog to the next, more efficient, technology. And though experience has left me too jaded to wax poetic over European economic policymaking, I believe that Europe just might succeed in addressing some of its structural economic challenges. Through German Chancellor Gerhard Schröder's "Agenda 2010" economic reform program, for example, Germany has at least begun to admit that its archaic labor laws might pose a problem.

Someday, too, Europe might realize that trade with more than 3 billion people in Asia is as important as internal trade within Europe. And finally, the Europeans might get lucky in a completely unexpected way that boosts their economic prospects. For example, one of Europe's biggest obstacles to deeper integration and economic growth is language. What if all Europeans are one day able to carry around small pocket computers that instantly and flawlessly translate languages? With the language barrier gone, competition and true regional integration would flourish in Europe. Stranger things have happened.

Yes, there is a fair chance that Europe's economy will fall farther and farther behind the United States and Asia. But there is also a significant chance—about one in three—that Europe is playing leapfrog and getting ready for a big jump. So don't write off the EU just yet. When all the experts agree that Europe is hopeless, you know it is time to take a second look. Maybe it will not happen this year or next, but there is every reason to believe that someday, Europe's economy just might be on top. No joke.

Kenneth Rogoff, Foreign Policy's economics columnist, is professor of economics and Thomas D. Cabot professor of public policy at Harvard University.

Putin Gambles on Raw Power

By STEVEN LEE MYERS

MOSCOW

Countries react differently to terror. After the Sept. 11 attacks, Americans rallied behind their government of their own free will. After the Madrid train bombings last March, Spaniards ousted theirs. President Vladimir V. Putin took steps last week that seem to ensure that Russians will do neither.

After modern Russia's worst terrorist act—the horrifying seizure of a school that ended with more than 300 hostages dead—Mr. Putin ordered an overhaul of the political system, stripping Russians of their right to elect their governors and district representatives in Parliament. Mr. Putin's response seemed like a non sequitur, since how the country conducts its elections on the regional level has little, if anything, to do with fighting the terrorism that war in Chechnya has spawned. But there was a logic to it, at least for Mr. Putin and his supporters, and it was one that dashed—perhaps decisively—hopes here and abroad that Russia had left behind its long, tortured history of authoritarianism when the Soviet Union collapsed.

The Kremlin has tried the iron hand before. In the end, it fails.

Democracy, Mr. Putin suggested in remarks after the school siege, does not result in stability, but rather instability. It does not unify, but rather divides. The principal threat posed by democracy in Russia today, he made clear on separate occasions in the last two weeks, lies in simmering ethnic and religious tensions along the rim of Russia where ethnically non-Russian people live. That division, he suggested, can only be controlled with an iron hand from above.

The attack on the school in Beslan was a watershed in a country that has had its share of them in history. And to Mr. Putin's critics, it confirmed their fears that, instinctively, he puts his faith in the Kremlin's unquestioned authority as the force to hold Russia together.

In the tragic arc of Russian history, it has always been so—even if, in the end, the rigid power of the center has always failed.

A theme of those who accepted Mr. Putin's prescription was distrust of the unruliness of electoral will in a country with deep ethnic, social, class and religious divisions.

It was those divisions that the fighters who seized the school—terrorists loyal to the Chechen separatist commander Shamil Basayev—seemed eager to stoke when they struck in multiethnic North Ossetia.

They seemed well aware that what Russia has failed to do in more than 13 years of post-Soviet politics is develop a sense of national identity that might overcome those divisions. Indeed, in the southern and Asian areas where Russia's Muslim groups live, an ardent religious identification is threatening to take its place.

"We live in conditions of aggravated internal conflicts and interethnic conflicts that before were harshly suppressed by the governing ideology," Mr. Putin said the night after the siege in Beslan ended on Sept. 3. In his speech, he lamented the demise of "a huge, great country," the Soviet Union, and rued the forces of disorder that its dissolution unleashed in Russia.

He returned to the theme four days later when he met with a group of American and European academics and analysts. Media accounts afterward focused on his pointed rebuff of calls to negotiate with Chechnya's separatists, whom he equated with Al Qaeda and Osama bin Laden. More telling about his plans to come was his reference to an obscure electoral dispute in Karachayevo-Cherkessia, one of the troubled republics of the North Caucasus.

In 1999, a disputed presidential election split the republic's two main ethnic groups, the Karachai and the Cherkess. As Mr. Putin recounted it, only his intervention—as prime minister, at the time—averted a civil war.

Clifford Kupchan, vice president of the Nixon Center in Washington, attended the meeting with Mr. Putin, and summarized Mr. Putin's dark view of democracy as "one man, one vote, one war."

"Given that Russia is not a melting pot, but rather a fragmented pot," Mr. Kupchan said in an interview, "he does not believe that democracy is the solution."

As he has before, Mr. Putin insisted last week that Russia remained on a democratic course, but he did so more reservedly than ever. When he announced his political overhaul on Monday, he said, "we must also, of course, react adequately to everything happening within the country."

In the turbulent years since the Soviet Union collapsed in 1991, Russia's embrace of democracy—and Mr. Putin's—has always been awkward.

The country's Constitution, written in 1993 after President Boris N. Yeltsin ordered the shelling of Parliament to roust defiant legislators, codifies basic democratic freedoms. In practice, though, democracy has been treated as little more than a license for a well-positioned few to steal and loot the old Soviet assets and to exploit Russians' baser instincts, especially when it comes to ethnic minorities.

Grigory A. Yavlinsky, one of the country's most prominent liberals, said the public's concept of democracy had been tainted by financial scandals and crises, by the consolidation of wealth in the hands of a few well-connected billionaires, by a decade of war in Chechnya, and lately by a wave of terrorist attacks, staged not in symbols of grandeur like skyscrapers and government buildings, but in places chillingly familiar to virtually every Russian: trains, subways, airplanes, a theater and, worst, a school.

On the southern rim, religion has begun to challenge the nation as a source of identity.

"All this period of time was called democracy," Mr. Yavlinsky said in an interview. "The people looked at it and said, 'If that is democracy, then, thank you very much.' " But he added, angrily: "All these things had nothing in common with democracy. It was Potemkin democracy."

During his presidency, Mr. Putin has shown little enthusiasm for the democratic experience. He has smothered political opponents, wrested control of independent television and manipulated the outcome of regional elections, none more so than the two presidential elections in Chechnya, where loyalists were elected by Soviet-like margins last October and again last month, after credible challengers were struck from the ballots.

Still, until Monday, Mr. Putin had never before reversed the fundamental democratic right of representation through the ballot—a right enshrined in the Constitution's letter and spirit, according to his critics. Under his proposal, which the Parliament will almost certainly adopt since it is dominated by parties loyal to him, Mr. Putin will appoint governors, presidents or other leaders who are now elected in each of country's 89 regions. Mr. Putin's proposals also would eliminate the district elections that choose half of the 450 seats in Parliament; instead, they will be selected based on national party lists drafted in Moscow in close consultation with Mr. Putin's Kremlin.

What was striking last week was how many Russian elected officials heartily endorsed Mr. Putin's plan.

"Elections are often dirty, with money from the shadow economy and criminal groups trying to influence the results," Valentina I. Matviyenko, the governor of St. Petersburg, told Itar-Tass on Wednesday as she fell into line behind a proposal that would deny her much of her electoral legitimacy and political authority. (She was elected last fall and, apparently, knew whereof she spoke.) "All this causes concern and alarm."

Her counterpart, Murat M. Zyazikov, president of the semi-autonomous republic of Ingushetia, who was elected with the Kremlin's help, echoed her fears. In a telephone interview, he said that elections had turned into "competitions between people with more money, which resulted in tensions in society."

"Western and human values are very close to us, but we have our own way of development," he said. "I think this was done in order to consolidate society."

In other words, it would seem, "the people have spoken" remains a phrase that strikes fear in Russia's ruling elite, which presumes to know better what is better for the country.

"It is soft Stalinism," Mr. Yavlinsky said.

He and others have spoken out against Mr. Putin's reordering, but they have done so from the margins. A rally organized by Mr. Yavlinsky's Yabloko party—with posters of Mr. Putin as Hitler—drew a handful of protesters. A few of the 15 independent members of Parliament voiced objections and then admitted there was little they could do to stop Mr. Putin.

The most prominent criticism came from the two men who, arguably, did much to create the system Russia has today, for better or worse. In twinned essays that appeared on Friday in the newsweekly Moskovskiye Novosti, Mr. Yeltsin and Mikhail S. Gorbachev wrote that Russia should preserve the democratic gains of the last 13 years.

"Strangling freedoms and curtailing democratic rights," Mr. Yeltsin wrote, "marks, among other things, the victory of terrorists."

What Does Putin Want?

"It is not hard to see Putin as an authoritarian. In most ways he is, based on Western standards. But, given Russia's current development trajectory, he probably has to be.... Either the Kremlin continues its very hard-handed approach to restructuring the economy or Russia risks becoming in effect a Burkina Faso with nuclear weapons."

PETER LAVELLE

With Russia seemingly returning to its opaque Soviet-like state, many Western journalists and analysts have also returned to their favorite Russia-watching pastime: asking the question, "Who is Putin?" Attempts at answers have rendered limited results, and they mostly overlook what is happening in Vladimir Putin's Russia. More times than not, perceptions of Russia remain at sharp variance with reality. Asking a better question—"What does Putin want?"—may tell us something about the Russia he intends to create.

President Putin's agenda is, if anything, straightforward. What may seem a lurch back to the Soviet past or a lunge forward to a new form of authoritarianism is in fact Russia overcoming the chaos of the first decade of postcommunism. Putin wants to develop a modern economy, end economic oligarchy, and assure that Russia's energy resources serve the national interest. He is willing to strengthen the state at the expense of democratic institutions if necessary. He wants to protect property rights, attract foreign investment, and restore an image of strength in the world. His pragmatism is evident for anyone who wishes to see it.

THE ECONOMIC REFORM AGENDA

Recently, much of the mainstream media and a number of academics have cast doubt on Putin's commitment to the development of a modern market economy in Russia. When Putin entered office, his support for liberalizing economic reform was clear to anyone who had taken care to note his past as a key aide to St. Petersburg Mayor Anatoly Sobchak, as well as his statements in his early days as acting president. Putin saw market reforms then as Russia's only credible future. A reasonable assessment of his economic agenda suggests he still does today—albeit to further the political goal of more broadly dispersed prosperity.

The economic reality presented to Putin when he assumed office in 2000 essentially consisted of competing claims made by the oil sector and the much weaker industrial lobby. The top five oil producers early on announced

a plan to significantly expand capacity, aggressively pushing for almost uninterrupted growth in oil production and exports. Market observers and analysts assessed the oil lobby's strategy as the "easy money" option. An eager and prepared market for oil and gas exports awaited in the United States, as well as in Russia's European and Asian neighbors, all seeking another source of energy besides the volatile Middle East.

The counterpoised agenda came from the weak but resurgent industrial lobby, which has been campaigning hard to have the Russian government diversify away from a dangerously high reliance on the oil and gas sector. This lobby petitions for government special preferences and investment incentives for Russia's other traditional industries, including aerospace, aviation, defense, and steel fabrication. Advocates argue that Russia still has a chance to develop global leadership in these areas, and they also push for building a domestic financial services industry.

Both lobbying groups have been forceful in the media in conveying their respective agendas to determine Russia's economic future. During Putin's first term the oil lobby appeared ascendant, and it has remained so to the present. But this ascendance may prove temporary.

Another plan for Russia's longer-term economic future has been aired, and repeatedly supported by none other than President Putin, yet analysts often neglect it. Announced at the start of 2000, this budgetary and economic policy calls for exploiting high inflows of cash from oil and gas exports to aggressively push broad-based growth across all economic sectors. Putin's objective, clearly and consistently stated over the past four years, is to eventually achieve a more diversified and balanced economy—an economy, that is, along lines seen in most European Union countries—with the intent of creating a greater and more egalitarian dispersion of wealth across the entire population.

A June 2004 study by the World Bank confirms Putin's political instincts. The report concludes, insofar as international comparisons are possible, that Russia has one of the most concentrated economies in the world, if not the most concentrated. A group of billionaires called the "oligarchs" largely controls the economy. Furthermore, ownership concentration is highly sector-specific: major owners dominate large industrial and raw materials sectors. Clearly, with these sectors constituting the Russian economy's main pillar (and primary source of exports), their owners can dominate the economy and, ultimately, politics and economic strategy. The World Bank analysis notes that, because of the immature market for ownership rights, "ownership in Russia's economy has not yet gone through the sort of 'remixing' which would have eliminated the most obvious traces of the transition from state to private ownership."

One key to creating a modern market economy in Russia is to reform, and in many cases gut, outdated and economically dysfunctional Soviet social services. To achieve this goal, Putin has risked his stellar public opinion ratings. He also has embarked on these structural changes while trying to break up economic and political oligarchy. This is no coincidence.

At the center of attempts to purge the Russian economy of residual Soviet elements is the monetization of the country's social benefits. Although Russia's economy was largely monetized between 1991 and 1992, it is often overlooked that the system of social benefits remained virtually unchanged from the Soviet era. The government continued to mandate discounts on pharmaceuticals, transportation, communications, and housing for retirees, military personnel, the disabled, and other dependent groups. As in the Soviet system, programs of in-kind benefits remained rife with corruption.

Putin's response has been to dismantle and remove the Soviet social programs, even though the political costs in doing so may rise as new benefit programs are put into place between now and 2006 and as the transition costs pile up. Thus far the reform project has been highly unpopular among recipients of outdated Soviet benefits, with Putin's popularity taking a strong hit for the first time during his presidency.

CUTTING DOWN THE OLIGARCHS

This is where the Yukos affair comes in. It would have been politically irresponsible, even dangerous, for Putin to impose additional sacrifices on ordinary Russians as part of structural reforms effected over the next few years without the recent demonstration of state power against the oligarchs. The prosecution of Mikhail Khodorkovsky, the head of Yukos Oil and Russia's richest man, has added to Putin's public support. The oligarchs, after all, are the personification of what went wrong during the 1990s, when a group of super-wealthy individuals essentially ruled Russia, and economic and political power was intensely concentrated as it had been during the Soviet era.

While trying to reduce the state's role in mandating costly entitlements, Putin has sought to increase the state's ability to govern by taking in more tax revenue that the growing economy generates. Only with effective tax collection can Moscow deal with the country's pervasive poverty and gross income differentials. And this, too, is related to the Yukos affair. The Kremlin has put on display an enormous legal arsenal in going after billions of dollars in taxes allegedly owed by Yukos. Other major tax offenders are unlikely to challenge the Kremlin again.

The effect is not lost on the public. Public opinion has long regarded the oligarchs as gross tax avoiders. Putin is attempting to completely reorder Russia's tax payment and collection system as part of his plans to modernize the economy. To convince ordinary Russians to honor their tax obligations, a public example had to be made of the oligarchs—with Yukos, Russia's largest privately held company, the signature demonstration. In this respect, Moscow is employing a strategy similar to one used by governments to prosecute organized crime. Since the state's resources are limited, it pursues the offender with the highest profile, hoping that others, along with ordinary Russians, will get the message and act accordingly.

The message appears to be working. Russian oil companies such as Tyumen Oil-British Petroleum, Sibneft, and Slavneft have announced that they will increase effective tax rates. In addition, as with most governments in oil-exporting nations, higher effective tax rates are expected during a time of extraordinarily high international petroleum prices. Overall, Russia's tax revenues during the first half of 2004 rose by 23 percent. Increased tax collection in the oil sector has allowed the government to lower tax obligations elsewhere.

With Yukos and its core shareholders serving as a test case, Russia's oligarchs will find themselves either cut down to size or allowed the kind of role that big business plays in other modernized economies. This outcome should not be regarded as regressive. Almost by definition, oligarchy represents a manner of fusing economic and political power within one person that institutions in the West have precluded since the 1920s.

In Russia, the concentration of both economic and political power in the hands of a few natural-resource oligarchs has been a brake on economic growth and diversification. Through their political influence, and in the face of weak state oversight and a weak industrial sector lobby, the oligarchs were generally able to divert public economic resources toward their own core business concerns and away from other parts of the investment-starved economy. The outcome of this arrangement has been all too obvious: cash generation, in the form of largely untaxed profits, was transferred abroad to avoid the tax authorities and the Russian public, should the state ever start questioning the legitimacy of the gains.

The Yukos affair represents a strong effort to alter the correlation of power between the regime and the oligarchs, designed to turn them into allies and servants rather than competitors and opponents of the state. Putin's thinking on the subject was revealed in a remarkable statement in 2003. "We have a category of people who have become rich and billionaires ... overnight," he said. "The state has appointed them billionaires, simply by giving away its assets practically free."

While more cases similar to the Yukos affair may occur, a comprehensive annihilation of the oligarchs appears unlikely. Putin wants a partial "nationalization" of the oligarch class, not the complete renationalization of their assets. Moving forward, the Kremlin will in effect appoint or dismiss or tolerate oligarchs-cum-big-businessmen based on their performance and their compatibility with national economic goals.

ENDING BIG OIL'S SELF-SERVICE

Seen in this light, the Kremlin's assault on Yukos is hardly an impulsive act of political and economic terrorism against property rights in the oil industry. Compared internationally, Russia is the only major oil exporter (and the only major oil-producing country with the two exceptions of the United States and United Kingdom) where the state is not the major operator drilling and lifting crude for production and export. The Kremlin is reordering the oil sector to roughly match international norms.

Putin is also looking to the future. Since 1999, Russia's petroleum production has increased 48 percent, primarily because of new wells. Turning out 9 million barrels of oil a day, Russia competes with Saudi Arabia as the world's largest exporter. Now Putin has called on his oil ministers to finalize plans for adding export pipelines to boost output to 11 million barrels per day by 2009. Russia's expected export increase, in conjunction with other world suppliers, could lower the cost of crude oil as early as 2006.

Because of almost unprecedented global demand and equally unprecedented high oil prices, the Kremlin's coffers receive an additional $1.5 billion per month over budget projections. A number of experts claim high petroleum prices last year accounted for almost half of Russia's 7.3 percent growth in gross domestic product. But who benefits from this? Putin has stated that "The government must base its decisions on the interests of the state as a whole and not on those of individual companies." And these are not just words; Russia's oil giants Lukoil and Sibneft are acutely aware that Putin means business.

Lukoil, Russia's second-largest petroleum firm, already has expressed its willingness to pay more taxes and work as a loyal foreign policy conduit on energy matters for the Kremlin. Sibneft, the third-ranked oil producer owned by oligarch and English football enthusiast Roman Abramovich, has also caught the Kremlin's attention. With investigations of Sibneft and Abramovich mushrooming, it appears only a matter of time before Sibneft will be under the Kremlin's heel as well.

The fate of Yukos's assets if it is forced into bankruptcy is open to speculation. The government-owned Rosneft Oil Company is rumored to be the Kremlin's favorite—some of Putin's key aides sit on Rosneft's board of directors. The natural gas monopoly Gazprom, government-owned as well, is also thought to be in the running. In the end it does not really matter. Yukos's transformation will essentially create what has been the Kremlin's goal from the advent of this affair: the creation of what could be called "KremPEC," the Kremlin Petroleum Export Corporation. This outcome would increase revenues and restore a large chunk of the economy under the state's purview for market reforms.

In addition to benefiting ordinary Russians, Putin wants the energy sector to serve the country's international political and economic interests. Russia has never had a meaningful relationship with the Organization of Petroleum Exporting Countries because independent domestic producers have been able to make petroleum policy without Kremlin consent. The impending breakup of Yukos and changes in ownership of the company's assets will allow the Kremlin to speak with a single voice when making international strategic petroleum alliances.

The international environment would appear to support KremPEC's ambitious goals. Terrorism threatens oil export giant Saudi Arabia, the cost of oil hovers around $45 a barrel, a gallon of gasoline costs up to $2.50 in the United States and far more in Europe, and continuing turmoil in Iraq limits the prospect of Iraqi oil significantly affecting international oil markets any time soon. Meanwhile, energy-hungry China and India are eager to find new and secure energy export markets to support their rapid economic growth.

The Kremlin has carefully thought out what the future might hold if Saudi Arabia, OPEC's powerbroker, becomes a target of larger and increased terrorist attacks. As the largest producer in the world, Russia might rethink its position concerning membership in the international petroleum cartel if Saudi exports were to face long-term risk.

In any event, the Yukos affair will quickly become part of history, its lessons absorbed. When that happens, Russia's oil patch will become more secure, attracting international petroleum investment, as well as providing Russia with needed cash flow to continue the reform of its economy. The difference is that energy negotiations and strategizing will take place behind Kremlin walls, instead of with oil oligarchs. For an energy-hungry world, doing business with KremPEC will become almost risk-free and eventually will make OPEC's current hold over world petroleum markets irrelevant. OPEC is about to be dethroned, with Putin's KremPEC its successor.

PROTECTING PROPERTY RIGHTS

The high-profile legal assault against Yukos has encouraged the perception that Putin is indifferent to property rights in Russia. But, beyond the state bureaucracy's sometimes aggressive, inefficient, or selective application of property rights law, the legal protection of private property is in fact being strengthened.

On June 10, 2004, Russia's parliament, the State Duma, adopted in the first of three readings 27 new bills introducing changes to the existing housing code, confirming the principle of private property by emphasizing the centrality of the state registry of property titles and by easing the property registry process and making it more transparent and affordable. The Kremlin designed all of these bills for the legislature. When the Western media comment that Putin is forcing legislation through without debate, these are the kinds of laws that are being passed.

Many observers claim that the Kremlin is most interested in asserting the "property rights" of the state, but this focus is overplayed. Putin is trying to redress the claims of property of the average Russian, which ultimately will create more confidence in property rights generally. Indeed, in Russia the government's treatment of Yukos is perceived as a reassertion of property-rights principles that were violated during the free-for-all privatization of public property in the 1990s.

Protecting property rights is one way Putin hopes to draw more foreign investment to his country. During five straight years of robust economic growth, Russia became an attractive investment target. Today, according to Western media, the Yukos affair has caused enormous concern that Putin is indifferent to minority shareholders in Russian companies. But the reality paints a different picture. Even though Russia is again experiencing net capital outflows (primarily from Russian nationals' expatriating funds), foreign investment has not stopped or reversed, and foreign companies continue to funnel money into Russia.

Final resolution of the Yukos affair could invite renewed interest in Russia as an investment target. If in fact smallish Kremlin-owned Rosneft becomes the flagship of Russia's oil sector, absorbing most of Yukos's lucrative assets, there is every reason to believe a company such as ExxonMobil would be interested in partnering with it or creating a joint venture. Such an arrangement would carry little if any political risk. Most analysts fail to understand that in Russia, just as with other emerging markets, the most solid and profitable business partner is the state. A number of Western oil giants have recognized this and are knocking on the Kremlin's door.

RUSSIA'S IMAGE IN THE WORLD

Since becoming president, Putin has demonstrated flexibility on a number of foreign policy issues that past Russian or Soviet leaders would have deemed unthinkable. Arms agreements can be concluded with a handshake. Expensive bases around the world are closed. Understanding and patience are shown when America establishes bases in parts of the former Soviet Union. Putin's foreign policy has emphasized constructively joining international institutions.

Yet the Kremlin's image in the world continues to suffer from charges of authoritarianism and revisionist imperialism. As mainstream analysts see it, the former KGB official has lived up to their expectations that he would clamp down on the "exuberance" of the 1990s; having established his "controlled democracy," Putin proceeds to choke Russia's nascent freedom to death.

A fairer assessment is that Putin will not be deterred from his domestic reform agenda, which includes a liberalized economy. The Russian leader has consistently adhered to the belief that his country can enjoy a good and strong image in the world only when it is economically competitive at home and abroad. Putin's regime is sending unambiguous signals that it is prepared to go to any length—including undermining its international reputation in the short term—to pursue its objective of rearranging the oligarchic economy inherited from the 1990s.

Putin also wants Russia to have strong neighbors and meaningful trading partners. What many call "Kremlin meddling" in the "near abroad" more often than not reflects efforts to promote political and economic stability on Russia's borders. It is often overlooked that millions of ethnic Russians live beyond the country's borders. Destabilized regimes and distressed economies in the countries that make up most of the Commonwealth of Independent States often negatively affect Russia's diaspora.

It is also often overlooked, and strangely so in light of the imperialist tendencies of czarist and Soviet forebears, that Putin is far more interested in promoting Russia's economic interests with neighboring countries than in pursuing heavy-handed military ambitions. Putin's Kremlin has learned well the cost of empire and is trying to avoid it.

THE NECESSARY AUTHORITARIAN?

All too often Russia watchers focus their analysis on what is called Russia's "managed democracy." Commentators are not wrong to worry about the present state of the country's political parties and weakened opposition, the Duma's tendency to rubberstamp Kremlin initiatives, the lack of checks and balances in government, and the electronic media's insufficient independence. Putin's decisions in September to abolish direct popular election of regional governors and to introduce legislation clearly designed to create Kremlin super majorities in the federal parliament have nothing to do with democracy in a Western sense. However, for democracy to have any meaning in Russia, the Kremlin must first create conditions in which the majority of Russians feel they have a stake in the country's destiny. This can come about with the kind of "managed capitalism" Putin is promoting. "Managed capitalism" is not state capitalism. The state does not want complete control of the economy. But Putin's government does want to help the economy find a more equitable and competitive balance.

Putin's crackdown on electronic media makes clear that the Kremlin will forgo public discussion of its policies as it reorders the country's economic priorities. Indeed, it is not hard to see Putin as an authoritarian. In most ways he is, based on Western standards. But, given Russia's current development trajectory, he probably has to be. Russia is at an extremely important juncture. Either the Kremlin continues its very hard-handed approach to restructuring the economy or Russia risks becoming in effect a Burkina Faso with nuclear weapons. It is very clear which future Putin wants.

Time is not on Russia's side. During Putin's presidency the country has experienced a remarkable economic recovery, but its infrastructure remains in a perilous state of disrepair, its demographic trends portend enormous difficulties, and domestic terror—the September hostage crisis in Beslan being the most horrific example—appears on the rise. This is why Putin is pushing the clock as hard as he can without engendering the kind of chaos that Russia experienced during the first failed decade of reform away from communism. The historical question—"Who is Putin?"—ultimately will find an answer. In the meantime, the Kremlin's economic-reform juggernaut continues its course, right on schedule.

PETER LAVELLE *is a Moscow-based senior analyst for United Press International and author of an electronic newsletter on Russia, "Untimely Thoughts" <untimely-thoughts.com>.*

Reprinted with permission from *Current History* Magazine (October 2004, pp. 314–318). © 2004 by Current History, Inc.

UNIT 4
Political Diversity in the Developing World

Unit Selections

Key Points to Consider

- What do developing countries have in common, and how are they diverse?

- How did the PRI maintain its dominance in Mexican politics for so long?

- What has caused the apparent impasse in Mexico's politics?

- How has multiracial democracy functioned in South Africa? What are some of the country's major political, economic, and social problems?

- How has Nigeria landed in its fourth republic since independence?

- How do you explain China's relative success in turning toward market reforms, as compared to the Soviet Union?

- How do you explain the apparent resilience of Indian democracy?

- What are some of the most common obstacles to the installation of a democracy in a country like Iraq or Afghanistan?

- Why is there so much attention paid to Turkey in the discussion of both the European Union and the development of the Middle East?

 **Links: www.dushkin.com/online/**
These sites are annotated in the World Wide Web pages.

Africa News Online
  http://allafrica.com/
ArabNet
  http://www.arab.net
Inside China Today
  http://www.einnews.com/china/
Organization for Economic Cooperation and Development
  http://www.oecd.org/home/
Sun SITE Singapore
  http://sunsite.nus.edu.sg/noframe.html

Until recently, the Third World was a widely used umbrella term for a disparate group of states that are now more frequently called the developing countries. Their most important shared characteristic may well be that these countries have not become relatively modern industrial societies. Most of these developing nations also share the problems of poverty and, though now less frequently, rapid population growth.

In many other ways, the developing countries vary tremendously in their socio-cultural and political characteristics. Some of them have representative systems of government, and a few of these, such as India, even have an impressive record of political stability. Many of them have been governed by authoritarian regimes that normally claim to represent the best interests of the people. Closer examination will often reveal that the avowed determination of self-appointed leaders to improve their societies is frequently less significant than their determination to maintain and expand their own power and privilege.

In recent years, market-oriented development has gained in favor in many countries that previously subscribed to some version of heavy state regulation or socialist planning of the economy. Their renewed interest in markets resembles the strategic policy shift that has also occurred in former Communist-ruled nations as well as the more advanced industrial countries. It usually represents a pragmatic acceptance of a "mixed economy" rather than a doctrinaire espousal of laissez-faire capitalism. In other words, targeted state intervention continues to play a role in economic development, but it is no longer as pervasive, rigid, or heavy-handed as often in the past.

In studying the attempts by developing countries to create institutions and policies that will promote their socioeconomic development, it is important not to leave out the international context. In the recent past, the political and intellectual leaders of these countries have often drawn upon some version of what is called dependency theory to explain their plight, sometimes combining it with demands for special treatment or compensation from the industrial world. In some of its forms, dependency theory is itself an outgrowth of the Marxist or Leninist theory of imperialism, according to which advanced capitalist countries have established exploitative relationships with the weaker economic systems of the less developed world. Such theories have often focused on external factors to explain a country's failure to generate self-sustained growth. They differ strikingly from explanations that give greater emphasis to a country's internal obstacles to development (whether socio-cultural, political, environmental, or a combination of these). Such theoretical disagreements are not merely of academic interest. The theories themselves are likely to provide the intellectual basis for strikingly different policy conclusions and development strategies. In other words, ideas and theory can have important consequences.

The debate has had some tangible consequences in recent years. It now appears that dependency theory, at least in its simplest and most direct form, has lost intellectual and political support. Instead of serving as an explanatory paradigm, it is now more fre-

quently encountered as part of more pluralist explanations of lagging development that recognize the tangled complexity of both internal and external factors likely to affect economic growth and change. There is much to be said for middle-range theory that pays greater attention to the contextual or situational aspects of each case of development. On the whole, multivariable explanations seem preferable to monocausal ones. That is also true for policy responses: Strategies of development that may work in one setting may come to naught in a different environment. One size rarely fits all.

Sometimes called the Group of 77, but eventually consisting of some 120 countries, the developing states used to link themselves together in the United Nations to promote whatever interests they may have had in common. They focused on promoting changes designed to improve their relative commercial position vis-à-vis the affluent industrialized nations of the North. Their common front, however, turned out to be more rhetorical than real, when interest divergences became apparent. It would be a mistake to assume that there must be a necessary identity of interest among these countries or that they pursue complementary foreign policies.

Outside the United Nations, some of these same countries have occasionally tried to increase and control the price of industrially important primary exports through the building of cartel agreements among themselves. Sometimes the result has been detrimental to other developing nations. The most successful of these cartels, the Organization of Petroleum Exporting Countries (OPEC), was established in 1973 and held sway for almost a decade. Its cohesion eventually eroded, resulting in drastic reductions in oil prices. While this latter development was welcomed in the oil-importing industrial world as well as in many developing countries, it left some oil-producing nations, such as Mexico, in economic disarray for a while. Moreover, the need to find outlets for the huge amounts of petrodollars, which had been deposited by some oil producers in Western banks during the period of cartel-induced high prices, led some financial institutions to make huge and often ill-considered loans to many developing nations. The frantic and often unsuccessful efforts to repay on schedule created new economic, social, and political dislocations, which hit particularly hard in Latin America during the 1980s.

Some of the poorer oil-producing nations recaptured a degree of economic leverage at the turn of the new century. In a reduced form, the situation resembled a déjà vu, as global energy consumption increased and the OPEC countries proved willing and able, at least for a while, to return to a coordinated policy of limiting the production and hence the supply of petroleum. As a result, energy prices rose rapidly, and the advanced industrial nations were once again made aware of their economic vulnerability, stemming from a dependence on a regular flow of relatively low-priced oil.

The problems of poverty, hunger, and malnutrition in much of the developing world are socially and politically explosive. In their fear of revolution and their opposition to meaningful reform, the privileged classes have often resorted to brutal repression as a means of preserving a status quo favorable to themselves. In Latin America, this led to a politicization during the 1970s of many lay persons and clergy of the Roman Catholic Church, who demanded social reform in the name of what was called liberation theology. For them, this variant of dependency theory filled a very practical ideological function by providing a relatively simple analytical and moral explanation of a complex reality. It also gave some strategic guidance for political activists who were determined to change this state of affairs. Their views on the inevitability of class struggle, and the need to take an active part in it, often clashed with the Vatican's far more conservative outlook. Like dependency theory, liberation theology today appears to have been effectively absorbed into more pluralist outlooks and pragmatic strategies for socioeconomic development.

The collapse of Communist rule in Europe has had a profound impact on the ideological explanation of the developing world's poverty and on the resulting strategies to overcome it. The Soviet model of modernization now appears to offer very little of practical value. The fact that even the Communists who remain in power in China have been eager to experiment widely with market reforms, including the private profit motive, has added to the general discredit of the centrally planned economy. Perhaps even more important, there seemed for a while to be a positive demonstration effect in some countries in Africa and Latin America that pursued more market-oriented strategies of development. On the whole, they appeared, at least until recently, to perform much better than some of their more statist neighbors tied to highly regulated and protected economies. This realization may help explain the intellectual journey of someone like the now-deceased Michael Manley, the former prime minister of Jamaica, who broke away from the combination of dependency theory and socialist strategies that he had once defended vigorously. During the 1980s, Manley made an intellectual U-turn as he gained a new respect for market-oriented economic approaches, without abandoning his interest in using reform politics to promote the interests of the poor. A similar political shift was taken by Fernando Henrique Cardoso, who came to embrace market economics before he became president of Brazil until 2002. In his youth, Cardoso had been exiled by the then-ruling military junta for having written a book on dependency and underdevelopment that became a primer of left-wing analysis in Latin America. More recently, the political scientist and activist Jorge G. Castañeda called upon the Left in Latin America to abandon utopian goals and seek social reforms within "mixed" market economies. Until his resignation in 2003,

he served as foreign minister of Mexico in President Fox's relatively market-friendly government.

Latin America illustrates the difficulty of establishing stable pluralist democracies in many parts of the developing world. Some authors have argued that its dominant political tradition is basically authoritarian and corporatist rather than competitively pluralist. They see the region's long tradition of centralized oligarchic governments, usually of the Right, as the result of an authoritarian "unitary" bias in the political culture. From this perspective, there would seem to be little hope for a lasting pluralist development, and the current trend toward democratization in much of Latin America would also appear unlikely to last. There are indeed signs pointing in that direction. Yet it is no mean accomplishment that one after the other dictatorship in the region has been replaced by an elected government. The demonstration effect of democratic governments in Spain and Portugal may well have played a role for the Latin American countries. Finally, the negative social, economic, and political experience with authoritarian rulers is one of the strongest cards held by their democratic successors.

In order to survive and develop, each of the new democracies must meet the pragmatic test ("Does it work?"), by providing evidence of social and economic progress. They may yet turn out to have been short interludes between authoritarian regimes. Strife-torn Venezuela is a case in point. The even grimmer case of Argentina, which was one of the world's most prosperous countries at the beginning of the twentieth century, serves as a warning that both authoritarian-populist and neoliberal policy directions can end in social and political disaster. On the other hand, the new president of Brazil appears to have had a promising start. Right after winning office as a politician with left-wing credentials, he sought to calm the financial markets by announcing a policy orientation that seeks to strike an optimum balance between the needs for greater social justice and efficiency.

In much of Latin America there seems to be a new questioning of the turn toward a greater emphasis on market economics that replaced the traditional commitment to strategies of statist interventions. It is too simple to explain this phenomenon as a product of impatience alone. A basic problem is that the benefits of economic growth do not "trickle down" as freely in practice as they do in economic theory. Instead, there are many instant losers in the economic dislocations that usually attend free market reforms.

There can be other serious problems as well, as shown in the attempt by former president Carlos Salinas of Mexico to move his country toward a more competitive form of market enterprise. His modernization strategy included Mexico's entry into the North American Free Trade Agreement (NAFTA) with the United States and Canada. In a time of enormous socioeconomic dislocations, however, Salinas showed considerable reluctance to move from an economic to a thorough political reform. Such a shift would have undermined the long-time hegemony of his own Institutional Revolutionary Party (PRI) and given new outlets for protest by self-perceived losers in the process. On the other hand, some observers criticized the market-oriented approach as too one-sidedly economic in its implicit assumption that modernization could be accomplished without a basic change of the political system. During his last year in office, Salinas was confronted by an armed peasant rebellion in the southern province of Chiapas, which gave voice to the demand for land reform and economic redistribution. Mexican criticism of Salinas intensified after he left office in December 1994 and 3 months later sought political exile abroad. Soon after, some top Mexican officials and their associates were accused of having links to major drug traffickers with a sordid record of corruption and political assassination.

The successor to Salinas was elected in August 1994, in a competitive contest that was reported as not seriously distorted by fraud. The ruling party won with 51 percent of the vote. The PRI's first presidential candidate, Luis Donaldo Colosio, had been assassinated in the early part of the campaign. His place was taken by Ernesto Zedillo, an economist and former banker who fit the technocratic mold of recent Mexican leaders. As president, he continued the basic economic policies of Salinas, but Zedillo appeared far more willing to listen to demands for meaningful political reform as well. In other ways too, his governmental performance was remarkable. Shortly after he took office at the beginning of December 1994, the Mexican peso collapsed and brought the economy into disarray. A major factor was the country's huge trade deficit and the resultant loss of confidence in the peso. This setback could have paralyzed the new president. Instead, he dealt energetically and skillfully with the problem. By early 1997, the Mexican government was able to announce that it had paid back a huge relief loan provided by the United States. The overall economic prospect for the struggling country appeared to improve considerably.

The Mexican elections of July 1997 represented something of a political milestone in the country's recent history. In retrospect, they were an omen of things to come. The basic result was a considerable setback for the Institutional Revolutionary Party—an outcome that would have been unthinkable in earlier years. In the lower house of Congress, the two main opposition parties deprived the ruling PRI of its habitual controlling majority. They began to transform what had been regarded as a rubber stamp chamber into a political check on the president.

Some months before the new presidential elections were held in the summer of 2000, the PRI appeared to have recovered electoral support. Many observers thought it could once again win the country's highest political office, which the party had occupied for 72 years. This time, however, the election process appeared to be more democratic than in the past, beginning with a much-touted, first-ever selection of the PRI candidate in a contested "primary" race that differed from the traditional "handpicking" used in the past. Looked at more closely, the political reality was not so very different, for the party apparatus was geared to promote Francisco Labastida, who eventually won the nomination.

In the end, the PRI lost its grip on power when Labastida was defeated decisively by the charismatic businessman, Vicente Fox. The latter's center-right National Action Party (PAN) also became the leading force in both houses of Congress. As a result, Mexico has now experienced a major political turnover as the result of a general election. It is necessary to add that the great experiment with political and economic liberty in Mexico has coincided with political gridlock and economic setbacks, as analyzed M. Delal Baer in the article, "Mexico at an Impasse." Here, as in much of the rest of Latin America, the high expectations that accompanied long-awaited political changes have been followed by disappointments.

South Africa faces the monumental task of making democracy work in a multiracial society where the ruling white minority had never shared political or economic power with black Africans or Asian immigrants. A new transitional constitution was adopted in late 1993, followed by the first multiracial national elections in April 1994. Former president F. W. de Klerk may go into history as a late reformer, but his political work was bound to displease many members of South African society. If the reforms were judged to have gone much too far and too fast by many members of the privileged white minority, they clearly did not go far enough or come quickly enough for many more people who demanded measures that went beyond formal racial equality.

Nelson Mandela, who succeeded de Klerk in the presidency, faced an even more difficult historical task. On the other hand, he possessed some strong political cards in addition to his undisputed leadership qualities. He represented the aspirations of a long-repressed majority, yet he was able to retain the respect of a large number of the white minority. It will be important that his successor continues to bridge the racial cleavages that otherwise threaten to ravage South African society. In an early interim constitution for post-apartheid South Africa, the reformers had sought political accommodation through an institutional form of power sharing. A new constitution, adopted in 1996, lays the foundation for creating simple majority-based governments that are bound to be dominated for now by the African National Congress (ANC), Mandela's political party. The new charter contains many guarantees of individual and group rights, but political prudence would seem to recommend some form of meaningful interracial coalition-building in South Africa's policy-making process. The continued task of finding workable forms of power sharing is only one of many problems. In order for the democratic changes to have much meaning for the long-suppressed majority, it will be necessary to find policies that reduce the social and economic chasm separating the races. The politics of redistribution will be no simple or short-term task, and one may expect many conflicts in the future. There is a host of other social problems confronting the leaders of this multiracial democracy. Nevertheless, for the first time since the beginning of colonization, South Africa now offers some hope for an improvement in interracial relations.

In December 1997, Mandela stepped down from the leadership of the ANC as a first step in his eventual retirement from politics. His place was taken by Thabo Mbeki, the country's deputy president, who became president in June 1999, soon after the parliamentary elections in which the ANC won 266 of the 400 seats, or one short of a two-thirds majority. The new leaders appear to have done their best to provide for political continuity instead of a divisive power struggle after Mandela's departure. Mbeki (and everyone else) lacks Mandela's great moral authority. He is widely described as "businesslike" and competent, but Mbeki's dismissive and poorly informed views on the country's serious AIDS problem have caused international alarm. Recently Mandela has stepped back into the public limelight by announcing his intention to play a leading role in promoting policies that will seriously identify and confront this issue.

Nigeria covers a large area and has more than 100 million inhabitants, making it the most populous country in Africa. The former British colony has returned to electoral politics after 15 years of oppressive military rule that brought economic havoc to the potentially rich nation. The path towards a stable and effective democratic governance in this culturally diverse country will be long and difficult. Ethnic and religious conflicts threaten the emergence of both a well-functioning civil society and a stable form of representative government. Nigeria bears close watching by students of comparative politics.

China is the homeland of nearly 1.3 billion people, or about one-fifth of the world's population. Here the reform Communists, who took power after Mao Zedong's death in 1976, began much earlier than their Soviet counterparts to steer the country toward a relatively decontrolled market economy. They also introduced some political relaxation, by ending Mao's recurrent ideological campaigns to mobilize the masses. In their place came a domestic tranquility such as China had not known for over half a century. But the regime encountered a basic dilemma: it wished to maintain tight controls over politics and society while freeing the economy. When a new openness began to emerge in Chinese society, comparable in some ways to the pluralism encouraged more actively by Gorbachev's glasnost policy of openness in the Soviet Union, it ran into determined opposition among hard-line Communist leaders. The aging reform leader, Deng Xiaoping, presided over a bloody crackdown on student demonstrations in Beijing's Tiananmen Square in May 1989. The regime has refused to let up on its tight political controls of society, but it continues to loosen the economic controls in the areas or zones designated for such reforms. In recent years, China has experienced a remarkable economic surge with growth rates unmatched elsewhere in the world. A still unanswered question is whether the emerging market-oriented society can long coexist with a tightly controlled political system. In February 1997 Beijing announced the death of Deng Xiaoping.

Jiang Zemin, chosen by Deng as his successor in 1989, had been the country's president since 1993. As government and party leader, he appeared determined to continue the relatively pragmatic course adopted by Deng. It needs to be added that the regime has revived a hard line in dealing with real, imagined, or potential political dissidence, which includes some forms of religious expression. Moreover, there are familiar signs of social tension, as China's mixed economy leaves both "winners" and "losers" in its wake. Despite the country's undeniable problems and shortcomings, China's leaders have steered clear of the chaos that has plagued post-Soviet Russia. They seem determined to continue with their tight political controls, even as their economy becomes freer and more market-oriented. Some observers believe that the basic economic and political norms will eventually begin to converge, but that remains to be seen. A test case is the movement known as Falun Gong, which the ruling Communists see as a threat because of its effective organization and solidarity—qualities that no longer characterize the Communist Party to the same degree as earlier.

It remains to be seen whether Hu Jintao, who was named party leader in the latter half of 2002, will turn out to move the country further in a technocratic direction, as many observers expect. What seems certain is that Hu Jintao has moved quietly to further concentrate power in his own hands. In September 2004 he replaced Jing Zemin as the country's military chief—a major political change, as Joseph Kahn explains.

India is often referred to as a subcontinent. With more than one billion people, this country ranks second only to China in population and ahead of the continents of Latin America and Africa combined. India is deeply divided by ethnic, religious, and regional differences. It is a secular state, but tense relations between politicized Hindu extremists and members of the large Muslim minority occasionally erupts in violence. For the vast majority of the huge population, a life of material deprivation has long seemed inescapable. That may be changing. There is now a possibility of meaningful relief if the country's struggling economy could be freed from heavy-handed state interference. The turn in that direction can be traced back to the early 1990s, when the market revolution cautiously touched India.

The economic changes have taken place in a context that carries the potential for political chaos. In 1992 the national elections were marred by the assassination of Rajiv Gandhi, a former prime minister. When his Congress party won the election, one of its veteran politicians, P.V. Narasimha Rao, headed the new government. He followed in the steps of other reformers in the developing world by loosening economic planning and controls on international trade and investment. These market-oriented policies brought substantial economic gains but were accompanied by a flurry of corruption scandals that tainted several members of Rao's cabinet. His Congress party was badly defeated in the general election of May 1996. There followed some short-lived multiparty coalition governments.

In the spring of 1998, parliamentary elections produced a result that seemed to promise even more instability for the world's largest democracy. The Bharatiya Janta Party (BJP), dominated by Hindu nationalists, won the most seats, but it was only able to govern in alliance with several smaller parties. The coalition provided a weak parliamentary majority, but it was able to survive just over a year, partly because the BJP leader, Prime Minister Atal Behari Vajpayee, was able to tame the rhetoric of his own party's more militant Hindu-nationalist members. As long expected, the government collapsed in April 1999, when a small coalition member defected.

Some 300 million Indian voters took part in the new elections that followed. The result was a clear victory for the incumbent governing coalition, now numbering 24 parties. It was the first time in 27 years that an incumbent prime minister won re-election in India. Once the dominant Congress party, which had hoped to revive and return to power, instead suffered its worst defeat since independence. In the elections of 2004, however, it recuperated and returned to power as key member of the United Progressive Alliance. The BJP returned to the opposition.

In the near future, at least, the dramatic political change seems likely to be accompanied by continuity of economic strategy, for the new Prime Minister, Mr. Singh, is also identified with market-friendly policies. Ironically, this deregulating and increasingly dynamic economy may be the source of "real change" in India, but the cumbersome political institutions provide the framework that holds the country together, as Rajan Menon observes. Some India watchers warn that the country's market reforms have caused social and economic dislocations that could spark new political turmoil and ethnic strife. As always, this huge multiethnic democracy bears watching.

Mexico at an Impasse

M. Delal Baer

THE EXPECTATIONS REVOLUTION

THE JULY 2000 DEFEAT of Mexico's Institutional Revolutionary Party (PRI) after more than 70 years of rule sparked a revolution in expectations. There were celebrations in the streets, glowing editorials in foreign newspapers, and expressions of undiluted optimism in investment and policy circles. Newly elected president Vicente Fox projected a triumphant image of strength and confidence that inflated hopes at home and abroad: private investment would flood in, the rule of law would prevail, the sins of the past would be punished, and the U.S.–Mexico relationship would flower. More profoundly, Mexico would elude its existential condition as an underdeveloped nation.

Three years into Mexico's democratic transition, few of these dreams have been realized. Mexican politics are more democratic but less governable and are suffering from gridlock between the executive and legislative branches. The economy is stable, but growth and competitiveness are lagging as the next generation of reforms—tax, energy, and labor—falls prey to partisan bickering in Mexico's Congress. And the friendship between Fox and President George W. Bush has cooled over differences about immigration and policy toward Iraq. Mexico shows no signs of an imminent crisis, but its triple political, economic, and diplomatic impasse is taking a toll. The price of unreasonably high expectations has been premature disillusionment. A breakthrough in at least one area must come fairly soon—lest Mexico's grant experiment with economic and political liberty fail to fulfill its potential.

UNGOVERNABLE DEMOCRACY

THE PRINCIPAL CONCERN of Mexico's political elite today is how to build governing majorities and achieve consensus. After three years of stalemate in Congress, there is debate over whether Mexico's political paralysis is the result of a constitutional structure that makes it inherently ungovernable or of weak leadership on the part of President Fox. The answer to this question is not insignificant. If the logjam is due to weak leadership, the presidential elections of 2006 might resolve the problem. If the logjam,

however, is structural in nature, it will be much more difficult to overcome.

Fox's leadership style is unconventional and ideologically heterogeneous. Some commentators find him refreshing and authentic, whereas others complain that he has not established clear priorities or consistent legislative strategies. But whatever Fox's shortcomings, it is clear that any leader, no matter how gifted, would have struggled with the challenge of assuming the presidency at Mexico's singular moment of regime change. Fox won only 42.5 percent of the vote in the 2000 elections, and his National Action Party (PAN) controls just 30 percent of seats in the lower house of Congress (the Chamber of Deputies) and 38 percent in the Senate. In most instances of regime change, the old regime is defeated and dismantled definitively. In Mexico, the PRI was defeated but far from dismantled: it remains ensconced in Congress as a legitimate opposition party.

Many Mexicans believe that a democratic transition must include a punitive settling of accounts with the PRI. As a result, Fox has found himself on the horns of a dilemma: he needs a juicy corruption case from the PRI era to prosecute, but he also needs the PRI's support to form congressional majorities. Fox has failed to reconcile these competing demands. His cabinet is divided between pragmatists who see accommodation with the PRI as inescapable and confrontationists who think that the president's legitimacy depends on destroying the PRI, root and branch. Fox has oscillated between these two approaches, launching vituperative attacks on the PRI one day and calling for congressional unity the next. The result has been stalemate: the government launched investigations of the PRI that were aggressive enough to undermine the chance of legislative cooperation but not decisive enough to satisfy the appetite for vengeance.

Striking a balance between governability and historical reckoning is most difficult during the early years of a democratic transition, as was the case in Argentina and Chile. Some will inevitably complain that Mexico's democratic transition did not settle accounts in any spectacular fashion, despite the fact that a special prosecutor is investigating former President Luis Echeverría for his alleged role in the 1968 Tlatelolco student massacre. Others will argue that the PRI never committed human rights abuses on the scale of Chile's Augusto Pinochet or Argentina's Jorge Rafael Videla, making an expurgation of past sins less necessary. But what is most important is that the first three years of Mexico's transition have not seen a single serious threat to democracy. This success speaks well of both President Fox, who has emphasized stability, and the PRI, which accepted its defeat with at least a modicum of grace. To the extent that the stalemate of the past three years is attributable to the unique dilemma of regime change, it is a small price to pay for democratic survival. When such one-time tensions have faded, Mexico's parties may be able to put aside the past and cooperate on national business.

Today's gridlock, however, also stems from structural flaws that make Mexico particularly susceptible to the frustrations of a divided government and a limited presidency. Traditionally, governability was ensured only by the PRI's ability to deliver overwhelming majorities in both houses of Congress, as the politician Manuel Camacho has noted. There is no constitutional mechanism to guarantee that a president can successfully govern in the face of an opposition Congress. Without a majority in either house, therefore, the Fox presidency was instantly cut down to size by PRI legislators more than willing to exercise the constitutional prerogatives accorded to them in their new role as the opposition (the PRI's Senate leader recently declared that his party would govern from Congress).

It is improbable that any Mexican political party will be able to reconstruct the electoral majorities formerly enjoyed by the PRI. The historic 2000 elections did not produce realignment in favor of the PAN, nor did the 2003 midterm elections result in a PRI majority in Congress. Instead, three major parties of roughly equal strength vie for dominance: the PRI, the PAN, and the left-wing Democratic Revolutionary Party (PRD). Each party, moreover, is riven by personal and ideological faults that undermine the negotiating capacity of party leaders in Congress. The system is further divided by three small parties that survive thanks mostly to the use of proportional representation (based on a party's percentage of the national vote tally) to elect a portion of Congress.

Looking ahead to the 2006 presidential election, one can envision a scenario similar to that of the 2000 election: weak parties and strong candidates who lack electoral coattails. Mexico City Mayor Andres Manuel Lopez Obrador, one of the country's most popular potential presidential candidates, consistently polls in the neighborhood of 52 percent even though his party, the PRD, has never won more than 25 percent of the vote in a national election. In the event that a ticket-splitting Mexican electorate gives him a victory but only 17 percent of Congress to his party, forming a governing alliance would be immensely difficult. Similarly, a PRI or PAN candidate could win a weak victory in the presidential race while his or her party achieved a tepid plurality in Congress.

Some analysts have advocated a major constitutional overhaul to install a parliamentary regime and guarantee majority support for the executive. But many Mexicans, understandably disconcerted by the impasse between the president and the Congress and fearful for the viability of democracy, instead look back nostalgically on the days of a strong president. Accustomed to a pyramidal presidency so powerful that it was once described as a six-year Aztec monarchy, they are bewildered by this upside-down world. But the possibility of restoring an all-powerful presidency is remote, and reengineering the Mexican constitution to implant a parliamentary system is similarly unlikely.

Disillusionment with the political parties may account for historically low voter turnout (42 percent) in the 2003 midterm elections and could cause the electorate to seek out more charismatic figures. Jorge Castañeda, formerly Fox's foreign minister, launched an exploratory bid for the presidency on this logic, arguing that Mexican voters go to the polls only when presented with a charismatic individual who offers hope of change. As one senior Mexican diplomat has wryly commented, "In Mexico we have egos, not institutions." This trend toward personalism and weak parties may be nothing to worry about. Mexico might simply go the way of the United States: weak but persistent parties that field strong candidates. In a more ominous scenario, however, the decay of party institutions and congressional gridlock could restore the authoritarian temptation and pave the way for wild-card leadership.

Gridlock could restore the authoritarian temptation.

Under current conditions, there are only two ways to create majorities in Mexico: alliance building or modest political reform aimed at consolidating the party system. Without strong parties that can achieve electoral majorities across the board, the negotiating skills of future presidents will be crucial. Mexican political culture has little experience with compromise, and the road to democracy has been paved with insult and calumny. Give-and-take is central to a well-functioning democracy, but the spirit of retribution has bogged down relations between Fox and the PRI-dominated legislature. In time, the public may blame all parties for such gridlock, thereby creating incentives to compromise. The elimination of proportional representation, meanwhile, would encourage the gradual consolidation of the party system. Instituting campaign finance reform, congressional reelection, and "second round" provisions in presidential elections (to guarantee majority victories) would further enhance party legitimacy.

If there is hope for ending gridlock in the remaining three years of the Fox administration, it stems from the fact that all three major parties have a shot at winning the presidency in 2006. None wishes to inherit an ungovernable nation, and none wishes to be accused of obstructionism. The hunger for power, therefore, may encourage a flurry of congressional activity toward the end of Fox's tenure.

Mexican democracy is not fated to be dysfunctional. But without some reform, it may end up in a peculiar state of institutional limbo and semipermanent gridlock: a constitutionally mandated presidential system that operates more like a majority-less parliamentary system.

THE COMPETITIVENESS DEFICIT

THE 2000 PRESIDENTIAL ELECTION was the first in close to 30 years to take place unaccompanied by a massive devaluation of the Mexican peso—thanks to former President Ernesto Zedillo's commitment to fiscal discipline and a free-floating currency. Three years later, Mexican democracy has passed an important economic test: both Congress and President Fox have resisted the temptation to engage in deficit spending and foreign borrowing in the face of a stubborn, painful recession. In fact, Fox's economic team has achieved unprecedented price and monetary stability—treasury bond rates are below five percent, and inflation is around four percent. Meanwhile, the federal deficit has fallen to less than one percent of GDP, foreign debt represents less than 20 percent of GDP, and Mexico's balance of trade is stable. Macroeconomic stability has permitted real wages to rise for three consecutive years, and, if growth returns in a low-inflation environment, Mexico will increase its per capita GDP for the first time in nearly 30 years.

In the meantime, however, Mexico is caught in a grinding stagnation that has led to a net loss of 2.1 million jobs, average GDP growth of less than one percent in the first three years of the Fox administration, and a surge in illegal immigration to the United States. The onset of recession in the United States hit Mexico hard, especially in the manufacturing sector. But there are signs that the Mexican recession is the result of a growing competitiveness deficit, not simply a matter of bad luck to be solved by an uptick in the U.S. economy. Mexico faces pressures from Chinese exports in the U.S. market and from foreign assembly plants moving to the Caribbean, China, and other Latin American nations.

The current congressional impasse over economic reform is especially damaging in this context. The stalemate is not simply partisanship run amok; it is a symptom of regime change, of fundamental disagreement over how much to preserve from the older order. Many of Mexico's market reforms were imposed from above by the PRI's ruling technocracy in the 1990s. Ironically, opposition to them now comes not from President Fox and the PAN but from the PRI itself—the continuation of a long-simmering conflict within the party that has erupted into an open rebellion since the PRI lost the presidency. (Many PRI-istas, however, have started to push for early passage of some

reforms to ease the task should the party recapture the presidency in 2006.) Although there is a cost to delaying reform, Mexico does need time to build a foundation of democratic support for its market economy. Competitiveness-enhancing reforms run headlong into taboos and have steep political costs.

Energy policy provides a good example of this deadlock. Energy has long served as a sacred symbol of Mexican sovereignty, and the constitution explicitly prohibits private ownership in energy sectors, even though the government does not have sufficient resources to finance its own oil and natural gas exploration. As a result, cheap energy does not offer the natural advantage to the Mexican economy that it should. Electricity costs there are, on average, higher than those in the United States, and there are frequent energy shortages that, among other things, keep investment away from many northern industrial parks. Although Mexico sits on one of the world's largest natural gas reserves, it has to import natural gas from the United States. (In fact, federal efforts to develop privately run, competitively priced electrical capacity have slowed to a crawl due to scarce gas supplies.) "A Mexican businessman can go to Texas and invest in natural gas production to sell to Mexico, but that businessman is unable to do the same at home in Mexico," one economic official has scoffed. Still, mustering the two-thirds congressional majority needed to change the constitution and liberalize the energy sector is a daunting task.

Reform of the judicial system, another crucial step in improving Mexico's economic situation, will not be easy either. Foreign investors are wary of wobbly courts (plagued by frivolous litigation and corrupt judges) and the capriciousness of the rule of law. The Dutch financial services company ING has been sued three times in three separate criminal courts for alleged underpayment on an insurance policy held by Fertinal, a nearly bankrupt company hoping to save itself with a huge reward. Senior ING executives have been arbitrarily jailed, and ING even saw its assets frozen on the order of a Mexico City court—a move that sent chills through the foreign financial community.

Raising taxes, also a necessary reform, is another political bombshell. Mexico's tax collection rate hovers around 11 percent of GDP—the lowest among the members of the Organization for Economic Cooperation and Development, which average collection rates of almost 27 percent. Future competitiveness depends on long-term investment in physical infrastructure and human capital, and Mexico's efforts in these areas will lag so long as its tax collection rate remains so low. Windfall resources from privatization and high oil prices have made it possible to postpone tax reform over the past two decades, but the moment of truth is fast approaching. Mexico is running out of public companies to privatize, oil prices are falling, and revenues derived from commercial tariffs have declined with the advent of free trade.

A coming demographic shift will only exacerbate these spending pressures. Although Mexico is typically considered a young country, the percentage of the population aged 65 and over is projected to increase to 13 percent in 2030 and to almost 25 percent by 2050 (from a low of 2.6 percent in 1930). In absolute terms, this means that there will be 17 million people older than 65 in 2030 and more than 30 million in 2050. The implications of this shift for health and pension costs are staggering. If Mexico cannot soon achieve economic modernity and tax efficiency, it will face a social catastrophe. As Richard Jackson, director of the Global Aging Initiative, puts it, Mexico must grow rich before it grows old.

Mexico has made enormous strides toward fiscal and monetary stability, but its economy cannot afford to idle while the rest of the world speeds ahead. Stalled reforms have dampened investor enthusiasm, costing Mexico $5 billion in direct foreign investment (which fell from $16 billion in 2000 to $11 billion in 2002). The failure to generate the more than one million jobs needed for new entrants into the labor market, meanwhile, could thrust hundreds of thousands of Mexicans out of their homes and toward the U.S. border. Still, some long-term investors are betting that the backlash against liberalization will fade as the wheels of generational change turn. Youthful Mexican politicians from all parties express positive convictions about the need for continued economic opening. Mexico may be closer than it seems to a true consensus on an open economy, but a breakthrough must occur soon if the competitiveness deficit is to be eliminated and the hemorrhage of Mexicans into the United States stanched.

BEYOND NAFTA

MEXICO'S DEMOCRATIC REVOLUTION raised hopes of a revolution in U.S.-Mexican relations. But ever since the North American Free Trade Agreement went into effect in 1994, the two countries have been searching for the next great advance in bilateral relations. Jorge Castaneda proposed transforming NAFTA into a European-style "North American Community," complete with free movement of labor and social development funds for poorer nations. Fox, enamored of Europe's success in helping to develop the formerly poor countries of Spain and Portugal, hoped that the United States might be willing to do the same for Mexico. He also asked that the Bush administration provide de jure recognition of the de facto residence of millions of Mexicans working illegally in the United States, the first step toward a free labor market.

A Mexican foreign policy that demanded sizeable amounts of aid and the legalization of millions of immigrants, however, was the last thing the Bush administration had expected. Washington tends to associate the European model with overregulation and excessive supranatural bureaucracy, and Mexico underestimated U.S. sensitivity to job competition and downward pressure on

wages in the face of looming recession. The free movement of labor remains unrealistic as long as Mexican wages are a fraction of wages in the United States. Plenty of U.S. policymakers remember that the last amnesty offered by Congress—the Simpson-Rodino Immigration Reform and Control Act of 1986—resulted in ever-larger waves of illegal immigration and undermined the credibility of U.S. law enforcement. Ultimately, the events of September 11 allowed the White House to gracefully sidestep the inconvenient requests of its southern neighbor.

Such setbacks do not mean that integration cannot continue or that nothing has been accomplished. Mexico has successfully broadened U.S. focus beyond its prior preoccupation with drug trafficking (thanks in part to the progress it has made in arresting cartel leaders, which allowed the U.S. Congress to modify its controversial certification process). The Partnership for Prosperity, a creative initiative launched by Bush and Fox in September 2001 to foster investment in Mexico's underdeveloped regions, has brought the Overseas Private Investment Corporation and the Peace Corps to Mexico for the first time. There is hope for coordination in developing border infrastructure and North American standards and certification procedures. Even in immigration policy, incremental progress is possible if care is taken to protect certain sensitive service and manufacturing sectors.

U.S.-Mexican relations are tied up in knots: each nation expects the impossible of the other.

Three lessons of enduring importance emerge from the experience of Bush and Fox thus far. The first is that it does not pay to hinge the success of the entire relationship on a single issue, as Mexico did when it defined success exclusively in terms of a comprehensive immigration accord. The second is the need for prior agreement when one partner seeks a sea change in relations. When the Fox administration announced its desire for changes in U.S. immigration policy without any prior negotiation, it created expectations that plague the relationship to this day. The third lesson is that issue linkage can prove fatal for bilateral harmony. With such a complex bilateral agenda, linking issues allows a fire in one area to spread to others, leading to multiple breakdowns in bilateral relations. Mexico tried to link the entire agenda to immigration; the United States has done the same with Iraq. As a result, U.S.-Mexican relations are tied up in knots: each nation expects the impossible of the other.

The next great shift in bilateral relations is within sight, but it awaits a more propitious moment. The United States and Mexico must first erect a new North American security architecture. Protection of the North American perimeter is essential to the security of both nations. (Consider the effects on Mexico of a contagious biological attack on Los Angeles or Dallas, or the economic costs should a terrorist attack on the United States be launched from Mexico.) Nonetheless, they have had no formal defense relations since the end of World War II, and, given Mexico's recent diplomatic choices, there is little chance that a strategic alliance will be forged in the short term. A few days before the first anniversary of September 11, Mexico withdrew from the Rio Pact, the western hemisphere equivalent of the NATO charter's provisions for collective self-defense. This move was a stunning blow from a neighbor presumed to be a friend. Mexico had taken to lambasting the pact as a militaristic relic of the Cold War, and the United States never actually expected that Mexican troops would participate in a Rio Pact—sponsored action. Nonetheless, Washington interpreted Mexico's withdrawal as a sign that the United States, in its darkest hour, could not expect even symbolic solidarity. So crippled was Mexico by its historic insecurity that, when confronted with the diplomatic challenges of September 11, it could not see the genuine vulnerability of its northern neighbor, let alone respond compassionately, without equating compassion with subordination.

Mexico's position in the run-up to the war on Iraq was also troubling. Its decision not to support the U.S. position can be attributed to domestic opposition and pressure from other allies, but it also had a tendency to indulge in what one senior U.S. official described as diplomatic "dancing in the end zone." Mexico may feel the need to burnish its anti-American credentials to play to a home audience upset by the lack of a new immigration accord. The result, however, has been a setback in bilateral relations.

Fortunately, U.S.-Mexican security cooperation is in better shape than such symbolic actions indicate. Mexico has pursued what one Mexican diplomat calls a "Janus-faced" policy: privately working to secure borders while publicly declaring diplomatic distance and issuing stern demands for immigration reform. In reality, a quiet revolution has begun. Both countries have stepped up efforts to secure the North American perimeter, sharing sensitive intelligence and jointly monitoring shared airspace. If there is anything to criticize, it is that the United States has not been quick enough to give Mexico the resources and technology it needs to upgrade its security infrastructure. Washington should grant Mexico observer status in the North American Aerospace Defense Command (NORAD, currently run with Canada's help) and create a joint bioterrorism task force to coordinate the epidemiological efforts and border health resources of both countries. Ultimately, the goal should be to build the institutional architecture necessary to turn bilateral relations into a strategic partnership, complementing the economic partnership established by NAFTA.

STOPPING THE DRIFT

THERE IS FRUSTRATINGLY LITTLE that the United States can do to enhance Mexico's economic competitiveness or to consolidate Mexican democracy; these are issues that Mexico must resolve on its own. But Washington can and should stop the drift in bilateral relations. The Bush administration must put Mexico back on its priority list, despite its recent disappointment with Mexican foreign policy.

President Bush should renew his commitment to the Partnership for Prosperity by naming a special envoy to marshal private investors and philanthropic interest to the high-migration regions of Mexico. Currently, less than one percent of foreign investment goes to rural Mexico; even a modest increase would make a meaningful difference for the almost 25 million Mexicans who live in these areas. The partnership is a bright spot in bilateral relations, but even it runs the risk of getting lost in the shuffle.

Washington should also take action on immigration policy, even though the interests of Mexico and the United States are not always perfectly aligned. Policymakers should begin with the agricultural sector, in which Mexican and U.S. workers do not compete. Mexican farm laborers should not have to face death in the desert to perform a vital function for the U.S. economy. Rather than wait for Congress to act on the politically thorny issue of immigration, Bush could increase the number of visas issued through the already existing agricultural worker program. The United States should also improve the consular services offered by its embassy in Mexico City. Consular and customs officers are the face of the United States to millions of Mexicans; too often, those faces are scowling and unfriendly, and demand for consular services far outstrips capacity. An infusion of money is necessary to increase the number and quality of officers.

As for Mexico, there is no better way to win the affection of the United States than to make it feel that it has a true partner in matters of mutual defense. Mexico should engage the security issue head-on as an equal partner, without hiding behind multilateral distractions and anachronistic shibboleths about losing national sovereignty.

Such steps, modest but not insignificant, will benefit both nations. The next three years will determine the outcome of Mexico's historic transition. Mexico and the United States, out of self-interest and mutual concern, must work to make the most of them.

M. DELAL BAER is Director of the Mexico Project at the Center for Strategic and International Studies and editor of *The NAFTA Debate*.

The New South Africa, a Decade Later

ANTOINETTE HANDLEY

"What has changed has been unexpected: the politics of the country have stabilized with astonishing speed . . ., [the ANC government] has implemented a conservative macroeconomic policy; and an epidemic has emerged as the single greatest threat to stability and prosperity."

Any traveller returning from South Africa since its first democratic elections in April 1994 is inevitably asked "What has changed?" And the paradox is that everything has changed and nothing has changed; . . . stability has depended on the illusion among whites that nothing has really changed and among blacks that everything has changed."—*Shula Marks*

The paradox at the heart of the South African miracle has been sustained by an illusion. The real test will come, the historian Shula Marks suggests, when whites realize that everything has changed and blacks realize that nothing has changed.

Few anticipated that white South Africans would voluntarily hand over political power to the African National Congress (ANC), the liberation movement that they for decades had vilified as "terrorists" and "communists," or that the leaders of this movement would prove remarkably moderate custodians of the country's economy. And yet for the most part that is what has occurred. Ten years ago the ANC won the country's first genuinely democratic elections and has governed since. This is a good time to assess what is new about the new South Africa.

What has changed has been unexpected: the politics of the country have stabilized with astonishing speed, moving from violent conflict to quotidian electoral politics in a few short years; the ANC government, despite its radical heritage and its electoral alliance with the South African Communist Party, has implemented a conservative macroeconomic policy; and an epidemic has emerged as the single greatest threat to stability and prosperity.

SINCE THE MORNING AFTER

When he came to office in 1994, President Nelson Mandela of the ANC faced a daunting range of challenges in three broad areas: stabilizing the political and social order; addressing issues of socioeconomic justice while maintaining the fiscal health of the country; and restoring growth, employment, and productivity to a long moribund economy.

A decade into the politics of the new South Africa, it is easy to forget how profoundly uncertain the political outlook was leading up to the first nationwide democratic elections in April 1994. Political violence had peaked in the early 1990s, averaging more than 3,000 deaths a year as political negotiations progressed and the governing National Party, the ANC, and other parties moved toward agreement on an interim constitution and elections. The threat by Mangosuthu Buthelezi, leader of the Inkatha Freedom Party, to boycott the country's first national democratic elections further raised political tensions and seemed sure to blight the birth of the new South Africa.

Only a week before the polling, Buthelezi decided to participate. The party's name, symbol, and its leader's photograph were hastily glued on to millions of ballots. Despite disorganization at many polling stations and threats of further violence, South Africans from every formerly defined racial category and all classes cast their ballots on April 26, 1994. The ANC won overwhelmingly, yet was gracious in its victory. Mandela headed up a "government of national unity" that initially drew potential dissidents into governing. The head of the National Party, F. W. De Klerk, was made vice president and Buthelezi was given a seat in the cabinet. With a clear eye to reassuring whites who continued to dominate the economy, the National Party (which later, in the spirit of the new South Africa, renamed itself the New National Party) was granted control of portfolios including finance, mineral and energy affairs, and agriculture.

Black South Africans woke up to a new president, to the decisive defeat of apartheid, and to a democracy that many had thought they would never see. White South Africans woke up in the same houses and drove their children to the same schools before heading to their usual jobs, while their homes were cleaned by the same maids. This seemingly banal reality—over a million women, overwhelmingly African, work in white households as maids—captures the cold fact that unequal access to jobs and education and consequent extreme levels of income inequality were perhaps the defining characteristic of apartheid. (A telling statistic: in 1994, while white South Africans could expect to live into their 70s, the average life expectancy for black South Africans was around 55 years.)

Since its founding in 1910, South Africa had been built on racial discrimination. After 1994, South Africans set about trying to bring some normalcy to the country's near pathological politics. De Klerk and Mandela quarreled in public, but for 14 months the government of national unity provided reassurance to the formerly powerful white minority, and political violence dropped to one-fourth its previous level. (The National Party, citing its inability to meaningfully shape government policy, withdrew from the national unity government in June 1996.)

Black South Africans, who make up 75 percent of the population, are generally considered to own between 2 percent and 7 percent of overall market capitalization in terms of stock shares.

However, not all of South Africa's problems could be resolved through political magnanimity. After 1994 the security of the average South African was more routinely threatened by violent crime than by political violence. A surge in reported crime from the early 1990s continued after 1994. Whether this surge represented a rise in actual incidents of crime or just improved reporting rates was unclear.

The new ANC government poured significant resources into policing and embarked on much needed reforms that were intended to improve the quality of policing and detective work and to increase public trust in the police. These efforts may have produced some success. After topping out in the late 1990s, overall crime rates have stabilized and violent crimes may even have declined. Still, crime remains at horrifyingly high levels: there are, for example, 45 murders per 100,000 people, a figure almost 10 times higher than the US average. Most South Africans (white and Indian South Africans in particular) continue to feel less safe now than they did when crime was at its highest.

Trust was crucial to social and political order in the new South Africa, but trust could not be built until the country as a whole began to come to terms with its past. In this respect, the Truth and Reconciliation Commission was central to the emergence of a new, more stable South African polity and society. The TRC made important compromises to advance political reconciliation. It chose to focus only on "gross human rights abuses" rather than examining the social, structural, and institutional foundations of the previous system, and it limited its purview to the period between 1960 and 1994. The commission recognized that an indefinitely drawn out series of hearings would place undue strain on an already fragile polity. Especially important was the decision effectively to eschew the pursuit of justice (that is, prosecution of offenders) in return for as full a telling of the "truth" as possible. The TRC relied on the testimony of thousands of victims and perpetrators alike, using the promise of amnesty to reward perpetrators for "full disclosure" of their misdeeds. This testimony, beamed by radio and television daily and directly into millions of living rooms across the country, represents the TRC's most significant achievement. It laid the groundwork for a common South African history that black and white South Africans might one day understand in the same way.

POLITICS AS USUAL?

Electoral coalitions that have emerged offer perhaps the most telling evidence of South Africa's new political stability. Many of today's political parties are the heirs of political forces that, prior to 1994, engaged in deadly military conflict with each other. Since then parties have engaged in all manner of extraordinary alliances—between Afrikaner and Zulu nationalists, between liberals and conservatives, and, most extraordinary, between the former liberation movement and its former oppressors—at local, regional, and national levels. In this respect, South Africa is well on the way to a reassuringly tedious brand of politics as usual.

The new constitution, adopted in 1996, is an impressive document that has greatly assisted in increasing social and political order. Alongside a comprehensive bill of rights (including social and economic rights), it established proportional representation in the legislature, a relatively centralized government with limited powers devolved to regional and local levels, and an independent judiciary together with a range of other independent agencies (such as a Human Rights Commission) to ensure government responsiveness. Given the extent of the ANC's electoral dominance (in 1999, it won two-thirds of the seats in the national legislature), such institutionalized protections may be vital. South Africa's opposition parties have not for the most part succeeded in broadening their support outside of narrow racially or regionally defined constituencies. Of course, the dominance of a single party is not new in South Africa; in the apartheid era the National Party controlled the country's white legislature for 46 years, hardly a reassuring precedent.

It is striking how quickly South Africa has achieved political and social stability. But that stability is threatened by the growing disorder in neighboring Zimbabwe. The deterioration of food security, political order, and economic growth in that country has profound negative repercussions for South Africa, given the highly integrated nature of the regional economy. (Zimbabwe is South Africa's largest trading partner in Africa, and has consistently ranked in the top 10 of South Africa's international trading partners. South Africa's exports in Zimbabwe also comprise a large share of high-value added and manufactured goods, precisely the kind of exports the country would like to see grow.)

South Africa publicly has yet to demonstrate any decisive leadership with respect to Zimbabwe. This public reticence can be traced to the new South Africa's first rather naïve and heavy-handed attempts to raise issues of human rights on the continent, which were resented by many African states accustomed to a style of diplomacy that prioritized solidarity in public and pressure only behind the scenes. When their early efforts served only to offend other leaders and isolate South Africa on the continent, South Africa's diplomats switched to a brand of foreign policy-making that addressed human rights issues less assertively.

South Africa has attempted to play a diplomatic role in conflict resolution elsewhere on the continent, most notably in the Democratic Republic of the Congo. But solutions to such multifaceted conflicts may be beyond the resources of a single country. The new South Africa is, after all, a mid-sized power with all the ambiguities and ambivalence that this entails for its international role, and it often finds itself regarded with some coolness on its home continent.

The country's leadership in international economic forums, such as the World Trade Organization, the Non-Aligned Movement, and the United Nations Conference on Trade and Development, has been more nuanced and assertive. South Africa has begun to demonstrate some ability to navigate the international political economy, which can be seen, for example, in the successful marketing of the New Economic Partnership for African Development (NE-PAD) to international donors. The real threat to South Africa's prospects has come from a different source.

THE AIDS CRISIS

The greatest challenge facing South Africa in the past decade, as well as the source of the ANC's most important failing, has been the HIV/AIDS epidemic. According to the country's Department of Health, less than 1 percent of the population was infected with HIV in 1990. By the end of the decade that figure had jumped to over 25 percent, one of the fastest growing infection rates in the world. The epidemic is now considered to have reached its "mature" phase: infection rates are slowing, and the next phase—the onset of full-blown AIDS, increased mortality rates, and the creation of large numbers of AIDS orphans—has begun. AIDS is expected to slash the average life expectancy of black South Africans to 40 years, undoing the impact of other improvements in health and welfare. HIV/AIDS is now the largest single cause of death in the country.

The ANC's failure to respond promptly and adequately to this threat has undoubtedly exacerbated the health crisis and weakened the government's international standing as well as public trust in the government. First as Mandela's deputy and later as the country's president, Thabo Mbeki reacted first with inaction, then denial, then reluctant engagement. His questioning of the link between HIV and the development of AIDS, a view he has since downplayed, and his defensive and hostile interactions with nongovernmental organizations and activists on the AIDS issue have undermined the government's response at every level.

The inadequate response may have resulted from an inability on the part of leading figures in the ANC to comprehend the sheer scale of the problem posed by HIV/AIDS, but this only explains the initial lack of a response. As the dimensions of the crisis became clearer, the epidemic and the question of how to respond to it became highly politicized. The ANC had a long tradition of regarding the state as central to any systematic attempt to combat poverty in South Africa. After decades of struggle against apartheid, democracy had granted the ANC control of the state and seemed to provide the long-awaited opportunity to finally begin to address the backlog of social needs. HIV/AIDS may have been seen as an unwelcome problem that threatened to undo all of the good that the ANC hoped to accomplish. The epidemic threatened also to confirm the trope of Africa as a source of disease and hopeless despair and to displace Mbeki's vision of an "African Renaissance," a resurgence of the continent, powered by home-grown solutions. This may have further confirmed the tendency to ignore or downplay the emerging crisis.

AIDS is expected to slash the average life expectancy of black South Africans to 40 years.

As the ANC and Mbeki cast about for solutions to the growing epidemic, they were predisposed toward and against certain diagnostic and policy options. After decades of attempts by an apartheid government to restrict the growth of the black population through birth control campaigns, they were inclined not to accept the diagnosis of AIDS as a sexually transmitted disease that the use of condoms could curb. As politicians speaking to a conservative popular culture that frowned on the public airing of anything related to sex, they were inclined not to promote a solution that would require a frank and public discussion of matters sexual. By contrast, as progressives and social activists, they were predisposed toward a solution that regarded AIDS as arising out of poverty—the very ill that they were primed to address—and hence they were open to the dissident view that questioned the causal link between HIV and AIDS and pointed instead to the impact of poverty (through chronic malnutrition, a lack of clean water and shelter, and constant exposure to disease and environmental stress) on the immune system.

Governmental inaction did not go unchallenged. The Treatment Action Campaign (TAC), part of South Africa's dynamic civil society, has lobbied energetically for expanded treatment. Most notably, the TAC filed a legal challenge to the government's policy of restricting the availability of nevirapine, an important antiretroviral drug used to treat the HIV infected. In a landmark ruling in 2002, South Africa's constitutional court ordered the government to make the drug available, progressively and within the limits of available resources, in all public health facilities and, likewise, to provide for testing and counseling across the country. But with roughly 5 million South Africans infected with HIV, the annual cost of treatment could run to billions of dollars.

THE INEQUALITY CHALLENGE

The AIDS crisis and the cost of antiretrovirals will inevitably affect the country's ability to deal with another of its challenges—socioeconomic justice—although the two issues are inextricably connected, as the TAC case showed. Beyond HIV/AIDS, the ANC leadership has made a concerted effort to reorient government spending toward the needs of the poorest stratum of society within existing budget constraints, even if this has not always been to the satisfaction of the courts.

The government's chosen instrument in this regard was the Reconstruction and Development Program (RDP). It outlined an exhaustive list of the country's outstanding social needs but failed to prioritize among them or specify how they were to be addressed. The list, moreover, included so many urgent needs—such as access to safe drinking water, basic health care, and housing—that the government's ability to address them would ultimately depend on the overall health of the economy.

Within just a couple of years, the government realized it needed to rethink the strategy. It dismantled the RDP ministry and reassigned core programs to the relevant line ministries. Provision of basic needs has since seen significant improvement. The percentage of households with access to clear water rose from 60 percent in 1996 to 85 percent in 2001, and those with sanitation increased from 49 percent in 1994 to 63 percent in 2003. The proportion of households with electricity rose from 32 percent in 1996 to 70 percent in 2001. The government has made free health care available to pregnant women and children under five years old. Progress on housing was initially less impressive, but 10 years later just over a million homes have been provided.

One of the greatest successes in improving the lives of the poor arose, almost inadvertently, from the racial equalization of pensions for the elderly. In the dying days of apartheid, the National Party, no doubt with an eye to the prospect of democratic elections, raised the level of state pensions for Africans, Indians, and coloreds (mixed race) to the level that whites had long enjoyed. In one stroke this authorized the monthly injection, into hundreds of thousands of households across the country, of $90 a month, roughly twice the median black monthly income. Close to 80 percent of age-qualified Africans now receive a state pension, prorated in terms of household income. Overall, 1.6 million elderly people receive a state pension. Because age in South Africa is closely correlated with household poverty, this has proved a remarkably effective way to target some of the country's poorest households. The state pension has brought dramatic benefits in the health and nutritional status of children, too, because of the prevalence in South Africa of the extended family structure.

The continuing expansion of welfare payments has proved an effective weapon in the battle against poverty. But there are concerns about its fiscal sustainability. If the number of households receiving state pensions continues to expand at the current rate, and if the value of the grant is maintained in real terms, the costs of the program may bankrupt the treasury, especially when added to the costs of providing medical care and welfare to all the South Africans affected by AIDS.

Many of apartheid's most pernicious economic and social effects resulted from the systematic undereducation of black South Africans. Since 1994, the ANC has continued the broadening of educational access that began under the National Party, but—again, as under the National Party—that education is of decidedly uneven quality. Education currently receives almost a quarter of the government's total budget, but that investment goes largely to meeting the salaries of teachers, many of whom are poorly trained and perform badly in the classroom. Combined with weak local governance, the overall result is an education system that continues to produce large numbers of underskilled graduates in an economy that suffers from a dramatic shortage of skilled labor.

THE ECONOMY IN GEAR

In 1994 the ANC inherited an economy that had only just begun to expand again after a recession in the early 1990s. In fact, the malaise was longstanding: the economy had not grown strongly or created enough jobs to keep up with the expanding labor pool since the late 1970s. In addition, while the relatively smooth political transition had stanched the worst of capital flight, capital inflows through the mid-1990s primarily took the form of easily liquidated portfolio flows, rather than direct investment in new productive enterprises. International investors, along with their domestic counterparts, adopted a wait-and-see attitude.

Key leaders within the ANC, including Mbeki, Trade and Industry Minister Alec Erwin, and Finance Minister Trevor Manuel, came to understand the importance of establishing their credibility with the markets. The result, launched in June 1996, was a policy entitled Growth, Employment and

141

Redistribution (GEAR). Despite its name, GEAR was essentially an orthodox stabilization package, almost indistinguishable in policy content from those imposed by the World Bank and International Monetary Fund in developing economies around the world. GEAR, however, was voluntary, undertaken without any direct pressure or conditionalities from the international financial institutions.

GEAR was based on the premise that in order to grow, South Africa's economy would have to become more competitive and export oriented. At the core of GEAR were requirements to lower government deficits and inflation, reduce tariff barriers, privatize existing state-owned enterprises, and move toward a more dynamic, deregulated market.

Some of these goals proved easier to meet than others. Under the National Party, the budget deficit had reached 8 percent of GDP. The ANC succeeded in lowering that to 2 percent, a significant achievement for a government that had been expected to face irresistible demands to boost spending. It helped that the new South African government had inherited from the apartheid government a relatively efficient and progressive tax system with high rates of compliance. The tax system has since been further strengthened, with happy consequences for the government's deficits.

Inflation has slowly come down, albeit not as dramatically, into single-digit rates. The government also has successfully lowered tariff barriers, though there is still some way to go before South African manufacturing experiences the full extent of competitive pressures. Privatization and commercialization of a panoply of state-owned enterprises—including the national airline, telecommunications, railways, and harbors—have proceeded much more slowly. The effort is complicated by sometimes conflicting objectives, seeking not only to maximize the selling price of state assets and improve their efficiency but also to extend service provision to previously unserved communities and promote black economic empowerment.

The finishing touches were being applied to the GEAR strategy in 1996 when South Africa's domestic currency, which had to that point been remarkably stable, came under attack from international currency speculators. The South African Reserve Bank did not handle the crisis well. In April 1994, the exchange rate had been 3.50 rand to the US dollar. By February 1996, it had plunged to R4.20 to the dollar. In part, the currency crisis was related to technical factors (including an arbitrage gap and the difference between South Africa's inflation rate and that of its major trading partners), but it also reflected financial markets' judgment about overall management of the economy and political stabilization. There were tremors, for example, when Mandela appointed the country's first black minister of finance, Trevor Manuel. The same reaction met the news that the National Party's outgoing governor of the Reserve Bank, Chris Stals, would be replaced by Tito Mboweni, a top-ranking ANC official without extensive financial sector experience. In 1998, international money markets subjected the ANC to a further set of lessons on the power of perceptions of risk, taking the rand down to R6.84 to the dollar. By the end of December 2001, the rand had plummeted to an all-time low of R13.10 to the dollar—an undervaluation by most accounts. Indeed, since that time, the currency has appreciated considerably and for much of 2003 and into 2004 has ranged between R6 and R7 to the dollar.

GEAR has done much to stabilize the South African economy and lay the basis for long-term growth, but it has not significantly shifted the racial basis of economic power. On the tenth anniversary of the new democracy, whites continue to dominate the economy. Black South Africans, who make up 75 percent of the population, are generally considered to own between 2 percent and 7 percent of overall market capitalization in terms of stock shares, hardly a dramatic improvement on 1994's figures. In addition, much of what has been achieved has benefited a tiny black shareowning elite. A sustained transformation of black South Africans' role in the economy has yet to emerge.

BIG BUSINESS, BAD BUSINESS

Economic stabilization aside, the failure of the economy to create large numbers of jobs threatens social stability. The modest revival of growth has been insufficient to generate a requisite increase in employment. Reform of the labor market was initially regarded as a critical part of the GEAR program, but there have been few effective policy innovations on this front. Instead, South Africa's elites have opted to continue with a highly corporatist decision-making model in which the interests of big business and organized labor are privileged over those of small and medium-sized businesses and the unemployed.

The prevalent labor framework aspires toward a high-value-added economy model, staffed by a skilled labor force suitably compensated for its productivity. The trouble is that most of South Africa's current work force is unskilled and not highly productive. The only basis on which this generation of workers conceivably can compete in international labor markets is on price—which, within the current regulatory framework, has not been possible. The result, effectively, has been to shut the unskilled unemployed out of labor markets and to reduce the hiring capacity of small and medium-sized firms.

It is easy to understand why organized labor would press for such a labor market; the trade unions' job after all is to secure the best possible terms for their members. It is less clear why big business would agree to this—at least until one considers the nature of big business in South Africa and, in particular, of its overall cost structure. Since the 1970s, South African big business has tended to be highly capital-intensive, labor costs forming a relatively small proportion of overall costs. Even high wages have not cost big business a huge amount in overall terms. By contrast, the cost of political unrest that could result from unpleasant wrangling over wages, in the form of strikes and industrial action, would be high. The preference of big business invariably has been for a high wage model that would at least ensure minimal disruption to industrial processes.

There is more evidence that big business may be bad for business. South Africa performs poorly in indexes intended to measure levels of entrepreneurship, possibly because of the historically high levels of concentration of ownership and the dearth of real competitiveness in the South African economy. The mark-up in the South African manufacturing sector is roughly twice that found in US manufacturing. The government has attempted to introduce pro-competitive policies to curb collusive behavior within the South African economy but without any great success so far.

A DEMOCRATIC BALANCE-SHEET

South Africans can celebrate with pride a series of significant achievements since 1994. A society that had been organized on the basis of separate and inequitable access to the most basic needs has been restructured into an open and democratic system in which all South Africans enjoy the right to representation and services. The government has made real progress in addressing some of the social welfare inequalities that apartheid created. And its macroeconomic policies have laid the foundation for sustainable long-term economic growth.

With the dawning of the new democracy's tenth anniversary, it is natural for black South Africans to also consider what it is that has *not* changed—or, at least, not for the better: their job prospects and their chances of living a long and healthy life. Both of these outlooks will be shaped by the state of the country's education system, the economy's capacity to create jobs, and the course of the HIV/AIDS epidemic. None of these factors, in origin, flow from the policies of the current government. Today's principals and teachers were, for example, the product of apartheid education; the economy's inability to create enough jobs is related to longstanding capital-to-labor ratios that resulted from business and government decisions made in the 1970s; and the HIV/AIDS epidemic likewise came from elsewhere (both geographically and historically in terms of the basic health care system set up by the National Party).

Yet it is evolving government policy that will shape how these three crises develop from this point. Attempts are being made to address the problems in the education system; in the interim, middle-class children will continue to receive a relatively good standard of education, but it will take some time before reforms are able to improve the quality of education in rural and working class areas. Similarly, the government is attempting to address job creation with public works programs—but here the problem is less amenable to policy tinkering. Only fundamental shifts in the labor relations framework and in the nature of the economy will create the requisite number and kind of jobs for the millions currently unemployed. An effective response to the HIV/AIDS epidemic, by contrast, may well require a change of leadership in the top ranks of the ANC.

ANTOINETTE HANDLEY is a professor of political science at the University of Toronto.

Nigeria's Democratic Generals

"If democracy firmly establishes itself in this African giant and economic reform leads to increasing wealth and stability, Nigeria could serve as a beacon of inspiration for a continent many view as hopeless."

ROBERT B. LLOYD

In April 2003 Nigerians reelected President Olusegun Obasanjo to a second term in polling generally accepted as free and fair, though marred by serious voting irregularities. Obasanjo's reelection marked the first time the country had successfully carried out a back-to-back election of a civilian government. Will the country's transition to democracy continue? Or will it, like past attempts to install elective governments, abort amid ethnic conflict or military coups? Much depends on the answer.

DIVIDED IT STANDS

Located on Africa's western shore, Nigeria has the potential to become one of the continent's powerhouses. Its population of 130 million is expected to nearly double to 245 million by 2015. Lagos, Nigeria's commercial capital, is itself home to an estimated 11 million people—edging out Cairo as the largest urban center on the African continent. The country possesses vast reserves of oil and natural gas, with estimates of proven oil reserves ranging from 24 billion to 32 billion barrels. Nigeria today produces about 2 million barrels of oil per day, the majority of which it exports to markets in the United States, Europe, and Asia. In 2002 it was the fifth-largest exporter of crude oil to the United States.

Already Nigeria has taken a leading role in the continent's political affairs. It has supplied peacekeeping troops both in Sierra Leone and Liberia to help stabilize those two failed states in West Africa. Along with South Africa and Australia, Nigeria has taken the lead in addressing Commonwealth concerns regarding the current political crisis in Zimbabwe. President Obasanjo, working closely with South Africa, also played a critical role in creating the New Partnership for African Development as a way to spur economic growth on the continent.

A large and growing population, abundant energy resources, and a regional leadership position might suggest a prosperous and peaceful country. Yet Nigeria has a troubled history of economic malaise, political and religious strife, and debates over the viability of the Nigerian federation. Nigerians have had to grapple with postcolonial nation-building in one of the most diverse states in the world. Approximately 500 languages are spoken, and the country remains deeply divided among three major ethnolinguistic groups. In the north are the Hausa-Fulani, who comprise nearly a third of the population. In southwestern Nigeria, including Lagos, are the Yoruba. Igbos, the third-largest group, live in southern Nigeria. These last two groups each comprise one-fifth of the population. Moreover, a stark religious divide splits the country roughly in half. Northern Nigeria is Muslim; the south is predominantly Christian.

These ethnic, linguistic, cultural, religious, and geographic divisions have repeatedly threatened the integrity of the Nigerian state. Nigerian politics, not surprisingly, has been marked by a competitive struggle for preferential control over the government and the resources it controls. Yet, despite forces that logically lead toward disintegration, the Nigerian state has survived. Furthermore, notwithstanding periodic bouts of military rule and corrupt civilian governments, Nigerians show a persistent inclination toward democracy. The recent elections evoke some optimism that Nigeria's transition to a durable democratic regime is continuing. Of particular importance is the growing acceptance of democracy as the best, if often flawed, way to manage conflict in a deeply divided country.

WHO RULES NIGERIA?

The genesis of the Nigerian state, like most in Africa, was rooted in the competitive logic of one European colonial power's trying to maximize its African territorial possessions while minimizing those of rival European states. In Nigeria's case Britain was the colonial power and its primary rival was France. In addition, control over the three major ethnolinguistic regions of Nigeria afforded Great Britain access to the mouth of the Niger River, its inland tributaries, and the immediate Atlantic coastline.

British colonial policies contributed to a deepening divide among the three regions. Opting to rule indirectly through Muslim Fulani leaders, the British discouraged Christian missionary activity in the north. In the largely animist south, missionaries and a stronger British colonial presence fostered education, employment, and urbanization. Although the British eventually consolidated the Muslim north with the animist and Christian south in 1914, it was not until after World War II that formal political interaction occurred between northern and southern Nigerians. The British essentially treated Nigeria's north, east, and west as separate and distinct administrative units rather than as one colony.

Nigeria achieved independence in October 1960 but was now left with the question: Who among Nigerians would govern the country? This led directly to a second, and related, question: How would Nigeria be governed? The answers to these two questions have framed much of the country's politics—and economics—since independence.

> *It is premature to conclude that Nigeria will trade military for de facto single party rule.*

The initial answer was a democratic regime that would allow access to power for all Nigerians and respond to demands placed on the state and its resources. The country's tripartite division meant, however, that Nigerian politics were inherently unstable. Furthermore, in practice access to political power meant direct access to economic resources for personal use. Putting additional strains on the system was the fact that the Muslim north made up just over 50 percent of the country's population. This meant that election results based largely on ethnic and religious criteria would lead to a northerner heading a country whose oil wealth lay largely in the south.

Intense competition among three regionally based monopolistic parties for power at the new federal level caused the democratic regime to collapse just six years after independence. Rather than channeling conflict in a constructive manner, the political system was seen as a winner-take-all contest for power and money. The rules of the game virtually guaranteed that two parties would always perceive themselves as losers and thus be marginalized in the new political dispensation.

COUP AND COUNTER-COUP

As conflict grew, in 1966 the Igbos in the east staged a coup against the democratic government, headed by northerners. This was the spark that led to civil war and the near dissolution of the Nigerian federation. Angry northern leaders staged a countercoup and also encouraged attacks on Igbos in the north. Many were killed, and many more returned to their homeland. Last-ditch attempts at negotiations failed, and the Eastern Region seceded as the Republic of Biafra in 1967. The military

ultimately defeated the Biafran rebellion in 1970, but at a high cost to the country. An estimated 1 million to 3 million Igbos died, most from starvation and disease. An estimated 3 million were refugees. Cities were in ruins. Schools and clinics were closed.

One long-lasting outcome was a perception of legitimacy attached to military rule because of its nationalist credentials. A unified military government acted as a salutary counterpoint to the potential disintegration of a diverse and divided state. Northern military leaders taking power through coups became a characteristic and persistent feature of Nigerian politics for the next three decades. Yet, throughout Nigeria's long history of military rule, the appeal of democracy remained strong. Even a tyrant like General Sani Abacha, who ruled the country from 1993 to 1998, paid lip service to the argument that he was serving Nigeria until democracy could be restored.

From 1967 until the establishment of the Second Republic in 1979, military leaders grappled with conflicting demands on the state. Successive regimes centralized finances, established methods of distributing rapidly increasing oil revenues among Nigeria's states, embarked on numerous bouts of subdividing the regions into more numerous states, and rewrote the constitution of the First Republic—most notably to replace the British parliamentarian system with an American presidential model. Instrumental in moving Nigeria toward democracy during this period was Lieutenant General Obasanjo, a Yoruba from the west. A commander in the Biafran War, Obasanjo came into power in 1976 after Nigerian leader Brigadier General Murtala Mohammed was assassinated during a failed coup attempt. Obasanjo won great respect for handing over power to a civilian government in 1979.

Alhaji Shehu Shagari, a Muslim Fulani from the north, was elected president of the Second Republic. The return to democratic rule caused many of the same political tensions to resurface. Once again the three regions, though modified by subdivision into numerous states, contended for access to political power and economic resources. Conflict grew over the appointment of federal liaisons who acted as alternate state governors, a federal quota system on education and bureaucracy that had the effect of favoring northerners, and the allocation of declining oil revenues. Government corruption reached epidemic proportions. Holding office in government, rather than being seen as a service to one's fellow citizens, had become the quickest and surest path to financial well-being. Despite these tensions, the civilian government managed to hold elections in 1983. Shagari's party won by a landslide, but his victory was secured by massive voting fraud.

A SUCCESSION OF GENERALS

The Second Republic, and Nigeria's first attempt at back-to-back civilian elections, ended that same year when a northern Muslim, General Mohammadu Buhari, staged a coup in December. At this point the Nigerian political system had shown a clear pattern of alternating between periods of civilian government (liberalization) and military rule (integration). Buhari launched a popular anti-corruption crusade and a very unpopular fiscal austerity policy. He also attempted to organize the life of generally disorderly Nigerians. Soldiers enforced bus queues and publicly humiliated government employees who showed up late to work. Complaints were addressed by passing decrees to restrict freedom of the press. A bloodless coup in 1985 ousted the unpopular Buhari and elevated General Ibrahim Babangida as head of Nigeria.

Babangida seized power during a time of severe economic crisis. Beginning in 1982 the oil boom was followed by an oil bust as worldwide oil production increased. The price of oil fell dramatically. Government spending, however, had continued to grow despite the fall in oil-derived revenues. Shortfalls were made up by borrowing, which led to large debts. Corruption remained endemic. Babangida, a Muslim, embarked on a policy of economic liberalization combined with political centralization, reform, and repression. Political dissent, and the deepening economic crisis, quickly eroded his support. In response, Babangida initiated, and manipulated freely, a rocky and contentious transition toward democracy. This process culminated in elections in 1993, won by a Yoruba businessman. But the Babangida government annulled the election results even before they were announced, bringing a quick end to the Third Republic.

In November 1993, General Sani Abacha, Babangida's minister of defense, staged his own coup. Under Abacha, Nigerian politics descended to lows never reached before. Abacha ended any semblance of democratic rule. He replaced civilian state and federal elected officials with military officers. He purged dissenting military officers, clamped down on the media, and established a police state. Together with his close military associates, he plundered the state's resources. He responded to protest with harsh repression. Outraged at his abuses, the European Union imposed sanctions and the Commonwealth suspended Nigeria. Once the bright star of Africa, Nigeria had deteriorated into an internationally isolated rogue state.

Domestic and international opposition to Abacha did, however, have an impact on his rule. The collapse of the Soviet Union also ushered in a new era of democratization across the African continent. The winds of change had even swept to South Africa where, in 1994, democracy was born on the rubble of apartheid. Sensing the unpopularity of military rule in a continent increasingly democratizing, Abacha convened a National Constitutional Conference. This body endorsed a draft constitution and announced a return to civilian government within two years. Abacha later pushed the date back two years to 1998. The delay gave him time to induce the five officially sanctioned parties to endorse him as their candidate. Clearly the democratic transition from military to "civilian" rule would leave Abacha in charge. But as the August 1998 date for a predicted landslide election victory came closer, one of history's unpredicted yet extraordinary Y-junctions occurred: Abacha died of an apparent heart attack (although it was rumored that he had been poisoned).

A provisional ruling council selected General Abdusalami Abubakar as Nigeria's new leader. Abubakar, a Muslim from the north, moved quickly to release political prisoners—including Olusegun Obasanjo, the former general who had handed power over to a civilian administration in 1979 and who had been imprisoned for opposing Abacha. Abubakar also announced a revamped democratic transition. Elections were scheduled for the spring of 1999.

THE DEMOCRATIC MOMENT

In assessing Nigeria's transition to democracy it is important to note that the country had provided an answer, if not a democratic one, to the two questions posed earlier: Who will rule Nigeria, and how will it be governed? By 1999, a largely northerndominated military had governed Nigeria for the previous 16 years. While military leaders presented themselves as guardians of Nigeria's integrity, they also had self-interest in serving in government. Official positions brought personal enrichment through access to oil-derived government revenues. Periodic military coups afforded new officers access to so-called time at the trough. By 1999, however, the Abacha government's repression and corruption, combined with a free-falling economy, had caused public support for a military answer to these two questions to wane.

In May 1999 Obasanjo was elected president of Nigeria's Fourth Republic. Election returns generally confirmed the regional, ethnic, and religious divides in the country, but also provided a hopeful sign for overcoming Nigeria's political fault lines. Obasanjo's People's Democratic Party (PDP) was largely northern-based and Muslim, but Obasanjo himself was a Yoruba Christian. His election mollified Yorubas still stinging from the election annulment in 1993 that had denied a Yoruba the presidency. Obasanjo won with 63 percent of the recorded vote. The results, though marred by serious voting irregularities, were nevertheless generally accepted as valid.

Nigeria would be a ripe target for Al Qaeda, given the state's political instability, its role as a major oil exporter to the United States, and its status as home to Africa's largest Muslim population after Egypt.

The establishment of democracy led to high expectations among Nigerians that many of the critical economic and political problems facing the country would be addressed, if not resolved. But Obasanjo immediately faced challenges from northerners, who now felt marginalized in the government. Growing tensions between Muslims and Christians over the implementation of sharia (Islamic law) in northern states led to widespread killings in the state of Kaduna. The economic crisis deepened as fuel shortages led to long lines at gasoline stations. Political instability in the oil-producing delta region disrupted production. Fighting between the Ijaw and Itsekiri ethnic groups caused Shell and ChevronTexaco to suspend operations. Growing militancy among oil workers and youth frustrated by the oil-rich region's poverty led to attacks on oil installations in the south and offshore and to further oil production cuts. Electrical blackouts became commonplace. Gang wars began to rock the sprawling urban area of Lagos. Obasanjo survived a movement in the National Assembly to impeach him on bribery charges.

Despite these challenges, Nigeria in April 2003 held its first successful civilian-led election that followed another civilian-led election. Obasanjo's PDP ran against the largely northwestern and Muslim All Nigeria Peoples Party (ANPP) led by Mohammadu Buhari. This meant that the presidential election pitted two former generals and heads of state against each other: one a Christian Yoruba, the other a northern Muslim. Two smaller regional parties also fielded candidates, but the largely Yoruba, southwestern based party, Alliance for Democracy (AD), made a critical decision to support Obasanjo. The elections returned Obasanjo to power with 62 percent of the vote. His closest rival, Buhari, garnered 32 percent. The elections, like the polling in 1999, were marked by serious irregularities. But, overall, despite complaints and threats from Buhari, Nigerians and international observers accepted the election's legitimacy.

The outcome changed Nigeria's political landscape. The Yoruba AD suffered disastrous losses in the southwest. AD voters marked PDP for Obasanjo, but out of confusion, ignorance, or design also voted for PDP in legislative and gubernatorial elections. An Igbo party (with about 3 percent of the total vote) did well only in its home states. As a result, Nigerian politics for the moment features two national parties—the PDP and ANPP—and a clutch of smaller parties based on region or personality. Of the two national parties, only the PDP has true national reach. The AD may be gradually losing the Yoruba vote as citizens in the south and west decide that access to political power at the federal level, especially with a fellow Yoruba as president, outweighs traditional party loyalty.

The PDP, since its rise to power five years ago, has gradually extended its influence throughout the country. Access to power gives the party a decided advantage in contesting future elections. Although the ANPP retains considerable popularity in the north, it has had less success in pushing beyond its Muslim base. Thus, for the first time in Nigerian history, de facto single party rule has become a possibility. Given the fractious polity, it is premature to conclude that Nigeria will trade military for de facto single party rule. But, given the prevalence of such rule in other African states, this possibility cannot be dismissed. Even South Africa's current political system is dominated by the African National Congress, and will likely remain so for some time. Political patronage, which supports single party rule, is a characteristic feature of African politics.

NIGERIA'S REGIONAL ROLE

Although flawed, the April 2003 elections marked an important milestone in the life of Nigeria. A civilian administration successfully oversaw new elections. Violence, by Nigerian standards, was relatively low and did not cause the elections to fail or be annulled. Nigeria, no longer an outcast, has taken its seat at the table as one of the world's most populous democratic states.

Nigeria is a leader on such international initiatives as the creation of the African Union that replaced the former Organization for African Unity. Along with South African President Thabo Mbeki, Obasanjo has given birth to the New Partnership for African Development, an initiative to foster economic growth and greater political accountability among African states. And President Obasanjo took the lead in suspending President Robert Mugabe's Zimbabwe from the Commonwealth for human rights violations. He has actively sought ways to mediate the political crisis in that troubled country.

In August 2003, as part of a settlement to end the longstanding conflict in Liberia, Nigeria provided sanctuary to Liberian President Charles Taylor. The decision was controversial, but it overcame a stubborn impasse and facilitated Taylor's relinquishing power and the end of the civil war. Concurrently, Nigerian troops moved into Liberia to help provide security for a failed state. The peaceful resolution of border disputes with neighboring Cameroon has also inched forward.

Nigeria's peacekeeping experience under the auspices of the Economic Community of West African States suggests the country is well placed to assist in providing security in the region. This role has been strongly supported by the United States. The Bush administration sees Nigeria, along with Ethiopia, Kenya, and South Africa, as one of the four key states in sub-Saharan Africa that can act as an anchor for regional stability through mediation and peacekeeping operations. (That it provides an alternate source of oil outside the Middle East is also noted.) Nigeria, generally pro-West, is seeking investment to spur economic growth. The African Growth and Economic Opportunity Act, signed into law on May 18, 2001, is the centerpiece of the Bush administration's efforts to foster trade, investment, and economic growth in Africa, and it is a natural fit for Nigeria's own leadership in the New Partnership for African Development.

THREATS TO DEMOCRACY

While Nigeria's international standing clearly has grown, the permanent establishment of a democratic polity remains vulnerable to a number of domestic threats. The economy's continued weakness, for one, could derail the democratic transition. Nigeria is a very poor country. Nearly two-thirds of the population make less than one dollar per day. The growth rate averaged 3.1 percent per year between 1990 and 2000. Population growth, however, averaged 2.7 percent between 1995 and 2000. Nigeria needs an annual growth rate of at least 7 percent to make a real dent in unemployment. While a steady stream of oil revenues provides income, the oil-based economy has failed to diversify, so Nigeria remains unusually exposed to rapid swings in world oil prices.

While the need to accelerate Nigeria's growth and broaden its economic base is obvious, the means to achieve these objectives are far from simple. Like many countries in Africa, Nigeria's economy is highly regulated. Earlier attempts to liberalize the economy have foundered on widespread political opposition. Well-connected political elites benefit financially from these regulations. In the case of fuel, Nigerians widely believe that cheap fuel is a birthright, even though state subsidies cost the government scarce tax revenue. Poor maintenance at the four state-owned oil refineries has led to the odd feature of an oil producer importing refined fuel.

A second challenge to Nigeria's democratic transition arises from Islamic activism. Like many other states with large Muslim populations, Nigeria has been affected by agitation to integrate Islamic teachings into state legal codes. In January 2000, shortly after the 1999 election that ended years of rule by northern Muslims, the state of Zamfara introduced legislation to impose Islamic law. Twelve states in the Muslim north have since implemented sharia. These actions have heightened tensions between Muslims and Christians: thousands have been killed in periodic bouts of fighting.

International attention focused on sharia in Nigeria following well-publicized death sentences against two young women who became pregnant outside of marriage. In October 2001, Safiya Hussaini was sentenced to death by stoning. A similar sentence against Amina Lawal followed in March 2002. Although sharia courts later overturned their sentences on technicalities, the precise relationship between sharia, state law, and federal law remains unclear. Sharia greatly exacerbates the Christian and Muslim divide in the country, and thus puts the federation's stability at risk.

The West has shown more interest in Islamist activism since Al Qaeda's attacks against the United States in 2001. There is no direct evidence that Al Qaeda cells are active in Nigeria and the government denies that any cells exist in the country. Nevertheless, the military recently crushed a small Islamic sect in the northeastern state of Yobe after it raided police stations to seize arms. The group apparently wanted to establish an Islamic state. Nigeria would be a ripe target for Al Qaeda, given the state's political instability, its role as a major oil exporter to the United States, and its status as home to Africa's largest Muslim population after Egypt.

Corruption is a third challenge facing Nigerian democracy. Nigeria's history is one of military leaders stepping in when the public grows weary of stunning levels of political corruption. The use of public goods for private gain is deeply ingrained. Transparency International recently ranked Nigeria as the second most corrupt country in the world. Unless the government can reduce corruption and firmly establish respect for property rights, many of the same dynamics that undermined earlier attempts at democratization could cause the Fourth Republic to founder. A formal inquiry into the bankruptcy of state-owned Nigeria Airways, initiated by President Obasanjo in 2001 and later made public in November 2003, revealed that the company's assets had been siphoned off to managers, government ministers, and officials. The government has demanded a return of some $400 million in stolen assets from those responsible. Although no one has yet been convicted, such high-profile cases do place increasing pressure on a culture of corruption.

Ethnic violence, too, continues to test democracy. In March 2004 more than 100 people died in conflict between the Ijaw and Itsekiri in Warri, an oil port city in the state of Delta. Ethnic rivalry, which also includes the Urhobo, has left Delta insecure. Further north, in the central states of Benue, Taraba, and Nassarawa, fighting between the Tiv and Jukun has led to hundreds of deaths. In October 2001, the army indiscriminately massacred more than 200 Tiv civilians in Benue as revenge for a Tiv ambush that killed 19 soldiers. In Lagos, fighting between Hausas and Yorubas led to the deaths of more than 300 people in January 2002. While bouts of ethnic fighting are less common in Lagos, security in the city has been widely eroded by the growth in organized crime.

Fifth, democracy in Nigeria historically has been halted when the military stages a coup. While there is no indication of this happening in the near future, it remains the surest and most likely way that the Fourth Republic would end. Triggers for a military takeover might include any number of grievances, including economic weakness, political corruption, or ethnic conflict.

DANGEROUS EXPECTATIONS?

Nigeria's democratic transition, like those of other countries such as South Africa, must deal with people's often unrealistic expectations of what democracy can actually deliver in the near term. For many in developing countries, democracy is seen as a means to become wealthy rather than as a system of government that protects civil rights, promotes liberty, and reflects the will of the governed. While a constitutional regime can hardly guarantee economic growth, failure to meet expectations for jobs can erode popular support for democracy. If the Fourth Republic is to prove durable, Nigeria will have to address directly and forcefully the economic reforms necessary to boost the country's economic growth. A shrinking economic pie exacerbates ethnic, regional, and religious tension in the country and disappoints those who had put their faith in democracy.

Despite its many challenges, Nigeria has come a long way politically in the past few years. Democracy in Nigeria will have a distinct Nigerian accent, but democratic habits have begun to take hold. The world has a vested interest in seeing this transition succeed, for Nigeria not only is Africa's most populous country, but also a regional power and major oil producer. It also is in some ways a microcosm of the African continent and of the tests it faces. If democracy firmly establishes itself in this African giant and economic reform leads to increasing wealth and stability, Nigeria could serve as a beacon of inspiration for a continent many view as hopeless.

ROBERT B. LLOYD *is an assistant professor of international relations at Pepperdine University and director of its international studies program.*

Hu Takes Full Power in China as He Gains Control of Military

Orderly Shift Adds to Reins Over State and Party

By Joseph Kahn

BEIJING, Sept. 19—China's president, Hu Jintao, replaced Jiang Zemin as the country's military chief and de facto top leader on Sunday, state media announced, completing the first orderly transfer of power in the history of China's Communist Party.

Mr. Hu, who became Communist Party chief in 2002 and president in 2003, now commands the state, the military and the ruling party. He will set both foreign and domestic policy in the world's most populous country, which now has the world's seventh-largest economy and is rapidly emerging as a great power.

The transition is a significant victory for Mr. Hu, a relatively unknown product of the Communist Party machine. He has solidified control of China's most powerful posts at a younger age—he is 61—than any Chinese leader since Mao Zedong, and is now likely to be able govern relatively unimpeded by powerful elders.

Mr. Jiang's resignation, which surprised many party officials who expected the tenacious elder leader to cling to power for several more years, came after tensions between Mr. Jiang and Mr. Hu began to affect policy making in the one-party state, some officials and political analysts said.

Mr. Jiang, 78, may be suffering from health problems, several people informed about leadership debates said. But he appeared robust in recent public appearances and was widely described as determined to keep his job—and even expand his authority—until he submitted a letter of resignation this month.

The leadership transition was announced Sunday in a terse dispatch by the New China News Agency, followed by a 45-minute broadcast on China Central Television. Mr. Jiang and Mr. Hu appeared side by side, smiling, shaking hands and praising each other profusely in front of applauding members of the Central Committee of the Communist Party, which formally accepted Mr. Jiang's resignation and Mr. Hu's promotion at the conclusion of its four-day annual session.

Mr. Jiang's offer to retire, which was first reported by The New York Times earlier this month, was given no advance publicity in state media. China Central Television read the text of Mr. Jiang's resignation letter on its evening broadcast,

emphasizing that his resignation was voluntary. The letter was dated Sept. 1.

"In consideration of the long-term development of the party's and people's collective endeavors, I have always looked forward to fully retiring from all leadership posts," Mr. Jiang wrote, according to an official transcript of his letter. He said Mr. Hu "is fully qualified to take up this position."

Even by the strict standards of secrecy within the party, the decision about Mr. Jiang's fate was closely held. For a vast majority of the 70 million party members, not to mention the general public, there had been no indication that he was planning to retire, and his abrupt departure seems likely to increase the sense that the most important personnel decisions are made without broad consultation. Since the Communists defeated the Nationalists in a civil war and took control of China in 1949, the party has repeatedly failed to execute orderly successions. All three of the men chosen by Mao Zedong to succeed him were purged before they could consolidate power, two of them by Mao himself and the third by Deng Xiaoping after Mao's death in 1976.

Deng also anointed and then cashiered two successors. In the aftermath of the bloody crackdown on dissent in 1989, he elevated Mr. Jiang from the middling rank of Shanghai party chief to China's highest posts.

The most recent transition looked similarly compromised when Mr. Jiang maneuvered to keep control of the military in 2002. Party officials said Mr. Hu had been slated to inherit full power at that time and that his failure to control the military forced him to operate in Mr. Jiang's shadow.

But Mr. Jiang's retirement suggests that the party now operates more according to the consensus of its elite members rather than the whims of its most senior leader.

Moreover, Mr. Jiang did not appear to have extracted any special concessions as the price of his retirement. Notably, he failed to arrange for Vice President Zeng Qinghong to be elevated to the Central Military Commission. Party officials had said they expected Mr. Zeng, a longtime protégé and ally of Mr. Jiang's, to become either a regular member or a vice chairman of the commission.

On Sunday, Xu Caihou, a military officer in charge of propaganda work, was promoted to replace Mr. Hu as a vice chairman of the commission. He will serve with Cao Gang-chuan, the defense minister, and Gen. Guo Boxiong.

The number of regular members of the commission was expanded to seven from four, adding representatives from the navy, air force and the unit in charge of China's nuclear arsenal.

Mr. Hu, a poker-faced bureaucrat who served most of his career in inland provinces and rarely if ever traveled outside China before he rose to the most senior ranks in the late 1990's, has sent mixed signals about how he intends to rule. He deftly handled the first big crisis of his leadership in the spring of 2003, when China faced the SARS epidemic that top health officials had initially covered up. Mr. Hu sacked two senior officials and ordered a broad mobilization to combat the disease, which was controlled within weeks.

He has sought to draw a contrast with Mr. Jiang's aristocratic image, making trips to China's poorest areas and shunning some conspicuous perks. He pledged to raise the incomes of workers and peasants and redirect more state spending to areas left behind in China's long economic boom.

"Use power for the people, show concern for the people and seek benefit for the people," Mr. Hu said in remarks early in his term as party chief. He has allowed state media to refer to him as a populist, though his rise through the ranks has not depended on popular support.

Little is known about Mr. Hu personally beyond a few random facts offered by the propaganda machine, including his enthusiasm for Ping-Pong and what is described as a photographic memory. In official settings, he is a much less colorful figure than Mr. Jiang, who crooned "Love Me Tender" at an Asian diplomatic gathering and was fond of quoting Jefferson and reciting the Gettysburg Address to visiting Americans.

It seems highly unlikely that Mr. Hu is a closet liberal. Editors and other journalists say he has tightened media controls. He has presided over a crackdown on online discussion by jailing people who express antigovernment views on the Internet.

"My general impression is that Hu is a Communist of the old mode," said Alfred Chan, professor of politics at Huron College in Canada, who is conducting a study of the new leadership. "His career has been totally shaped by the Communist system. I think many expectations of him are exaggerated because he works under the constraints of party discipline."

In a speech delivered last week, he referred to Western-style democracy as a "blind alley" for China. He has a plan for political change, but it mostly involves injecting some transparency and competitiveness within the single-party system to make officials police themselves better.

In foreign affairs, Mr. Hu deferred largely to Mr. Jiang. Mr. Jiang relished his role as a statesman and was proud of having built a nonconfrontational, sometimes even cordial relationship with the United States.

Mr. Hu is not expected to alter course substantially. But party officials say that he has tended to emphasize relations with China's neighbors and with Europe over ties with the United States and Japan.

He faces two major foreign policy tests that Mr. Jiang leaves unresolved. One involves North Korea, China's long-time ally, which American officials say is on the verge of becoming a full-scale nuclear power. Chinese officials worry that if Pyongyang formally goes nuclear, other Asian countries, notably Japan, could follow.

China is also deeply worried about how to deal with Taiwan under President Chen Shui-bian, who many here believe intends to move the island, which China claims as its sovereign territory, toward independence.

Mr. Jiang steered China toward a tougher rhetorical and military posture toward Taiwan, even as the Bush administration expanded military aid to the island. Mr. Hu has not shown any signs of changing course, but some analysts say he may experiment with a more flexible approach if he does not have to worry about having his nationalist credentials second-guessed by Mr. Jiang.

Mr. Hu and Mr. Jiang did not publicly spar. But there were signs that their relationship had become strained. Mr. Jiang rejected a framework for China's emergence as a great power that Mr. Hu supported. The policy framework, known by the slogan "peaceful rise," was dismissed by Mr. Jiang as too soft when China was threatening Taiwan with military force.

Mr. Hu and his prime minister, Wen Jiabao, have also had to battle internally to curtail wasteful state spending and cool the overheated economy. Some regional leaders are thought to have looked to Mr. Jiang as a counterweight to Mr. Hu because they see the elder leader as a champion of fast economic growth supported by heavy state investment.

"It may be that Hu will no longer have to worry that Jiang will contest his decisions, and that could make decision-making smoother," said Frederick Teiwes, an expert on elite politics at the University of Sydney.

Some people who have visited Mr. Jiang or spoken with his relatives say he has suffered health problems lately, offering one possible explanation for his unexpected retirement.

But Mr. Jiang is also thought to have come under heavy pressure within the party, and even within the military, to follow the example of Deng and withdraw from public life before health problems force him to do so. Mr. Hu also made a veiled call for Mr. Jiang to step aside when he lavished praise on Mr. Deng's decision to retire early during ceremonies to commemorate the 100th anniversary of the late leader's birth in August.

China
The Quiet Revolution
The Emergence of Capitalism

Doug Guthrie

When Deng Xiaoping unveiled his vision of economic reform to the Third Plenum of the 11th Central Committee of the Chinese Communist Party in December 1978, the Chinese economy was faltering. Reeling from a decade of stagnation during the Cultural Revolution and already falling short of the projections set forth in the 1976 10-year plan, China needed more than a new plan and the Soviet-style economic vision of Deng's political rival, Hua Guofeng, to improve the economy. Deng's plan was to lead the country down a road of gradual and incremental economic reform, leaving the state apparatus intact, while slowly unleashing market forces. Since that time, the most common image of China, promulgated by members of the US Congress and media, is of an unbending authoritarian regime that has grown economically but seen little substantive change.

There is often a sense that China remains an entrenched and decaying authoritarian government run by corrupt Party officials; extreme accounts depict it as an economy on the verge of collapse. However, this vision simply does not square with reality. While it is true that China remains an authoritarian one-party system, it is also the most successful case of economic reform among communist planned economy in the 20th century. Today, it is fast emerging as one of the most dynamic market economies and has grown to be the world's sixth largest. Understanding how this change has come about requires an examination of three broad changes that have come together to shape China's transition to capitalism: the state's gradual recession from control over the economy, which caused a shift in economic control without privatization; the steady growth of foreign investment; and the gradual emergence of a legal-rational system to support these economic changes.

Reform Without Privatization

During the 1980s and 1990s, economists and institutional advisors from the West advocated a rapid transition to market institutions as the necessary medicine for transforming communist societies. Scholars argued that private property provides the institutional foundation of a market economy and that, therefore, communist societies making the transition to a market economy must privatize industry and other public goods. The radical members of this school argued that rapid privatization—the so-called "shock therapy" or "big bang" approach to economic reforms—was the only way to avoid costly abuses in these transitional systems.

The Chinese path has been very different. While countries like Russia have followed Western advice, such as rapidly constructing market institutions, immediately removing the state from control over the economy, and hastily privatizing property, China has taken its time in implementing institutional change. The state has gradually receded from control over the economy, cautiously experimenting with new institutions and implementing them incrementally within existing institutional arrangements. Through this gradual process of reform, China has achieved in 20 years what many developing states have taken over 50 to accomplish.

The success of gradual reform in China can be attributed to two factors. First, the gradual reforms allowed the government to retain its role as a stabilizing force in the midst of the turbulence accompanying the transition from a planned to a market economy. Institutions such as the "dual-track" system kept large state-owned enterprises partially on the plan and gave them incentives to generate extra income by selling what they could produce above the plan in China's nascent markets. Over time, as market economic practices became more successful, the "plan" part of an enterprise's portfolio was reduced and the "market" part grew. Enterprises were thus given the stability of a continued but gradually diminishing planned economy system as well as the time to learn to set prices, compete for contracts, and produce efficiently. Second, the government has gradually promoted ownership-like control down the government administrative hierarchy to the localities. As a result, the central government was able to give economic control to local administrators without privatization. But with economic control came accountability, and local administrators became very invested in the successful economic reform of the villages, townships, and municipalities under their jurisdictions. In a sense, as Professor Andrew Walder of Stanford University has argued, pushing economic responsibilities onto local administrators created an incentive structure much like those experienced by managers of large industrial firms.

Change From Above

Even as economic reform has proceeded gradually, the cumulative changes over two decades have been nothing short of radical. These reforms have proceeded on four levels: institutional changes instigated by the highest levels of government; firm-level institutions that reflect the legal-rational system emerging at the state level; a budding legal system that allows workers institutional backing outside of the factory and is heavily influenced by relationships with foreign investors; and the emergence of new labor markets, which allow workers the freedom and mobility to find new employment when necessary. The result of these changes has been the emergence of a legal-rational regime of labor, where the economy increasingly rests upon an infrastructure of ordered laws that workers can invoke when necessary.

Under Deng Xiaoping, Zhao Ziyang brought about radical change in China by pushing the country toward constitutionality and the rule of law to create rational economic processes. These changes, set forth ideologically as a package of reforms necessary for economic development, fundamentally altered the role of politics and the Communist Party in Chinese society. The early years of reform not only gave a great deal of autonomy to enterprise managers and small-scale entrepreneurs, but also emphasized the legal reforms that would undergird this process of change. However, by creating a body of civil and economic law, such as the 1994 Labor Law and Company Law and the 1995 National Compensation Law upon which the transforming economy would be based, the Party elites held themselves to the standards of these legal changes. Thus the rationalization of the economy led to a decline in the Party's ability to rule over the working population.

In recent years, this process has been continued by global integration and the tendency to adopt the norms of the international community. While championing global integration and the Rule of Law, Zhu Rongji also brought about broader political and social change, just as Zhao Ziyang did in China's first decade of economic reform. Zhu's strategy has been to ignore questions of political reform and concentrate instead on the need to adopt economic and legal systems that will allow the country to integrate smoothly into the international community. From rhetoric on "linking up with the international community" to laws such as the 2000 Patent Law to institutions such as the State Intellectual Property Office and the Chinese International Economic Trade and Arbitration Commission, this phase of reform has been oriented toward enforcing the standards and norms of the international investment community. Thus, Zhu's

objective is to deepen all of the reforms that have been discussed above, while holding these changes to the standards of the international community.

After two decades of transition, the architects of the reforms have established about 700 new national laws and more than 2,000 new local laws. These legal changes, added regulations, and experiments with new economic institutions have driven the reform process. A number of laws and policies in the 1980s laid the groundwork for a new set of policies that would redefine labor relations in fundamental ways. For example, the policies that set in motion the emergence of labor contracts in China were first introduced in an experimental way in 1983, further codified in 1986, and eventually institutionalized with the Labor Law in 1994. While there are economic incentives behind Chinese firms' willingness to embrace labor contracts, including the end of lifetime employment, these institutional changes have gradually rationalized the labor relationship, eventually providing a guarantee of due process in the event of unfair treatment and placing workers' rights at the center of the labor relationship. Incremental changes such as these have been crucial to the evolution of individual rights in China.

The obvious and most common response to these changes is that they are symbolic rather than substantive, that a changing legal and policy framework has little meaning when an authoritarian government still sits at the helm. Yet the scholarship that has looked extensively at the impact of these legal changes largely belies this view. Workers and managers take the new institutions seriously and recognize that the institutions have had a dramatic impact on the structure of authority relations and on the conception of rights within the workplace.

Other research shows that legal and policy changes that emphasize individual civil liberties are also significant. In the most systematic and exhaustive study to date of the prison system, research shows that changes in the treatment of prisoners have indeed resulted in the wake of the Prison Reform Law. And although no scholarship has been completed on the National Compensation Law, it is noteworthy that 97,569 suits were filed under this law against the government in 1999, a proportional increase of over 12,000 percent since the beginning of the economic reforms. These institutions guarantee that, for the first time in the history of the People's Republic of China, individuals can have their day in court, even at the government's expense.

The 1994 Labor Law and the Labor Arbitration Commission (LAC), which has branches in every urban district, work hand-in-hand to guarantee workers their individual rights as laborers. Chapter 10 of the Labor Law, entitled "Labor Disputes," is specifically devoted to articulating due process, which laborers are legally guaranteed, should a dispute arise in the workplace. The law explicitly explains the rights of the worker to take disputes to outside arbitration (the district's LAC) should the resolution in the workplace be unsatisfactory to the worker. Further, many state-owned enterprises have placed all of their workers on fixed-term labor contracts, which significantly rationalize the labor relationships beyond the personalized labor relations of the past. This

An Age of Jurisprudence

Lawyers

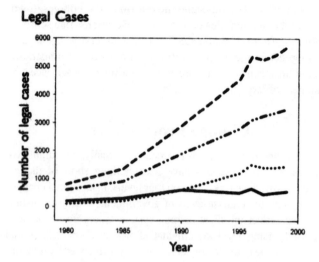

Legal Cases

The above graphs depict two recent trends in China: a growing body of lawyers and an increasing number of legal cases. As the graph at left indicates, the number of lawyers in China has increased dramatically in the past 20 years, rising from fewer than 10,000 in 1980 to over 100,000 in 2000. The graph at right shows the growth in various types of legal cases over the same period. In particular, there have been significant increases in civil, economic, and first-trial cases.

2002 Statistical Yearbook of China

bundle of changes has fundamentally altered the nature of the labor relationship and the mechanisms through which authority can be challenged. For more than a decade, it has been possible for workers to file grievances against superiors and have those grievances heard at the LACs. In 1999, 52 percent of the 120,191 labor disputes settled by arbitration or mediation were decided wholly in favor of the workers filing the suits. These are official statistics from the Chinese government, and therefore should be viewed skeptically. However, even if the magnitude is incorrect, these numbers illuminate an important trend toward legal activity regarding workers' rights.

Many of these changes in labor practices were not originally adopted with workers' rights in mind, but the unintended consequence of the changes has been the construction of a regime of labor relations that emphasizes the rights of workers. For instance, extending the example of labor contracts that were being experimented with as early as 1983, these were originally intended as a form of economic protection for ailing enterprises, allowing a formal method of ending lifetime employment. However, workers began using the terms of employment codified in the contracts as the vehicle for filing grievances when contractual agreements were not honored. With the emergence of the LACs in the late 1980s and the further codification of these institutions in the Labor Law, the changes that were in progress became formalized in a set of institutions that ultimately benefited workers in the realm of rights. In a similar way, workers' representative committees were formed in the

state's interest, but became an institution workers claimed as their own. These institutions, which many managers refer to as "our own little democracy," were adopted early in the reforms to co-opt the agitation for independent labor unions. These committees do not have the same power or status as independent labor unions in the West, but workers have made them much more significant in factories today than they were originally intended to be.

Foreign Investment's Impact

At the firm level, there is a process of rationalization in which firms are adopting a number of rational bureaucratic systems, such as grievance filing procedures, mediation committees, and formal organizational processes, that are more often found in Western organizations. In my own work on these issues, I have found that joint venture relationships encourage foreign joint ventures to push their partner organizations to adopt stable legal-rational structures and systems in their organizations. These stable, legal-rational systems are adopted to attract foreign investors, but have radical implications for the structure of authority relations and the lives of individual Chinese citizens. Chinese factories that have formal relationships with foreign, and particularly Western, firms are significantly more likely to have institutionalized formal organizational rules, 20 times more likely to have formal grievance filing procedures, five times

154

more likely to have worker representative committee meetings, and about two times more likely to have institutionalized formal hiring procedures. They also pay about 50 percent higher wages than other factories and are more likely to adopt China's new Company Law, which binds them to abide by the norms of the international community and to respect international legal institutions such as the Chinese In-ternational Economic Arbitration and Trade Commission. Many managers openly acknowledge that the changes they have set in place have little to do with their own ideas of efficient business practices and much more to do with pressure brought on them by their foreign partners. Thus, there is strong evidence that foreign investment matters for on-the-ground change in China.

> Foreign investors and Chinese firms are not interested in human rights per se, but the negotiations in the marketplace lead to transformed workplaces, which affect millions of Chinese citizens on a daily basis.

Given the common image of multinational corporations seeking weak institutional environments to capitalize on cheap labor, why would joint venture relationships with Western multinationals have a more positive impact in the Chinese case? The answer has to do with the complex reasons for foreign investment there. Corporations are rarely the leading advocates of civil liberties and labor reform, but many foreign investors in China are more interested in long-term investments that position them to capture market share than they are in cheap labor. They generally seek Chinese partners that are predictable, stable, and knowledgeable about Western-style business practices and negotiations. Chinese factories desperately want to land these partnerships and position themselves as suitable investment partners by adopting a number of the practices that Western partners will recognize as stable and reform-minded. Among the basic reforms they adopt to show their fitness for "linking up" with the international community are labor reforms. Thus, the signaling of a commitment to stable Western-style business practices through commitments to labor reform has led to fundamental changes in Chinese workplace labor relations. Foreign investors and Chinese firms are not interested in human rights per se, but the negotiations in the marketplace lead to transformed workplaces, which affect millions of Chinese citizens on a daily basis.

However, changes at the firm level are not meaningful if they lack the legal infrastructure upon which a legal-rational system of labor is built. The construction of a legal system is a process that takes time; it requires the training of lawyers and judges, and the emergence of a culture in which individuals who are part of the legal system come to process claims. This process of change is difficult to assess because it relies on soft variables about the reform process, such as, for example, how judges think about suits and whether a legal-rational culture is emerging. But we can look at some aspects of fundamental shifts in society. All of these changes, in turn, rest upon a legal-rational system that is slowly but surely emerging in China.

Finally, beyond the legal and institutional changes that have begun to transform Chinese society fundamentally, workers are no longer tied to workplaces in the way that they once were. In the pre-reform system, there was very little mobility of labor, because workers were generally bound to their "work units" for life. The system created a great deal of stability for workers, but it also became one of the primary means through which citizens were controlled. Individuals were members of their work units, which they were dependent on for a variety of fundamental goods and services.

This manufactured dependence was one of the basic ways that the Party exercised control over the population. Writing about the social uprisings that occurred in 1989, Walder points out that the erosion of this system is what allowed citizens to protest with impunity on a scale never before observed in communist China: "[W]hat changed in these regimes in the last decade was not their economic difficulties, widespread cynicism or corruption, but that the institutional mechanisms that served to promote order in the past—despite these long-standing problems—lost their capacity to do so." It is precisely because labor markets have opened up that workers are no longer absolutely dependent upon the government for job placements; they now have much more leverage to assert the importance of their own rights in the workplace. And while the private sector was nonexistent when the economic reforms began, the country has seen this sector, which includes both private enterprises and household businesses, grow to more than 30 million individuals. With the growth of the private sector, there is much greater movement and autonomy among laborers in the economy. This change has afforded workers alternative paths to status attainment, paths that were once solely controlled by the government.

Quiet Revolution

Much like the advocates of rapid economic reform, those demanding immediate political and social reform often take for granted the learning that must occur in the face of new institutions. The assumption most often seems that, given certain institutional arrangements, individuals will naturally know how to carry out the practices of capitalism. Yet these assumptions reflect a neoclassical view of human nature in which rational man will thrive in his natural environment—free markets. Completely absent from this view are the roles of history, culture, and pre-existing institutions; it is a vision that is far too simplistic to comprehend the challenge of making rational economic and legal systems work in the absence of stable institutions and a history to which they can be linked. The transition from a command economy to a market economy can be a wrenching experience, not only at the institutional level but also at the level of individual practice. Individuals must learn the rules of the market and new institutions must be in place long enough to gain stability and legitimacy.

The PRC government's methodical experimentation with different institutional forms and the Party's gradual relinquishing of control over the economy has brought about a "quiet revolution." It is impossible to create a history of a legal-rational economic system in a dramatic moment of institutional change. The architects of China's transition to capitalism have had success in reforming the economy because they have recognized that the transition to a radically different type of economic system must occur gradually, allowing for the maximum possible institutional stability as economic actors slowly learn the rules of capitalism. Capitalism has indeed arrived in China, and it has done so via gradual institutional reform under the communist mantle.

DOUG GUTHRIE is Associate Professor of Sociology at New York University.

In March Toward Capitalism, China Has Avoided Russia's Path

Asia: Unlike its onetime idol, Beijing has used a gradual approach to developing a market-oriented economy.

By HENRY CHU
TIMES STAFF WRITER

BEIJING—If the Soviet Union always seemed like the terrifying embodiment of Big Brother to the West, then for years it was something of a big brother to China toward the south.

Inspired by the same Marxist-Leninist ideals that first took root in Russia, Beijing alternately held up Moscow as its role model and, in times of disillusionment, its nemesis.

But since the Soviet Union's collapse, China has come to regard Russia as one thing only: its worst nightmare—a country with a political system in disarray; a society in sometimes violent flux; and, now, an economy in free fall.

In attempting to remake itself from a Communist behemoth into a capitalist beacon, China has studiously tried to avoid the path of its onetime idol, preferring a more gradual approach to change. Over the last 20 years, the result has been shaky but mostly upward progress: steady economic growth, an emerging middle class, a new breed of entrepreneurs.

As world leaders and economists reassess the wisdom of free markets amid today's global turmoil, the China model—from the perspective of Russia's collapse and the pain in lesser Asian countries that wholeheartedly embraced capitalism—looks wise enough.

Yet even as Beijing silently congratulates itself on the wisdom of its go-slow approach, analysts say that historical conditions here have been nearly as big

a contributor to China's improvement as current policy.

And as in Russia, major domestic reforms—especially China's latest efforts to shed its money-losing state enterprises and streamline its bloated bureaucracy—have brought about a whole new set of problems, making the final outcome of one of the most ambitious economic transitions in history far from certain.

"It is too soon to say whether China's reforms will succeed," Nicholas Lardy, an economist with the Brookings Institution in Washington, wrote recently.

Like Russia, China has struggled to redesign a planned economy into a market-oriented one. But even though both were Communist in name, the two countries launched their modernization drives at very different stages in their development.

"The Communist revolution in the former Soviet Union was over 70 years old; the Communist revolution in China was 30," said Harry Harding, a Sinologist at George Washington University. "The former Soviet Union was more industrialized; China was still an agricultural, rural society."

China embarked on its transformation when Deng Xiaoping, the nation's late "paramount leader," officially ended Beijing's isolation in 1978 with a series of measures designed to open up and liberalize the world's most populous country.

The enormous rural communes set up by Mao Tse-tung were dismantled. Peasant farmers were permitted to sell food on the private market. Two years later, the doors to foreign investment were thrown open in specially designated zones along the southern coast.

Setting the Stage

Radical Maoism was dead, discredited after the 1966–76 Cultural Revolution, one of China's darkest periods, during which hundreds of thousands of citizens were killed.

Ironically, however, many scholars now argue that some of Mao's wrongheaded policies actually fostered the political climate and infrastructure necessary for the success of China's long march toward capitalism—or, in Deng's wordplay, "socialism with Chinese characteristics." Fanaticism was replaced by pragmatism and a thirst for a new national direction.

"The Cultural Revolution deinstitutionalized the political system and de-legitimized the Communist Party in ways that made reform both necessary and more possible," Harding said.

Under Mao, much of China's economic decision-making and planning had already devolved to local authorities. After Deng's reforms began, local officials used their knowledge and the fledgling industrial development across China to push for rapid industrialization of the countryside through a combination of tax breaks and enterprising schemes.

Labor was cheap—and plentiful. Three of every four Chinese toiled in the fields and could be redirected into industrial jobs and big, capital-intensive projects. In the Soviet Union, by contrast, industrialization was largely complete when the Soviet empire collapsed, leaving 75% of workers scrambling for hard-to-find jobs in new sectors of the economy.

Chinese cities such as Shenzhen, the first of the special economic zones, mushroomed with activity.

Shiny new skyscrapers now rise from a robust manufacturing base. Millions of Barbie dolls roll off assembly lines into the eager hands of children worldwide. The population of Shenzhen, a onetime fishing village with 30,000 inhabitants across from the Hong Kong border, skyrocketed a hundredfold to 3 million.

Traders work the Shenzhen stock market. This year, foreign investment through July totaled an impressive $1.6 billion.

Much of the investment in Shenzhen and throughout the rest of China comes from a natural resource that Russia does not have: the ethnic Chinese around the world who still feel strong ties with "the motherland" and who have become one of China's primary engines for growth.

Whereas the Soviet Union splintered along nationalist and ethnic lines after its breakup, overseas Chinese, about 55 million in all, have remained remarkably unified through their common cultural heritage across boundaries of state and time.

"Hong Kong, Taiwan, Singapore and the Chinese diaspora in South [and] East Asia and North America are filled with ethnic Chinese entrepreneurs who have proved to be valuable sources of knowledge and investment and who have served as important bridges to the world economy," Andrew G. Walder, sociologist and specialist in China market reforms at Stanford University, observed in the China Quarterly magazine.

Amazingly, between 75% and 80% of all foreign investment in China (including money from Hong Kong) comes out of the pockets of ethnic Chinese across the globe, whose ranks boasted three dozen billionaires in East Asia in 1994.

Although the regional financial crisis has pinched some of the capital flow from the outside, economists say that money keeps pouring in at a fast clip.

In addition to abundant foreign investment, a comparatively low foreign debt— thanks to Mao's insistence on national self-sufficiency—has been crucial to China's revival as one of the world's major economies.

In stark contrast to Russia, China has not had to resort to crushing bailout packages by the International Monetary Fund to shore up its economy. While the government is struggling to keep expenditures in check as central tax revenue dwindles, Beijing does not need to devote huge resources to servicing short-term foreign debt; 80% of its debt is long-term, according to Hu Biliang, a senior economist with a French securities firm here.

Moscow, meanwhile, has buckled under the weight of $31.2 billion in IMF cash since 1992. And those loans have invariably come with political strings attached, reflecting one of the widest and most important divergences between China and Russia on the way to the free market: their different political systems.

For Russia, economic reform has gone hand in hand with political restructuring. At about the same time that Moscow relinquished its stranglehold on the economy, the Russian people also flung off the totalitarian Communist regime in one violent shudder.

Since then, prescriptions for a free market have been intertwined with efforts to build a free society. Economic shock treatment and the massive unloading of nationalized industries in Russia are bound up with ending the political monopoly of the Communist Party and building a raucous, but functional democracy.

Beijing, on the other hand, represents the last great bastion of Communist control, a one-party dictatorship that oversees one-fifth of humanity. Its authoritarian rule has greatly loosened over the last two decades—some detect the signs of a civil society emerging—but the one-party Communist regime remains China's government.

As such, China's leaders can still rule by fiat, pushing through relatively unpopular measures when necessary, although the regime is careful not to push too hard lest it provoke a popular uprising such as the 1989 Tiananmen Square demonstrations. Even the ensuing massacre that year put only a temporary crimp in the economy, which flagged until Deng launched a "southern tour" of China in 1992 to jump-start greater economic liberalization.

Now many Chinese appear content to ignore the government so long as it allows some personal freedom, such as easier internal movement within China, and the liberty to pursue a higher living standard.

Beijing knows its legitimacy increasingly rests on its handling of the economy, and it has tried to help its citizens discover the truth of Deng's famous maxim: "To get rich is glorious." China's leaders are hoping that an economic overhaul is enough, without knitting it together with a political one, as happened in the former Soviet bloc.

"Where in Eastern Europe [economic] shock therapy and mass privatization are designed in part to dismantle communism and strip former Communists of power and privilege," Walder wrote, "in China gradual reform is intended to allow the party to survive as an instrument of economic development."

As a multi-party state, Russia is now full of vested interests jockeying for position. Politicians, elected by popular vote, must cater to them to stay in power.

The result has been a crony capitalism and democracy stage-managed by a handful of "oligarchs" behind the scenes, who have gobbled up the wealth and used it to wrest favors from Moscow.

So far, China has stayed largely immune to such stresses. But it has spawned a crony capitalism of its own that threatens the stability that the government is obsessed with maintaining.

Among those who have enriched themselves the most from Beijing's market reforms are not the *laobaixing,* or common people, but the families of high officials, who have used their connections to gain control of some of the most lucrative businesses in China.

Indeed, such corruption was one of the main grievances that drove the *laobaixing* to Tiananmen Square in 1989, marching for an end to Communist Party privilege and nepotism.

Fighting Corruption

The issue still ranks as China's No. 1 public beef. Frustrated locals and foreigners alike complain that preferential treatment for party "princelings" or through money passed under the table kills competition and undermines their ability to do honest business.

The Asian financial crisis has put enormous pressure on the government as exports have slowed and the economy tightens. Production surpluses in industries such as steel sit untouched in huge stockpiles. Devastating flooding across China has made government promises of an 8% economic growth rate this year ring hollow.

Unemployment, officially at 3.5% but probably higher, is rising as local authorities eagerly shed their small and medium-sized state-owned enterprises at a speed the government was evidently not prepared for. In some cases, the enterprises were sold for pennies on the dollar to friends and relatives of local officials, though not on the scale of the "false" privatization in Russia that concentrated assets in just a few hands, analysts say.

"There are as yet no media moguls like [Boris] Berezovsky or energy czars like [Viktor] Chernomyrdin, but localities are seething with resentment against those who appropriated local collective enterprises over the past five to 10 years," said Douglas Paal, president of the Asia Pacific Policy Center in Washington and former National Security Council senior staffer under Presidents Reagan and Bush.

Last month, in a sign of growing alarm, the Communist regime issued an official editorial calling for a halt to "blind selling of state-owned firms."

"Leaders in some localities have simplified these serious and complicated reforms, and have taken them to mean merely selling such enterprises," the New China News Agency said. Local authorities should "carefully study" the proper guidelines regulating such sales, it added.

With joblessness on the rise, Beijing has backed off from ambitious plans to make residents buy their own homes and to slash China's bureaucracy in half, a potential loss of 4 million jobs.

Worker protests have already broken out, from Sichuan province in central China to Heilongjiang in the northeast, but are not reported in the official media.

These days, no one is willing to write off China as a potential economic success story, but pessimism hangs in the air among economists and some citizens here over the current state of China's gradual, multi-pronged reform program. It seems clear, however, that the Russian strategy is not an alternative.

"There probably are no panaceas in this world," said Harding. "Neither the Russian model nor the Chinese model is perfect. Or, as the cynic once said, 'The grass is brown on both sides of the fence.'"

Sonia: and yet so far

Formed in a shambles, India's new government can only get better

THE comparisons that have been drawn with the Buddha and Mohandas Gandhi seem a bit overblown. But India reveres renunciation, and the decision by Sonia Gandhi (no relation to the Mahatma) to forgo the chance to become India's prime minister has mightily enhanced her stature. It has probably also been good for her party, Congress, and the prospects of the government it will lead under Manmohan Singh, her anointee, who was due to be sworn in on May 22nd.

The party itself found this hard to accept. Its members of parliament seemed to think they had wandered into a production of "King Lear", a less happy tale of renunciation. In an emotional—nay, hysterical—meeting on May 18th they hectored, cajoled and begged Mrs Gandhi to change her mind and take the job. The unbridled sycophancy was a reminder of the party's feudal attachment to the Nehru-Gandhi dynasty, and fear that, without her as a neutral figurehead, its kingdom will fall apart.

Mrs Gandhi was swayed neither by them nor by the several hundred equally high-pitched party activists gathered outside her front gate, some of whom felt genuinely cheated. They had worked hard to help her achieve the election result announced on May 13th, bringing a Congress-led coalition back to power against all expectations. They had rooted for her right to be prime minister despite being born in Italy. Some argued, incredibly, that if she was unwilling to serve, then her son Rahul, a 33-year-old first-time MP, should step in. Others complained she was yielding to a xenophobic campaign that should have been confronted.

That may indeed have been one factor in Mrs Gandhi's decision. The Bharatiya Janata Party (BJP), the former ruling party, and its coalition partners had said they would boycott her swearing-in, though the BJP's leader and former prime minister, Atal Behari Vajpayee, would attend. One former BJP government minister, Sushma Swaraj, and her husband were to resign their seats in the upper house of parliament in protest at the "national shame" of installing an Italian-born prime minister. Similarly, another senior BJP leader, Uma Bharti, had resigned as chief minister of the state of Madhya Pradesh. After Mrs Gandhi's sacrifice though, Miss Bharti, a *sanyasin,* or religious renunciate, looked rather silly.

Other groups linked to the Rashtriya Swayamsevak Sangh (RSS), the Hindu-nationalist mass organisation that spawned the BJP, had already taken this campaign to the streets. Ram Madhav, an RSS spokesman, blamed the BJP's electoral defeat in part on its failure to find "any real national-level emotive or ideological issue". There was a risk that Mrs Gandhi's Italian origins might fill that void and prove the dominant theme of the new government's early days. Rahul Gandhi and his sister Priyanka were also said to oppose their mother's taking office, fearing for her life, though Rahul denied this. Their father, Mrs Gandhi's husband Rajiv, and grandmother, Indira, both former prime ministers, were each assassinated.

Mr Madhav claims that even some Congress voters were uneasy about being ruled by a native Italian, and he probably has a point. She speaks Hindi, wears sarees and says she prefers *naan* to pasta. But her foreign birth would always have been a stick to beat her with. Her party's mandate in the election was hardly a clear-cut endorsement either of its policies or its leader. Congress gained just under 27% of the national vote, about 1.5 percentage points less than in the last election in 1999. Its coalition won almost exactly the same share of the votes, about 36%, as the BJP's.

Mrs Gandhi herself had always been careful not to promote herself as a prime-ministerial candidate. During the campaign, this was seen as a shrewd tactic to stop the BJP turning it into a presidential-style contest between an untested, foreign-born novice and the popular, statesmanlike Mr Vajpayee. It now seems that Mrs Gandhi all along saw her duty as limited to rescuing her late husband's party from its recent slump and, in her words, to providing India with "a secular government that is strong and stable"; but not leading it.

Outside the Congress hot-house, some were relieved at that. The political drama in Delhi was played out against the distant thud of a crashing stockmarket. The Mumbai exchange suffered its worst-ever day on May 17th, at one point having fallen by more than 17%. The next day, news that Mrs Gandhi was thinking of stepping aside helped spur a recovery.

One reason for the market's cheer was the assumed identity of Mrs Gandhi's replacement. Having attributed to her the

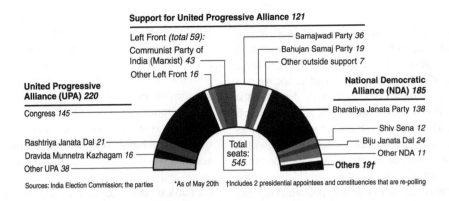

Support for United Progressive Alliance *121*

Left Front *(total 59)*:
Communist Party of India (Marxist) *43*
Other Left Front *16*

Samajwadi Party *36*
Bahujan Samaj Party *19*
Other outside support *7*

United Progressive Alliance (UPA) *220*
Congress *145*

Rashtriya Janata Dal *21*
Dravida Munnetra Kazhagam *16*
Other UPA *38*

Total seats: 545

National Democratic Alliance (NDA) *185*
Bharatiya Janata Party *138*
Shiv Sena *12*
Biju Janata Dal *24*
Other NDA *11*

Others *19†*

Sources: India Election Commission; the parties   *As of May 20th   †Includes 2 presidential appointees and constituencies that are re-polling

wisdom of the Buddha it was inevitable that Mrs Gandhi's parliamentary colleagues would ask her to nominate one. Her choice, Manmohan Singh, is popular with investors as the author of India's economic liberalisation. An academic economist, he was Congress's finance minister in 1991, when, in response to a balance-of-payments crisis, the government launched a package of reforms, beginning the dismantling of the "licence raj" of state planning, import controls and excessive regulation that was Nehru's legacy.

So his presence is heartening for investors who have two worries about the new government: first, that it will be hostile to business and reluctant to continue or accelerate the liberalisation Mr Singh began; second, that it will be unstable and short-lived. The fears stem partly from its status as a minority government. Not only will Congress rely on a coalition—to be known as the United Progressive Alliance (UPA)—but the UPA will itself be a minority (see chart), relying on the "outside support" of other parties, of which much the biggest is a "Left Front" dominated by the Communist Party of India (Marxist), or CPI (M).

Playing the red card

The CPI (M) has been in power in the state of West Bengal since 1977, and like ruling communist parties elsewhere, has become pragmatic in office. Once notorious for red tape and strikes, the state has recently been hard-selling its attractions as a destination for inward investment in information technology and services such as call-centres. The Communist chief minister, Buddhadeb Bhattacharjee, boasts of its success in promoting enterprise: exporting roses to the Netherlands, and housing potato-processing facilities for PepsiCo. It has even, with the help of British government aid, been closing down some of its loss-making state enterprises.

But during the election, Mr Bhattacharjee said that the CPI (M) could never join a Congress-led coalition, because of differences on economic policy. Mr Singh, whom the Communists are now happy to accept as a prime minister, was "the first torch-bearer for the IMF". One cause of the stockmarket crash was a suggestion by a Communist spokesman that the disinvestment ministry, which oversees India's privatisation programme, should be abolished (not a bad idea in itself, but he appeared to want to abolish privatisation as well).

The possibility of an end to the "disinvestment" of state enterprises, which in recent months helped fuel a surging stockmarket, is a specific fear of investors. A broader concern is that all economic policy will likewise be hostage to the populist demands of Congress's coalition partners. A number of the reforms that economists argue are most needed will probably not make much headway. Labour laws, for example, which make it hard to shed staff without state-government permission, are unlikely to be tackled.

The same is true of the reform that Arun Shourie, the outgoing BJP disinvestment minister, believed the most important of all, to the system by which funds are allocated to government departments and states. He argued that these reward poor performance—"the bigger the deficit, the bigger the grant". But tampering with this system may not appeal to state leaders whose support Congress needs, such as Laloo Prasad Yadav of Bihar, a state notorious for economic underperformance.

However, fears that reforms are about to be shelved, and the markets' reaction, seem excessive. The reform process has always involved more stops than starts, and Congress may be no worse placed to pursue it than was the BJP. Surjit Bhalla, of Oxus Fund Management, a hedge fund in Delhi, says that, since 1991, every government that has taken power in India has accelerated the reforms, and he expects this one to be no different. The Left, he says, is to Congress as the RSS was to the BJP, minus the RSS's communal tendencies. Just as the BJP had to resist the protectionist "self-reliant" economic tendency within the RSS, so Congress will be fending off leftist conservatism.

The markets are now awaiting the "common minimum programme" Congress and its partners are drafting. To the extent that this mirrors Congress's own manifesto, it will differ little from the BJP's approach, though privatisation is to be "more selective", and not pursued, in Mr Singh's phrase, "as an ideology".

The national vote was too evenly split, and too driven by local factors, to be interpreted as a clear mandate; much less, despite some attempts to do so, could it be seen as a national indictment of the reforms. But it has been taken as a slap in the face for the BJP from the mass of Indians who live in poverty in the countryside. Every new government pays them lip-service. This one, relishing the shock of victory, knows better than most how much it needs to concentrate on agriculture and rural infrastructure. That, however, is itself an argument for accelerated reform.

Stability pacts

The other fear about the new government is that it will prove shaky. Because it tends to be a competitor for power at the state level with its potential partners, Congress has in the past found it hard to forge national coalitions. Many UPA members have a price: one wants a new state carved out of Andhra Pradesh; another demands the ditching of harsh anti-terrorist legislation. Others, notably the Left parties and the Samajwadi ("Socialist") Party, which won 36 seats in India's largest state, Uttar Pradesh, are not actually joining the coalition: a form of power without accountability. Not having the responsibility that goes with cabinet seats, they could blackmail the government on issue after issue, and risk turning policymaking into a saga of serial brinksmanship.

Power in Indian politics is a great adhesive. Having touched it, the Left will be loth to let it slip. But managing such a complex and potentially fissile arrangement will demand great political skill. Mr Singh is, in this respect, untried. He is much admired as a kind, courteous and clever man. As a Sikh, he is India's first non-Hindu prime minister and living testimony to its secular traditions. But he sits in the upper house of parliament and has never won a direct election, though he will now have to do so in the next six months.

His first challenge will be to form a government that satisfies his coalition partners without sacrificing his policy goals. He is fortunate in being able to fill most jobs from Congress ranks. Besides the economic portfolios, much interest focuses on the foreign ministry and the post of national security adviser.

The next stage in the peace process with Pakistan—talks on measures to build confidence about the two countries' nuclear arsenals—is due next week. In August, foreign ministers are to meet, and by then the two sides should have begun to discuss the hardest issue, the status of Kashmir. Congress has supported the peace initiative Mr Vajpayee launched last year.

But it may find it harder to negotiate on Kashmir than would the BJP, whose Hindu-nationalist background makes it less vulnerable to attack from chauvinists. The peace process was to be Mr Vajpayee's claim to a place in history. It would be good if, in opposition, he ensured that it enjoys bipartisan support. But his party's willingness to stoke racist antipathy to Mrs Gandhi, and his own silence as it did so, do not bode well for restraint.

India's Democracy Provides Lessons

The struggling nation has integrated its diversity in a way that could be an example to Iraq.

Rajan Menon

NORTH SUTTON, N.H.—India's failures are legion and impossible to ignore. Poverty and desperation abound. Infant mortality is unacceptably high. Schools and healthcare are substandard—if available at all.

Roads and other infrastructure are primitive or in poor repair. The Indian government seems unable to adequately protect the country's Muslim minority (about 12% of the population) from periodic pogroms, and violence against lower castes erupts regularly.

Conflicts with Pakistan over Kashmir continue, made more alarming by the fact that both countries now possess nuclear weapons.

But despite these very real problems, most of what we read about India misses what is most remarkable about the country: its sheer survival.

As the United States attempts to shape a new government in Iraq, the lessons of India are perhaps worth considering, not least because the challenge Iraq faces—keeping a multiethnic country whole without sliding into dictatorship—is one that India, despite all its difficulties, has faced and overcome against considerable odds.

When India gained independence in 1947, it seemed too big and too diverse to hold together. Though a majority of the country's 400 million people were Hindus, there were Muslims, Christians (Protestants and Catholics), Jews, Jains, Buddhists and Zoroastrians. An array of languages (18 now have official status), thousands of dialects and a labyrinthine system of castes and sub-castes added to this bewildering complexity. Few outside

India believed that such an unwieldy behemoth could remain a single country.

But the system has held together, and it has done so despite some fearsome shocks, starting with the assassination of Mahatma Gandhi soon after Indian independence and continuing with the slaying of two prime ministers, three wars and numerous crises with neighboring Pakistan, the emasculation of democracy during the "emergency" proclaimed from 1975 to 1977 by then-Prime Minister Indira Gandhi, widespread and devastating riots sparked by plans to declare Hindi the national language, and separatist movements of Muslims in Kashmir, Sikhs in the Punjab and Nagas and Mizos in India's remote northeast.

Not only has Indian polity proved sturdy enough to weather these shocks, it has done so without abandoning democracy. With the exception of Indira Gandhi's "emergency," there has not been an interruption in—or even a real threat to—democratic institutions. Political power in the country has been passed from party to party frequently in federal and local elections, and voter turnout is high. The military has remained thoroughly under civilian control. Furthermore, India has consistently allowed a free press—in English and the many Indian languages. And a staggering array of civic groups promotes the interests of women, castes and language groups, professions and the environment. Labor unions engage in collective bargaining and strike regularly. Political demonstrations are a daily occurrence.

If the survival of India as a unified country is remarkable, the survival of its democracy is astonishing. When India became independent, it lacked any tradition of modern democracy. It had an abysmally low per capita income and a minuscule middle class, and most of its people were illiterate. Democracy, so social scientists tell us, cannot survive under such circumstances.

The standard explanation for how India has managed to reconcile diversity and unity while also fostering democracy invokes the country's colonial legacy. The British, so the explanation goes, transplanted their hallowed traditions, ideas and institutions of civil liberties and the rule of law.

Yet this account doesn't hold up on closer inspection. Let's leave aside for the moment the fact that most expansions of democratic rights in colonial India were not the products of benevolent tutelage but necessary and shrewd responses to the gathering momentum of an Indian nationalist movement. The main problem with crediting the British with India's success at democracy is that there is no shortage of former British colonies that, upon becoming independent, turned thoroughly undemocratic, with the military seizing power and ruling through naked force. Consider, for example, the post-colonial histories of Egypt, Iraq, Ghana, Nigeria, Kenya and Burma. Consider, in particular, India's neighbor and cultural cousin Pakistan, which has been ruled by the military for most of its existence.

There is no simple explanation for why India has not only survived but also maintained a fairly robust democracy. But what is clear is that the first could not have been attained without the other. A democratic order has been critical in preventing India's fragmentation.

Elections, a free press and civil society have provided multiple mechanisms for political participation—for power to be pursued, for grievances to be aired and for resources and remedies to be sought. India's democratic institutions work as a series of safety valves that prevent conflict from becoming the prevalent mechanism for deciding the most basic societal questions: who gets what, and when and how.

Moreover, India's federal system of 28 states, which were created to represent major linguistic and cultural groups, provides for substantial decentralization and autonomy, both of which have increased as local parties representing the interests of particular peoples have grown in number. The design is at times unwieldy and untidy, but it has served to prevent contentious issues from being automatically projected onto the national stage.

This arrangement, along with India's heterogeneity, has helped prevent crises in one region of the country from rattling the entire political system; instead, disturbances remain localized. In distant Kerala (both spatially and culturally removed), Kashmir's violence is viewed with a degree of detachment. Likewise, the bloodshed that accompanied Sikh separatism in the northern state of Punjab did not inflame passions in the southern state of Tamil Nadu.

The paradox, then, is that India's diversity and its seemingly cumbersome political system have enabled unity and democracy to combine. Seeming weaknesses have proved to be assets.

Now that economic reform, which was initiated in 1991, is well underway, India's growth rates have picked up, averaging 6% since 1992, compared with 3.5% in the 1970s and early 1980s. Foreign investment is increasing as barriers to entry are being dismantled. And a wealth of English-speaking scientists and engineers is enabling India to exploit the opportunities provided by globalization.

India's democratic politics rule out any Chinese-style economic reform by fiat. Nor will there be any counterpart to Deng Xiaoping, the all-powerful moving force behind the Chinese economic miracle. Democracy, which requires compromise, will ensure that India's pace of change is slow and that there are plenty of setbacks.

But the gradualism necessitated by participation and the reconciliation of differences will give the reforms that emerge greater legitimacy. And if, in its lumbering fashion, India does get its economic act together, it will combine unity, democracy and prosperity. It will then have performed a miracle of its own. Whether Iraq, like India, can defy the odds remains to be seen, but Iraq's leaders could certainly look east for some useful lessons.

Rajan Menon is Monroe J. Rathbone professor of international relations at Lehigh University and a fellow at the New America Foundation.

MIDDLE EAST DEMOCRACY

People in the Middle East want political freedom, and their governments acknowledge the need for reform. Yet the region appears to repel democracy. Arab regimes only concede women's rights and elections to appease their critics at home and abroad. If democracy arrives in the Middle East, it won't be due to the efforts of liberal activists or their Western supporters but to the very same Islamist parties that many now see as the chief obstacle to change.

By Marina Ottaway and Thomas Carothers

"The Middle East Is the Last Holdout Against the Global Democratic Trend"

No. The Middle East is on the wrong side of the global democratic divide, but unfortunately it does not lack company. As Russia slides into authoritarianism, the former Soviet Union is becoming a democratic wasteland with only a few shaky pockets of pluralism, such as Georgia, Ukraine, and Moldova. Central Asia is no better off than the Arab world in terms of democracy. A depressingly large swath of East and Southeast Asia from North Korea and China down through Vietnam, Laos, and Burma to Malaysia and Singapore—is a democracy-free zone that shows few signs of change.

Nor was the Middle East immune to the "Third Wave," the decisive expansion of democracy that started in southern Europe and Latin America 30 years ago and subsequently spread to other parts of the world. During the 1980s, several Arab countries, including Egypt, Tunisia, and Jordan, initiated political reforms to permit multiparty competition. These reforms lost momentum or were undone in the 1990s, however, as Arab leaders proved unwilling to risk their own power through genuine processes of democratization. Tunisia, for example, moved back to rigid authoritarian rule.

Today, political reform is percolating again in the region, amid growing public frustration over chronic corruption, poor socio-economic performance, and a pervasive sense of stagnation. The Sept. 11, 2001, terrorist attacks also created pressure for reform—from both the United States and some Arabs who began to question why their societies were so widely viewed as dangerous political cesspools. Talk about political reform and democracy is rife even in the Gulf monarchies where such issues had been taboo. The steps taken thus far in most countries, however, are modest. Although the Arab world is not impervious to political change, it has yet to truly begin the process of democratization.

"Democracy in the Middle East Is Impossible Until the Arab-Israeli Conflict Is Resolved"

Wrong. Arab governments curb political participation, manipulate elections, and limit freedom of expression because they do not want their power challenged, not because tension with Israel requires draconian social controls. When the government of Kuwait refuses to give women the right to vote, it does so out of deference to the most conservative elements of its population, not out of fear that voting women will undermine the country's security. Fear of competition, not of a Zionist plot, leads the Egyptian ruling party to oppose competitive presidential elections. When it comes to democratic reform, the Zionist threat is merely a convenient excuse.

Yet failure to resolve the Arab-Israeli conflict prevents the United States from gaining credibility as an advocate of democracy in the Middle East. Liberal Arabs perceive claims by the United States that it wants democracy in the Middle East as hypocritical, pointing to what they see as American indifference to the rights of the Palestinians and unconditional support for Israel. For their part, many Arab governments do not take U.S. pressure to democratize their region seriously, believing that the need for oil and fear of upsetting regimes that recognize Israel will trump Washington's desire for democratic change. U.S. credibility in the Middle East will not be restored—and the unprecedented level of anti-American resentment will not abate-until the United States makes a serious, balanced effort to tackle the conflict. Without such credibility, Washington's effort to stimulate democratization in the region will be severely constrained.

"The United States Wants Democracy in the Middle East"

Up to a point. The democratic transformation of the Middle East emerged as a central objective of U.S. foreign policy during the Bush administration. This new policy is a sharp reversal of several decades of steadfast support for many autocratic regimes in the region, such as those in Egypt, Saudi Arabia, and Jordan. It reflects the new post-9/11 conventional wisdom that Middle East democracy is the best antidote to Islamist terrorism.

Although this desire for democracy may be heartfelt, the United States has a lengthy laundry list of other priorities in the region: access to oil, cooperation and assistance on counterterrorism, fostering peace between Israel and its neighbors, stemming the proliferation of weapons of mass destruction, and preventing Islamist radicals from seizing power.

The newfound U.S. enthusiasm for democracy competes for a place in this mix. Fighting Islamist militants and safeguarding oil still compels the United States to cooperate with authoritarian regimes. People in the region watched as the United States took a tough line against Iran and Syria while failing to push Saudi Arabia, Egypt, Tunisia, or other friendly tyrants very hard. The Bush administration launched new diplomatic endeavors and aid programs to support positive change, such as the Broader Middle East and North Africa Initiative and the Middle East Partnership Initiative. But they consist of mild, gradual measures designed to promote democratic change without unduly challenging the authority of incumbent governments.

Moreover, despite the president's conviction that democratic change in the Middle East is necessary, a great deal of ambivalence remains within the U.S. policy bureaucracy about the prospect of any rapid political openings in the region. This sentiment is particularly true of the State Department and the intelligence community. Some experts worry that, given the political mood of most Arab citizens—who are angry at the United States and sympathetic to political Islam—free and open elections could result in some distinctly unfriendly regimes.

"The War in Iraq Advanced the Cause of Democracy in the Middle East"

Not yet. The U.S.-led war in Iraq removed from power one of the most heinous, repressive dictators in the region and opened up the possibility that Iraq will one day have a pluralistic political system held together by consensus rather than violence. The actual achievement of democracy in Iraq, however, remains distant and uncertain. The Path to that goal will be measured in years rather than months.

The war's political effects in the rest of the region—especially the way it exposed the hollowness of Saddam Hussein's regime—has contributed to increased calls for political reform in many Arab countries. Real progress toward democracy, however, is minimal. In addition, the war provoked some Arab governments, such as Egypt, to limit the already constrained political space they allow as a defensive gesture against public protests and as an excuse for prosecuting opponents.

Regrettably, President George W. Bush's repeated justification of the war as a democratizing mission has discredited some Western-oriented Arab democrats in the eyes of their fellow citizens. Many Arabs have come to view democracy itself as a code word for U.S. regional domination. The unpopularity of the war and the abuses against Iraqis at Abu Ghraib prison have further tarnished the reputation of the United States and fueled Islamist extremism.

Proponents of democratic contagion argue that if Iraq holds successful elections in early 2005, this example will resound loudly in the Arab world. But much of the Arab world will likely view such elections, even if they come off well, as highly flawed. Some parts of the predominantly Sunni areas of Iraq are not expected to participate in the elections, and many Arabs will inevitably accuse the United States of manipulation, because the elections will be held under U.S. occupation. Few Arabs will be dazzled into holding a new view of democracy on the basis of one election. Many countries in the region already hold elections of varying degrees of seriousness and importance, including one in Algeria earlier this year, which a Western observer described as "one of the best conducted elections, not just in Algeria, but in Africa and much of the Arab world."

Promoting democracy throughout the Middle East will require doing away with fantasies of a sudden U.S.-led transformation of the region and taking seriously the challenge of building credibility with Arab societies. Moreover, if the United States is to play a constructive supporting role, it must seriously revise its cozy relations with autocratic regimes, show a sustained ability to apply nuanced diplomatic pressure for political change at key junctures, and back up this pressure with well-crafted and well-funded assistance. Washington must prepare to accept emboldened political forces, and eventually new governments, that are uninterested in doing the United States' bidding. Embracing Middle East democracy in principle is easy; truly supporting it remains an enormous challenge.

"Islamists Are the Main Obstacle to Arab Democracy"

Think again. The standard fear is the "one person, one vote, one time" scenario: Islamists would only participate in elections to win power and put an end to democracy immediately. Hence, the argument goes, they should not be allowed to participate.

True, the commitment to democracy of even moderate Islamists is uncertain and hedged by the caveat that democratic governments must accept Islamic law. However, the chances of an overwhelming electoral victory that would allow Islamists to abrogate all freedoms at once is remote in the Arab world. During the last decade, Islamist parties and candidates have participated in elections in eight Arab countries (Algeria, Bahrain, Egypt, Jordan, Kuwait, Lebanon, Morocco, and Yemen), always with modest results. (These elections suffered from various degrees of government interference, but there is no indication that the Islamists would have won in a more open environment.) And Turkey, a country where an Islamist party took power with a large majority, is becoming an encouraging example of democratic success.

Although the prediction that Islamist electoral victories would lead to democracy's demise in the Middle East have so far proved unfounded, the possibility cannot be ruled out. Fear of such takeovers remains in many Arab countries and the United States. Many Arab regimes use this fear to justify meddling in elections and placing restrictions on political participation. The presence of Islamist parties thus complicates the process of democratization.

But Islamist parties are also integral to democratization because they are the only nongovernmental parties with large constituencies. Without their participation, democracy is impossible in the Middle East. The future of democracy in the region depends on whether a sufficient number of such parties moderate their political views and become actors in a democratic process, rather than spoilers in the present autocratic states, and whether incumbent governments stop hiding behind the Islamist threat and accept that all their citizens have a right to participate.

Arab Countries Have a Historic Propensity Toward Authoritarianism"

Yes. But so what? Most societies have lived under authoritarian rule for some time, often for a long time. Democracy is a relatively recent historical phenomenon. Even in the United States and Europe it was only consolidated through universal suffrage in the last century.

Arab rulers have been highly authoritarian, but no more so than European or Asian rulers for most of history. Arabs developed a political system based on Islam through the caliph, an individual who served as supreme leader of all Muslims. Europeans clung to the concept of the Holy Roman Empire for centuries after it ceased to exist in practice, fought ferocious religious wars for hundreds of years, and adopted the concept of separation of

church and state rather late and incompletely. The Arab world, for most of its history, was quite similar to the rest of the world.

Even in the 1960s and 1970s, much of the Arab world was highly representative of the major political trends of the day. Most Arab countries outside the Gulf displayed the combination of nationalism and socialism that constituted typical Third World ideology at the time. Gamal Abdel Nasser in Egypt, alongside Jawaharlal Nehru in India and Marshal Tito in Yugoslavia, was a major champion of this ideology, which waned in the 1980s with the end of the Cold War and the rise of globally connected economies.

To ascribe the lingering Arab absence of democracy to some unique historic affinity for authoritarianism, stemming from Arab culture, Islam, or anything else is thus factually incorrect. It is also politically defeatist, attributing a quality of inevitability that belies the experience of political change in other parts of the world.

"Promoting Women's Rights Is Crucial for Democratic Change"

False. This myth, a favorite of women's organizations and Western governments, reflects the combination of correct observation and false logic. No country can be considered fully democratic if a part of its population (in some cases, the majority) is discriminated against and denied equal rights. But efforts to change the status quo by promoting women's rights are premature. The main problem at present is that Arab presidents and kings have too much power, which they refuse to share with citizens and outside institutions. This stranglehold on power must be broken to make progress toward democracy. Greater equality for women does nothing to diminish the power of overly strong, authoritarian governments.

Arab leaders know this truth all too well. Many autocrats implement policies to improve women's rights precisely to give themselves reformist credentials and score points with Western governments, media outlets, and nongovernmental organizations. These efforts, however, often amount to a trick of smoke and mirrors designed to disguise the governments' refusal to cede any real power. In the last few years, several Arab states have appointed women to high positions and hurriedly implemented or proposed reforms concerning marriage, divorce, inheritance, and other personal status issues. These are welcome steps, but they do not address the core issue of promoting democracy: breaking the authoritarian pattern of Arab politics.

"Arab Democrats Are the Key to Reform"

Paradoxically, no. All Arab countries boast a small number of Westernized liberals who advocate respect for human rights, freedom of thought and speech, and democratic change. But democratic transformation requires more than the ideological commitment of a few individuals. In Western societies, a small democratic cadre sufficed in the distant past, when political participation was the preserve of public-minded intellectual elites and wealthy property owners. But the Arab world of today is not the United States or Europe of the 18th century. The political elite faces a growing challenge by Islamist movements, which are developing a popular support base. As a result, democratic transformation also requires broad-based political parties and movements capable of transforming abstract democratic ideals into concrete programs that resonate with a public whose main concern is survival.

Arab democrats have so far shown little capacity—and less inclination—to translate abstract ideas into programs with mass appeal. Because they talk to Western organizations and each other more than to their fellow citizens, opposition political parties with a liberal agenda find themselves unable to build broad constituencies. This failure leaves the field open to government parties, which can build a following on the basis of patronage, and to Islamist parties, which build their following in the best tradition of mass parties, with a mixture of ideological fervor and grassroots social services.

Government repression and, at times, co-optation have also undermined Arab democrats' effectiveness. Some regimes—notably Saudi Arabia's—move quickly to clamp down on any nascent liberal debate. Others are more tolerant, giving liberals some intellectual space to write and discuss issues openly, as long as their talk is not followed by action. Arab democrats in countries such as Egypt are not a persecuted group. Rather, they tend to be professionals comfortably ensconced in the upper-middle class. Therefore, they are hesitant to demand genuine reforms that might lead to a hard-line takeover and content to advocate democratization from the top.

Under such conditions, it would be a serious mistake for U.S. and European democracy advocates to focus on Arab democrats as the key to political change. These individuals will play a role if democracy becomes a reality. But during this period of transition, they have neither the inclination to push for reform nor the political clout to do so successfully.

"Middle East Democracy Is the Cure for Islamist Terrorism"

No. This view is rooted in a simplistic assumption: Stagnant, repressive Arab regimes create positive conditions for the growth of radical Islamist groups, which turn their sights on the United

States because it embodies the liberal sociopolitical values that radical Islamists oppose. More democracy, therefore, equals less extremism.

History tells a different story. Modern militant Islam developed with the founding of the Muslim Brotherhood in Egypt in the 1920s, during the most democratic period in that country's history. Radical political Islam gains followers not only among repressed Saudis but also among some Muslims in Western democracies, especially in Europe. The emergence of radical Islamist groups determined to wreak violence on the United States is thus not only the consequence of Arab autocracy. It is a complex phenomenon with diverse roots, which include U.S. sponsorship of the mujahideen in Afghanistan in the 1980s (which only empowered Islamist militants); the Saudi government's promotion of radical Islamic educational programs worldwide; and anger at various U.S. policies, such as the country's stance on the Arab-Israeli conflict and the basing of military forces in the region.

Moreover, democracy is not a cure-all for terrorism. Like it or not, the most successful efforts to control radical Islamist political groups have been antidemocratic, repressive campaigns, such as those waged in Tunisia, Egypt, and Algeria in the 1990s. The notion that Arab governments would necessarily be more effective in fighting extremists is wishful thinking, no matter how valuable democratization might be for other reasons.

The experience of countries in different regions makes clear that terrorist groups can operate for sustained periods even in successful democracies, whether it is the Irish Republican Army in Britain or the ETA (Basque separatists) in Spain. The ETA gained strength during the first two decades of Spain's democratization process, flourishing more than it had under the dictatorship of Gen. Francisco Franco. In fragile democratic states—as new Arab democracies would likely be for years—radical groups committed to violence can do even more harm, often for long periods, as evidenced by the Tamil Tigers in Sri Lanka, Abu Sayyaf in the Philippines, or the Maoist rebels in Nepal.

Marina Ottaway and Thomas Carothers are senior associate and director, respectively, at the Democracy and Rule of Law Project of the Carnegie Endowment for International Peace. They are coeditors of Uncharted Journey: Democracy Promotion in the Middle East *(Washington: Carnegie Endowment, 2005).*

From *Foreign Policy*, November–December 2004, pp. 22-24, 26-28. © 2004 by the Carnegie Endowment for International Peace. **www.foreignpolicy.com** Permission conveyed through Copyright Clearance Center, Inc.

Bin Laden, the Arab "Street," and the Middle East's Democracy Deficit

"Bin Laden speaks in the vivid language of popular Islamic preachers, and builds on a deep and widespread resentment against the West and local ruling elites identified with it. The lack of formal outlets to express opinion on public concerns has created [a] democracy deficit in much of the Arab world, and this makes it easier for terrorists such as bin Laden, asserting that they act in the name of religion, to hijack the Arab street."

DALE F. EICKELMAN

In the years ahead, the role of public diplomacy and open communications will play an increasingly significant role in countering the image that the Al Qaeda terrorist network and Osama bin Laden assert for themselves as guardians of Islamic values. In the fight against terrorism for which bin Laden is the photogenic icon, the first step is to recognize that he is as thoroughly a part of the modern world as was Cambodia's French-educated Pol Pot. Bin Laden's videotaped presentation of self intends to convey a traditional Islamic warrior brought up-to-date, but this sense of the past is a completely invented one. The language and content of his videotaped appeals convey more of his participation in the modern world than his camouflage jacket, Kalashnikov, and Timex watch.

Take the two-hour Al Qaeda recruitment videotape in Arabic that has made its way to many Middle Eastern video shops and Western news media.[1] It is a skillful production, as fast paced and gripping as any Hindu fundamentalist video justifying the destruction in 1992 of the Ayodhya mosque in India, or the political attack videos so heavily used in American presidential campaigning. The 1988 "Willie Horton" campaign video of Republican presidential candidate George H. W. Bush—in which an off-screen announcer portrayed Democratic presidential candidate Michael Dukakis as "soft" on crime while showing a mug shot of a convicted African-American rapist who had committed a second rape during a weekend furlough from a Massachusetts prison—was a propaganda masterpiece that combined an explicit although conventional message with a menacing, underlying one intended to motivate undecided voters. The Al Qaeda video, directed at a different audience—presumably alienated Arab youth, unemployed and often living in desperate conditions—shows an equal mastery of modern propaganda.

The Al Qaeda producers could have graduated from one of the best film schools in the United States or Europe. The fast-moving recruitment video begins with the bombing of the USS *Cole* in Yemen, but then shows a montage implying a seemingly coordinated worldwide aggression against Muslims in Palestine, Jerusalem, Lebanon, Chechnya, Kashmir, and Indonesia (but not Muslim violence against Christians and Chinese in the last). It also shows United States generals received by Saudi princes, intimating the collusion of local regimes with the West and challenging the legitimacy of many regimes, including Saudi Arabia. The sufferings of the Iraqi people are attributed to American brutality against Muslims, but Saddam Hussein is assimilated to the category of infidel ruler.

Osama bin Laden… is thoroughly imbued with the values of the modern world, even if only to reject them.

Many of the images are taken from the daily staple of Western video news—the BBC and CNN logos add to the videos' authenticity, just as Qatar's al-Jazeera satellite television logo rebroadcast by CNN and the BBC has added authenticity to Western coverage of Osama bin Laden.

Alternating with these scenes of devastation and oppression of Muslims are images of Osama bin Laden: posing in front of bookshelves or seated on the ground like a religious scholar, holding the Koran in his hand. Bin Laden radiates charismatic authority and control as he narrates the Prophet Mohammed's flight from Mecca to Medina, when the early Islamic movement was threatened by the idolaters, but returning to conquer them. Bin Laden also stresses the need for jihad, or struggle for the cause of Islam, against the "crusaders" and "Zionists." Later images show military training in Afghanistan (including target practice at a poster of Bill Clinton), and a final sequence—the word "solution" flashes across the screen—captures an Israeli soldier in full riot gear retreating from a Palestinian boy throwing stones, and a reading of the Koran.

THE THOROUGHLY MODERN ISLAMIST

Osama bin Laden, like many of his associates, is imbued with the values of the modern world, even if only to reject them. A 1971 photograph shows him on family holiday in Oxford at the age of 14, posing with two of his half-brothers and Spanish girls their own age. English was their common language of communication. Bin Laden studied English at a private school in Jidda, and English was also useful for his civil engineering courses at Jidda's King Abdul Aziz University. Unlike many of his estranged half-brothers, educated in Saudi Arabia, Europe, and the United States, Osama's education was only in Saudi Arabia, but he was also familiar with Arab and European society.

The organizational skills he learned in Saudi Arabia came in to play when he joined the mujahideen (guerrilla) struggle against the 1979 Soviet invasion of Afghanistan. He may not have directly met United States intelligence officers in the field, but they, like their Saudi and Pakistani counterparts, were delighted to have him participate in their fight against Soviet troops and recruit willing Arab fighters. Likewise, his many business enterprises flourished under highly adverse conditions. Bin Laden skillfully sustained a flexible multinational organization in the face of enemies, especially state authorities, moving cash, people, and supplies almost undetected across international frontiers.

The organizational skills of bin Laden and his associates were never underestimated. Neither should be their skills in conveying a message that appeals to some Muslims. Bin Laden lacks the credentials of an established Islamic scholar, but this does not diminish his appeal. As Sudan's Sorbonne-educated Hasan al-Turabi, the leader of his country's Muslim Brotherhood and its former attorney general and speaker of parliament, explained two decades ago, "Because all knowledge is divine and religious, a chemist, an engineer, an economist, or a jurist" are all men of learning.[2] Civil engineer bin Laden exemplifies Turabi's point. His audience judges him not by his ability to cite authoritative texts, but by his apparent skill in applying generally accepted religious tenets to current political and social issues.

THE MESSAGE ON THE ARAB "STREET"

Bin Laden's lectures circulate in book form in the Arab world, but video is the main vehicle of communication. The use of CNN-like "zippers"—the ribbons of words that stream beneath the images in many newscasts and documentaries—shows that Al Qaeda takes the Arab world's rising levels of education for granted. Increasingly, this audience is also saturated with both conventional media and new media, such as the Internet.[3] The Middle East has entered an era of mass education and this also implies an Arabic lingua franca. In Morocco in the early 1970s, rural people sometimes asked me to "translate" newscasts from the standard transnational Arabic of the state radio into colloquial Arabic. Today this is no longer required. Mass education and new communications technologies enable large numbers of Arabs to hear—and see—Al Qaeda's message directly.

Bin Laden's message does not depend on religious themes alone. Like the Ayatollah Ruhollah Khomeini, his message contains many secular elements. Khomeini often alluded to the "wretched of the earth." At least for a time, his language appealed equally to Iran's religiously minded and to the secular left. For bin Laden, the equivalent themes are the oppression and corruption of many Arab governments, and he lays the blame for the violence and oppression in Palestine, Kashmir, Chechnya, and elsewhere at the door of the West. One need not be religious to rally to some of these themes. A poll taken in Morocco in late September 2001 showed that a majority of Moroccans condemned the September 11 bombings, but 41 percent sympathized with bin Laden's message. A British poll taken at about the same time showed similar results.

Osama bin Laden and the Al Qaeda terrorist movement are thus reaching at least part of the Arab "street." Earlier this year, before the September terrorist attacks, United States policymakers considered this "street" a "new phenomenon of public accountability, which we have seldom had to factor into our projections of Arab behavior in the past. The information revolution, and particularly the daily dose of uncensored television coming out of local TV stations like al-Jazeera and international coverage by CNN and others, is shaping public opinion, which, in turn, is pushing Arab governments to respond. We don't know, and the leaders themselves don't know, how that pressure will impact on Arab policy in the future."[4]

Director of Central Intelligence George J. Tenet was even more cautionary on the nature of the "Arab street." In testimony before the Senate Select Committee on Intelligence in February 2001, he explained that the "right catalyst—such as the outbreak of Israeli-Palestinian violence—can move people to act. Through access to the Internet and other means of communication, a restive public is increasingly capable of taking action without any identifiable leadership or organizational structure."

Because many governments in the Middle East are deeply suspicious of an open press, nongovernmental organizations, and open expression, it is no surprise that the "restive" public, increasingly educated and influenced by hard-to-censor new media, can take action "without any identifiable leadership or organized structure." The Middle East in general has a democracy deficit, in which "unauthorized" leaders or critics, such as Egyptian academic Saad Eddin Ibrahim—founder and director of the Ibn Khaldun Center for Development Studies, a nongovernmental organization that promotes democracy in Egypt—suffer harassment or prison terms.

One consequence of this democracy deficit is to magnify the power of the street in the Arab world. Bin Laden speaks in the vivid language of popular Islamic preachers, and builds on a deep and widespread resentment against the West and local ruling elites identified with it. The lack of formal outlets to express opinion on public concerns has created the democracy deficit in much of the Arab world, and this makes it easier for terrorists such as bin Ladin, asserting that they act in the name of religion, to hijack the Arab street.

The immediate response is to learn to speak directly to this street. This task has already begun. Obscure to all except specialists until September 11, Qatar's al-Jazeera satellite television is a premier source in the Arab world for uncensored news and opinion. It is more, however, than the Arab equivalent of CNN. Uncensored news and opinions increasingly shape "public opinion"—a term without the pejorative overtones of "the street"—even in places like Damascus and Algiers. This public opinion in turn pushes Arab governments to be more responsive to their citizens, or at least to say that they are.

Rather than seek to censor al-Jazeera or limit Al Qaeda's access to the Western media—an unfortunate first response of the United States government after the September terror attacks—we should avoid censorship. Al Qaeda statements should be treated with the same caution as any other news source. Replacing Sinn Fein leader Gerry Adams' voice and image in the British media in the 1980s with an Irish-accented actor appearing in silhouette only highlighted what he had to say, and it is unlikely that the British public would tolerate the same restrictions on the media today.

Ironically, at almost the same time that national security adviser Condoleezza Rice asked the American television networks not to air Al Qaeda videos unedited, a former senior CIA officer, Graham Fuller, was explaining in Arabic on al-Jazeera how United States policymaking works. His appearance on al-Jazeera made a significant impact, as did Secretary of State Colin Powell's presence on a later al-Jazeera program and former United States Ambassador Christopher Ross, who speaks fluent Arabic. Likewise, the timing and content of British Prime Minister Tony Blair's response to an earlier bin Laden tape suggests how to take the emerging Arab public seriously. The day after al-Jazeera broadcast the bin Laden tape, Blair asked for and received an opportunity to respond. In his reply, Blair—in a first for a Western leader—directly addressed the Arab public through the Arab media, explaining coalition goals in attacking Al Qaeda and the Taliban and challenging bin Laden's claim to speak in the name of Islam.

PUTTING PUBLIC DIPLOMACY TO WORK

Such appearances enhance the West's ability to communicate a primary message: that the war against terrorism is not that of one civilization against another, but against terrorism and fanaticism in all societies. Western policies and actions are subject to public scrutiny and will often be misunderstood. Public diplomacy can significantly diminish this misapprehension. It may, however, involve some uncomfortable policy decisions. For instance, America may be forced to exert more diplomatic pressure on Israel to alter its methods of dealing with Palestinians.

Western public diplomacy in the Middle East also involves uncharted waters. As Oxford University social linguist Clive Holes has noted, the linguistic genius who thought up the first name for the campaign to oust the Taliban, "Operation Infinite Justice," did a major disservice to the Western goal. The expression was literally and accurately translated into Arabic as *adala ghayr mutanahiya,* implying that an earthly power arrogated to itself the task of divine retribution. Likewise, President George W. Bush's inadvertent and unscripted use of the word "crusade" gave Al Qaeda spokesmen an opportunity to attack Bush and Western intentions.

Mistakes will be made, but information and arguments that reach the Arab street, including on al-Jazeera, will eventually have an impact. Some Westerners might condemn al-Jazeera as biased, and it may well be in terms of making assumptions about its audience. However, it has broken a taboo by regularly inviting official Israeli spokespersons to comment live on current issues. Muslim religious scholars, both in the Middle East and in the West, have already spoken out against Al Qaeda's claim to act in the name of Islam. Other courageous voices, such as Egyptian playwright Ali Salem, have even employed humor for the same purpose.[5]

We must recognize that the best way to mitigate the continuing threat of terrorism is to encourage Middle Eastern states to be more responsive to participatory demands, and to aid local nongovernmental organizations working toward this goal. As with the case of Egypt's Saad Eddin Ibrahim, some countries may see such activities as subversive. Whether Arab states like it or not, increasing levels of education, greater ease of travel, and the rise of new communications media are turning the Arab street into a public sphere in which greater numbers of people, and not just a political and economic elite, will have a say in governance and public issues.

NOTES

1. It is now available on-line with explanatory notes in English. See <http://www.ciaonet.org/cbr/cbr00/video/excerpts_index.html>.

2. Hasan al-Turabi, "The Islamic State," in *Voices of Resurgent Islam,* John L. Esposito, ed. (New York: Oxford University Press, 1983), p. 245.

3. On the importance of rising levels of education and the new media, see Dale F. Eickelman, "The Coming Transformation in the Muslim World," *Current History,* January 2000.

4. Edward S. Walker, "The New US Administration's Middle East Policy Speech," *Middle East Economic Survey,* vol. 44, no. 26 (June 25, 2001). Available at <http://www.mees.com/news/a44n26d01.htm>.

5. See his article in Arabic, "I Want to Start a Kindergarten for Extremism," *Al-Hayat* (London), November 5, 2001. This is translated into English by the Middle East Media Research Institute as Special Dispatch no. 298, Jihad and Terrorism Studies, November 8, 2001, at <http://www.memri.org>.

DALE F. EICKELMAN *is Ralph and Richard Lazarus Professor of Anthropology and Human Relations at Dartmouth College. His most recent book is* The Middle East and Central Asia: An Anthropological Approach, *4th ed. (Englewood Cliffs, N. J.: Prentice Hall, 2002). An earlier version of this article appeared as "The West Should Speak to the Arab in the Street," Daily Telegraph (London), October 27, 2001.*

Reprinted from *Current History,* January 2002, pp. 36-39. © 2002 by Current History, Inc. Reprinted by permission.

UNIT 5

Comparative Politics: Some Major Trends, Issues, and Prospects

Unit Selections

Key Points to Consider

• What is meant by the first, second, and third waves of democratization? Discuss the reversals that followed the first two. Where are most of the countries affected by the third wave located? What factors appear to have contributed to their democratization? What are the signs that the third wave may be over?

• What are some main problems and dilemmas of old and new democracies, as discussed by Thomas Carothers?

• In what ways can market capitalism and liberal democracy be said to be mutually supportive, according to Gabriel Almond?

• How do Martin Wolf and David Held differ in their approach to free market economics? What is the implication of the argument that in economics, one model or "size" is unlikely to "fit all"?

• What does Benjamin Barber mean when he warns that democracy is threatened by globalism and tribalism?

 **Links: www.dushkin.com/online/**
These sites are annotated in the World Wide Web pages.

Commission on Global Governance
http://www.sovereignty.net/p/gov/gganalysis.htm
IISDnet
http://www.iisd.org/default.asp
ISN International Relations and Security Network
http://www.isn.ethz.ch
United Nations Environment Program
http://www.unep.ch/

The articles in this unit deal with three major political trends or patterns of development that can be observed in much of the contemporary world. It is important at the outset to stress that, with the possible exception of Benjamin Barber, none of the authors predict some form of global convergence in which all political systems would become alike in major respects. On closer examination, even Barber turns out to argue that a strong tendency toward global homogenization is offset by a concurrent tendency toward intensified group differentiation and fragmentation.

Thus the trends or patterns discussed should be seen as widespread but neither unidirectional nor universal. They are situationally defined, and therefore come in a great variety. They may well turn out to be temporary or partly reversible. Moreover, they do not always reinforce one another, but show countervailing tensions as well. Indeed, their different forms of development are the very stuff of comparative politics, which seeks an informed understanding of the political dimension in social life by making careful comparisons across time and space.

After such cautionary preliminaries, we can proceed to identify three recent developments that singly and together have had a very important role in changing the political world in which we live. One is the process of democratization, which has been sweeping much of the world. This refers to a widespread trend toward some form of popularly chosen, accessible and accountable government. In the last quarter of the twentieth century, it often took the form of a search for representative, pluralist democracy in countries that were previously ruled by some form of authoritarian oligarchy or dictatorship.

A second trend, sometimes labeled the capitalist revolution, is the even more widespread shift toward some form of market economy. It includes a greater reliance on private enterprise and the profit motive, and involves a concurrent move away from strong regulation, central planning, and state ownership. The "social market economy," found in much of Western Europe, remains a form of capitalism, but one which includes a major role for the state in providing public goods and services, redistributing income, and setting overall societal goals. In some of the Asian Communist-ruled countries, above all China, we have become used to seeing self-proclaimed revolutionary socialists introduce a considerable degree of capitalist practice in their formerly planned economies. Ironically, capitalism seems to have come to China by courtesy of its ideological opponents.

The third major trend could be called the revival of ethnic or cultural politics. This refers to a growing emphasis on some form of an exclusive group identity as the primary basis for political expression. In modern times, it has been common for a group to identify itself by its special ethnic, religious, linguistic, or other cultural traits and to make this identity the basis for a claim to special recognition and, sometimes, to rule by and for itself.

The article that makes up the first section covers democratization as the first of these trends, that is, the spread of representative forms of government in recent years. Even if this development is often fragile and likely to be reversed in some countries, we need to remember how remarkable it was in the first place. Using very different criteria and data, skeptics on both right and left for a long time doubted

whether representative government was sufficiently efficient, attractive or legitimate to spread or even survive in the modern world.

Samuel Huntington's widely discussed thesis concerning a recent wave of democratization underlies the article by Thomas Carothers. Huntington is one of the best-known observers of this trend, who in the past emphasized the existence of cultural, social, economic, and political obstacles to the spread of representative government in most of the world. Even before the collapse of the communist regimes in Europe, he had begun to identify a broad pattern of democratization that had started in the mid-1970s, when the three dictatorships in Southern Europe came to an almost simultaneous end (in Greece, Portugal, and Spain). In the following decade, democratization spread to most of Latin America. The countries of the Soviet bloc in Central and Eastern Europe then followed. The trend also reached some states in East and South Asia like Taiwan or South Korea as well as some parts of Africa, above all South Africa and now, more tentatively, Nigeria. The recent transfer of political power in Mexico, after more than seven decades of one-party hegemony, can also be seen in this context.

In a widely adopted phrase, Huntington identified this widespread trend as the "third" in a series of successive "waves" of democratization in modern history. The "first wave" had been slow to develop but long in its reach. It began in the 1820s and lasted about one century, until the 1920s. During this period the United States and subsequently 28 other countries established governments based on a wide franchise that eventually came to include women as well as men. Democratization was not only a drawn-out process in these countries, it was also a flawed and imperfect one. Thus it has been pointed out that in 1900 not a single one of them would have met today's stricter minimum standards of what constitutes a democracy. Soon after the end of the war "to make the world safe for democracy," its spread came to a halt. In the first half of the 1920s, Mussolini's capture and consolidation of power in Italy began a period of severe democratic setbacks—a first "reverse wave," as it has been called—that lasted until the mid-1940s. During those two decades, the number of democracies in the world plunged from 29 by more than half, as many became victims of indigenous dictatorial takeovers or subsequent military conquests. In the middle of World War II, there were only four full-fledged democratic states left in Europe, Britain and the three neutrals, Ireland, Sweden, and Switzerland. Possibly Finland could be added to this small group.

A "second wave" of democratization started with the Allied victory in World War II and continued during the early post–war years. This trend lasted until the early 1960s and included the liberated countries in Western Europe that immediately restored their democratic institutions and practices—countries like the Netherlands, Belgium, Luxembourg, Denmark, Norway, and France. In addition, the major defeated nations, Western Germany and Japan, were steered to democratic politics by the occupying powers. Finally, in the process of decolonization, the newly independent countries often started out with a formal democratic framework—one that often proved to be fragile and sometimes of very short duration. They and some countries in Latin America were the main settings for the authoritarian revival—the relatively short second "reverse wave"—that only lasted a little over a decade, until the mid-1970s. During this period of democratic setbacks, the number of democracies fell from 36 to 30 and the number of non-democracies rose from 75 to 95, as various former colonies or newly minted democracies fell under authoritarian or dictatorial rule.

Then, in the mid-1970s, the important "third wave" of democratization got its start. It turned out to be more sweeping and universal than its predecessors. Already by beginning of the 1990s, Huntington counted about 60 democracies in the world. Larry Diamond, another prominent authority on the subject, reported in 2000 that 120 states out of a world total of 192 independent states (63 percent) met at least the electoral requirements for being classified as democracies. The number was reduced to 71 (or 37 percent) when he applied the stricter standards of liberal democracy—basic civil rights and liberties, rule of law, political independence and neutrality of the judiciary, an open, pluralist society, and civilian control of the military. That is still an impressive change, when one considers Robert Dahl's finding that only 22 countries have a continuous history as democracies since 1950. Both Huntington and Diamond's findings lend support to the conclusion that democracy's advance has been at best a "two steps forward, one step back" kind of process.

Writing in 2004, Thomas Carothers finds that the "third wave" has come to a standstill. The expectations associated with the coming of democracy were in some countries so high that disappointments were bound to follow. Already some earlier "third wave" democratic advances in countries like the Sudan, Algeria, and Peru have been followed by authoritarian reversals. Haiti (like Nigeria) has gone through its own double wave. The prospects for democracy on that poverty-stricken Caribbean island do not seem bright. There are ominous signs of authoritarian revivals elsewhere in the world.

What are the general conditions that inhibit or encourage the spread and stabilization of democracy? Huntington and Diamond are among the scholars who have identified specific historical factors that contributed to the third wave. One important factor was the loss of legitimacy by both right- and left-wing authoritarian regimes, as they have became discredited by failures. Another factor was the expansion in some developing countries of an urban middle class, with a strong interest in representative government and the rule of law. In Latin America, especially, the influence of a recently more liberal Catholic Church was important. There have also been various forms of external influence by the United States and the European Community, as they have tried, however tentatively, to promote a human rights agenda. A different but crucial instance of external influence took the form of Mikhail Gorbachev's shift toward nonintervention by the Soviet Union in the late 1980s, when he abandoned

the Brezhnev Doctrine's commitment to defend established communist regimes in Central and Eastern Europe and elsewhere against "counterrevolution." Finally, there is the "snowballing" or demonstration effect with the successful early transitions to democracy in countries like Spain or Poland, which served as models for other countries in similar circumstances.

Huntington's rule of thumb is that a democratic form of government can be considered to have become stable when a country has had at least two successive peaceful turnovers of power. Such a development may take a generation or longer to complete, even under fortunate circumstances. Many of the new democracies have little historical experience with a democratic way of life. Where there has been such an experience, it may have been spotty and not very positive. There may be important cultural or socioeconomic obstacles to democratization, according to Huntington. Like most other observers, he sees extreme poverty as a principal obstacle to successful democratization. The stunted growth of democratization in Muslim societies has drawn a lot of attention, but there are exceptions as Marina Ottaway and Thomas Carothers point out in their article, "Middle East Democracy," in unit four.

Germany provides a valuable case study for testing some of these interpretations of democracy. After World War I, antidemocratic forces in Germany identified its democratic Weimar Republic with national disaster, socioeconomic ruin, and political weakness and instability. In the wake of the Great Depression, they supported Adolf Hitler's Nazi movement that came to power in January 1933 and abolished the fledgling constitutional democracy. After World War II, by contrast, the Federal Republic of Germany became increasingly credited with stability and growing prosperity. At first accepted passively, the West German democratic system soon generated an increasing measure of pragmatic support from its citizenry, based primarily on its widely perceived effectiveness. In time, the new republic also appeared to gain a deeper affection from much of the population. Careful observers, like David Conradt, detected a transformation of German values in a liberal democratic direction already in the early 1970s. The Federal Republic faced another test after Germany's unification with its accompanying wrenching changes and inevitable disappointments for many people in Eastern Germany. For many of them, national unification had been linked to unrealistic expectations of almost immediate socioeconomic alignment with the prosperous West. When the new order failed to deliver quite as promptly or bountifully as they had expected, some East Germans used their new freedom to protest. In dealing with this challenge, the Federal Republic is fortunate to have a stable set of institutions, a well-developed democratic tradition, and a solid economic structure.

The second section of this unit covers the trend toward capitalism or, better, some form of market economy. Here Gabriel Almond explores the complex and ambiguous connections between capitalism and democracy in an article that draws upon both theory and empirical studies. His systematic discussion shows that there are ways in which capitalism and democracy support each other, and ways in which they tend to undermine each other. Is it possible to have the best of both? Almond answers at length that there is a nonutopian manner in which capitalism and democracy can be reconciled, namely in democratic welfare capitalism.

Almond's discussion can be linked to a theme emphasized by some contemporary political economists. They point out that the economic competition between capitalism and socialism, at least in the latter's traditional meaning of state ownership and centralized planning, has become a largely closed chapter in contemporary history. The central question now is which form of capitalism or market economy will be more successful and acceptable. A similar argument has been made by the French theorist, Michel Albert, who also distinguished between the British-American and the continental "Rhineland" models of capitalism. The former is more individualistic, anti-governmental, and characterized by such traits as high employee turnovers and short-term profit-maximizing. It differs considerably from what the Germans themselves like to call their "social market economy." The latter is more team-oriented, emphasizes cooperation between management and organized labor, and leaves a considerable role for government in the setting of general economic strategy, the training of an educated labor force, and the provision of social welfare services.

These different conceptions of capitalism can be linked to different histories. Both Britain and the United States experienced a head start in their industrial revolutions and felt no great need for deliberate government efforts to encourage growth. By contrast, Germany and Japan both played the role of latecomers, who looked to government protection in their attempts to catch up. To be sure, governments were also swayed by military considerations to promote German and Japanese industrialization. But the emergence of a kind of "social capitalism" in other continental countries of Europe suggests that cultural and institutional rather than military factors played a major role in this development. We should continue to expect very differently mixed market economies, because one economic model or size is unlikely ever to fit all.

A crucial question is whether the relative prosperity and social security associated with this kind of mixed economy can be maintained in a time of technological breakthroughs and global competition. Those who expected a practical answer to come from the policies and strategies adopted by the "red-green" government in Germany were at first disappointed. In 1999, Gerhard Schröder issued a joint statement with Tony Blair, in which the two Europeans distinguished between "a market economy" and "a market society." They supported the former but not the latter, without really clarifying the intriguing distinction. More than five years after it assumed office, however, the German government has presented a major reform project, "Agenda 2010," discussed in an article by Bertrand Benoit in unit one.

Two articles in this unit can be read as a debate on the role of the free market. Martin Wolf argues strongly for a market-based globalization as the best way to create wealth, reduce inequality and poverty, and increase the life chances of human beings. He considers a stable and effective political system, based on the nation state, to be a prerequisite for a well functioning market economy. All the same, David Held finds Wolf's position to be too one-sidedly neo-liberal and economic. Held argues that a social democratic orientation needs to be introduced if liberty is to be accompanied by social justice.

The third section deals with the revival of the ethnic and cultural dimension in politics. Until recently, relatively few observers foresaw that this element would play such a divisive role in the contemporary world. There were forewarnings, such as the ethnonationalist stirrings in the late 1960s and early 1970s in peripheral areas of such countries as Britain, Canada, or Spain. It also lay behind many of the conflicts in the newly independent countries of the developing world. But most Western observers seem to have been poorly prepared for the task of anticipating or understanding the resurgence of politicized religious, ethnic, or other cultural forces. Many non-Westerners were taken by surprise as well. Mikhail Gorbachev, for example, grossly underestimated the centrifugal force of the nationality question in his own country.

The politicization of religion in many parts of the world falls into this development of a "politics of identity." In recent years, religious groups in parts of Latin America, Asia, the Middle East, sub-Saharan Africa, Asia, and Southern Europe have set out on the political road in the name of their faith. As Max Weber warned in a classic lecture shortly before his death, it can be dangerous to seek "the salvation of souls" along the path of politics. The coexistence of people of divergent faiths is possible only because religious conviction need not fully determine or direct a person's or a group's politics. Where absolute and fervent convictions take over, they make it difficult to compromise pragmatically and live harmoniously with people who believe differently. Pluralist democracy requires an element of tolerance, which for many takes the form of a casual "live and let live" attitude.

There is an important debate among political scientists concerning the sources and scope of politics based on ethnic, religious, and cultural differences. Samuel Huntington argues that our most important and dangerous future conflicts will be based on clashes of civilizations. In his view, they will be far more difficult to resolve than those rooted in socioeconomic or even ideological differences. His critics, including the German political observer, Josef Joffe, argue that Huntington distorts the differences among civilizations and trivializes the differences within civilizations as sources of political conflict. Chandra Muzaffar, a Malaysian commentator, goes further by contending that Huntington's thesis provides a rationalization for a Western policy goal of dominating the developing world. Others have pointed out that ethnic conflicts are in fact often the result of political choices made by elites. This can turn out to be a hopeful thesis because it would logically follow that such conflicts are avoidable if other political choices were made. In her article, Amy Chua reminds us that markets have short-run impacts that can have devastating consequences in multi-ethnic societies. This can happen whenever ethnic minorities turn out to be "market-dominant" and become viewed as outside exploiters. The result has been very bitter ethnic conflict in a number of countries.

In a widely discussed article, Benjamin Barber brings a broad perspective to the discussion of identity politics in the contemporary world. He sees two major tendencies that threaten democracy. One is the force of globalism, brought about by modern technology, communications, and commerce. Its logical end station is what he calls a "McWorld," in which human diversity, individuality, and meaningful identity are erased. The second tendency works in the opposite direction. It is the force of tribalism, which drives human beings to exacerbate their group differences and engage in holy wars or "jihads" against each other. Barber argues that globalism is at best indifferent to liberal democracy, while militant tribalism is deeply antithetical to it. He argues in favor of seeking a confederal solution, based on democratic civil societies, which could provide human beings with a nonmilitant, parochial communitarianism as well as a framework that suits the global market economy fairly well.

175

DEMOCRACY'S SOBERING STATE

"Democracy still occupies the high ground in the world.... Yet, just a few years into the new century, the grand hope that it will prove the age of democracy's global triumph appears far more tenuous than it seemed just 10 or 15 years ago."

THOMAS CAROTHERS

What Samuel Huntington called the "third wave" of democracy—the multitude of democratic openings that began in southern Europe in the mid-1970s and then spread during the next two decades throughout Latin America, Asia, the former Soviet bloc, and sub-Saharan Africa—has come to a standstill. According to Freedom House, an organization that tracks democratization around the world, there were 118 electoral democracies in 1996. Today, eight years later, there are 117. The relative proportions of countries that Freedom House rates as free, partly free, or not free have been largely static since the end of the 1990s.

POLITICS
The World, 2005

Of course, good news about democracy around the globe can still be found. Indonesians, for example, are making impressive strides in building democracy in the world's most populous Muslim country and have just inaugurated their first democratically elected president. A year ago Georgians threw off the decaying rule of President Eduard Shevardnadze and embarked on a bold effort to breathe new life into their country's shaky democratic experiment. South Africans recently celebrated the tenth anniversary of their postapartheid democracy, a democracy that is holding together despite myriad challenges. Tens of millions of Central and Eastern Europeans are now citizens of both democratic states and the European Union. And millions of Afghans took part in successful presidential elections in Afghanistan in October. More generally, key prodemocratic values, like government accountability and citizen empowerment, continue to spark interest and activism on every continent. And the community of people, organizations, and governments committed to advancing democracy's fortunes worldwide continues to grow.

Still, the grand hopes that energized some of democracy's most ardent optimists in the heady peak years of the third wave have not been realized. The former Soviet Union has gone from democratic frontier to democratic wasteland in just over a decade. South America is facing a crisis of democracy marked by political instability, rising conflict, and declining public belief in democratic institutions. Significant parts of East Asia, including China, North Korea,

Vietnam, Burma, Laos, and Singapore, remain under authoritarian rule, with little sign of change in sight. Dozens of African countries have seen once-promising democratic openings deliver only weak pluralism at best, or destructive civil conflict at worst. And, the US occupation of Iraq notwithstanding, the Arab world remains a democracy-free zone—despite increased international pressure for reform and some mild efforts by Arab rulers to move a few steps away from long-established patterns of autocracy.

Behind these signs of trouble in different regions lies a diverse set of factors that are coalescing in the first decade of this century to blunt democracy's global advance. No one of the factors is determinative in and of itself, but when combined they present a daunting new context. Understanding this context is vital to shaping an effective response.

THE AUTHORITARIAN REBOUND

The first factor inhibiting democratization is the persistence and even rejuvenation of authoritarian forces and structures in many countries that appeared, at least for a short time, to be experiencing democratic openings. Authoritarian forces were able to lie low or become dormant during the initial period of political change, even as dictatorial regimes fell. The apparent democratic transitions often turned out to be relatively shallow, despite their grand early moments and the high hopes they spawned. Dramatic first-time elections were held, new constitutions written, civil society unleashed, and government reforms announced. But the process of change in many cases did not penetrate the resilient, adaptable institutions behind the day-to-day screen of pluralistic politics—institutions that often harbored authoritarian mindsets, legacies, and actors such as domestic security services, militaries, and crony-dominated, state-owned businesses. In an unfortunately large number of cases, nondemocratic forces have been able to reassert themselves, taking advantage of the often fractious or feckless character of fledgling democratic governments. The rising economic and personal insecurity that many nascent democracies have produced for average citizens has eased the task of resurgent authoritarians since these conditions render citizens susceptible to the argument that a strong hand can set daily life back on track.

There is a significant gap between the soaring rhetoric about freedom in the Middle East and actual Western policy in most of the region.

This phenomenon has been vividly present in the former Soviet Union as well as in parts of sub-Saharan Africa. Post-Soviet authoritarians have gained a grip throughout a region that in the early 1990s seemed to be opening itself to genuine political change. Pluralism is hanging on in a few former Soviet republics, such as Ukraine, Georgia, Kyrgyzstan, and Moldova. But most have become mired again in authoritarian or semi-authoritarian rule.

Russia's authoritarian slide under President Vladimir Putin has been especially damaging and dispiriting. Putin has methodically hollowed out or co-opted every major institution—including the national broadcast media, the Russian Duma, political parties, and regional governorships—that had achieved any real degree of independence. The systematic disassembling of his country's nascent democratic system has been a textbook case of dedemocratization that will be studied, unfortunately, by both political scientists and would-be autocrats for years to come. With Russia's democratic experiment at least alive, albeit troubled, throughout the 1990s, the overall political direction of the region appeared to be still up for grabs, despite bad news out of Central Asia and the Caucasus. But Russia's recent turn, although not necessarily permanent, throws the weight of regional political life firmly in the wrong corner, where it is likely to stay for years.

Adding to the disappointment of the post-Soviet political record is the fact that neither the United States nor Europe really has done much to try to slow or reverse the backsliding. Western governments are comfortable doing business with strongmen leaders as long as access to oil and gas continues uninterrupted, and because these leaders remain helpful on Western counterterrorism concerns.

Although sub-Saharan Africa generally has made substantial progress toward greater political pluralism and openness in the past 15 years, a discouraging number of countries continue to suffer persistent authoritarian rule, especially in francophone Africa, but in other parts of the region as well, including Sudan, Zimbabwe, Eritrea, and Equatorial Guinea. In some cases, such as Ivory Coast and Zimbabwe, authoritarian rule has returned after what looked like an encouraging political opening. In most of the others, authoritarian leaders or parties that may have learned to say a few of the right things about democracy in the early 1990s have reverted fully to type.

THE PERFORMANCE PROBLEM

Although a troubling number of countries that were initially counted as part of the third wave have experienced a reassertion of authoritarian forces, quite a few others have managed to go from initial democratic openings to the establishment of reasonably open pluralistic systems. Many of these countries, however, are facing a different challenge to the consolidation of

democracy: they are not succeeding in providing better lives for their citizens socially or economically. The economic reform measures that many new democracies adopt, though helping to reduce government deficits and stabilize currencies, have often produced only tepid growth. Citizens of these countries face higher prices for basic goods, an increased threat of unemployment, and stagnant incomes. Moreover, they are often beset with heightened social problems, especially rising crime and a breakdown of the traditional social safety net.

This overall problem, which has come to be known as the problem of democratic performance, can be debilitating to struggling democracies. It may not be fair in some philosophical sense for people to judge democracy on the basis of the socioeconomic performance of a given weak democratic regime. Democracy is in a strict sense about political values, choices, and processes; it does not per se provide answers to economic and social problems. Yet, fair or not, this is what citizens of new democracies (and for that matter, established ones as well) do. And when the performance is poor over time, the effects can be negative. In many new democracies, citizens are seriously disenchanted with their governments. This disenchantment is turning into a larger loss of belief in democracy itself and, in some more aggravated cases, into instability and political conflict.

The war on terrorism has hurt America's status as a model of democracy and weakened America's credibility as a prodemocratic actor.

South America has been sharply afflicted with this problem, although the challenge of democratic performance has also dogged various countries in Central America, southeastern Europe, South Asia, and Southeast Asia as well. In South America, unlike in the former Soviet Union and some other regions, authoritarians were largely overcome or at least sent back to the barracks after democratic openings occurred. Almost all South American countries achieved flawed but real democratic systems, with most of the main institutional and procedural forms of democracy. Yet, in the past three or four years, the region has experienced what many South Americans and external observers increasingly view as a crisis of democracy. Argentina hit a frightening bump in its political road in 2001 when an economic crisis (itself partly caused by deficiencies in the political system, above all low levels of elite accountability) produced a period of vertiginous political instability; during one three-week spell the country went through five presidents. Venezuela has been suffering serious political polarization and conflict since the 1998 election of Hugo Chávez, a populist strongman with dubious fidelity to democratic norms who survived a recall referendum this year. Peru is undergoing a period of deep political malaise, marked by a hollow party system and the collapse of support for President Alejandro Toledo, whose election in 2001 was heralded as a rebirth of Peruvian democracy after the authoritarian reign of Alberto Fujimori. Bolivia and Ecuador have both experienced the ouster of presidents and the rise of serious new political fissures and tensions. Alongside these punishing developments are two longstanding political problems: the deeply corrupted dominant-power rule by the Colorado Party in Paraguay and the continuing civil war in Colombia.

South America's democratic woes derive from many causes and vary in nature from place to place. They are discouraging precisely because they highlight that democracy can corrode in so many different ways. But the problem of democratic performance—rooted in weak state institutions, entrenched, corrupted political elites, and poor systems of political representation and accountability—plays a role in much of the region. Fifteen to twenty years after the return of democracy, many South Americans do not feel that greater political freedom and choice have improved their lives very much, or at all, especially in terms of economic well-being and personal security. Given the high expectations that many people in the region had for what the end of dictatorship would bring, frustration over poor democratic performance turns easily into bitterness. The result has been a rising tide of cynicism, anger, and hostile actions against political parties, legislatures, governments, and even democracy itself.

DOING WELL UNDER DICTATORS

A third factor contributing to a newly challenging environment for global democracy is the sense that quite a few authoritarian countries have been doing well economically in recent years, giving new life to the old idea that dictatorship is better than democracy at producing socioeconomic development. This idea was popular in the 1960s and 1970s, both in the West and in developing countries. In the West it was an article of faith among economists worried about populist-oriented policy making and a convenient excuse by diplomats for supporting friendly tyrants who were useful on security issues. In developing countries, ruling elites found it a handy justification for their repressive grip on power. The idea lost some steam in the 1980s, weakened by the accumulated socioeconomic failures of dictatorial regimes in many developing countries, especially in sub-Saharan Africa. Across the 1990s the opposite idea gained considerable ground in international development circles—that democracy and economic development go hand in hand—or even more strongly, that democracy, with its presumably better systems of representation and accountable governance, actually facilitates economic development. The experience in the 1990s of much of the postcommunist world—where for a time progress on political reform and economic growth correlated strongly—added weight to the new view.

China's extraordinary economic success has presented a serious problem for those arguing that democracy is necessary for development or that dictatorial regimes cannot produce sustained economic development. In the current context, in which citizens of many developing countries are dissatisfied with the socioeconomic performance of their new democratic regimes, China's continued very rapid growth and its increasing economic muscle on the world stage have made it an increasingly powerful example. Talk of the "China model" has become much more common around the developing world than 10 years ago, both among ruling elites and average citizens. Magnifying this effect in the past several years are other authoritarian or

semi-authoritarian countries, including Russia, Ukraine, Kazakhstan, and Vietnam, that have also been turning in high growth rates. Indeed, of the ten fastest-growing economies in the developing world between 1999 and 2002, only one—Albania—was led by a (somewhat) democratic government. This trend can be explained in part by the high price of oil, which has buoyed the economies of a number of oil-rich autocracies. Nevertheless, the trend fuels the belief in the developing world that a strong hand is best for development. And it undercuts the efforts of the international development community to make the case for a democracy-development link.

THE WAR ON TERRORISM

A fourth complicating element for democracy in today's international context is the US war on terrorism. The ouster of the Taliban regime in Afghanistan and of Saddam Hussein in Iraq have opened the possibility, still far from being realized, of establishing stable, peaceful, democratic rule in these countries. President George W. Bush has also made a declared push for democratic transformation of the Middle East a part of his antiterrorism campaign, although this has been problematic in implementation. Other elements of the war on terrorism, however, have hurt democracy's cause. The US government's strongly felt need for closer counterterrorism cooperation with governments in many parts of the world has led it to warm relations with various autocratic regimes, such as those in Pakistan and Uzbekistan, and to go easy on the democratic backsliding of others, such as Russia.

In addition, the war on terrorism has hurt America's status as a model of democracy and weakened America's credibility as a prodemocratic actor. The world has watched closely, and often with disappointment, America's troubled effort to balance heightened law enforcement concerns with domestic political and civil rights, above all for Muslim citizens or residents of the United States. And the abusive treatment of detainees in US-run prisons or detention facilities in Iraq, Afghanistan, and Guantánamo has badly tarnished America's standing as a defender of human rights. Americans may have largely moved on past the stories and images that emerged from the Abu Ghraib prison outside Baghdad, but in many other parts of the world the negative emotions produced by those events are still strongly felt. A further negative consequence of the war on terrorism for global democracy has been the tendency of governments in the Middle East and many parts of Asia to use the antiterrorism banner as an excuse to crack down on political opponents, a tendency the United States has protested too little.

AND NOW FOR THE HARD PART

The most pressing as well as complex and difficult issue concerning the advance of democracy over the next decade and beyond is the question of whether the Middle East can make any significant democratic progress. Policy makers in Washington and other Western capitals advance the idea that the arrival of democracy in the Middle East is necessary to eliminate the roots of radical Islamist terrorism. Although this proposition is badly oversimplified and potentially misleading as a policy credo, it has raised to an unprecedented degree the level of international attention paid to the Arab world's democratic deficit.

The Bush administration's push for democracy in the Middle East has consisted of both a massive military-led effort to reconstruct Iraqi politics on a democratic template and an interrelated series of much less intrusive measures in the rest of the region, including new aid programs, multilevel diplomatic steps like the Broader Middle East and North Africa Initiative, and some high-level jawboning of Arab leaders by top US officials. The region's skeptical and recalcitrant response to the new push has demonstrated how hard a prodemocratic policy toward the Middle East will be in practice. The political reconstruction of Iraq has been much more difficult and costly (in financial, human, and diplomatic terms) than those in charge of the intervention ever thought it would be. Certainly, many of the political forces in post-Saddam Iraq support some kind of pluralistic outcome, yet the road to achieving it remains littered with daunting obstacles. And although Iraq is less repressive today than it was under Saddam, it has not yet proved a positive model for the region. Arabs largely view Iraq as a violent, chaotic, frightening place, one where thousands of Arabs have died as a direct or indirect result of a foreign invasion and occupation and whose political life is still controlled, deep down, by the United States.

The new international attention to the absence of democracy in the Arab world, including the various US and European initiatives to encourage or stimulate positive movement, has helped engender more discussion in Arab countries about the need for political reform and democracy. A few governments, most notably perhaps that of Morocco, have continued along paths of reform that have led to some real pluralism, albeit still within a monarchical framework. And some of the more authoritarian Arab governments, such as those in Egypt and Saudi Arabia, have announced minor new reform steps, both to respond to these internal debates and to win some international favor.

But in general the region remains stuck in deeply entrenched patterns of autocratic rule. Arab states are willing to engage in limited off-again, on-again political reforms, but more as a liberalizing strategy to avoid democracy rather than to achieve it. Arab ruling elites do not share the new Western view that democratic change is necessary to combat Islamist extremism. In fact, they hold the opposite view: that democracy would likely unleash radical forces that could be harmful to both the region and the West. Pressure from below for democratic change is weak at best throughout the region, despite the stepped-up activities of some civic groups and others speaking out on behalf of reform. Those who advocate for democracy (usually secular Western-oriented intellectuals) lack organized constituencies behind them. And the groups that do have mass-based constituencies—Islamist organizations—often do not frame their political objectives in terms of democracy and are placed under strict limits by regimes nervous about any mass-based processes of political change.

It is by no means impossible that the Arab world will over time make progress toward democracy. But the process is likely to be much slower than the current fervor for reform in Washington and other Western capitals might imply, not to mention more conflictive and unsettling to Western interests than the new policy credo suggests. Despite the rhetoric coming from the White House, in practice US and other Western policy makers are not at all sure that opening up Arab political systems to popular choice would actually serve Western economic and security interests overall. In some cases, dangerous instability or even civil conflict might result. Other Arab societies might choose Islamist leaders who are not inclined to be helpful on the Israeli-Palestinian conflict or other important issues. There is a significant gap between the soaring rhetoric about freedom in the Middle East and actual Western policy in most of the region. Policies more cautious in deeds than in words are likely to persist.

GETTING SERIOUS

The state of democracy in the world is sobering. Democracy still occupies the high ground across the world both as the only political ideology to command widespread legitimacy and as the political system of most of the world's wealthy or powerful countries. Yet, only a few years into the new century, the grand hope that it will prove the age of democracy's global triumph appears far more tenuous than it seemed just 10 or 15 years ago.

American policy makers determined to make democracy promotion a major element of US foreign policy will have to do better than rely on attractive but superficial slogans like "freedom is on the march." It is necessary to move away from the mindset that a democratic trend is advancing in the world and that US policy should aim to support it. The challenges now are more fundamental: how to stimulate democracy in regions where authoritarianism has bested the democratic trend, and how to support democracy where it is under siege because of poor performance. Responding to these challenges will require a greater willingness to pressure authoritarian leaders who offer short-term economic and security benefits to the United States but spell long-term trouble, especially in the former Soviet Union and the Middle East. And it will require the United States to construct more effective partnerships with South America and other regions where democracy is under siege. Democracy promotion is a convenient, even easy rhetorical framework for a global policy, especially in the context of the war on terrorism. Making it work in practice is neither convenient nor easy, and the state of democracy in the world is only getting more complex and demanding with each passing year.

THOMAS CAROTHERS is director of the Democracy and Rule of Law Project at the Carnegie Endowment for International Peace. He is coeditor with Marina Ottaway of *Uncharted Journey: Democracy Promotion in the Middle East* (Carnegie Endowment, forthcoming January 2005).

Capitalism and Democracy*

Gabriel A. Almond

Joseph Schumpeter, a great economist and social scientist of the last generation, whose career was almost equally divided between Central European and American universities, and who lived close to the crises of the 1930s and '40s, published a book in 1942 under the title, *Capitalism, Socialism, and Democracy*. The book has had great influence, and can be read today with profit. It was written in the aftergloom of the great depression, during the early triumphs of Fascism and Nazism in 1940 and 1941, when the future of capitalism, socialism, and democracy all were in doubt. Schumpeter projected a future of declining capitalism, and rising socialism. He thought that democracy under socialism might be no more impaired and problematic than it was under capitalism.

He wrote a concluding chapter in the second edition which appeared in 1946, and which took into account the political-economic situation at the end of the war, with the Soviet Union then astride a devastated Europe. In this last chapter he argues that we should not identify the future of socialism with that of the Soviet Union, that what we had observed and were observing in the first three decades of Soviet existence was not a necessary expression of socialism. There was a lot of Czarist Russia in the mix. If Schumpeter were writing today, I don't believe he would argue that socialism has a brighter future than capitalism. The relationship between the two has turned out to be a good deal more complex and intertwined than Schumpeter anticipated. But I am sure that he would still urge us to separate the future of socialism from

that of Soviet and Eastern European Communism.

Unlike Schumpeter I do not include Socialism in my title, since its future as a distinct ideology and program of action is unclear at best. Western Marxism and the moderate socialist movements seem to have settled for social democratic solutions, for adaptations of both capitalism and democracy producing acceptable mixes of market competition, political pluralism, participation, and welfare. I deal with these modifications of capitalism, as a consequence of the impact of democracy on capitalism in the last half century.

At the time that Adam Smith wrote *The Wealth of Nations*, the world of government, politics and the state that he knew—pre-Reform Act England, the French government of Louis XV and XVI—was riddled with special privileges, monopolies, interferences with trade. With my tongue only half way in my check I believe the discipline of economics may have been traumatized by this condition of political life at its birth. Typically, economists speak of the state and government instrumentally, as a kind of secondary service mechanism.

I do not believe that politics can be treated in this purely instrumental and reductive way without losing our analytic grip on the social and historical process. The economy and the polity are the main problem solving mechanisms of human society. They each have their distinctive means, and they each have their "goods" or ends. They necessarily interact with each other, and transform each other in the process. Democracy in particular generates goals and programs. You cannot give people the suffrage,

and let them form organizations, run for office, and the like, without their developing all kinds of ideas as to how to improve things. And sometimes some of these ideas are adopted, implemented and are productive, and improve our lives, although many economists are reluctant to concede this much to the state.

My lecture deals with this interaction of politics and economics in the Western World in the course of the last couple of centuries, in the era during which capitalism and democracy emerged as the dominant problem solving institutions of modern civilization. I am going to discuss some of the theoretical and empirical literature dealing with the themes of the positive and negative interaction between capitalism and democracy. There are those who say that capitalism supports democracy, and those who say that capitalism subverts democracy. And there are those who say that democracy subverts capitalism, and those who say that it supports it.

The relation between capitalism and democracy dominates the political theory of the last two centuries. All the logically possible points of view are represented in a rich literature. It is this ambivalence and dialectic, this tension between the two major problem solving sectors of modern society—the political and the economic —that is the topic of my lecture.

Capitalism Supports Democracy

Let me begin with the argument that capitalism is positively linked with democracy, shares its values and culture, and facilitates its development. This case has been made in historical, logical, and statistical terms.

Albert Hirschman in his *Rival Views of Market Society* (1986) examines the values, manners and morals of capitalism, and their effects on the larger society and culture as these have been described by the philosophers of the 17th, 18th, and 19th centuries. He shows how the interpretation of the impact of capitalism has changed from the enlightenment view of Montesquieu, Condorcet, Adam Smith and others, who stressed the *douceur* of commerce, its "gentling," civilizing effect on behavior and interpersonal relations, to that of the 19th and 20th century conservative and radical writers who described the culture of capitalism as crassly materialistic, destructively competitive, corrosive of morality, and hence self-destructive. This sharp almost 180-degree shift in point of view among political theorists is partly explained by the transformation from the commerce and small-scale industry of early capitalism, to the smoke blackened industrial districts, the demonic and exploitive entrepreneurs, and exploited laboring classes of the second half of the nineteenth century. Unfortunately for our purposes, Hirschman doesn't deal explicitly with the capitalism–democracy connection, but rather with culture and with manners. His argument, however, implies an early positive connection and a later negative one.

Joseph Schumpeter in *Capitalism, Socialism, and Democracy* (1942) states flatly, "History clearly confirms… [that]… modern democracy rose along with capitalism, and in causal connection with it… modern democracy is a product of the capitalist process." He has a whole chapter entitled "The Civilization of Capitalism," democracy being a part of that civilization. Schumpeter also makes the point that democracy was historically supportive of capitalism. He states, "… the bourgeoisie reshaped, and from its own point of view rationalized, the social and political structure that preceded its ascendancy…" (that is to say, feudalism). "The democratic method

was the political tool of that reconstruction." According to Schumpeter capitalism and democracy were mutually causal historically, mutually supportive parts of a rising modern civilization, although as we shall show below, he also recognized their antagonisms.

Barrington Moore's historical investigation (1966) with its long title, *The Social Origins of Dictatorship and Democracy; Lord and Peasant in the Making of the Modern World*, argues that there have been three historical routes to industrial modernization. The first of these followed by Britain, France, and the United States, involved the subordination and transformation of the agricultural sector by the rising commercial bourgeoisie, producing the democratic capitalism of the 19th and 20th centuries. The second route followed by Germany and Japan, where the landed aristocracy was able to contain and dominate the rising commercial classes, produced an authoritarian and fascist version of industrial modernization, a system of capitalism encased in a feudal authoritarian framework, dominated by a military aristocracy, and an authoritarian monarchy. The third route, followed in Russia where the commercial bourgeoisie was too weak to give content and direction to the modernizing process, took the form of a revolutionary process drawing on the frustration and resources of the peasantry, and created a mobilized authoritarian Communist regime along with a state-controlled industrialized economy. Successful capitalism dominating and transforming the rural agricultural sector, according to Barrington Moore, is the creator and sustainer of the emerging democracies of the nineteenth century.

Robert A. Dahl, the leading American democratic theorist, in the new edition of his book (1990) *After the Revolution? Authority in a Good Society*, has included a new chapter entitled "Democracy and Markets." In the opening paragraph of that chapter, he says:

It is an historical fact that modern democratic institutions… have existed only in countries with predominantly privately owned, market-oriented economies, or

capitalism if you prefer that name. It is also a fact that all "socialist" countries with predominantly state-owned centrally directed economic orders—command economies—have not enjoyed democratic governments, but have in fact been ruled by authoritarian dictatorships. It is also an historical fact that some "capitalist" countries have also been, and are, ruled by authoritarian dictatorships.

To put it more formally, it looks to be the case that market-oriented economies are necessary (in the logical sense) to democratic institutions, though they are certainly not sufficient. And it looks to be the case that state-owned centrally directed economic orders are strictly associated with authoritarian regimes, though authoritarianism definitely does not require them. We have something very much like an historical experiment, so it would appear, that leaves these conclusions in no great doubt. (Dahl 1990)

Peter Berger in his book *The Capitalist Revolution* (1986) presents four propositions on the relation between capitalism and democracy:

Capitalism is a necessary but not sufficient condition of democracy under modern conditions.

If a capitalist economy is subjected to increasing degrees of state control, a point (not precisely specifiable at this time) will be reached at which democratic governance becomes impossible.

If a socialist economy is opened up to increasing degrees of market forces, a point (not precisely specifiable at this time) will be reached at which democratic governance becomes a possibility.

If capitalist development is successful in generating economic growth from which a sizable proportion of the population benefits, pressures toward democracy are likely to appear.

This positive relationship between capitalism and democracy has also been sustained by statistical studies. The "Social Mobilization" theorists of the 1950s and 1960s which included

Daniel Lerner (1958), Karl Deutsch (1961), S. M. Lipset (1959) among others, demonstrated a strong statistical association between GNP per capita and democratic political institutions. This is more than simple statistical association. There is a logic in the relation between level of economic development and democratic institutions. Level of economic development has been shown to be associated with education and literacy, exposure to mass media, and democratic psychological propensities such as subjective efficacy, participatory aspirations and skills. In a major investigation of the social psychology of industrialization and modernization, a research team led by the sociologist Alex Inkeles (1974) interviewed several thousand workers in the modern industrial and the traditional economic sectors of six countries of differing culture. Inkeles found empathetic, efficacious, participatory and activist propensities much more frequently among the modern industrial workers, and to a much lesser extent in the traditional sector in each one of these countries regardless of cultural differences.

The historical, the logical, and the statistical evidence for this positive relation between capitalism and democracy is quite persuasive.

Capitalism Subverts Democracy

But the opposite case is also made, that capitalism subverts or undermines democracy. Already in John Stuart Mill (1848) we encounter a view of existing systems of private property as unjust, and of the free market as destructively competitive—aesthetically and morally repugnant. The case he was making was a normative rather than a political one. He wanted a less competitive society, ultimately socialist, which would still respect individuality. He advocated limitations on the inheritance of property and the improvement of the property system so that everyone shared in its benefits, the limitation of population growth, and the improvement of the quality of the labor force through the provision of high quality education for all by the state. On the eve of the emergence of the modern democratic capitalist order John Staurt Mill wanted to control the excesses of both the market economy and the majoritarian polity, by the education of consumers and producers, citizens and politicians, in the interest of producing morally improved free market and democratic orders. But in contrast to Marx, he did not thoroughly discount the possibilities of improving the capitalist and democratic order.

Marx argued that as long as capitalism and private property existed there could be no genuine democracy, that democracy under capitalism was bourgeois democracy, which is to say not democracy at all. While it would be in the interest of the working classes to enter a coalition with the bourgeoisie in supporting this form of democracy in order to eliminate feudalism, this would be a tactical maneuver. Capitalist democracy could only result in the increasing exploitation of the working classes. Only the elimination of capitalism and private property could result in the emancipation of the working classes and the attainment of true democracy. Once socialism was attained the basic political problems of humanity would have been solved through the elimination of classes. Under socialism there would be no distinctive democratic organization, no need for institutions to resolve conflicts, since there would be no conflicts. There is not much democratic or political theory to be found in Marx's writings. The basic reality is the mode of economic production and the consequent class structure from which other institutions follow.

For the followers of Marx up to the present day there continues to be a negative tension between capitalism, however reformed, and democracy. But the integral Marxist and Leninist rejection of the possibility of an autonomous, bourgeois democratic state has been left behind for most Western Marxists. In the thinking of Poulantzas, Offe, Bobbio, Habermas and others, the bourgeois democratic state is now viewed as a class struggle state, rather than an unambiguously bourgeois state. The working class has access to it; it can struggle for its interests, and can attain partial benefits from it. The state is now viewed as autonomous, or as relatively autonomous, and it can be reformed in a progressive direction by working class and other popular movements. The bourgeois democratic state can be moved in the direction of a socialist state by political action short of violence and institutional destruction.

Schumpeter (1942) appreciated the tension between capitalism and democracy. While he saw a causal connection between competition in the economic and the political order, he points out "... that there are some deviations from the principle of democracy which link up with the presence of organized capitalist interests.... [T]he statement is true both from the standpoint of the classical and from the standpoint of our own theory of democracy. From the first standpoint, the result reads that the means at the disposal of private interests are often used in order to thwart the will of the people. From the second standpoint, the result reads that those private means are often used in order to interfere with the working of the mechanism of competitive leadership." He refers to some countries and situations in which "... political life all but resolved itself into a struggle of pressure groups and in many cases practices that failed to conform to the spirit of the democratic method." But he rejects the notion that there cannot be political democracy in a capitalist society. For Schumpeter full democracy in the sense of the informed participation of all adults in the selection of political leaders and consequently the making of public policy, was an impossibility because of the number and complexity of the issues confronting modern electorates. The democracy which was realistically possible was one in which people could choose among competing leaders, and consequently exercise some direction over political decisions. This kind of democracy was possible in a capitalist society, though some of its propensities impaired its performance. Writing in the early years of World War II, when the future of democracy and of capitalism were uncertain, he leaves unresolved the questions of "... Whether or not democracy is one of those products of capitalism which are to die out with it..." or "... how well or ill capitalist society qualifies for the task of working the democratic method it evolved."

Non-Marxist political theorists have contributed to this questioning of the reconcilability of capitalism and democracy. Robert A. Dahl, who makes the point that capitalism historically has been a necessary precondition of democracy, views contemporary democracy in the United States as seriously compromised, impaired by the inequality in resources among the citizens. But Dahl stresses the variety in distributive patterns, and in politico-economic relations among contemporary democracies. "The category of capitalist democracies" he writes, "includes an extraordinary variety... from nineteenth century, laissez faire, early industrial systems to twentieth century, highly regulated, social welfare, late or postindustrial systems. Even late twentieth century 'welfare state' orders vary all the way from the Scandinavian systems, which are redistributive, heavily taxed, comprehensive in their social security, and neocorporatist in their collective bargaining arrangements to the faintly redistributive, moderately taxed, limited social security, weak collective bargaining systems of the United States and Japan" (1989).

In *Democracy and Its Critics* (1989) Dahl argues that the normative growth of democracy to what he calls its "third transformation" (the first being the direct city-state democracy of classic times, and the second, the indirect, representative inegalitarian democracy of the contemporary world) will require democratization of the economic order. In other words, modern corporate capitalism needs to be transformed. Since government control and/or ownership of the economy would be destructive of the pluralism which is an essential requirement of democracy, his preferred solution to the problem of the mega-corporation is employee control of corporate industry. An economy so organized, according to Dahl, would improve the distribution of political resources without at the same time destroying the pluralism which democratic competition requires. To those who question the realism of Dahl's solution to the

problem of inequality, he replies that history is full of surprises.

Charles E. Lindblom in his book, *Politics and Markets* (1977), concludes his comparative analysis of the political economy of modern capitalism and socialism, with an essentially pessimistic conclusion about contemporary market-oriented democracy. He says

We therefore come back to the corporation. It is possible that the rise of the corporation has offset or more than offset the decline of class as an instrument of indoctrination.... That it creates a new core of wealth and power for a newly constructed upper class, as well as an overpowering loud voice, is also reasonably clear. The executive of the large corporation is, on many counts, the contemporary counterpart to the landed gentry of an earlier era, his voice amplified by the technology of mass communication.... [T]he major institutional barrier to fuller democracy may therefore be the autonomy of the private corporation.

Lindblom concludes, "The large private corporation fits oddly into democratic theory and vision. Indeed it does not fit.

There is then a widely shared agreement, from the Marxists and neo-Marxists, to Schumpeter, Dahl, Lindblom, and other liberal political theorists, that modern capitalism with the dominance of the large corporation, produces a defective or an impaired form of democracy.

Democracy Subverts Capitalism

If we change our perspective now and look at the way democracy is said to affect capitalism, one of the dominant traditions of economics from Adam Smith until the present day stresses the importance for productivity and welfare of an economy that is relatively free of intervention by the state. In this doctrine of minimal government there is still a place for a framework of rules and services essential to the productive and efficient performance of the economy. In part the government has to protect the market from itself. Left to their

own devices, according to Smith, businessmen were prone to corner the market in order to exact the highest possible price. And according to Smith businessmen were prone to bribe public officials in order to gain special privileges, and legal monopolies. For Smith good capitalism was competitive capitalism, and good government provided just those goods and services which the market needed to flourish, could not itself provide, or would not provide. A good government according to Adam Smith was a minimal government, providing for the national defense, and domestic order. Particularly important for the economy were the rules pertaining to commercial life such as the regulation of weights and measures, setting and enforcing building standards, providing for the protection of persons and property, and the like.

For Milton Friedman (1961, 1981), the leading contemporary advocate of the free market and free government, and of the interdependence of the two, the principal threat to the survival of capitalism and democracy is the assumption of the responsibility for welfare on the part of the modern democratic state. He lays down a set of functions appropriate to government in the positive interplay between economy and polity, and then enumerates many of the ways in which the modern welfare, regulatory state has deviated from these criteria.

A good Friedmanesque, democratic government would be one "... which maintained law and order, defended property rights, served as a means whereby we could modify property rights and other rules of the economic game, adjudicated disputes about the interpretation of the rules, enforced contracts, promoted competition, provided a monetary framework, engaged in activities to counter technical monopolies and to overcome neighborhood effects widely regarded as sufficiently important to justify government intervention, and which supplemented private charity and the private family in protecting the irresponsible, whether madman or child ...."
Against this list of proper activities for a free government, Friedman pinpointed more than a dozen activities

of contemporary democratic governments which might better be performed through the private sector, or not at all. These included setting and maintaining price supports, tariffs, import and export quotas and controls, rents, interest rates, wage rates, and the like, regulating industries and banking, radio and television, licensing professions and occupations, providing social security and medical care programs, providing public housing, national parks, guaranteeing mortgages, and much else.

Friedman concludes that this steady encroachment on the private sector has been slowly but surely converting our free government and market system into a collective monster, compromising both freedom and productivity in the outcome. The tax and expenditure revolts and regulatory rebellions of the 1980s have temporarily stemmed this trend, but the threat continues. "It is the internal threat coming from men of good intentions and good will who wish to reform us. Impatient with the slowness of persuasion and example to achieve the great social changes they envision, they are anxious to use the power of the state to achieve their ends, and confident of their own ability to do so." The threat to political and economic freedom, according to Milton Friedman and others who argue the same position, arises out of democratic politics. It may only be defeated by political action.

In the last decades a school, or rather several schools, of economists and political scientists have turned the theoretical models of economics to use in analyzing political processes. Variously called public choice theorists, rational choice theorists, or positive political theorists, and employing such models as market exchange and bargaining, rational self interest, game theory, and the like, these theorists have produced a substantial literature throwing new and often controversial light on democratic political phenomena such as elections, decisions of political party leaders, interest group behavior, legislative and committee decisions, bureaucratic, and judicial behavior, lobbying activity, and substantive public policy areas such as constitutional arrangements, health and environment policy, regulatory policy, national security and foreign policy, and the like. Hardly a field of politics and public policy has been left untouched by this inventive and productive group of scholars.

The institutions and names with which this movement is associated in the United States include Virginia State University, the University of Virginia, the George Mason University, the University of Rochester, the University of Chicago, the California Institute of Technology, the Carnegie Mellon University, among others. And the most prominent names are those of the leaders of the two principal schools: James Buchanan, the Nobel Laureate leader of the Virginia "Public Choice" school, and William Riker, the leader of the Rochester "Positive Theory" school. Other prominent scholars associated with this work are Gary Becker of the University of Chicago, Kenneth Shepsle and Morris Fiorina of Harvard, John Ferejohn of Stanford, Charles Plott of the California Institute of Technology, and many others.

One writer summarizing the ideological bent of much of this work, but by no means all of it (William Mitchell of the University of Washington), describes it as fiscally conservative, sharing a conviction that the "... private economy is far more robust, efficient, and perhaps, equitable than other economies, and much more successful than political processes in efficiently allocating resources...." Much of what has been produced "... by James Buchanan and the leaders of this school can best be described as contributions to a theory of the failure of political processes." These failures of political performance are said to be inherent properties of the democratic political process. "Inequity, inefficiency, and coercion are the most general results of democratic policy formation." In a democracy the demand for publicly provided services seems to be insatiable. It ultimately turns into a special interest, "rent seeking" society. Their remedies take the form of proposed constitutional limits on spending power and checks and balances to limit legislative majorities.

One of the most visible products of this pessimistic economic analysis of democratic politics is the book by Mancur Olson, *The Rise and Decline of Nations* (1982). He makes a strong argument for the negative democracy–capitalism connection. His thesis is that the behavior of individuals and firms in stable societies inevitably leads to the formation of dense networks of collusive, cartelistic, and lobbying organizations that make economies less efficient and dynamic and polities less governable. "The longer a society goes without an upheaval, the more powerful such organizations become and the more they slow down economic expansion. Societies in which these narrow interest groups have been destroyed, by war or revolution, for example, enjoy the greatest gains in growth." His prize cases are Britain on the one hand and Germany and Japan on the other.

The logic of the argument implies that countries that have had democratic freedom of organization without upheaval or invasion the longest will suffer the most from growth-repressing organizations and combinations. This helps explain why Great Britain, the major nation with the longest immunity from dictatorship, invasion, and revolution, has had in this century a lower rate of growth than other large, developed democracies. Britain has precisely the powerful network of special interest organization that the argument developed here would lead us to expect in a country with its record of military security and democratic stability. The number and power of its trade unions need no description. The venerability and power of its professional associations is also striking.... In short, with age British society has acquired so many strong organizations and collusions that it suffers from an institutional sclerosis that slows its adaptation to changing circumstances and technologies. (Olson 1982)

By contrast, post-World War II Germany and Japan started organizationally from scratch. The organizations that led them to defeat were all dissolved, and under the occupation inclusive organizations like the general trade union movement and general organizations of the industrial and commercial community were first formed. These inclusive organizations had more regard for the general national interest and exercised some discipline on the narrower interest organizations. And both countries in the post-war decades experienced "miracles" of economic growth under democratic conditions.

The Olson theory of the subversion of capitalism through the propensities of democratic societies to foster special interest groups has not gone without challenge. There can be little question that there is logic in his argument. But empirical research testing this pressure group hypothesis thus far has produced mixed findings. Olson has hopes that a public educated to the harmful consequences of special interests to economic growth, full employment, coherent government, equal opportunity, and social mobility will resist special interest behavior, and enact legislation imposing anti-trust, and anti-monopoly controls to mitigate and contain these threats. It is somewhat of an irony that the solution to this special interest disease of democracy, according to Olson, is a democratic state with sufficient regulatory authority to control the growth of special interest organizations.

Democracy Fosters Capitalism

My fourth theme, democracy as fostering and sustaining capitalism, is not as straightforward as the first three. Historically there can be little doubt that as the suffrage was extended in the last century, and as mass political parties developed, democratic development impinged significantly on capitalist institutions and practices. Since successful capitalism requires risk-taking entrepreneurs with access to investment capital, the democratic propensity for redistributive and regulative policy tends to reduce the incentives and the resources available for risk-taking and creativity. Thus it can be argued that propensities inevitably resulting from democratic politics, as Friedman, Olson and many

others argue, tend to reduce productivity, and hence welfare.

But precisely the opposite argument can be made on the basis of the historical experience of literally all of the advanced capitalist democracies in existence. All of them without exception are now welfare states with some form and degree of social insurance, health and welfare nets, and regulatory frameworks designed to mitigate the harmful impacts and shortfalls of capitalism. Indeed, the welfare state is accepted all across the political spectrum. Controversy takes place around the edges. One might make the argument that had capitalism not been modified in this welfare direction, it is doubtful that it would have survived.

This history of the interplay between democracy and capitalism is clearly laid out in a major study involving European and American scholars, entitled *The Development of Welfare States in Western Europe and America* (Flora and Heidenheimer 1981). The book lays out the relationship between the development and spread of capitalist industry, democratization in the sense of an expanding suffrage and the emergence of trade unions and left-wing political parties, and the gradual introduction of the institutions and practices of the welfare state. The early adoption of the institutions of the welfare state in Bismarck Germany, Sweden, and Great Britain were all associated with the rise of trade unions and socialist parties in those countries. The decisions made by the upper and middle class leaders and political movements to introduce welfare measures such as accident, old age, and unemployment insurance, were strategic decisions. They were increasingly confronted by trade union movements with the capacity of bringing industrial production to a halt, and by political parties with growing parliamentary representation favoring fundamental modifications in, or the abolition of capitalism. As the calculations of the upper and middle class leaders led them to conclude that the costs of suppression exceeded the costs of concession, the various parts of the welfare state began to be put in place—accident, sickness, unemployment insurance, old age insurance,

and the like. The problem of maintaining the loyalty of the working classes through two world wars resulted in additional concessions to working class demands: the filling out of the social security system, free public education to higher levels, family allowances, housing benefits, and the like.

Social conditions, historical factors, political processes and decisions produced different versions of the welfare state. In the United States, manhood suffrage came quite early, the later bargaining process emphasized free land and free education to the secondary level, an equality of opportunity version of the welfare state. The Disraeli bargain in Britain resulted in relatively early manhood suffrage and the full attainment of parliamentary government, while the Lloyd George bargain on the eve of World War I brought the beginnings of a welfare system to Britain. The Bismarck bargain in Germany produced an early welfare state, a postponement of electoral equality and parliamentary government. While there were all of these differences in historical encounters with democratization and "welfarization," the important outcome was that little more than a century after the process began all of the advanced capitalist democracies had similar versions of the welfare state, smaller in scale in the case of the United States and Japan, more substantial in Britain and the continental European countries.

We can consequently make out a strong case for the argument that democracy has been supportive of capitalism in this strategic sense. Without this welfare adaptation it is doubtful that capitalism would have survived, or rather, its survival, "unwelfarized," would have required a substantial repressive apparatus. The choice then would seem to have been between democratic welfare capitalism, and repressive undemocratic capitalism. I am inclined to believe that capitalism as such thrives more with the democratic welfare adaptation than with the repressive one. It is in that sense that we can argue that there is a clear positive impact of democracy on capitalism.

We have to recognize, in conclusion, that democracy and capitalism are both positively and negatively related, that they both support and subvert each other. My colleague, Moses Abramovitz, described this dialectic more surely than most in his presidential address to the American Economic Association in 1980, on the eve of the "Reagan Revolution." Noting the decline in productivity in the American economy during the latter 1960s and '70s, and recognizing that this decline might in part be attributable to the "tax, transfer, and regulatory" tendencies of the welfare state, he observes,

> The rationale supporting the development of our mixed economy sees it as a pragmatic compromise between the competing virtues and defects of decentralized market capitalism and encompassing socialism. Its goal is to obtain a measure of distributive justice, security, and social guidance of economic life without losing too much of the allocative efficiency and dynamism of private enterprise and market organization. And it is a pragmatic compromise in another sense. It seeks to retain for most people that measure of personal protection from the state which private property and a private job market confer, while obtaining for the disadvantaged minority of people through the state that measure of support without which their lack of property or personal endowment would amount to a denial of individual freedom and capacity to function as full members of the community. (Abramovitz 1981)

Democratic welfare capitalism produces that reconciliation of opposing and complementary elements which makes possible the survival, even enhancement of both of these sets of institutions. It is not a static accommodation, but rather one which fluctuates over time, with capitalism being compromised by the tax-transfer-regulatory action of the state at one point, and then correcting in the direction of the reduction of the intervention of the state at another point, and with a learning process over time that may reduce the amplitude of the curves.

The case for this resolution of the capitalism-democracy quandary is made quite movingly by Jacob Viner who is quoted in the concluding paragraph of Abramovitz's paper, "... If... I nevertheless conclude that I believe that the welfare state, like old Siwash, is really worth fighting for and even dying for as compared to any rival system, it is because, despite its imperfection in theory and practice, in the aggregate it provides more promise of preserving and enlarging human freedoms, temporal prosperity, the extinction of mass misery, and the dignity of man and his moral improvement than any other social system which has previously prevailed, which prevails elsewhere today or which outside Utopia, the mind of man has been able to provide a blueprint for" (Abramovitz 1981).

References

Abramovitz, Moses. 1981. "Welfare Quandaries and Productivity Concerns." *American Economic Review*, March.

Berger, Peter. 1986. *The Capitalist Revolution*. New York: Basic Books.

Dahl, Robert A. 1989. *Democracy and Its Critics*. New Haven: Yale University Press.

____. 1990. *After the Revolution: Authority in a Good Society*. New Haven: Yale University Press.

Deutsch, Karl. 1961. "Social Mobilization and Political Development." *American Political Science Review*, 55 (Sept.).

Flora, Peter, and Arnold Heidenheimer. 1981. *The Development of Welfare States in Western Europe and America*. New Brunswick, NJ: Transaction Press.

Friedman, Milton. 1981. *Capitalism and Freedom*. Chicago: University of Chicago Press.

Hirschman, Albert. 1986. *Rival Views of Market Society*. New York: Viking.

Inkeles, Alex, and David Smith. 1974. *Becoming Modern: Individual Change in Six Developing Countries*. Cambridge, MA: Harvard University Press.

Lerner, Daniel. 1958. *The Passing of Traditional Society*. New York: Free Press.

Lindblom, Charles E. 1977. *Politics and Markets*. New York: Basic Books.

Lipset, Seymour M. 1959. "Some Social Requisites of Democracy." *American Political Science Review*, 53 (September).

Mill, John Stuart. 1848, 1965. *Principles of Political Economy*, 2 vols. Toronto: University of Toronto Press.

Mitchell, William. 1988. "Virginia, Rochester, and Bloomington: Twenty-Five Years of Public Choice and Political Science." *Public Choice*, 56: 101–119.

Moore, Barrington. 1966. *The Social Origins of Dictatorship and Democracy*. New York: Beacon Press.

Olson, Mancur. 1982. *The Rise and Decline of Nations*. New Haven: Yale University Press.

Schumpeter, Joseph. 1946. *Capitalism, Socialism, and Democracy*. New York: Harper.

*Lecture presented at Seminar on the Market, sponsored by the Ford Foundation and the Research Institute on International Change of Columbia University, Moscow, October 29—November 2.

Gabriel A. Almond, professor of political science emeritus at Stanford University, is a former president of the American Political Science Association.

We need more globalisation—
but we will only get it if we have better states

Political fragmentation is a huge obstacle to reducing worldwide poverty and inequality, writes **Martin Wolf,** the FT's chief economics commentator, in this exclusive extract from the final chapter of his forthcoming book

Martin Wolf

The 1980s and 1990s witnessed the collapse of the Soviet communist tyranny, an unprecedentedly rapid spread of democracy and nigh on universal economic liberalization. East and South Asia, home to 55 per cent of humanity, enjoyed an unprecedented leap towards prosperity.

Yet critics of Globalisation talk of this period of great hope and remarkable achievement as if it were a catastrophe. Many do so because they lament the death of the revolutionary tradition that held sway over the imaginations of so many over two centuries. Most compare the imperfect world in which we live with a perfect one of their imagining. It is in their way of viewing what has happened in the world, rather than the details of their critique, that those hostile to global economic integration are most in error.

What we must do is build upon what has been achieved, not, as so many critics wish, throw it all away. In the era after September 11 2001, that cooperative task has certainly become far more difficult. For peoples to sustain openness to one another is far harder at a time of fear than one of confidence. But the task has also become more urgent. A collapse of economic integration would be a calamity. Not only would it deprive much of humanity of hope for a better life. It would also, inevitably, lead to growing friction among the countries of the world.

Global economic integration has gone into reverse before. Between 1914 and 1945, the combined force of international rivalry, instability, interests and ideas caused the disintegration of this earlier form of globalisation.

History is unlikely to repeat itself. There is little chance of war between the great powers, who, in any case, are committed to market-led economic development and co-operation. The move to floating rates has significantly reduced the risk of a second Great Depression. Protectionist interests have been significantly modified and ameliorated by contemporary economic developments, including the rise of the international integrated transnational company. Finally, while vocal groups oppose global capitalism, they are very different from, and much less intellectually coherent than, the opponents of liberalism of a century ago.

Yet the danger to our open world economy is not small. The combination of fears of terrorism, economic instability, protectionist reactions to economic change and the rise of new competitors, particularly China, and protesters against economic integration could yet do grave damage. Global economic integration may not collapse, but that does not mean it will advance in ways that provide the greatest possible opportunities for the largest possible proportion of humanity.

Consider the biggest obstacle to a more even spread of global prosperity and the provision of essential global public goods: not global economic integration or transnational companies, as critics allege, but the multiplicity of independent sovereigns. It is not just the failure of states, but their existence, that creates the problems we now confront.

Think, first of all, of global inequality. Inequality among individuals has exploded over much of the past two centuries, not because of increased inequality within countries, but because of the divergent growth of different societies. Over the past two decades, the accelerated growth of a number of very large, poor countries above all, China and India—has reduced global interpersonal inequality. But a huge number of countries containing some 1.5bn people lags ever further behind. The overwhelming probability is that some, though certainly not all, of these countries will continue to

Martin Wolf's Ten Commandments of Globalisation

1. The market economy is the only arrangement capable of generating sustained increases in prosperity, providing the underpinnings of liberal democracy and giving individual human beings the opportunity to strive for what they desire in life.
2. Individual states remaining the locus of political debate and legitimacy. Supranational institutions gain their legitimacy and authority from the states that belong to them.
3. It is in the interest of both states and their citizens to participate in international treaty-based regimes and institutions that deliver global public goods, including open markets, environmental protection, health and international security.
4. Such regimes need to be specific and focused. But they also need means of enforcement.
5. The World Trade Organisation has been enormously successful. But it has already strayed too far from its primary function of promoting trade liberalisation. The arguments for a single undertaking binding all members also need to be reconsidered, since that brings into the negotiations a large number of small countries with negligible impact on world trade.
6. The case for regimes covering investment and global competition is strong. But such regimes do not need to be imposed on all the world's countries. It would be better to create regimes that include fewer countries, but contain higher standards.
7. It is in the long-term interest of countries to integrate into global financial markets. But they need to understand the need for an appropriate exchange rate regime, often a floating rate, and a sound and well-regulated financial system.
8. In the absence of a global lender of last resort, it is necessary to accept standstills and renegotiation of sovereign debt. A particularly strong case can be made for developing ways to write off 'odious debt'—debt contracted by politically illegitimate regimes.
9. Official development assistance is very far indeed from a guarantee of successful development. But the sums now provided are so small, a mere 0.22 per cent of the gross domestic product of the donor countries in 2001, that more should help, if used wisely. Aid should go to countries with sound policy regimes, but it should never be large enough to free a government from the need to raise most of its money from its own people.
10. Countries should normally be allowed to learn from their own mistakes, even if that means that some make no progress. But the global community also needs the capacity and will to intervene effectively where states fail altogether.

---

lag in the decades to come. If so, not only the absolute, but even proportionate, gaps in average living standards between the richest and the poorest countries in the world will continue to grow. Today, that ratio is some 75 to one. A century ago, it was about 10 to one. In half a century, it could easily be 150 to one.

What then lies behind such massive divergences in performance? A large part of the answer, as we have seen, is cumulative historical forces causing divergence. As countries grow richer, they are better able to afford high standards of education, health and public services. As citizens become better informed and more prosperous, they insist on higher standards in public life. At a certain point, economic growth becomes a routine. A positive cycle of reinforcement goes from the economy, to polity and society, and back again.

Meanwhile, at the opposite end of the spectrum from success to failure, societies seem stuck in an equally powerful vicious cycle. Very low standards of living mean correspondingly limited ability to provide any of the necessary public goods that underpin economic growth. Education is inadequate and illiteracy rife. Economic activity remains unsophisticated. Ambitious people view poli-

tics as a way to extract the wealth unavailable in normal economic activity. The result is corruption or, at worst, outright civil war. Among large states, the US may be seen as an exemplar of the first kind of society and Nigeria as the exemplar of the second.

The forces at work do not, fortunately, only cause divergence. There are also powerful forces for convergence. The accumulated know-how, as well as the markets, of the high-income countries offer opportunities for economic catch-up. But the evidence suggests that some societies are far better able to catch up than others. Natural resource abundance has proved a handicap for a host of reasons, not least the opportunities it gives to political rent-seeking. In contrast, labour abundance seems to work well, in the right policy environment, partly because it creates a direct connection between effort and reward. In an economy whose wealth is based on the efforts of its citizens, rather than on riches that come out of the ground, a government's ability to extract resources while failing to provide valuable services in return is relatively limited. The mutual dependence of the citizens and state forms the basis of a functioning social contract. If the state breaks

that contract, by extortion, the economy fails to grow, or, if it has attained wealth, retrogresses.

IF we ask further what would be the most powerful mechanism for ensuring that the forces of economic convergence overwhelm those of divergence, the answer has to be jurisdictional integration. The European Union is a regional system of jurisdictional integration. It imposes an obligation on all its members to accept freedom to trade, migrate and move capital. Such integration is not just an obligation, it is a credible commitment. These commitments have made the EU an extraordinarily successful machine for generating economic catch-up among previously poorer members, from Italy in the 1950s and 1960s to Ireland in the 1990s.

If similarly credible obligations could be spread globally, there can be little doubt that convergence would accelerate. At present capital flows to developing countries are remarkable for their modesty. But if the commitments to protecting property and allowing capital to move freely were credible everywhere, the movement of capital to poor countries would increase hugely. Again, if

The Dangerous Cacophony of the Critics

How are we to reconcile the reality of a world divided into unequal sovereignties with exploitation of the opportunities offered by international economic integration? That is the challenge we confront. How far, in turn, do the critics of market-led globalisation help us to answer this question? The answer is: hardly at all, partly because of the divergence of opinions they offer and partly because many live in a fantasy world.

Anarchists, for example, believe in the possibility of a society without government and coercion. But, without a state, power rests with gangsters: Sierra Leone is hardly a model on which the world can—or should—be expected to build. Those in favour of economic localisation apparently believe the power of corporations would be smaller if they were freed from the pressures of global competition. Again, deep greens want to halt economic advance, whatever the wishes of humanity. Protest may be fun. But it is a basis for neither effective policy nor mature politics.

Many of the critics argue that more sovereign discretion should be granted to countries than at present, particularly in relation to the World Bank and International Monetary Fund, but also in relation to the rules of the World Trade Organisation. Yet many—sometimes even the same people—argue that such discretion should be limited in order to ensure environmental protection. In this case, then, the argument is not over the principle of sovereign autonomy, but rather over what countries should be required to do and not to do. Yet others argue in favour of autonomy for developing countries to pursue the strategies they desire, while expecting high-income countries to maintain open borders and provide more development assistance. Others, in turn, argue that high-income countries should be free to protect their workers from unfair competition from developing countries, while forcing developing countries to accept minimum environmental and labour standards. This is a cacophony, with loud disagreements over whether countries should be free to do as they wish, over which countries should enjoy such freedom, and over what areas of policy they should be allowed to choose.

A narrower set of questions is how far the specific criticisms of these groups should inform our ideas about the appropriate direction for reform. Analysis suggests that at least some of the points that critics have made should be taken into account. Among the most important are:

- The case for permitting infant industry promotion in developing countries;
- The arguments for high-income countries to open their markets in favour of exports from developing countries;
- The need to be aware of the risks of mismanaged liberalisation of capital controls;
- The risk that institutions might be captured by special interests, as was the case for the agreement on trade-related intellectual property in the Uruguay Round;
- The case for international regimes ensuring effective responses to global environmental challenges;
- The need to set the case for international economic integration in a wider policy framework which also emphasises sound public finances, macroeconomic stability, financial stability, adequate investment in education, health and infrastructure, encouragement for innovation and, above all, the rule of law.

These are legitimate, albeit limited, concerns. But the hysterical complaints of the critics about the impact of international economic integration are nonsense. Transnational companies do not rule the world. Neither the WTO nor the IMF can force countries to do what they would prefer not to do. Crises do not afflict sound financial systems. Global economic integration does not render states helpless. Nor has it created unprecedented poverty and inequality.

The critics represent the latest—and least intellectually impressive—of a long series of assaults on the market economy. Yet, however unimpressive their arguments, these critics are dangerous, because they can give protectionist interests a legitimacy they do not deserve.

They allow protectionists to claim that they benefit the poor of the world as they deprive them of the opportunity to earn their living on world markets.

---

people could move freely from poor and failing countries to richer ones, global inequality and extreme poverty would both fall substantially.

We can go much further than this. Imagine not just jurisdictional integration in the sense of the contemporary EU, but in the sense of a contemporary state, say the US. Consider then a world in which the US was not one of the world's countries, but a global federation with equal voting rights for all. Far greater resources would then flow to the poorer regions of this imaginary "world-country", to finance infrastructure, education, health and the machinery of law and order.

This should not be surprising. We know very well that money is spent by a country on those with a political voice. In 2001, total official assistance from all rich countries to all developing countries amounted to $52bn. This was substantially less than the sums spent by the British government on the education of the country's young people and roughly a seventh of what the rich countries spend on assistance to their farmers. Provided such a "world-country" avoided imposing unnecessarily high costs on labour in the poorer regions, as Germany did after unification in the early 1990s, convergence should be accelerated still further.

These thought experiments illuminate what is far and away the most important source of inequality and persistent poverty: the fact that humanity is locked into almost 200 distinct countries, some of which are prosperous, well governed and civilised, while most others remain poor, badly governed and apparently incapable of providing the basis of a tolerable existence. Since the success of the economy depends on the quality of the state, this inequality in the quality of states guarantees persistent inequality among individuals.

The multiplicity of countries, their divergent historical experiences and the differences in the quality of the regimes they live under do not merely help perpetuate mass poverty and global inequality. They also make it almost impossible to ensure the provision of global public goods. The underlying constraint here is free-riding. While everybody should be better off if countries combined to provide global public goods, it is normally in the interests of individual countries to let others bear the cost.

This, however, is not the only difficulty. Some public goods may be of far greater importance to some countries than to others. Elimination of HIV/Aids from southern Africa is an obvious example: it is of vast importance to the countries concerned, but of somewhat less moment to others far away. But the resources needed to tackle such a disease may well be unavailable in the countries most directly affected. Similarly, those likely to be most damaged by global warming may well not be those that do most to cause it.

These are not trivial obstacles to the world many wish to inhabit. They are created by deep-seated conflicts among the values the contemporary world holds most dear. We believe in self-governing sovereignty, democracy, and, if not in greater global equality, at the least in alleviation of global poverty. But rich sovereign democracies will always use the bulk of their resources to tackle the problems of their own citizens, and protect themselves against disruption from abroad. They will control immigration tightly and be strongly inclined towards protecting adversely affected citizens against the impact of imports from the rest of the world. Similarly, an impoverished sovereign state must rely largely on its own resources. At worst, an incompetent, plundering, even murderous regime may assail its people without hindrance. At best, it will struggle to create the conditions for greater prosperity.

This is not an argument for world government. Even if it were achievable, such a leviathan would almost certainly crush the enterprise and competition that generate economic advance. Nor could such a world-state be meaningfully democratic. Even in the EU, differences in culture, language and sense of identity make it virtually impossible to generate anything approximating to a European politics. Elections without a shared political space are barren. At best, they generate remote technocracies. At worst, they can easily end up with the tyranny not so much of the majority as of enraged and self-interested minorities. But the globe's political fragmentation is, nonetheless, a huge obstacle to the achievement of many of the objectives the critics of globalisation hold dear.

Only a few lunatics—the localisers believe that the prosperity of the citizens of existing countries would be enhanced by fragmenting the integrated markets of contemporary national economies into self-sufficient village or manorial economies. But the world economy is fragmented, notwithstanding the progress made towards exploiting at least the potential gains from economic integration in recent decades. For that, the principal explanation is political fragmentation.

What sort of world should people who understand the power of market forces for human betterment now support? What role should international institutions play? And what are the proper limits of national sovereignty? These are not simple questions. Difficult choices arise. There is no one set of right answers. My suggestions come in "10 commandments of globalisation".

All these commandments matter. But the first two are the most important. The view that states and markets are in opposition to one another is the obverse of the truth. The world needs more globalisation, not less. But we will only have more and better globalisation if we have better states. We must reject the critics' fantasies and nightmares. Above all, we must recognize that inequality and persistent poverty are the consequence not of the still limited integration of the world economy, but of the globe's political fragmentation. If we wish to make our world a better place, we must look not at the failures of the market economy, but at the hypocrisy, greed and stupidity that so often mar our politics. As for the critics of market-led globalisation, they are not the antidote to the poison of bad politics. They are among its purveyors.

The sight of the affluent young of the west wishing to protect the poor of the world from the processes that delivered their own remarkable prosperity is unutterably depressing. So, too, is the return of all the old anti-capitalist cliches. It is as if the collapse of Soviet communism had never happened. The self-righteous indignation of those who have been so signally and repeatedly on the wrong side of history would be astonishing, if it were not so predictable. We must, and can, make the world a better place to live in. But we will do so only by ignoring these siren voices. The open society has, as always, its enemies, both within and without. Our time is no exception. We owe it to posterity to ensure that they do not triumph.

From *Financial Times*, May 10, 2004, p. 11, extracted from the final chapter of *Why Globalization Works*, by Martin Wolf. Copyright © 2004 by Yale University Press. Reprinted by permission of Yale University Press.

Global left turn

BY DAVID HELD

Martin Wolf and I come from similar backgrounds and agree about much in the globalisation debate. But while he regards liberal markets as sufficient, I think the globe needs a turn to social democracy

MARTIN WOLF, THE chief economics commentator of the *Financial Times,* has written a remarkable but flawed defence of the global market economy: *Why Globalisation Works: The Case for the Global Market Economy* (Yale University Press). Wolf conceives globalisation in essentially economic terms. The book says little about the political, social, cultural and environmental aspects of globalisation, although he does argue that nation states remain the locus of political debate and legitimacy and that the best way to combine economic globalisation with political stability is via liberal democracy. But it is economic globalisation—meaning greater openness of trade, free movement of capital, expansion of foreign direct investment—which is the focus because it is, in Wolf's view, the key to boosting prosperity and the life opportunities of all.

Wolf's mission is to dispel the illusions about globalisation promulgated by the forces of what he calls anti-globalisation.com, or the "new millennium collectivists." The book is about the intellectual clash between liberal capitalism and its opponents. Wolf is on the streets fighting a new wave of dark forces. The stakes are high: disorder and the fragmentation of the global economy threaten unless they are defeated. And defeating them requires both showing them they are wrong and offering hope for a better future.

Wolf's voice is clear, serious and didactic, and his book offers a carefully crafted account of the global market economy and the strengths and limits of his opponents' views. Yet there is also something anachronistic about the book and the territory it covers: its agenda seems to have been set a few years ago when the anti-globalisation movement was at its peak and hundreds of thousands were marching against the forces of economic globalisation. These days, after 9/11 and the war in Iraq, it is seldom asked whether we are for or against globalisation.

The ground has shifted to a debate about the *type* of globalisation we want. On these grounds, Wolf's contribution is less impressive.

I HAVE BEEN thinking and writing about globalisation and global governance arrangements for over a decade, and have considered much of the material that informs Wolf's book. It is therefore interesting to reflect on the points of similarity and difference in our background and approach.

Wolf begins his book with a brief autobiographical essay, describing his recent family history and its influence upon him. His father was an Austrian Jewish refugee who came to Britain before the second world war, and his mother was from a Dutch Jewish family. My parents were both Jewish and born in Germany, one in Leipzig and the other in Berlin. Both came to Britain in the early 1930s fleeing the Nazis. Wolf, like myself, was brought up with a strong sense of the menace of authoritarian dictatorships, and we both learned early about the importance of the values of an open society and of the forces, from the left and right, which might threaten it.

Both Wolf and I grew up in communities strongly committed to the Enlightenment ideals of freedom, democracy and the pursuit of reason—the impartial pursuit of truth—and with a strong sense of the fragility of the world's commitment to them. But while he believes that the liberal market economy is the best means of embedding these ideals, and that markets and liberal states create a framework for humans to be free and equal, I consider that the Enlightenment ideals remain unfulfilled in important respects and that the neoliberal form of globalisation to which Wolf subscribes is a challenge to them.

We have both been influenced by Friedrich Hayek. Wolf takes him as one of the great champions of personal liberty, of the market economy as a necessary condition of democracy, and of the dangers of intrusive government. I, like Wolf, take Hayek as one of the great theorists of the market, and of its advantages over other systems. But I also think that Hayek failed to grasp the nature of markets as systems of power which can also threaten liberty and democracy. Wolf conceives of markets as powerless mechanisms of co-ordination, while I understand them as highly fluid and risk-laden—often generating damaging externalities with regard to health, welfare, income distribution and the environment.

This is not an argument for abandoning the market, but it is an argument—explored in my new book *Global Covenant*—for reframing it. If we want to guarantee personal liberty and the efficient and just operation of the market, we must build bridges between economic and human rights, between the commercial and the environmental, and between national and international jurisdictions. Hayek does not help here at all. For both Hayek and Wolf, at the feast of the global market, power is largely absent.

Nevertheless, both Wolf and I believe that globalisation has been much misrepresented. We agree, for example, that globalisation is more than Americanisation; that there has been no straightforward collapse in welfare, labour or environmental standards (although there are big challenges); globalisation does not mean the end of the state; it has not just compounded the globe's inequities; the gap between the world's richest and and poorest states is greater than it has ever been and is growing, yet there is some evidence that the proportion of those living in extreme poverty is falling; global economic processes have not always reinforced corporate power; developing countries do not always lose out in world trade; and economic globalisation and the current structure of economic governance do *not* exclude the voice and influence of developing countries. Most of Wolf's book is devoted to examining propositions such as these, and while he does not paint a wholly rosy picture of economic globalisation, the force of the book is to show that anti-globlisation.com has precious little to offer.

We agree on the need to dispel these myths, but Wolf's portrait of economic globalisation does not get to the heart of the problems of globalisation in its current neoliberal form. I will stress three of them here: global market integration is not the indispensable condition of development; a "market first" political philosophy cannot provide adequate terms of reference for thinking about a range of transborder problems and the capacities of multilateral organisations to cope with them; and liberal market philosophy is the wrong philosophy for the age in which we live. We require, instead, a cosmopolitan social democratic philosophy to guide a world of overlapping communities.

Wolf's main argument is that "a successful move to the market, including increasing integration in the world economy, explains the success stories of the past two decades." Developing countries which have prospered, notably in Asia, have all followed this path. But his argument needs questioning in a number of respects.

First, the experience of China and India—along with Japan, South Korea and Taiwan earlier—shows that countries do not have to adopt liberal trade or capital market policies in order to benefit from enhanced trade and faster growth. All these countries have grown relatively fast behind protective barriers. It is true that as these countries have become richer, they have tended to liberalise their trade policy, but there is not a simple causal relationship at work. As Dani Rodrik, the Harvard economist, has shown, the only thing that can be said with certainty is that countries become more open as they become richer.

Furthermore, recent research has found that one of the main factors limiting the capacity of the poorest countries to develop is the liberalisation of capital. Geoffrey Garrett, a professor of political science at UCLA, has shown that what hurts developing countries faced with a broad liberalisation programme is not the pursuit of free trade per se, but the free movement of capital. While tariff liberalisation can be broadly beneficial for low-income countries, rapid capital liberalisation in the absence of sound domestic capital markets can be a recipe for "volatility, unpredictability and booms and busts in capital flows." Countries that have rapidly opened their capital accounts have performed significantly less well in terms of economic growth and income inequality than countries that have maintained tight control on capital movements but cut tariffs. An IMF study published in March 2003 found that there is no consistent support for the theory that financial globalisation per se delivers a higher rate of economic growth.

Economic protectionism does not work as a general strategy, but there is evidence to suggest that a country's internal economic integration—the development of its human capital and national market institutions, and the replacement of imports with national production where feasible—can be stimulated by state-led industrial policy. The evidence indicates that the development of state regulatory capacity, a sound public domain, the ability to focus investment on job creating sectors in competitive and productive areas and the protection of infant industries are more important priorities than integration into world markets. This finding should not come as a surprise, since nearly all today's rich countries began their growth behind tariff barriers and only lowered them once their economies were relatively robust.

The argument here should not be taken, as Wolf might suspect, as a simple endorsement of old leftist, state-centred development. Public objectives can be delivered by a diversity of actors, public and private. And the development of civil society is an indispensable part of national development. Although there can, of course, be conflicts between economic development and the strengthening of civil society, all countries need sufficient autonomy to work out their own ways of managing this conflict.

Developing nations need the latitude to create individual polices and institutions which may depart from the orthodoxy of global market integration. Similarly, organisations such as the WTO need a broader range of policies to encourage the different national economic systems to flourish within an equitable, rules-based global market order.

Wolf acknowledges elements of these arguments throughout his book, especially in his discussions of the work of Dani Rodrik and Ha-Joon Chang (see Michael Lind's essay in *Prospect*, January 2003). He accepts that there is much more involved in successful development than trade liberalisation, and that financial liberalisation carries risks. He does concede some ground to the critics of market liberalisation and global economic integration. But he never allows that these concessions have implications for the very basis of his liberal market approach—for its explanatory power and prescriptive value.

For both Friedrich Hayek and for Martin Wolf, at the feast of the global market economy, power is largely absent

---

THERE ARE many ways of conceiving and categorising the global challenges that we face. Jean-François Rischard, vice-president for Europe of the World Bank, usefully thinks of them as forming a triumvirate of problems, concerned with sharing our planet (global warming, water deficits, biodiversity and ecosystem losses), our humanity (poverty, global infectious diseases, conflict prevention), and our rulebook (intellectual property rights, unsustainable debt, trade, finance and tax rules). Wolf seems to think that global challenges such as these can be addressed by the current interstate order, even if it does require reform (notably in relation to the IMF and the WTO). But how urgent global problems might be resolved is far from clear, for the problem-solving capacity of the international system is not effective, accountable or fast enough. There are three main difficulties.

To begin with, there is no clear division of labour among the many international governmental agencies: functions overlap, mandates conflict, and aims and objectives get blurred. This is true, for example, in the area of health and social policy, where the World Bank, the IMF and the World Health Organisation often have competing priorities.

A second, related set of problems surrounds those issues which have both domestic and international dimensions. These are often insufficiently understood or acted upon. There is an ultimate lack of responsibility

for problems such as global warming and the loss of global biodiversity. Institutional fragmentation means that these issues fall between agencies. This latter problem is also manifest between the global level and national governments.

A third set of difficulties relates to an accountability deficit in the international agencies which stems from power imbalances among states. Multilateral bodies need to be more representative of the states involved with them. Developing countries are under-represented in many international organisations. There must also be arrangements in place to ensure consultation and co-ordination between state and non-state actors, and these conditions are seldom met in multilateral decision-making bodies.

Underlying these institutional difficulties is a lack of symmetry or congruence between decision-makers and decision-takers. The point has been well articulated recently by Inge Kaul and her associates at the UNDP in their work on global public goods and what they term the "forgotten principle of equivalence." At its simplest, the principle suggests that those who are significantly affected by a global development, good or bad, should have a say in its provision or regulation. Yet all too often there is a breakdown of "equivalence" between decision-makers and decision-takers. For example, a decision to permit the "harvesting" of rainforests may contribute to ecological damage far beyond the borders which formally limit the responsibility of a given set of decision-makers. A decision to build a nuclear plant near the frontiers of a neighbouring country is likely to be taken without consulting that country, despite the risks for it.

Systematising the provision of global public goods requires extending and reshaping multilateral institutions. Pressing issues include the need to develop criteria for fair international negotiations; strengthen the negotiating capacity of developing countries; create advisory scientific panels for major global issues (following the example of the intergovernmental panel on climate change); create negotiating arenas for new priority issues (such as access to water), together with appropriate grievance panels (such as a world water court); and expand the remit of the UN security council to examine and, where necessary, intervene in the full gambit of human crises—physical, social, biological, environmental.

LIBERAL MARKET philosophy offers too narrow a view, but clues to an alternative strategy can be found in an old rival—social democracy—which Wolf explicitly rejects. Traditionally, social democrats have sought to deploy the democratic institutions of individual countries on behalf of a particular national project—a compromise between the powers of capital, labour and the state. They have accepted that markets are central to generating economic wellbeing, but recognised that in the absence of appropriate regulation they suffer serious flaws—especially the generation of unwanted risks for their citizens, and an unequal distribution of those risks.

Social democracy at the global level means pursuing an economic agenda which calibrates the freeing of markets with poverty reduction and the protection of basic labour and environmental standards. What is required is not only the enactment of existing human rights and environmental agreements and the clear articulation of these with the ethical codes of particular industries (where they exist or can be developed), but also the introduction of new terms of reference into the ground rules or basic laws of the free market and trade system. Precedents exist: in the social chapter of the EU's Maastricht treaty, for example, or in the attempt to attach labour and environmental conditions to the Nafta regime.

Social democratic globalisation requires three interrelated transformations. The first would involve engaging companies in the promotion of core UN principles (as the UN's global compact does at present). To the extent that this led to the entrenchment of human rights and environmental standards in corporate practices, it would be a significant step forward. And to avoid these principles being sidestepped, they need to be elaborated in due course as a set of mandatory rules. The second set of transformations would thus involve the entrenchment of revised codes, rules and procedures—concerning health, child labour, trade union activity, environmental protection, stakeholder consultation and corporate governance, among other matters—in the terms of reference of economic organisations and trading agencies.

But this cannot be implemented without a third set of transformations, focused on alleviating the harshest cases of economic suffering. This means that development policies must challenge unequal access to the global market, and ensure that global market integration, particularly of capital markets, happens in sequence with the growth of sustainable public sectors, which guide long-term investment in healthcare, human capital and physical infrastructure, and the development of transparent, accountable political institutions. Moreover, it means eliminating unsustainable debt, seeking ways to reverse the outflow of net capital assets from the south to the north, and creating new finance facilities for development purposes. In addition, if such measures were combined with a (Tobin) tax on the turnover of financial markets,

and/ or a consumption tax on fossil fuels, and/or a shift of priorities from military expenditure (running at over $950bn a year globally) to the alleviation of severe need (direct aid amounts to $50bn a year globally), then the developed world might really begin to accommodate those nations struggling for survival and minimum welfare.

This is a big agenda, which cannot, of course, be realised all at once. Yet, as I argue in *Global Covenant*, it is feasible, and can be pursued on a step by step basis. And unless we move in this direction, and make social justice a priority alongside liberty, then tens of millions of people will continue to die unnecessarily every year of poverty, disease and environmental degradation.

The shift in the agenda of globalisation I am arguing for—a move from liberal to social democratic globalisation—would also have payoffs for today's most pressing security concerns. If developed countries want rapid progress towards global legal codes that will enhance security and ensure action against the threat of terrorism, then they should also participate in a wider process of reform that addresses the insecurity of life experienced in developing societies. Across the developing world, human rights and democracy are seldom perceived as legitimate concerns in the abstract. They must be connected with humanitarian issues of social and economic wellbeing, such as education and clean water.

To be concerned today with the Enlightenment ideals of freedom, democracy and reason, one needs to think about their entrenchment in an era in which political communities and states matter, but not solely and exclusively. States are hugely important vehicles for aiding the delivery of effective public regulation, equality and social justice, but they should not be thought of as occupying a privileged level of politics. They can be judged by how far they deliver these public goods and how far they fail. The question is not why globalisation works, but rather how it can be made to work better to bridge the gaps between liberty and social justice, economic and human rights concerns, the accelerating affluence of some and the continuing poverty of many. Liberal economic philosophy does not equip us adequately for this task.

David Held is a professor of political science at the LSE and author of "Global Covenant: The Social Democratic Alternative to the Washington Consensus" (Polity Press)

THE IMPERATIVE OF STATE-BUILDING

Francis Fukuyama

State-building—the creation of new governmental institutions and the strengthening of existing ones—is a crucial issue for the world community today. Weak or failed states are close to the root of many of the world's most serious problems, from poverty and AIDS to drug trafficking and terrorism. While we know a lot about state-building, there is a great deal that we do not know, particularly about how to transfer strong institutions to developing countries. We know how to transfer resources, people, and technology across cultural borders. But well-functioning public institutions require certain habits of mind, and operate in complex ways that resist being moved. We need to focus a great deal more thought, attention, and research on this area.

The idea that building up, rather than limiting or cutting back the state, should be at the top of our agenda may strike some as odd or even perverse. After all, the dominant trend in world politics for the past generation has been the critique of "big government" and the attempt to move activities from the state sector to private markets or to civil society. Yet particularly in the developing world, weak, incompetent, or nonexistent government has been and continues to be a source of severe difficulties.

For example, the AIDS epidemic in Africa has infected more than 25 million people and will take a staggering toll of lives. AIDS can be treated, as it has been in the developed world, with anti-retroviral drugs. There has been a strong push to provide foreign assistance for AIDS medicines or else to force pharmaceutical companies to permit the marketing of cheaper forms of their products in Africa and other parts of the Third World.

While part of the AIDS problem is a matter of resources, another important aspect is the government capacity to manage health programs. Anti-retroviral drugs are not only costly, but complicated to administer. Unlike one-shot vaccines, they must be taken in complex doses over long periods of time; failure to follow the proper regimen may actually make the epidemic worse by allowing the HIV virus to mutate and develop drug resistance. Effective treatment requires a strong public-health infrastructure, public education, and knowledge about the epidemiology of the disease in specific regions. Even if the resources were there, the institutional capacity to treat the disease is lacking in most countries in sub-Saharan Africa (though some, like Uganda, have done a much better job than others). Dealing with this epidemic thus requires helping afflicted countries develop the institutional capacity to use what resources they may acquire.

Lack of state capacity in poor countries has come to haunt the developed world much more directly. The end of the Cold War left a band of failed or weak states stretching from the Balkans through the Caucasus, the Middle East, Central Asia, and South Asia. State collapse or weakness had already created major humanitarian and human rights disasters with hundreds of thousands of victims during the 1990s in Somalia, Haiti, Cambodia, Bosnia, Kosovo, and East Timor. For a while, the United States and other countries could pretend that these problems were just local, but the terrorist attacks of September 11 proved that state weakness constituted a huge strategic challenge as well. Radical Islamist terrorism combined with the availability of weapons of mass destruction added a major security dimension to the burden of problems created by weak governance. In the wake of military actions taken since 9/11, the United States has taken on major new responsibilities for nationbuilding and state-building in Afghanistan and Iraq. Suddenly the ability to shore up or create from whole cloth missing state capabilities and institutions has risen to the top of the global agenda and seems likely to be a major condition for the possibility of security in important parts of the world. Thus state weakness is both a national and an international issue today of the first order.

Governance and Modernity

The problem of weak states and the need for state-building have existed for many years; the September 11 attacks have made them more obvious. Poverty is not the proximate cause of terrorism: The organizers of the 9/11 terror plot came from relatively well-off backgrounds and became recruits of violent Islamism not in their native countries, but while pursuing higher studies in Western Europe. The attack, however, brought attention to a central problem for the West: The modern world offers an attractive package, combining the market economy's material prosperity with liberal democracy's heritage of political and cultural freedom. It is a package that many people in the world want, as evidenced by the largely one-way flows of immigrants and refugees from less-developed to more-developed countries.

The modernity of the liberal West is difficult to achieve for many societies around the world. While some countries in East Asia have made this transition successfully over the past two generations, others in the developing world have either been stuck or have actually regressed over the same period. At issue is the question of whether the institutions and values of the liberal West are indeed universal, or whether they represent, as Samuel P. Huntington argued in *The Clash of Civilizations*, merely the outgrowth of cultural habits of a certain part of the northern European world.[1] The fact that Western governments and multilateral development agencies have not been able to provide much useful advice or help to developing countries undercuts the higher ends that they seek to foster.

Controversies over the size and strength of the state heavily shaped the politics of the twentieth century. It began with a liberal international order presided over by the world's leading liberal state, Great Britain. The scope of nonmilitary state activity was relatively narrow in Britain and all the other leading European powers, and in the United States it was even more restricted. As the century proceeded through war, revolution, depression, and war again, that liberal world order crumbled. Across much of the world, the minimalist liberal state gave way to a much more centralized and active one.

One stream of development led by way of two branches toward the "totalitarian" state, which focused on wholly abolishing civil society as an independent sphere and subordinating it to state purposes instead. In a sense, both branches came to a stop in Berlin: the right-wing branch when Hitler's bunker there was overrun and the Nazi Third Reich crushed in 1945, and the left-wing branch when the Berlin Wall was torn down in 1989 and the communist experiment crumbled under the weight of its own contradictions across Eastern Europe and the former Soviet Union.

Yet the first three-quarters of the century saw the size, functions, and scope of the state increase in nontotalitarian countries as well, including virtually all the democracies. In 1900, state sectors in Western Europe and the United States generally consumed no more than 10 percent of annual Gross Domestic Product (GDP); by the 1980s that figure approached 50 percent, and in the case of social-democratic Sweden, 70 percent.

This growth, and the inefficiencies and unanticipated consequences that it brought, led to a vigorous counter-trend in the form of Thatcherism and Reaganism. The politics of the last two decades of the century were characterized by the reascendancy of liberal ideas throughout much of the developed world, and attempts to control if not reverse state-sector growth. The collapse of the most extreme form of statism—communism—gave extra impetus to the movement to reduce the size of the state in noncommunist countries. At midcentury, the Austrian-American economist and classical-liberal thinker Friedrich A. Hayek was pilloried for suggesting that there was a connection between totalitarianism and the modern welfare state. By the time of Hayek's death in 1992, his ideas were being taken much more seriously.[2] This was true not just in the political world, where conservative and center-right parties came to power, but in academia as well, where neoclassical economics gained enormously in prestige as the leading social science.

Reducing the size of the state sector was the dominant theme of policy during the critical years of the 1980s and early 1990s when a wide variety of countries in the former communist world, Latin America, Asia, and Africa were emerging from authoritarian rule. There was no question that the all-encompassing state sectors of the former communist world needed to be dramatically scaled back. But state bloat had affected many noncommunist developing countries as well.

In response to these trends, the advice offered by the U.S. government and by international financial institutions such as the International Monetary Fund (IMF) and the World Bank stressed measures meant to reduce the degree of state intervention in economic affairs. One of the formulators of these measures would dub them the "Washington Consensus."[3] Detractors, particularly in Latin America, referred to them as "neoliberalism." In recent years, the Washington Consensus has come under relentless attack not only from antiglobalization protesters but also from academic critics with serious credentials in economics.[4]

In retrospect, there was nothing wrong with the Washington Consensus per se: Many developing-country state sectors were in fact obstacles to growth, and in the long run only economic liberalization could fix them. The problem was rather that while states needed to be cut back in certain areas, they needed to be simultaneously strengthened in others. The economists who promoted liberalizing economic reform understood this perfectly well in theory. But the relative emphasis in this period lay heavily on the reduction of state activity, which could often be honestly confused with or deliberately misconstrued as an effort to cut back state capacity across the board. The state-building agenda, which was at least as important as the state-reducing one, received no particular thought or emphasis. The result was that liberalizing economic reform failed to deliver on its promise in many countries. Some particularly ill-equipped countries even found that the lack of a proper institutional framework left them worse off after liberalization than they would have been had it never occurred. The problem lay in basic conceptual failures to unpack the different dimensions of "stateness," and to understand how they relate to economic development.

Measuring the State: Scope versus Strength

A good way to begin analyzing the role of the state in development is to ask whether the United States has a strong or a weak state. One clearcut answer comes from scholars such as Seymour Martin Lipset, who argue that U.S. political institutions are deliberately designed to weaken or limit the exercise of state power. The United States was born in a revolution against state authority, and the resulting antistatist political culture asserted itself through such constraints on state power as constitutional government with clear protections for individual rights, the separation of powers, federalism, and the like. Lipset points out that the American welfare state was established later and remains much more limited (for example, no comprehensive national health-care system) than those of other developed democracies, that U.S. markets are much less regulated, and that the United States was in the forefront of the movement to contain or roll back the welfare state in the 1980s and 1990s.[5]

On the other hand, there is another sense in which the United States lives under a very strong state. The eminent German sociologist Max Weber famously defined the state as "a human community that (successfully) claims the *monopoly of the legitimate use of physical force* within a given territory."[6] In other words, the essence of stateness is *enforcement*: the ability, ultimately, to send someone with a uniform and a gun to force people to comply with the state's laws. In this respect, the United States as a state is extraordinarily strong: Across its territory there exists a plethora of police and other agencies—local, state, and federal— to enforce everything from traffic rules and commercial-law regulations to criminal statutes and the Bill of Rights.

The United States, in other words, has a system of limited government that carefully restricts the *scope* of state activity. But within that scope, the state has ample power— and not just on paper—to frame and carry out laws and policies. Of course U.S. citizens often give voice to a certain justified cynicism regarding the efficiency and good sense of their own public authorities. In colloquial American English, saying that a job has been done to standards that are "close enough for government work" is not a term of praise. Yet there is no mistaking that the U.S. rule of law is and ought to be the envy of much of the rest of the world: Americans who complain about how their local motor-vehicles bureau treats them should try getting a driver's license or dealing with a traffic ticket in Mexico City or Jakarta.

It therefore makes sense to distinguish between the *scope* of state activities, which refers to the different functions and goals taken on by governments, and the *strength* of state power, which has to do with the ability of states to plan and execute policies, and to enforce laws cleanly and transparently—what is now commonly referred to as state or institutional capacity. One of the confusions in our understanding of stateness is the fact that the word "strength" is often used indifferently to refer both to what is here labeled "scope," and to "strength" or capacity.

Distinguishing between these two dimensions of stateness allows us to create a matrix that will help us to differentiate the degrees of stateness in a variety of countries around the world. We can array the scope of state activities along a continuum that stretches from necessary and important to merely desirable to optional and in certain cases counterproductive or even destructive. There is of course no agreed hierarchy of state functions, particularly when it comes to questions of redistribution and social policy. Most people would agree that there has to be some degree of hierarchy: States need to provide public order and defense from external invasion before they provide universal health insurance or free higher education. The World Bank's 1997 *World Development Report* provides one plausible list of state functions, divided into three categories that range from "minimal" to "intermediate" to "activist." This list is obviously not exhaustive, but provides useful benchmarks for gauging state scope.

Different countries of course fall at different points along the minimal-to-activist continuum depending on how ambitious they are in terms of what their governments seek to accomplish. There are countries that attempt complex governance tasks like running parastatal business enterprises or allocating investment credits, while at the same time failing to provide such basic public goods as law and order or public infrastructure. It is best to array countries along the continuum according to the most ambitious functions they seek to perform, even if they fail at or do not care much about more basic ones.

Another continuum, which we may think of as running perpendicular to the first, can be used to rate the comparative strength of various states' overall institutional capabilities. Strength in this sense includes, as noted above, the ability to enact statutes and to frame and execute policies; to administer the public business with relative efficiency; to control graft, corruption, and bribery; to maintain high levels of transparency and accountability in governmental institutions; and most importantly, to *enforce* laws. There is obviously no commonly accepted standard of measurement by which to assess the precise strength of state institutions. Moreover, different state agencies may perform at varying levels. In Egypt, for instance, the state-security apparat is brutally effective while other government agencies routinely mishandle simple tasks like processing visa applications or licensing small businesses.[7] The governments of Mexico and Argentina have shown themselves fairly skillful at reforming state institutions such as central banks, but not so adept at controlling fiscal policy or providing high-quality public schooling or health care. Thus we should think of state capacity as a mostly uneven rather than a smooth phenomenon, since it can vary so strongly from one type of state function to another within the same country.

With the renewed emphasis on institutional quality in the 1990s, a number of relevant indices now exist that can help place countries on the effectiveness scale. One of these is Transparency International's Corruption Perception Index, which draws primarily upon surveys answered by businesspeople who operate in different countries. Another is the privately produced International Country Risk Guide, which breaks the numbers down into categories measuring corruption, law and order, and bureaucratic quality. In addition, the World Bank has recently developed a composite indicator of governance covering 199 countries.[8] Finally, there are broader, politically oriented measures such as Freedom House's annual global survey of political rights and civil liberties, as well as the Polity IV dataset.[9]

Figure 1 above combines these two dimensions into a single graph that arrays scope against strength. The matrix divides neatly into quadrants. From the economists' standpoint, the optimal place to be is in quadrant I, which combines a limited scope for state functions with strong institutional effectiveness. Economic growth will cease, of

FIGURE 1—STATE SCOPE AND STRENGTH

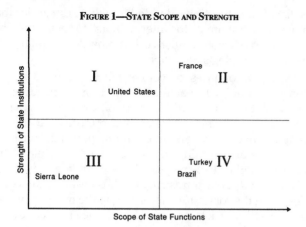

FIGURE 2—CHANGES IN STATE SCOPE AND STRENGTH

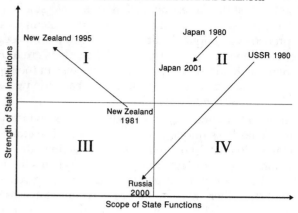

course, if a state moves too far to the left and fails to perform minimal functions such as protecting property rights, but the presumption is that growth will fall as states become more interventionist and move further right on the horizontal axis.

Economic efficiency is not, of course, the only reason for preferring a given scope of state functions. Many Europeans would argue that U.S.-style efficiency comes at the price of social justice and that they are happy to be in quadrant II rather than quadrant I. On the other hand, the worst place to be in efficiency terms is in quadrant IV, where an ineffective state takes on an ambitious range of activities that it cannot perform well. Unfortunately, this is exactly where a large number of developing countries are to be found.

The United States belongs in quadrant I rather than quadrant II because it has a less extensive state than either France or Japan; the United States has not attempted to manage broad sectoral transitions through credit allocation, as Japan did with its industrial policy during the 1960s and 1970s. Nor does the United States boast the same kind of high quality top-level bureaucracy as France with its *grandes écoles*. In this sense at least, the French state has a higher capacity. On the other hand, the quality of public bureaucracies in the United States is considerably higher than in most developing countries. Turkey and Brazil, by contrast, have funneled large proportions of GDP through their state sectors, run nationalized industries, and regulated and protected a wide range of economic activities.

It is not possible to be highly precise about where to locate countries along either axis, if only because state capacity almost always varies from agency to agency within the same country, and measures applied across several countries at once may not adequately capture all the phenomena. If one goes by outright transfers of income or social-program budgets, for instance, Japan has a smaller welfare state relative to the size of its economy than either France or Germany. Yet Japan provides an equivalent social safety net through the use of regulations (such as rules protecting small family-owned retail businesses), as well as through its use of private-sector microeconomic institutions like lifetime employment and the seniority wage system. On

the other hand, Japan's industrial policies historically have been more interventionist than those of most West European states, and its level of domestic regulation is very high. So is the Japanese state more active and administratively ambitious than a typical European welfare state? It is difficult to say.

It should also be clear that over time countries can change their location within the matrix, which also is useful in helping us to understand the dynamic nature of changes in stateness (see Figure 2). Thus the former USSR went from being a state of extensive scope (private property did not exist) with a moderate degree of administrative strength to being a state of narrower scope with an equally diminished degree of state capacity. The same can be said of Japan over the past two decades. It has made hesitant efforts at market liberalization, privatizing some state-owned companies and deregulating some domestic industries (largely under international pressure). At the same time, Japan's vaunted bureaucracies (particularly the finance ministry) have deteriorated in quality or have been captured by interest groups within society. Hence both Japan and Russia saw their state sectors move in the same direction—decreasing in both scope and strength—between about 1980 and 2000, though obviously starting from different places and moving at different speeds.

These cases stand in sharp contrast to that of New Zealand, which began a series of liberalizing reforms in the mid-1980s under the guidance of the Labour Party and its finance minister, Roger Douglas. By the start of that decade, New Zealand had developed one of the world's most extensive welfare states, but one that was clearly heading for crisis with the ballooning of national debt and a steady decline in the current account. The initial set of reforms begun in 1984 floated the New Zealand dollar; abolished currency controls; did away with agricultural and consumer subsidies, import licenses and export incentives; changed the tax structure from income and sales taxes to a broad-based consumption tax; and privatized state industries.[10] All of these were classic measures to reduce the scope of the state in New Zealand. But with passage of the State Sector Act in 1988, a second phase of reform began that sought to strengthen the administrative capacity of those core state agencies that remained. These reforms required departments to file monthly financial reports using commercial accounting standards; put the departments under the direction of chief executives who were hired under term contracts that set out conditions for employment; increased managerial discretion to permit shifting of the mix of inputs to be used to produce agreed outputs; and established a system of accountability using contract-like arrangements within the government. By the mid-1990s, therefore, New Zealand had gone some way along the optimal vector described by a state that has managed both to moderate its scope and raise its level of effectiveness.

Scope, Strength, and Economic Development

The development agenda for many international financial institutions shifted dramatically during the 1990s in a way that can be illustrated as follows. Look again at the Figure 1. There is no question that it is better to be in quadrant I than in quadrant IV, but is it better to be in quadrant II, with strong institutions and an extensive state, or quadrant III, with weak institutions and a limited state? A decade ago, many economists would have preferred quadrant III, on the grounds that markets would be self-organizing or that institutions and residual state capabilities would somehow take care of themselves. The Washington Consensus was a perfectly sensible list of economic-policy measures designed to reduce state scope through lower tariffs, privatization, subsidy cuts, deregulation, and the like. There is no reason, after all, for the Brazilian government to operate steel mills, or for Argentina to have a domestic automobile industry. In many cases, transitional and emerging-market countries were advised to move as rapidly as possible toward smaller state scope, on the grounds that the political window for engaging in this kind of reform would close quickly, and that it was better to get the pain of adjustment over with all at once.

The problem for many countries was that in the process of reducing state scope they either decreased state strength, or else generated demands for new types of state capabilities that were either weak or nonexistent. The austerity required by stabilization and structural adjustment policies became an excuse for cutting state capacity across the board, and not just in more-ambitious activities. In other words, while the optimal reform path would have been to decrease scope while increasing strength, many countries actually decreased both scope and strength. Instead of ending up in quadrant I, they ended up in quadrant III.

Something like this occurred in sub-Saharan Africa in the last quarter of the twentieth century. It is common to characterize regimes in this region as "neopatrimonial"—that is, with political power used to service a clientalist network of supporters. In some cases, like Mobutu's Zaire, the neopatrimonial state could only be described as predatory. In other cases, it led to simple rent-seeking by families, tribes, regions, or ethnic groups. As Nicolas van de Walle points out, the neopatrimonial regime, usually embodied in the office of the president, exists side-by-side with a Weberian rational bureaucracy, often created in colonial

times, that exists to perform the routine tasks of public administration.[11] The neopatrimonial regime is often threatened by the existence of the "modern" state sector and is a competitor with it for resources.

The dual nature of the African state meant that donor-imposed stabilization and structural-adjustment programs during the 1980s and 1990s had an unintended and counterproductive effect. The international lending community called for cutbacks in state scope through implementation of orthodox adjustment and liberalization programs. But neopatrimonial regimes, given their ultimate political dominance, used external conditionality as an excuse for cutting back on the modern state sectors while protecting and often expanding the scope of the neopatrimonial state. Thus basic investments in roads, primary schooling, agriculture, and public health plummeted during the last decades of the century, while "sovereignty expenditures" on armed forces, diplomatic posts, and jobs connected to African presidential offices increased dramatically. In Kenya, for example, the size of the president's office more than doubled, growing from about 18,000 employees in 1971 to more than 43,000 in 1990. No international lender or bilateral donor wanted to see this happen, yet no lender or donor could devise a form of conditionality to keep this from happening.

Many proponents of the Washington Consensus now say that they *of course* understood the importance of institutions, rule of law, and the proper sequencing of reforms. But questions of state capacity and statebuilding were largely absent from policy discussion in the late 1980s and early 1990s, and few policy makers in Washington warned of how liberalization might fail or be turned to perverse ends without proper political, legal, and administrative institutions to provide a context within which the reforms could work. Indeed, the general inclination among policy makers at the time was that any liberalization was likely to be better than no liberalization at all.[12]

Shaking Up the Washington Consensus

Thinking on these issues began to shift only after the East Asian economic crisis of 1997-98 and the problems experienced by Russia and other postcommunist countries. The financial crises in Thailand and South Korea were directly related to premature capital-account liberalization. In both countries, foreign short-term capital suddenly flooded into domestic banks while regulatory institutions lagged in effectiveness.[13] It is clear in retrospect that, under such circumstances, a little liberalization can be more dangerous than no liberalization at all. South Korea, for example, liberalized its capital account as a condition for OECD entry but without a corresponding opening of its equity markets or greater foreign direct investment. As a result, foreign investors who wanted a piece of the Korean economic miracle had their money in short-term accounts that could be withdrawn at the first sign of trouble. When Korea's current account began to deteriorate in 1996-97, the national currency came under irresistible pressure as short-term capital was withdrawn. This then set the stage for the economic crisis of late 1997.

Russia and other postcommunist countries faced a different problem. The privatization of state-owned enterprises is of course an appropriate goal of economic reform, but it takes institutional capacity to do this properly. Privatization inevitably creates huge information asymmetries that governments have the duty to correct. Assets and ownership rights have to be properly identified, valued, and transferred transparently; the rights of new minority shareholders have to be protected to prevent asset-stripping, tunneling, and other abuses. Thus while privatization involves a reduction in the scope of state functions, it requires a high degree of state capacity to implement. This capacity did not exist in Russia, and the stealing of public resources by the so-called oligarchs did much to delegitimize the postcommunist Russian state.

This new recognition of the priority of strength over scope is reflected in a comment made by Milton Friedman, the dean of orthodox free-market economists, in 2001. He noted that a decade earlier he would have had just three words of advice for countries making the transition from socialism: "privatize, privatize, privatize." To this he added: "But I was wrong. It turns out that the rule of law is probably more basic than privatization."[14]

From the standpoint of economic efficiency, is it more important to reduce state scope or increase state strength? Which will lead to greater growth? It is of course impossible to generalize, since economic performance will depend on the specific institutional capacities and state functions in question. There is evidence, however, that the strength of state institutions is more important, broadly speaking, than the scope of state functions. We have, after all, the growth record of Western Europe, whose scope of state functions is far larger than that of the United States, but whose institutions are strong as well. And why have East Asia's economies grown more robustly than their Latin American counterparts over the last 40 years? The likely answer has more to do with the former region's higher-quality state institutions than with any differences in state scope.[15] East Asian states have scopes that range from minimal (Hong Kong) to highly interventionist (South Korea), yet all achieved extraordinarily high rates of per capita GDP growth. By contrast, Latin America as a region scores worse than Asia on virtually every dimension of governance.

A further reason for thinking that strength is more important than scope in determining long-term economic-growth rates is the fact that there is a fairly strong positive correlation across a wide variety of countries between per capita GDP and percentage of GDP extracted by governments in taxes. That is, richer countries tend to funnel higher proportions of national wealth through their state sectors.[16] The rate of tax extraction is, of course, a measure of state scope, particularly for countries with higher levels of per capita GDP, but it is also a measure of administrative capacity (and is increasingly used as a metric by international financial institutions). That is, there are any number of countries that would like to be able to take in a larger share of GDP in taxes, but which cannot do so because their capacities for collecting taxes and enforcing tax laws are too weak. The fact that a strong positive correlation exists between tax extraction and level of development suggests that, generally and over time, the positive effects of greater administrative capacity counterbalance the negative effects of excessive state scope.[17]

The New Conventional Wisdom

Those who make and study development policy now take for granted much that has been said so far about the importance of state strength. "Institutions matter" has been a watchword since at least 1997. The concern over state strength, which goes under a variety of headings including governance, state capacity, or institutional quality, has in some sense always been around in development economics. In 1989, Hernando de Soto's *The Other Path: The Invisible Revolution in the Third World* reminded the development community that formal property rights made a difference, and more broadly, that smoothly functioning legal institutions promoted economic efficiency. De Soto sent researchers to find out what it would take to get a small business licensed in Lima, Peru. Ten months, 11 offices, and US$1,231 later, they came back with the papers.[18] In the United States or Canada, the same process would take less than two days. Noting the inefficiencies and barriers to new business startups caused by such a slow, tortuous, and expensive process, de Soto observed that it was no wonder poor entrepreneurs were electing to stay in the "informal" sector of licit yet unlicensed businesses. That sector was dynamic and often served as the only source for certain goods and services in poor neighborhoods. Yet the insecurity and unpredictability that go with the lack of formal, enforceable property rights narrowed investment horizons and prevented small businesses from becoming big ones with more jobs to fill and the like.

The development-policy community thus finds itself in an ironic position. The post-Cold War era began under the intellectual dominance of economists, who pushed strongly for liberalization and a minimal state. Ten years later, many economists have concluded that some of the most important variables affecting development are not economic but institutional and political in nature. There was an entire missing dimension of stateness—that of state-building—and hence of development studies that had been ignored amid all the talk about state scope. Many economists found themselves blowing the dust off half-century-old books on public administration, or else reinventing the wheel with regard to anticorruption strategies.

The new conventional wisdom that institutions are the critical variable in development now stands backed by a host of studies providing empirical documentation that this is so. There has, in addition, been a large and evolving literature on institutions and institutional development.[19] As in the case of all forms of conventional wisdom, the very fact that this view has become received wisdom should make us cautious. Michael Woolcock and Lant Pritchett talk about the problem of "getting to Denmark," where "Denmark" stands generically for a developed country with well-functioning state institutions.[20] We know what "Denmark" looks like, and something about how the actual Denmark came to be historically. But to what extent is that knowledge transferable to countries as far away historically and culturally from Denmark as Somalia or Moldova?

Unfortunately, the problem of how to get to Denmark is one that probably cannot be solved for quite a few countries. The obstacle is not a cognitive one: We know by and large how they differ from Denmark, and what a Denmark-like solution would be; the problem is that we do not have the political means of arriving there because there is insufficient local demand for reform. Well-meaning developed countries have tried a variety of strategies for stimulating such local demand, from loan conditionality to outright military occupation. The record, however, if we look at it honestly, is not an impressive one, and in many cases our interventions have actually made things worse.

NOTES

1. Samuel P. Huntington, *The Clash of Civilizations and the Remaking of World Order* (New York: Simon & Schuster, 1996).
2. Friedrich A. Hayek, *The Road to Serfdom* (Chicago: University of Chicago Press, 1944).
3. John Williamson, *The Political Economy of Policy Reform* (Washington, D.C.: Institute for International Economics, 1994), 26-27.
4. Dani Rodrik, *Has Globalization Gone Too Far?* (Washington, D.C.: Institute for International Economics, 1997); Joseph E. Stiglitz, Globalization and Its Discontents (New York: W.W. Norton, 2002).
5. Seymour Martin Lipset, *American Exceptionalism: A Double-Edged Sword* (New York: W.W. Norton, 1995).
6. Max Weber, *From Max Weber: Essays in Sociology* (New York: Oxford University Press, 1946), 78.
7. Diane Singerman, *Avenues of Participation: Family, Politics, and Networks in Urban Quarters of Cairo* (Princeton: Princeton University Press, 1995).
8. Indicators for six aspects of governance are available at *www.worldbank.org/wbi/governance/govdata2002*.
9. Adrian Karatnycky, "The 2003 Freedom House Annual Survey: National Income and Liberty," *Journal of Democracy* 15 (January 2004): 82-93. The Polity IV data are available at *www.cidcm.umd.edu/inscr/polity*.
10. New Zealand State Services Commission (1998), "New Zealand's State Sector Reform: A Decade of Change," at *www.ssc.govt.nz/display/document.asp?docid=2384*.
11. Nicolas van de Walle, *African Economies and the Politics of Permanent Crisis, 1979-1999* (Cambridge: Cambridge University Press, 2001).
12. This characterized the thinking of Clinton administration officials at the time of the South Korean entry into the OECD and in policy toward Thailand in the early 1990s, for

example, when there was little evidence of warnings concerning premature capital-account liberalization. See David Sanger and Nicholas Kristof, "How U.S. Wooed Asia To Let Cash Flow In," *New York Times*, 16 February 1999, A1.
13. Anthony Lanyi and Young Lee, *Governance Aspects of the East Asian Financial Crisis* (College Park, Md.: IRIS Working Paper 226, 1999); Stephan Haggard, *The Political Economy of the Asian Financial Crisis* (Washington: Institute for International Economics, 2000).
14. Interview with Milton Friedman in the Preface to *Economic Freedom of the World Annual Report* (Vancouver, B.C.: Fraser Institute, 2002), xvii.
15. Francis Fukuyama and Sanjay Marwah, "Comparing East Asia and Latin America: Dimensions of Development," *Journal of Democracy* 11 (October 2000): 80-99.
16. World Bank, *Building Institutions for Markets: World Development Report 2002* (Washington, D.C.: Oxford University Press, 2002).
17. Some forms of taxation are unambiguously bad for growth, like tariffs and other taxes on international trade. World Bank, *Building Institutions for Markets*.
18. Hernando de Soto, *The Other Path: The Invisible Revolution in the Third World* (New York: Harper & Row, 1989), 134.
19. For empirical reinforcement of the new conventional wisdom, see, among others, James A. Robinson and Daron Acemoglu, et al., "The Colonial Origins of Comparative Development: An Empirical Investigation" (Washington, D.C., NBER Working Paper 7771, 2000; William R. Easterly, *The Elusive Quest for Growth: Economists' Adventures and Misadventures in the Tropics* (Cambridge: MIT Press, 2001); Nicolas van de Walle, *African Economies and the Politics of Permanent Crisis, 1979-1999*. On institutions and how they develop, see Robert E. Klitgaard, *Controlling Corruption* (Berkeley, Calif.: University of California Press, 1988); Merilee S. Grindle, *Getting Good Government: Capacity Building in the Public Sector of Developing Countries* (Cambridge: Harvard Institute For International Development, 1997); Merilee S. Grindle, *Audacious Reforms: Institutional Invention and Democracy in Latin America* (Baltimore: Johns Hopkins University Press, 2000); Judith Tendler, *Good Government in the Tropics* (Baltimore: Johns Hopkins University Press, 1997); World Bank, et al., *The State in a Changing World* (Oxford: Oxford University Press, 1997); World Bank, *Reforming Public Institutions and Strengthening Governance* (Washington, D.C.: World Bank, 2000); World Bank, *Building Institutions for Markets*.
20. Michael Woolmark and Lant Pritchett, "Solutions When the Solution Is the Problem: Arraying the Disarray in Development, Center for Global Development," Washington, D.C., September 2002.

Francis Fukuyama is Bernard L. Schwartz Professor of International Political Economy at the Paul H. Nitze School of Advanced International Studies at Johns Hopkins University and the author of The Great Disruption: Human Nature and the Reconstitution of Social Order *(1999). Excerpted from the book,* State-Building: A New Agenda, *by Francis Fukuyama, published May 2004 by Cornell University Press. Copyright © 2004 by Francis Fukuyama.*

CULTURAL EXPLANATIONS

The man in the Baghdad café

Which "civilisation" you belong to matters less than you might think

GOERING, it was said, growled that every time he heard the word culture he reached for his revolver. His hand would ache today. Since the end of the cold war, "culture" has been everywhere—not the opera-house or gallery kind, but the sort that claims to be the basic driving force behind human behaviour. All over the world, scholars and politicians seek to explain economics, politics and diplomacy in terms of "culture-areas" rather than, say, policies or ideas, economic interests, personalities or plain cock-ups.

Perhaps the best-known example is the notion that "Asian values" explain the success of the tiger economies of South-East Asia. Other accounts have it that international conflict is—or will be—caused by a clash of civilisations; or that different sorts of business organisation can be explained by how much people in different countries trust one [an]other. These four pages review the varying types of cultural explanation. They conclude that culture is so imprecise and changeable a phenomenon that it explains less than most people realise.

To see how complex the issue is, begin by considering the telling image with which Bernard Lewis opens his history of the Middle East. A man sits at a table in a coffee house in some Middle Eastern city, "drinking a cup of coffee or tea, perhaps smoking a cigarette, reading a newspaper, playing a board game, and listening with half an ear to whatever is coming out of the radio or the television installed in the corner." Undoubtedly Arab, almost certainly

Muslim, the man would clearly identify himself as a member of these cultural groups. He would also, if asked, be likely to say that "western culture" was alien, even hostile to them.

Look closer, though, and the cultural contrasts blur. This coffee-house man probably wears western-style clothes—sneakers, jeans, a T-shirt. The chair and table at which he sits, the coffee he drinks, the tobacco he smokes, the newspaper he reads, all are western imports. The radio and television are western inventions. If our relaxing friend is a member of his nation's army, he probably operates western or Soviet weapons and trains according to western standards; if he belongs to the government, both his bureaucratic surroundings and the constitutional trappings of his regime may owe their origins to western influence.

The upshot, for Mr Lewis, is clear enough. "In modern times," he writes, "the dominating factor in the consciousness of most Middle Easterners has been the impact of Europe, later of the West more generally, and the transformation—some would say dislocation—which it has brought." Mr Lewis has put his finger on the most important and least studied aspect of cultural identity: how it changes. It would be wise to keep that in mind during the upsurge of debate about culture that is likely to follow the publication of Samuel Huntington's new book, "The Clash of Civilisations and the Remaking of World Order".

The clash of civilisations

A professor of international politics at Harvard and the chairman of Harvard's Institute for Strategic Planning, Mr Huntington published in 1993, in *Foreign Affairs*, an essay which that quarterly's editors said generated more discussion than any since George Kennan's article (under the by-line "x") which argued in July 1947 for the need to contain the Soviet threat. Henry Kissinger, a former secretary of state, called Mr Huntington's book-length version of the article "one of the most important books... since the end of the cold war."

The article, "The Clash of Civilisation?", belied the question-mark in its title by predicting wars of culture. "It is my hypothesis", Mr Huntington wrote, "that the fundamental source of conflict in this new world will not be primarily ideological or primarily economic. The great division among humankind and the dominating source of conflict will be cultural."

After the cold war, ideology seemed less important as an organising principle of foreign policy. Culture seemed a plausible candidate to fill the gap. So future wars, Mr Huntington claimed, would occur "between nations and groups of different civilisations"—western, Confucian, Japanese, Islamic, Hindu, Orthodox and Latin American, perhaps African and Buddhist. Their disputes would "dominate global politics" and the battle-lines of the future would follow the fault-lines between these cultures.

No mincing words there, and equally few in his new book:

Culture and cultural identities… are shaping the patterns of cohesion, disintegration and conflict in the post-cold war world… Global politics is being reconfigured along cultural lines.

Mr Huntington is only one of an increasing number of writers placing stress on the importance of cultural values and institutions in the confusion left in the wake of the cold war. He looked at the influence of culture on international conflict. Three other schools of thought find cultural influences at work in different ways.

• **Culture and the economy.** Perhaps the oldest school holds that cultural values and norms equip people—and, by extension, countries—either poorly or well for economic success. The archetypal modern pronouncement of this view was Max Weber's investigation of the Protestant work ethic. This, he claimed, was the reason why the Protestant parts of Germany and Switzerland were more successful economically than the Catholic areas. In the recent upsurge of interest in issues cultural, a handful of writers have returned to the theme.

It is "values and attitudes—culture", claims Lawrence Harrison, that are "mainly responsible for such phenomena as Latin America's persistent instability and inequity, Taiwan's and Korea's economic 'miracles', and the achievements of the Japanese." Thomas Sowell offers other examples in "Race and Culture: A World View". "A disdain for commerce and industry", he argues, "has… been common for centuries among the Hispanic elite, both in Spain and in Latin America." Academics, though, have played a relatively small part in this debate: the best-known exponent of the thesis that "Asian values"—a kind of Confucian work ethic—aid economic development has been Singapore's former prime minister, Lee Kuan Yew.

• **Culture as social blueprint.** A second group of analysts has looked at the connections between cultural factors and political systems. Robert Putnam, another Harvard professor, traced Italy's social and political institutions to its "civic culture", or lack thereof. He claimed that, even today, the parts of Italy where democratic institutions are most fully developed are similar to the areas which first began to generate these institutions in the 14th century. His conclusion is that democracy is not something

that can be put on like a coat; it is part of a country's social fabric and takes decades, even centuries, to develop.

Francis Fukuyama, of George Mason University, takes a slightly different approach. In a recent book which is not about the end of history, he focuses on one particular social trait, "trust". "A nation's well-being, as well as its ability to compete, is conditioned by a single, pervasive cultural characteristic: the level of trust inherent in the society," he says. Mr Fukuyama argues that "low-trust" societies such as China, France and Italy—where close relations between people do not extend much beyond the family—are poor at generating large, complex social institutions like multinational corporations; so they are at a competitive disadvantage compared with "high-trust" nations such as Germany, Japan and the United States.

• **Culture and decision-making.** The final group of scholars has looked at the way in which cultural assumptions act like blinkers. Politicians from different countries see the same issue in different ways because of their differing cultural backgrounds. Their electorates or nations do, too. As a result, they claim, culture acts as an international barrier. As Ole Elgstrom puts it: "When a Japanese prime minister says that he will 'do his best' to implement a certain policy," Americans applaud a victory but "what the prime minister really meant was 'no'." There are dozens of examples of misperception in international relations, ranging from Japanese-American trade disputes to the misreading of Saddam Hussein's intentions in the weeks before he attacked Kuwait.

What are they talking about?

All of this is intriguing, and much of it is provocative. It has certainly provoked a host of arguments. For example, is Mr Huntington right to lump together all European countries into one culture, though they speak different languages, while separating Spain and Mexico, which speak the same one? Is the Catholic Philippines western or Asian? Or: if it is true (as Mr Fukuyama claims) that the ability to produce multinational firms is vital to economic success, why has "low-trust" China, which has few such companies, grown so fast? And why has yet-more successful "low-trust" South Korea been able to create big firms?

This is nit-picking, of course. But such questions of detail matter because behind

them lurks the first of two fundamental doubts that plague all these cultural explanations: how do you define what a culture is?

In their attempts to define what cultures are (and hence what they are talking about), most "culture" writers rely partly on self definition: cultures are what people think of themselves as part of. In Mr Huntington's words, civilisation "is the broadest level of identification with which [a person] intensely identifies."

The trouble is that relatively few people identify "intensely" with broad cultural groups. They tend to identify with something narrower: nations or ethnic groups. Europe is a case in point. A poll done last year for the European Commission found that half the people of Britain, Portugal and Greece thought of themselves in purely national terms; so did a third of the Germans, Spaniards and Dutch. And this was in a part of the world where there is an institution—the EU itself—explicitly devoted to the encouragement of "Europeanness".

The same poll found that in every EU country, 70% or more thought of themselves either purely in national terms, or primarily as part of a nation and only secondly as Europeans. Clearly, national loyalty can coexist with wider cultural identification. But, even then, the narrower loyalty can blunt the wider one because national characteristics often are—or at least are often thought to be—peculiar or unique. Seymour Martin Lipset, a sociologist who recently published a book about national characteristics in the United States, called it "American Exceptionalism". David Willetts, a British Conservative member of Parliament, recently claimed that the policies espoused by the opposition Labour Party would go against the grain of "English exceptionalism". And these are the two components of western culture supposedly most like one another.

In Islamic countries, the balance between cultural and national identification may be tilted towards the culture. But even here the sense of, say, Egyptian or Iraqi or Palestinian nationhood remains strong. (Consider the competing national feelings unleashed during the Iran-Iraq war.) In other cultures, national loyalty seems pre-eminent: in Mr Huntington's classification, Thailand, Tibet and Mongolia all count as "Buddhist". It is hard to imagine that a Thai, a Tibetan and a Mongolian really have that much in common.

So the test of subjective identification is hard to apply. That apart, the writers define

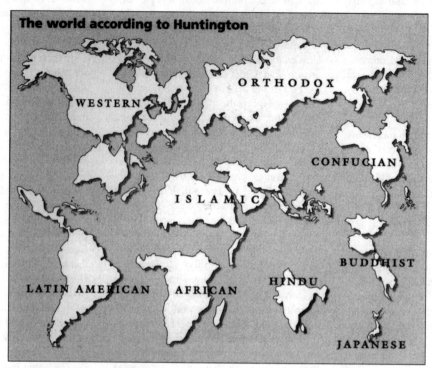

The world according to Huntington

Source: Adapted by The Economist from "The Clash of Civilisations and the Remaking of World Order" by Samuel Huntington

a culture in the usual terms: language, religion, history, customs and institutions and so on. Such multiple definitions ring true. As Bernard Lewis's man in the Levantine café suggests, cultures are not singular things: they are bundles of characteristics.

The trouble is that such characteristics are highly ambiguous. Some push one way, some another.

Culture as muddle

Islamic values, for instance, are routinely assumed to be the antithesis of modernising western ones. In Islam, tradition is good; departure from tradition is presumed to be bad until proven otherwise. Yet, at the same time, Islam is also a monotheistic religion which encourages rationalism and science. Some historians have plausibly argued that it was the Islamic universities of medieval Spain that kept science and rationalism alive during Europe's Dark Ages, and that Islam was a vital medieval link between the ancient world of Greece and Rome and the Renaissance. The scientific-rationalist aspect of Islam could well come to the fore again.

If you doubt it, consider the case of China and the "Confucian tradition" (a sort of proxy for Asian values). China has been

at various times the world's most prosperous country and also one of its poorest. It has had periods of great scientific innovation and times of technological backwardness and isolation. Accounts of the Confucian tradition have tracked this path. Nowadays, what seems important about the tradition is its encouragement of hard work, savings and investment for the future, plus its emphasis on co-operation towards a single end. All these features have been adduced to explain why the tradition has helped Asian growth.

To Max Weber, however, the same tradition seemed entirely different. He argued that the Confucian insistence on obedience to parental authority discouraged competition and innovation and hence inhibited economic success. And China is not the only country to have been systematically misdiagnosed in this way. In countries as varied as Japan, India, Ghana and South Korea, notions of cultural determination of economic performance have been proved routinely wrong (in 1945, India and Ghana were expected to do best of the four—partly because of their supposed cultural inheritance).

If you take an extreme position, you could argue from this that cultures are so complicated that they can never be used to explain behaviour accurately. Even if you

do not go that far, the lesson must be that the same culture embraces such conflicting features that it can produce wholly different effects at different times.

That is hard enough for the schools of culture to get to grips with. But there is worse to come. For cultures never operate in isolation. When affecting how people behave, they are always part of a wider mix. That mix includes government policies, personal leadership, technological or economic change and so on. For any one effect, there are always multiple causes. Which raises the second fundamental doubt about cultural explanations: how do you know whether it is culture—and not something else—that has caused some effect? You cannot. The problem of causation seems insoluble. The best you can do is work out whether, within the mix, culture is becoming more or less important.

Culture as passenger

Of the many alternative explanations for events, three stand out: the influence of ideas, of government and what might be called the "knowledge era" (shorthand for globalisation, the growth of service-based industries and so forth). Of these, the influence of ideas as a giant organising principle is clearly not what it was when the cold war divided the world between communists and capitalists. We are all capitalists now. To that extent, it is fair to say that the ideological part of the mix has become somewhat less important—though not, as a few people have suggested, insignificant.

As for the government, it is a central thesis of the cultural writers that its influence is falling while that of culture is rising: cultures are in some ways replacing states. To quote Mr Huntington again "peoples and countries with similar cultures are coming together. Peoples and countries with different cultures are coming apart."

In several respects, that is counter-intuitive. Governments still control what is usually the single most powerful force in any country, the army. And, in all but the poorest places, governments tax and spend a large chunk of GDP—indeed, a larger chunk, in most places, than 50 years ago.

Hardly surprising, then, that governments influence cultures as much as the other way around. To take a couple of examples. Why does South Korea (a low-trust culture, remember) have so many internationally competitive large firms? The answer is that the government decided that it should. Or another case: since 1945 German politicians of every stripe have been insisting that they want to "save Germany from itself"—an attempt to assert political control over cultural identity.

South Korea and Germany are examples of governments acting positively to create something new. But governments can act upon cultures negatively: ie, they can destroy a culture when they collapse. Robert Kaplan, of an American magazine *Atlantic Monthly*, begins his book, "The Ends of the Earth", in Sierra Leone: "I had assumed that the random crime and social chaos of West Africa were the result of an already-fragile cultural base." Yet by the time he reaches Cambodia at the end of what he calls "a journey at the dawn of the 21st century" he is forced to reconsider that assumption:

Here I was... in a land where the written script was one thousand two hundred years old, and every surrounding country was in some stage of impressive economic growth. Yet Cambodia was eerily similar to Sierra Leone: with random crime, mosquito-borne disease, a government army that was more like a mob and a countryside that was ungovernable.

His conclusion is that "The effect of culture was more a mystery to me near the end of my planetary journey than at its beginning." He might have gone further: the collapse of governments causes cultural turbulence just as much as cultural turbulence causes the collapse of governments.

Culture as processed data

Then there is the "knowledge era". Here is a powerful and growing phenomenon. The culture writers do not claim anything different. Like the Industrial Revolution before it, the knowledge era—in which the creation, storage and use of knowledge becomes the basic economic activity—is generating huge change. Emphasising as it does rapid, even chaotic, transformation, it is anti-traditional and anti-authoritarian.

Yet the cultural exponents still claim that, even in the knowledge era, culture remains a primary engine of change. They do so for two quite different reasons. Some claim that the new era has the makings of a world culture. There is a universal language, English. There are the beginnings of an international professional class that cuts across cultural and national boundaries: increasingly, bankers, computer programmers, executives, even military officers are said to have as much in common with their opposite numbers in other countries as with their next-door neighbors. As Mr Fukuyama wrote in his more famous book: the "unfolding of modern natural science... guarantees an increasing homogenisation of all human societies." Others doubt that technology and the rest of it are producing a genuinely new world order. To them, all this is just modern western culture.

Either way, the notion that modernity is set on a collision course with culture lies near the heart of several of the culture writers' books. Summing them up is the title of Benjamin Barber's "Jihad versus McWorld". In other words, he argues that the main conflicts now and in future will be between tribal, local "cultural" values (Jihad) and a McWorld of technology and democracy.

It would be pointless to deny that globalisation is causing large changes in every society. It is also clear that such influences act on different cultures differently, enforcing a kind of natural selection between those cultures which rise to the challenge and those which do not.

But it is more doubtful that these powerful forces are primarily cultural or even western. Of course, they have a cultural component: the artefacts of American culture are usually the first things to come along in the wake of a new road, or new television networks. But the disruptive force itself is primarily economic and has been adopted as enthusiastically in Japan, Singapore and China as in America. The world market is not a cultural concept.

Moreover, to suggest that trade, globalisation and the rest of it tend to cause conflict, and then leave the argument there, is not enough. When you boil the argument down, much of its seems to be saying that the more countries trade with each other, the more likely they are to go to war. That seems implausible. Trade—indeed, any sort of link—is just as likely to reduce the potential for violent conflict as to increase it. The same goes for the spread of democracy, another feature which is supposed to encourage civilisations to clash with each other. This might well cause ructions within countries. It might well provoke complaints from dictators about "outside interference". But serious international conflict is a different matter. And if democracy really did spread round the world, it might tend to reduce violence; wealthy democracies, at any rate, are usually reluctant to go to war (though poor or angrily nationalist ones may, as history has shown, be much less reluctant).

In short, the "knowledge era" is spreading economic ideas. And these ideas have three cultural effects, not one. They make cultures rub against each other, causing international friction. They also tie different cultures closer together, which offsets the first effect. And they may well increase tensions within a culture-area as some groups accommodate themselves to the new world while others turn their back on it. And all this can be true at the same time because cultures are so varied and ambiguous that they are capable of virtually any transformation.

The conclusion must be that while culture will continue to exercise an important influence on both countries and individuals, it has not suddenly become more important than, say, governments or impersonal economic forces. Nor does it play the all-embracing defining role that ideology played during the cold war. Much of its influence is secondary, ie, it comes about partly as a reaction to the "knowledge era". And within the overall mix of what influences people's behaviour, culture's role may well be declining, rather than rising, squeezed between the greedy expansion of the government on one side, and globalisation on the other.

The books mentioned in this article are:

Benjamin Barber. Jihad versus McWorld (Random House; 1995; 400 pages; $12.95).

Francis Fukuyama. The End of History and the Last Man (Free Press; 1992; 419 pages; $24.95. Hamish Hamilton; £20.) and Trust: The Social Virtues and the Creation of Prosperity (Free Press; 1995; 480 pages; $25. Hamish Hamilton; £25).

Lawrence E. Harrison. Who Prospers? How Cultural Values Shape Economic and Political Success (Basic Books; 1992; 288 pages; $14).

Samuel Huntington. The Clash of Civilisations? *Foreign Affairs* Vol. 72 (Summer 1993) and The Clash of Civilisations and the Remaking of World Order (Simon & Schuster; 1996; 367 pages; $26).

Robert Kaplan. The Ends of the Earth (Random House; 1996; 475 pages; $27.50. Papermac; £10).

Bernard Lewis. The Middle East (Wiedenfeld & Nicolson; 1995; 433 pages; £20. Simon & Schuster; $29.50).

Seymour Martin Lipset. American Exceptionalism (Norton; 1996; 352 pages; $27.50 and £19.95).

Robert Putnam. Making Democracy Work: Civic Traditions in Modern Italy (Princeton; 1993; 288 pages; $24.95 and £18.95).

Thomas Sowell. Race and Culture: A World View (Basic Books; 1994; 331 pages; $14).

An explosive combination

Capitalism, democracy don't always go together as planned

By AMY CHUA

In May 1998, Indonesian mobs swarmed the streets of Jakarta, looting and torching more than 5,000 ethnic Chinese shops and homes. One hundred and fifty Chinese women were gang-raped, and more than 2,000 people died.

In the months that followed, anti-Chinese hate-mongering and violence spread throughout Indonesia's cities. The explosion of rage can be traced to an unlikely source: the rapid combination of democracy and free markets—the very prescription wealthy democracies have promoted for healing the ills of underdevelopment.

How did things go so wrong?

During the 1980s and 1990s, Indonesia's aggressive shift to unrestrained free-market policies allow the country's Chinese minority, just 3 percent of the population, to take control of 70 percent of the private economy.

When Indonesians ousted President General Suharto in 1998, the country's poor majority rose up in a violent backlash against the Chinese minority and against markets. The democratic elections that abruptly followed 30 years of autocratic rule, while free and fair, were rife with ethnic scapegoating by indigenous politicians and calls for confiscation of Chinese wealth and a "People's Economy."

Today, the Indonesian government sits on $58 billion worth of nationalized assets, almost all formerly owned by Chinese tycoons. These once-productive assets now lie stagnant, while unemployment and poverty deepen.

What occurred in Indonesia is part of a pattern. It is the rule of unintended—but reasonably predicted—consequences. It is also a lesson for U.S. policy-makers in running postwar Iraq.

The reality is that given the conditions that actually exist now in many post colonial countries—conditions created by history, colonialism, divide-and-conquer policies, corruption, autocracy—the combination of laissez-faire capitalism and unrestrained majority rule may well have catastrophic consequences.

Roots of resentment

The notion that market democracy promotes peaceful prosperity has not always held sway. In the 18th and 19th centuries, most leading political philosophers and economists believed that market capitalism and democracy could only coexist in fundamental tension with each other. It is one of history's great surprises that Western nations succeeded so spectacularly in integrating markets and democracy.

Conditions in today's developing world, however, make the combination of markets and democracy much more volatile than was the case when Western nations embarked on their own paths to market democracy.

One reason has to do with scale: The poor are vastly more numerous, and poverty far more entrenched, in the developing world today.

Another has to do with process: Universal suffrage in developing countries is often implemented wholesale and abruptly—a destabilizing approach that is quite removed from the gradual enfranchisement seen during Western democratization.

But the most formidable problem the developing world faces is structural—and it's one that the West has little experience with.

It's the phenomenon of the market-dominant minority, ethnic minorities who tend under market conditions to dominate economically, often to an astounding extent, the impoverished "indigenous" majorities around them.

They're the Chinese in Southeast Asia, Indians in East Africa and the West Indies, Lebanese in West Africa, Kikuyu in Kenya, Ibo in Nigeria, Jews in post-Communist Russia, and whites in Zimbabwe, South Africa, and Bolivia, to name just a few.

It is crucial to recognize that groups can be market-dominant for widely different reasons, ranging from superior entrepreneurialism to a history of apartheid or colonial oppression. If, for example, as with whites in South Africa, a minority uses force to relegate the indigenous majority to inferior education and inhumane conditions for over a century, then that minority is likely to be market-dominant, for reasons that have nothing to do with culture.

In countries with a market-dominant minority, the rich are not just rich but belong to a resented "outsider" ethnic group.

In free-market environments, these minorities, together with foreign investors (who are often their business partners), tend to accumulate starkly disproportionate wealth, fueling ethnic envy and resentment among the poor majorities.

When democratic reforms give voice to this previously silenced majority, opportunistic demagogues can swiftly marshal majoritarian animosity into powerful ethnonationalist movements that can subvert both markets and democracy.

That's what happened in Indonesia and is happening around the world. The same dynamic—in which markets and democracy pit a poor, frustrated majority against a rich "outsider" minority—has produced retaliation, violence, and even mass slaughter of market-dominant minorities, from Croats in the former Yugoslavia to Tutsi in Rwanda.

A stake in the game

How can Western nations advance capitalism and democracy in the developing world without encouraging conflagration and bloodshed? They must stop promoting unrestrained, bare-knuckled capitalism (a form of markets that the West, itself, has repudiated) and unrestrained, overnight majority rule (a form of democracy Western nations have also repudiated).

Instead of encouraging a caricature of free-market democracy, they should follow their own successful model and sponsor the gradual introduction of democratic reforms, tailored to local circumstances.

They also should cultivate stabilizing institutions and programs such as social safety nets, tax-and-transfer programs, antitrust laws, philanthropy, constitutionalism and property protections. Most crucially, they must find ways to give the poor majorities of the world an ownership stake in their countries' corporations and capital markets.

In the United States, a solid majority of Americans, even members of the lower middle classes, own shares in major U.S. companies, often through pension funds, and thus have a stake in the U.S. market economy.

This is not the case in the developing world, where corporations are typically owned by single families belonging to a market-dominant minority. In South Africa as of June 2002, for example, blacks, although making up 77 percent of the population, controlled only 2 percent of the Johannesburg Stock Exchange's total capitalization.

Continued global democratization seems inevitable. But in this climate, international businesses, Western in-

vestors and market-dominant minorities should heed the lessons from Jakarta. It is an act of enlightened self-interest to launch highly visible local corporate responsibility initiatives and innovative profit-sharing programs.

Consider these models:
- In East Africa, powerful families of Indian descent include Africans in top management positions in their companies and provide education, training, and wealth-sharing schemes for their African employees
- In Russia, where anti-Semitism is rampant, the Jewish billionaire Roman Abramovich was recently elected governor of Chukotka after spending tens of millions of dollars of his personal fortune to airlift food, medicine, computers and textbooks into the poverty-stricken region.
- In Central America, a few Western companies have started to contribute to local infrastructure development and to offer stock options to local employees.

In these ways, foreign investors and market-dominant minorities can give local populations a stake in their local economy and businesses. This is perhaps the best way to defuse tensions that, history tells us, can sabotage both markets and democracy, the very structures businesses need to thrive.

The Bush administration might consider these lessons as it decides how to rebuild Iraq.

Perhaps because of beliefs in the "melting pot" and America's own relatively successful-though halting and incomplete-history of ethnic assimilation, Americans don't always understand the significance of ethnicity, both in the United States and especially in other countries. Interestingly, British colonial governments were fastidiously conscious of ethnic divisions.

Of course, their ethnic policies are a dangerous model. When it was the British Empire's turn to deal with nation-building and ethnicity, the British engaged in divide-and-conquer policies, not only protecting but favoring ethnic minorities, and simultaneously aggravating ethnic resentments.

Laissez-faire markets and overnight democracy in Iraq could well favor different ethnic or religious groups in the short run, creating enormous instability.

As a result, when the British decamped, the time bombs often exploded, from Africa to India to Southeast Asia. This contrast can be seen in how the United States and Britain looked at the situation in postwar Iraq.

At least before the war, the U.S. government's ethnic policy for Iraq was essentially to have no ethnic policy. Instead, U.S. officials seemed strangely confident that Iraq's ethnic, religious, and tribal divisions would dissipate in the face of democracy and market-generated wealth.

But in countries as deeply divided as Iraq, everything—even freedom and wealth—has ethnic and sectarian ramifications. Who will comprise the police? Who has experience in engineering and oil or the skills to run a stock exchange? Given Saddam Hussein's sadistically unfair and repressive regime, some groups—namely, the Sunni minority, particularly the Ba'athists—will almost certainly have a head start in terms of education, capital, and economic and managerial experience.

Consequently, as is true in so many other non-Western countries, laissez-faire markets and overnight democracy in Iraq could well favor different ethnic or religious groups in the short run, creating enormous instability.

At the same time, because by analogy at the global level, the United States has come to be seen as a kind of global market-dominant minority—wielding wildly disproportionate power relative to our size and numbers—every move we make with respect to Iraq is being closely—and perhaps even unfairly—scrutinized.

Despite Hussein's barbarous gulags, gross human-rights violations and repeated refusals to comply with U.N. requirements, international public opinion was overwhelmingly against the United States going to war with Iraq.

It is important to see that this opposition to U.S. policies was closely bound up with deep feelings of resentment and fear of U.S. power and cynicism about American motives.

Deep ethnic and religious divisions remain in Iraq, but ironically one theme unifying the Iraqi people at the mo-

ment is their intensifying opposition to American and British occupation.

Many Americans are bewildered—outraged—at the depth and pervasiveness of anti-Americanism in the world today. "Why do so many people want to come here if we're so terrible?" frustrated Americans demand. "What would France be doing if it were the world's superpower?" "Why do they hate us?" These are reasonable points.

But the fact of the matter is that because the United States is the world's sole superpower, we are going to be held to a higher standard than everyone else—market-dominant minorities always are.

For this reason, it is in the United States' own interest to avoid taking actions that suggest hypocrisy, look glaringly exploitative, or display lack of concern for the rest of the world, including of course the people of Iraq.

It is easy to criticize the United States, just as it is easy to hide behind facile calls for "free-market democracy." With the international community watching, I prefer to view this moment as a critical opportunity for the United States to surprise a skeptical world.

One thing, however, is clear:

The United States cannot simply call for elections and universal suffrage and at the same time support an economic system that is seen as benefiting only a tiny, privileged minority—whether an ethnic or religious minority or U.S. and British companies.

To do so would be a recipe for disaster.

Amy Chua is a professor of law at Yale University in New Haven, Conn., and the author of World on Fire: How Exporting Free Market Democracy Breeds Ethnic Hatred and Global Instability (Doubleday, 2003). Portions of this article previously appeared in the Harvard Business Review.

Jihad vs. McWorld

The two axial principles of our age—tribalism and globalism—clash at every point except one: they may both be threatening to democracy

Benjamin R. Barber

Just beyond the horizon of current events lie two possible political figures—both bleak, neither democratic. The first is a retribalization of large swaths of humankind by war and bloodshed: a threatened Lebanonization of national states in which culture is pitted against culture, people against people, tribe against tribe—a Jihad in the name of a hundred narrowly conceived faiths against every kind of interdependence, every kind of artificial social cooperation and civic mutuality. The second is being borne in on us by the onrush of economic and ecological forces that demand integration and uniformity and that mesmerize the world with fast music, fast computers, and fast food—with MTV, Macintosh, and McDonald's, pressing nations into one commercially homogenous global network: one McWorld tied together by technology, ecology, communications, and commerce. The planet is falling precipitantly apart and coming reluctantly together at the very same moment.

These two tendencies are sometimes visible in the same countries at the same instant: thus Yugoslavia, clamoring just recently to join the New Europe, is exploding into fragments; India is trying to live up to its reputation as the world's largest integral democracy while powerful new fundamentalist parties like the Hindu nationalist Bharatiya Janta Party, along with nationalist assassins, are imperiling its hard-won unity. States are breaking up or joining up: the Soviet Union has disap-. peared almost overnight, its parts forming new unions with one another or with like-minded nationalities in neighboring states. The old interwar national state based on territory and political sovereignty looks to be a mere transitional development.

The tendencies of what I am here calling the forces of Jihad and the forces of McWorld operate with equal strength in opposite directions, the one driven by parochial hatreds, the other by universalizing markets, the one re-creating ancient subnational and ethnic borders from within, the other making national borders porous from without. They have one thing in common: neither offers much hope to citizens looking for practical ways to govern themselves democratically. If the global future is to pit Jihad's centrifugal whirlwind against McWorld's centripetal black hole, the outcome is unlikely to be democratic—or so I will argue.

McWORLD, OR THE GLOBALIZATION OF POLITICS

Four imperatives make up the dynamic of McWorld: a market imperative, a resource imperative, an information-technology imperative, and an ecological imperative. By shrinking the world and diminishing the salience of national borders, these imperatives have in combination achieved a considerable victory over factiousness and particularism, and not least of all over their most virulent traditional form—nationalism. It is the realists who are now Europeans, the utopians who dream nostalgically of a resurgent England or Germany, perhaps even a resurgent Wales or Saxony. Yesterday's wishful cry for one world has yielded to the reality of McWorld.

The market imperative. Marxist and Leninist theories of imperialism assumed that the quest for ever-expanding markets would in time compel nation-based capitalist economies to push against national boundaries in search of an international economic imperium. Whatever else has happened to the scientist predictions of Marxism, in this domain they have proved farsighted. All national economies are now vulnerable to the inroads of larger, transnational markets within which trade is free, currencies are convertible, access to banking is open, and contracts are enforceable under law. In Europe, Asia, Africa, the South Pacific, and the Americas such markets are eroding national sovereignty and giving rise to entities—international banks, trade associations, transnational lobbies like OPEC and Greenpeace, world news services like CNN and the BBC, and multinational corporations that increasingly lack a meaningful national identity—that neither reflect nor respect nationhood as an organizing or regulative principle.

The market imperative has also reinforced the quest for international peace and stability, requisites of an efficient international economy. Markets are enemies of parochialism, isolation, fractiousness, war. Market psychology attenuates the psychology of ideological and religious cleavages and assumes a concord among producers and consumers—categories that ill fit narrowly conceived national or religious cultures. Shopping has little tolerance for blue laws, whether dictated by pub-closing British paternalism, Sabbath-observing Jewish Orthodox fundamentalism, or no-Sunday-liquor-sales Massachusetts puritanism. In the context of common markets, international law ceases to be a vision of justice and becomes a workaday framework for getting things done—enforcing contracts, ensuring that governments abide by deals, regulating trade and currency relations, and so forth.

Common markets demand a common language, as well as a common currency, and they produce common behaviors of the kind bred by cosmopolitan city life everywhere. Commercial pilots, computer programmers, international bankers, media specialists, oil riggers, entertainment celebrities, ecology experts, demographers, accountants, professors, athletes—these compose a new breed of men and women for whom religion, culture, and nationality can seem only marginal elements in a working identity. Although sociologists of everyday life will no doubt continue to distinguish a Japanese from an American mode, shopping has a common signature throughout the world. Cynics might even say that some of the recent revolutions in Eastern Europe have had as their true goal not liberty and the right to vote but well-paying jobs and the right to shop (although the vote is proving easier to acquire than consumer goods). The market imperative is, then, plenty powerful; but, notwithstanding some of the claims made for "democratic capitalism," it is not identical with the democratic imperative.

The resource imperative. Democrats once dreamed of societies whose political autonomy rested firmly on economic independence. The Athenians idealized what they called autarky, and tried for a while to create a way of life simple and austere enough to make the polis genuinely self-sufficient. To be free meant to be independent of any other community or polis. Not even the Athenians were able to achieve autarky, however: human nature, it turns out, is dependency. By the time of Pericles, Athenian politics was inextricably bound up with a flowering empire held together by naval power and commerce—an empire that, even as it appeared to enhance Athenian might, ate away at Athenian independ-

ence and autarky. Master and slave, it turned out, were bound together by mutual insufficiency.

The dream of autarky briefly engrossed nineteenth-century America as well, for the underpopulated, endlessly bountiful land, the cornucopia of natural resources, and the natural barriers of a continent walled in by two great seas led many to believe that America could be a world unto itself. Given this past, it has been harder for Americans than for most to accept the inevitability of interdependence. But the rapid depletion of resources even in a country like ours, where they once seemed inexhaustible, and the maldistribution of arable soil and mineral resources on the planet, leave even the wealthiest societies ever more resource-dependent and many other nations in permanently desperate straits.

Every nation, it turns out, needs something another nation has; some nations have almost nothing they need.

The information-technology imperative. Enlightenment science and the technologies derived from it are inherently universalizing. They entail a quest for descriptive principles of general application, a search for universal solutions to particular problems, and an unswerving embrace of objectivity and impartiality.

Scientific progress embodies and depends on open communication, a common discourse rooted in rationality, collaboration, and an easy and regular flow and exchange of information. Such ideals can be hypocritical covers for power-mongering by elites, and they may be shown to be wanting in many other ways, but they are entailed by the very idea of science and they make science and globalization practical allies.

Business, banking, and commerce all depend on information flow and are facilitated by new communication technologies. The hardware of these technologies tends to be systemic and integrated—computer, television, cable, satellite, laser, fiber-optic, and microchip technologies combining to create a vast interactive communications and information network that can potentially give every person on earth access to every other person, and make every datum, every byte, available to every set of eyes. If the automobile was, as George Ball once said (when he gave his blessing to a Fiat factory in the Soviet Union during the Cold War), "an ideology on four wheels," then electronic telecommunication and information systems are an ideology at 186,000 miles per second—which makes for a very

small planet in a very big hurry. Individual cultures speak particular languages; commerce and science increasingly speak English; the whole world speaks logarithms and binary mathematics.

Moreover, the pursuit of science and technology asks for, even compels, open societies. Satellite footprints do not respect national borders; telephone wires penetrate the most closed societies. With photocopying and then fax machines having infiltrated Soviet universities and *samizdat* literary circles in the eighties, and computer modems having multiplied like rabbits in communism's bureaucratic warrens thereafter, *glasnost* could not be far behind. In their social requisites, secrecy and science are enemies.

The new technology's software is perhaps even more globalizing than its hardware. The information arm of international commerce's sprawling body reaches out and touches distinct nations and parochial cultures, and gives them a common face chiseled in Hollywood, on Madison Avenue, and in Silicon Valley. Throughout the 1980s one of the most-watched television programs in South Africa was *The Cosby Show*. The demise of apartheid was already in production. Exhibitors at the 1991 Cannes film festival expressed growing anxiety over the "homogenization" and "Americanization" of the global film industry when, for the third year running, American films dominated the awards ceremonies. America has dominated the world's popular culture for much longer, and much more decisively. In November of 1991 Switzerland's once insular culture boasted best-seller lists featuring *Terminator 2* as the No. 1 movie, *Scarlett* as the No. 1 book, and Prince's *Diamonds and Pearls* as the No. 1 record album. No wonder the Japanese are buying Hollywood film studios even faster than Americans are buying Japanese television sets. This kind of software supremacy may in the long term be far more important than hardware superiority, because culture has become more potent than armaments. What is the power of the Pentagon compared with Disneyland? Can the Sixth Fleet keep up with CNN? McDonald's in Moscow and Coke in China will do more to create a global culture than military colonization ever could. It is less the goods than the brand names that do the work, for they convey lifestyle images that alter perception and challenge behavior. They make up the seductive software of McWorld's common (at times much too common) soul.

Yet in all this high-tech commercial world there is nothing that looks particularly democratic. It lends itself to surveillance as well as liberty, to new forms of manipulation and covert control as well as new kinds of participation, to skewed, unjust market outcomes as well as greater productivity. The consumer society and the open society are not quite synonymous. Capitalism and democracy have a relationship, but it is something less than a marriage. An efficient free market after all requires that consumers be free to vote their dollars on competing goods, not that citizens be free to vote their values and beliefs on competing political candidates and programs. The free market flourished in junta-run Chile, in military-governed Taiwan and Korea, and, earlier, in a variety of autocratic European empires as well as their colonial possessions.

The *ecological imperative.* The impact of globalization on ecology is a cliché even to world leaders who ignore it. We know well enough that the German forests can be destroyed by Swiss and Italians driving gas-guzzlers fueled by leaded gas. We also know that the planet can be asphyxiated by greenhouse gases because Brazilian farmers want to be part of the twentieth century and are burning down tropical rain forests to clear a little land to plough, and because Indonesians make a living out of converting their lush jungle into toothpicks for fastidious Japanese diners, upsetting the delicate oxygen balance and in effect puncturing our global lungs. Yet this ecological consciousness has meant not only greater awareness but also greater inequality, as modernized nations try to slam the door behind them, saying to developing nations, "The world cannot afford your modernization; ours has wrung it dry!"

Each of the four imperatives just cited is transnational, transideological, and transcultural. Each applies impartially to Catholics, Jews, Muslims, Hindus, and Buddhists; to democrats and totalitarians; to capitalists and socialists. The Enlightenment dream of a universal rational society has to a remarkable degree been realized—but in a form that is commercialized, homogenized, depoliticized, bureaucratized, and, of course, radically incomplete, for the movement toward McWorld is in competition with forces of global breakdown, national dissolution, and centrifugal corruption. These forces, working in the opposite direction, are the essence of what I call Jihad.

JIHAD, OR THE LEBANONIZATION OF THE WORLD

OPEC, the World Bank, the United Nations, the International Red Cross, the multinational corporation… there are scores of institutions that reflect globalization. But they often appear as ineffective reactors to the world's real actors: national states and, to an ever greater degree, subnational factions in permanent rebellion against uniformity and integration—even the kind represented by universal law and justice. The headlines feature these players regularly: they are cultures, not countries; parts, not wholes; sects, not religions; rebellious factions and dissenting minorities at war not just with globalism but with the traditional nation-state. Kurds, Basques, Puerto Ricans, Ossetians, East Timoreans, Quebecois, the Catholics of Northern Ireland, Abkhasians, Kurile Islander Japanese, the Zulus of Inkatha, Catalonians, Tamils, and, of course, Palestinians—people without countries, inhabiting nations not their own, seeking smaller worlds within borders that will seal them off from modernity.

A powerful irony is at work here. Nationalism was once a force of integration and unification, a movement aimed at bringing together disparate clans, tribes, and cultural fragments under new, assimilationist flags. But as Ortega y Gasset noted more than sixty years ago, having won its victories, nationalism changed its strategy. In the 1920s, and again today, it is more often a reactionary and divisive force, pulverizing the very nations it once helped cement together. The force that creates nations is "inclusive," Ortega wrote in *The Revolt of the Masses*. "In periods of consolidation, nationalism has a positive value, and is a lofty standard. But in Europe everything is more than consolidated, and nationalism is nothing but a mania.…"

This mania has left the post–Cold War world smothering with hot wars; the international scene is little more unified than it was at the end of the Great War, in Ortega's own time. There were more than thirty wars in progress last year, most of them ethnic, racial, tribal, or religious in character, and the list of unsafe regions doesn't seem to be getting any shorter. Some new world order!

The aim of many of these small-scale wars is to redraw boundaries, to implode states and resecure parochial identities: to escape McWorld's dully insistent impera-

tives. The mood is that of Jihad: war not as an instrument of policy but as an emblem of identity, an expression of community, an end in itself. Even where there is no shooting war, there is fractiousness, secession, and the quest for ever smaller communities. Add to the list of dangerous countries those at risk: In Switzerland and Spain, Jurassian and Basque separatists still argue the virtues of ancient identities, sometimes in the language of bombs. Hyperdisintegration in the former Soviet Union may well continue unabated—not just a Ukraine independent from the Soviet Union but a Bessarabian Ukraine independent from the Ukrainian republic; not just Russia severed from the defunct union but Tatarstan severed from Russia. Yugoslavia makes even the disunited, ex-Soviet, nonsocialist republics that were once the Soviet Union look integrated, its sectarian fatherlands springing up within factional motherlands like weeds within weeds within weeds. Kurdish independence would threaten the territorial integrity of four Middle Eastern nations. Well before the current cataclysm Soviet Georgia made a claim for autonomy from the Soviet Union, only to be faced with its Ossetians (164,000 in a republic of 5.5 million) demanding their own self-determination within Georgia. The Abkhasian minority in Georgia has followed suit. Even the good will established by Canada's once promising Meech Lake protocols is in danger, with Francophone Quebec again threatening the dissolution of the federation. In South Africa the emergence from apartheid was hardly achieved when friction between Inkatha's Zulus and the African National Congress's tribally identified members threatened to replace Europeans' racism with an indigenous tribal war. After thirty years of attempted integration using the colonial language (English) as a unifier, Nigeria is now playing with the idea of linguistic multiculturalism—which could mean the cultural breakup of the nation into hundreds of tribal fragments. Even Saddam Hussein has benefited from the threat of internal Jihad, having used renewed tribal and religious warfare to turn last season's mortal enemies into reluctant allies of an Iraqi nationhood that he nearly destroyed.

The passing of communism has torn away the thin veneer of internationalism (workers of the world unite!) to reveal ethnic prejudices that are not only ugly and deep-seated but increasingly murderous. Europe's old scourge, anti-Semitism, is back with a vengeance, but it is only one of many antagonisms. It appears all too easy to throw the historical gears into reverse and pass from a Communist dictatorship back into a tribal state.

Among the tribes, religion is also a battlefield. ("Jihad" is a rich world whose generic meaning is "struggle"—usually the struggle of the soul to avert evil. Strictly applied to religious war, it is used only in reference to battles where the faith is under assault, or battles against a government that denies the practice of Islam. My use here is rhetorical, but does follow both journalistic practice and history.) Remember the Thirty Years War? Whatever forms of Enlightenment universalism might once have come to grace such historically related forms of monotheism as Judaism, Christianity, and Islam, in many of their modern incarnations they are parochial rather than cosmopolitan, angry rather than loving, proselytizing rather than ecumenical, zealous rather than rationalist, sectarian rather than deistic, ethnocentric rather than universalizing. As a result, like the new forms of hypernationalism, the new expressions of religious fundamentalism are fractious and pulverizing, never integrating. This is religion as the Crusaders knew it: a battle to the death for souls that if not saved will be forever lost.

The atmospherics of Jihad have resulted in a breakdown of civility in the name of identity, of comity in the name of community. International relations have sometimes taken on the aspect of gang war—cultural turf battles featuring tribal factions that were supposed to be sublimated as integral parts of large national, economic, postcolonial, and constitutional entities.

THE DARKENING FUTURE OF DEMOCRACY

These rather melodramatic tableaux vivants do not tell the whole story, however. For all their defects, Jihad and McWorld have their attractions. Yet, to repeat and insist, the attractions are unrelated to democracy. Neither McWorld nor Jihad is remotely democratic in impulse. Neither needs democracy; neither promotes democracy.

McWorld does manage to look pretty seductive in a world obsessed with Jihad. It delivers peace, prosperity, and relative unity—if at the cost of independence, community, and identity (which is generally based on difference). The primary political values required by the global market are

order and tranquility, and freedom—as in the phrases "free trade," "free press," and "free love." Human rights are needed to a degree, but not citizenship or participation—and no more social justice and equality than are necessary to promote efficient economic production and consumption. Multinational corporations sometimes seem to prefer doing business with local oligarchs, inasmuch as they can take confidence from dealing with the boss on all crucial matters. Despots who slaughter their own populations are no problem, so long as they leave markets in place and refrain from making war on their neighbors (Saddam Hussein's fatal mistake). In trading partners, predictability is of more value than justice.

The Eastern European revolutions that seemed to arise out of concern for global democratic values quickly deteriorated into a stampede in the general direction of free markets and their ubiquitous, television-promoted shopping malls. East Germany's Neues Forum, that courageous gathering of intellectuals, students, and workers which overturned the Stalinist regime in Berlin in 1989, lasted only six months in Germany's mini-version of McWorld. Then it gave way to money and markets and monopolies from the West. By the time of the first all-German elections, it could scarcely manage to secure three percent of the vote. Elsewhere there is growing evidence that *glasnost* will go and *perestroika*—defined as privatization and an opening of markets to Western bidders—will stay. So understandably anxious are the new rulers of Eastern Europe and whatever entities are forged from the residues of the Soviet Union to gain access to credit and markets and technology—McWorld's flourishing new currencies—that they have shown themselves willing to trade away democratic prospects in pursuit of them: not just old totalitarian ideologies and command-economy production models but some possible indigenous experiments with a third way between capitalism and socialism, such as economic cooperatives and employee stock-ownership plans, both of which have their ardent supporters in the East.

Jihad delivers a different set of virtues: a vibrant local identity, a sense of community, solidarity among kinsmen, neighbors, and countrymen, narrowly conceived. But it also guarantees parochialism and is grounded in exclusion. Solidarity is secured through war against outsiders. And solidarity often means obedience to a hierarchy in governance, fanaticism in beliefs,

and the obliteration of individual selves in the name of the group. Deference to leaders and intolerance toward outsiders (and toward "enemies within") are hallmarks of tribalism—hardly the attitudes required for the cultivation of new democratic women and men capable of governing themselves. Where new democratic experiments have been conducted in retribalizing societies, in both Europe and the Third World, the result has often been anarchy, repression, persecution, and the coming of new, non-communist forms of very old kinds of despotism. During the past year, Havel's velvet revolution in Czechoslovakia was imperiled by partisans of "Czechland" and of Slovakia as independent entities. India seemed little less rent by Sikh, Hindu, Muslim, and Tamil infighting than it was immediately after the British pulled out, more than forty years ago.

To the extent that either McWorld or Jihad has a *natural* politics, it has turned out to be more of an antipolitics. For McWorld, it is the antipolitics of globalism: bureaucratic, technocratic, and meritocratic, focused (as Marx predicted it would be) on the administration of things—with people, however, among the chief things to be administered. In its politico-economic imperatives McWorld has been guided by laissez-faire market principles that privilege efficiency, productivity, and beneficence at the expense of civic liberty and self-government.

For Jihad, the antipolitics of tribalization has been explicitly antidemocratic: one-party dictatorship, government by military junta, theocratic fundamentalism—often associated with a version of the *Führerprinzip* that empowers an individual to rule on behalf of a people. Even the government of India, struggling for decades to model democracy for a people who will soon number a billion, longs for great leaders; and for every Mahatma Gandhi, Indira Gandhi, or Rajiv Gandhi taken from them by zealous assassins, the Indians appear to seek a replacement who will deliver them from the lengthy travail of their freedom.

THE CONFEDERAL OPTION

How can democracy be secured and spread in a world whose primary tendencies are at best indifferent to it (McWorld) and at worst deeply antithetical to it (Jihad)? My guess is that globalization will eventually vanquish retribalization. The ethos of material "civilization" has not yet encountered an obstacle it has been unable to thrust aside. Ortega may have grasped in the 1920s a clue to our own future in the coming millennium.

Everyone sees the need of a new principle of life. But as always happens in similar crises—some people attempt to save the situation by an artificial intensification of the very principle which has led to decay. This is the meaning of the "nationalist" outburst of recent years… things have always gone that way. The last flare, the longest; the last sigh, the deepest. On the very eve of their disappearance there is an intensification of frontiers—military and economic.

Jihad may be a last deep sigh before the eternal yawn of McWorld. On the other hand, Ortega was not exactly prescient; his prophecy of peace and internationalism came just before blitzkrieg, world war, and the Holocaust tore the old order to bits. Yet democracy is how we remonstrate with reality, the rebuke our aspirations offer to history. And if retribalization is inhospitable to democracy, there is nonetheless a form of democratic government that can accommodate parochialism and communitarianism, one that can even save them from their defects and make them more tolerant and participatory: decentralized participatory democracy. And if McWorld is indifferent to democracy, there is nonetheless a form of democratic government that suits global markets passably well—representative government in its federal or, better still, confederal variation.

With its concern for accountability, the protection of minorities, and the universal rule of law, a confederalized representative system would serve the political needs of McWorld as well as oligarchic bureaucratism or meritocratic elitism is currently doing. As we are already beginning to see, many nations may survive in the long term only as confederations that afford local regions smaller than "nations" extensive jurisdiction. Recommended reading for democrats of the twenty-first century is not the U.S. Constitution or the French Declaration of Rights of Man and Citizen but the Articles of Confederation, that suddenly pertinent document that stitched together the thirteen American colonies into what then seemed a too loose confederation of independent states but now appears a new form of political realism, as veterans of

Yeltsin's new Russia and the new Europe created at Maastricht will attest.

By the same token, the participatory and direct form of democracy that engages citizens in civic activity and civic judgment and goes well beyond just voting and accountability—the system I have called "strong democracy"—suits the political needs of decentralized communities as well as theocratic and nationalist party dictatorships have done. Local neighborhoods need not be democratic, but they can be. Real democracy has flourished in diminutive settings: the spirit of liberty, Tocqueville said, is local. Participatory democracy, if not naturally apposite to tribalism, has an undeniable attractiveness under conditions of parochialism.

Democracy in any of these variations will, however, continue to be obstructed by the undemocratic and antidemocratic trends toward uniformitarian globalism and intolerant retribalization which I have portrayed here. For democracy to persist in our brave new McWorld, we will have to commit acts of conscious political will—a possibility, but hardly a probability, under these conditions. Political will requires much more than the quick fix of the transfer of institutions. Like technology transfer, institution transfer rests on foolish assumptions about a uniform world of the kind that once fired the imagination of colonial administrators. Spread English justice to the colonies by exporting wigs. Let an East Indian trading company act as the vanguard to Britain's free parliamentary institutions. Today's well-intentioned quickfixers in the National Endowment for Democracy and the Kennedy School of Government, in the unions and foundations and universities zealously nurturing contacts in Eastern Europe and the Third World, are hoping to democratize by long distance. Post Bulgaria a parliament by first-class mail. Fed Ex the Bill of Rights to Sri Lanka. Cable Cambodia some common law.

Yet Eastern Europe has already demonstrated that importing free political parties, parliaments, and presses cannot establish a democratic civil society; imposing a free market may even have the opposite effect. Democracy grows from the bottom up and cannot be imposed from the top down. Civil society has to be built from the inside out. The institutional superstructure comes last. Poland may become democratic, but

then again it may heed the Pope, and prefer to found its politics on its Catholicism, with uncertain consequences for democracy. Bulgaria may become democratic, but it may prefer tribal war. The former Soviet Union may become a democratic confederation, or it may just grow into an anarchic and weak conglomeration of markets for other nations' goods and services.

Democrats need to seek out indigenous democratic impulses. There is always a desire for self-government, always some expression of participation, accountability, consent, and representation, even in traditional hierarchical societies. These need to be identified, tapped, modified, and incorporated into new democratic practices with an indigenous flavor. The tortoises among the democratizers may ultimately outlive or outpace the hares, for they will have the time and patience to explore conditions along the way, and to adapt their gait to changing circumstances. Tragically, democracy in a hurry often looks something like France in 1794 or China in 1989.

It certainly seems possible that the most attractive democratic ideal in the face of the brutal realities of Jihad and the dull realities of McWorld will be a confederal union of semi-autonomous communities smaller than nation-states, tied together into regional economic associations and markets larger than nation-states—participatory and self-determining in local matters at the bottom, representative and accountable at the top. The nation-state would play a diminished role, and sovereignty would lose some of its political potency. The Green movement adage "Think globally, act locally" would actually come to describe the conduct of politics.

This vision reflects only an ideal, however—one that is not terribly likely to be realized. Freedom, Jean-Jacques Rousseau once wrote, is a food easy to eat but hard to digest. Still, democracy has always played itself out against the odds. And democracy remains both a form of coherence as binding as McWorld and a secular faith potentially as inspiring as Jihad.

Benjamin R. Barber is the Whitman Professor of Political Science at Rutgers University. Barber's most recent books are Strong Democracy *(1984),* The Conquest of Politics *(1988), and* An Aristocracy of Everyone.

Published originally in *The Atlantic Monthly*, March 1992, pp. 53–55, 58–63, as an introduction to the book, *Jihad vs. McWorld* (Ballantine, 1996), a volume that discusses and extends the themes of the original article. Copyright © 1992 by Benjamin R. Barber. Reprinted by permission of the author.

Index

Index

Test Your Knowledge Form

We encourage you to photocopy and use this page as a tool to assess how the articles in *Annual Editions* expand on the information in your textbook. By reflecting on the articles you will gain enhanced text information. You can also access this useful form on a product's book support Web site at *http://www.dushkin.com/online/*.

NAME:

DATE:

TITLE AND NUMBER OF ARTICLE:

BRIEFLY STATE THE MAIN IDEA OF THIS ARTICLE:

LIST THREE IMPORTANT FACTS THAT THE AUTHOR USES TO SUPPORT THE MAIN IDEA:

WHAT INFORMATION OR IDEAS DISCUSSED IN THIS ARTICLE ARE ALSO DISCUSSED IN YOUR TEXTBOOK OR OTHER READINGS THAT YOU HAVE DONE? LIST THE TEXTBOOK CHAPTERS AND PAGE NUMBERS:

LIST ANY EXAMPLES OF BIAS OR FAULTY REASONING THAT YOU FOUND IN THE ARTICLE:

LIST ANY NEW TERMS/CONCEPTS THAT WERE DISCUSSED IN THE ARTICLE, AND WRITE A SHORT DEFINITION:

We Want Your Advice

ANNUAL EDITIONS revisions depend on two major opinion sources: one is our Advisory Board, listed in the front of this volume, which works with us in scanning the thousands of articles published in the public press each year; the other is you—the person actually using the book. Please help us and the users of the next edition by completing the prepaid article rating form on this page and returning it to us. Thank you for your help!

ANNUAL EDITIONS: Comparative Politics 05/06

ARTICLE RATING FORM

Here is an opportunity for you to have direct input into the next revision of this volume.
We would like you to rate each of the articles listed below, using the following scale:

1. **Excellent: should definitely be retained**
2. **Above average: should probably be retained**
3. **Below average: should probably be deleted**
4. **Poor: should definitely be deleted**

Your ratings will play a vital part in the next revision.
Please mail this prepaid form to us as soon as possible.
Thanks for your help!

RATING	ARTICLE	RATING	ARTICLE
	1. A Constitutional Revolution in Britain?		36. Middle East Democracy
	2. Judgment Day		37. Bin Laden, the Arab "Street," and the Middle East's Democracy Deficit
	3. Does New Labour Deserve a Third Term?		38. Democracy's Sobering State
	4. A Divided Self: A Survey of France		39. Capitalism and Democracy
	5. French Secularism Unwraps Far More than Headscarves in the Classroom		40. We Need More Globalisation—But We Will Only Get It If We Have Better States
	6. The Nicolas v Jacques Show		41. Global Left Turn
	7. Gerhard Schröder Clings On		42. The Imperative of State-Building
	8. Schröder Looks at the Stars Again		43. Cultural Explanations: The Man in the Baghdad Café
	9. The German Question		44. An Explosive Combination
	10. Japanese Spirit, Western Things		45. Jihad vs. McWorld
	11. Public Opinion: Is There a Crisis?		
	12. Political Parties: Empty Vessels?		
	13. Interest Groups: Ex Uno, Plures		
	14. Women in National Parliaments		
	15. Europe Crawls Ahead …		
	16. What Democracy Is … and Is Not		
	17. Judicial Review: The Gavel and the Robe		
	18. Referendums: The People's Voice		
	19. The Great Divide		
	20. Living With a Superpower		
	21. The Case for a Multi-Party U.S. Parliament? American Politics in Comparative Perspective		
	22. A Difficult Birth		
	23. What the EU Constitution Says		
	24. The Voters Take Their Revenge		
	25. Europe's Quiet Leap Forward		
	26. Putin Gambles on Raw Power		
	27. What Does Putin Want?		
	28. Mexico at an Impasse		
	29. The New South Africa, A Decade Later		
	30. Nigeria's Democratic Generals		
	31. Hu Takes Full Power in China as He Gains Control of Military		
	32. China: The Quiet Revolution		
	33. In March Toward Capitalism, China Has Avoided Russia's Path		
	34. Sonia: And Yet So Far		
	35. India's Democracy Provides Lessons		

(Continued on next page)

ABOUT YOU

Name _____   Date _____

Are you a teacher? ☐   A student? ☐
Your school's name _____

Department _____

Address _____   City _____   State _____   Zip _____

School telephone # _____

YOUR COMMENTS ARE IMPORTANT TO US!

Please fill in the following information:
For which course did you use this book?
_____

Did you use a text with this ANNUAL EDITION?   ☐ yes ☐ no
What was the title of the text?
_____

What are your general reactions to the *Annual Editions* concept?
_____

Have you read any pertinent articles recently that you think should be included in the next edition? Explain.
_____

Are there any articles that you feel should be replaced in the next edition? Why?
_____

Are there any World Wide Web sites that you feel should be included in the next edition? Please annotate.
_____

May we contact you for editorial input?   ☐ yes ☐ no
May we quote your comments?   ☐ yes ☐ no